# RELIGION AMONG THE PRIMITIVES

# RELIGION

# AMONG

# THE

# PRIMITIVES

# BY WILLIAM J. GOODE

WITH AN INTRODUCTION BY KINGSLEY DAVIS

**THE FREE PRESS OF GLENCOE**
**COLLIER-MACMILLAN LIMITED, LONDON**

FIRST FREE PRESS PAPERBACK EDITION 1964

*For information, address:*
The Free Press of Glencoe
A Division of The Macmillan Company
The Crowell-Collier Publishing Company
60 Fifth Avenue, New York, N.Y., 10011

Collier-Macmillan Canada, Ltd., Toronto, Ontario

DESIGNED BY SIDNEY SOLOMON

# CONTENTS

*To Pinù, who helped me begin it*
*and to Rifke, who helped me complete it*

# PREFACE

MODERN DEVELOPMENTS in social research have proceeded along two major fronts: A. The increasing precision and reliability of *techniques;* and B. Attacks on increasingly more difficult and significant *problems.* We are thus witnessing an integration of the "positivist" tradition, with a tradition bent on solving "more important" problems. It is to be hoped that this integration will finally be accomplished by the generation now being trained as sociologists. If this is achieved, perhaps we shall soon witness a period when the work of each past generation is rarely read. This would be the most significant tribute to the fruitfulness of its contribution. When only the historians are interested in our works, we shall know by that poignant fact that the foundations of social science have been properly laid. Until that time, however, the present work may serve as an approximation to such breadth and detailed specification of event and process as we may yet be privileged to witness.

The resumption of systematic cross-cultural studies is one step in the right direction. However, such studies indicate that even for kinship materials the gaps are enormous, and for such a phenomenon as religion the lacunae are great enough that even this modest study may be a contribution.

Except by helping the following generation, one can never adequately pay one's intellectual debts. Nevertheless, this is a welcome opportunity to record my gratefulness to a number of men who have helped me in this work. It is the more appropriate, since not all of them can be aware of the fact that they have actually played such a role.

It is to Kingsley Davis, primarily, that I owe a major debt. It was his original suggestion that aroused my interest in the subject of primitive religion, and his unpublished paper before the Philadelphia Anthropological Society in 1939 which was most instrumental in clearly focussing the relevant intellectual problems.

9

Wilbert E. Moore also aided me in understanding many difficult problems in social analysis, both town and gown, and more than once prevented me from making an obvious blunder. Both Davis and Moore have been mentors, colleagues, and friends, and I am fortunate to have met them early in my career.

Like so many social scientists who were trained in part at the University of Texas, I am grateful to Clarence E. Ayres. My first encounter with his stirring personality is still vivid to me after fifteen years: he was a gifted teacher who made his students hunger for growth. In breadth of interest, in eloquence of language, and in depth of thought, he was superb; and his warm personal qualities made him an inspiration to all who met him.

To George Eaton Simpson, now of Oberlin, thanks are due for the untiring care with which he read an earlier version of this manuscript. His insistence on accuracy in detail was very helpful.

A debt to Robert K. Merton and Talcott Parsons must also be recorded, since they cannot otherwise know its extent. In neither case is there any presumption of familiarity. Rather, personal contacts have stimulated an interest in work which was intrinsically of importance. However, in addition to their published works, I have obtained records of seminars, conferences, and lecture notes; and from all these I have often found solutions to difficult problems of analysis, usually without their learning of it.

To my former colleagues at Wayne University and Pennsylvania State College, I am grateful for genuine forbearance, advice, and friendship. Particular thanks are due to Seth Russell and to Frank E. Hartung, Harold Sheppard, Henry Baker, Norman D. Humphrey, and H. Warren Dunham; and to Cy Greenfield whose help in many bibliographical problems was gratefully received.

Let me add deep recognition of good fortune in having Melvin Tumin as my friend. In stress and relaxation he has been a good companion, and has given me intellectual stimulation of a high order.

Finally, I wish to offer my thankfulness, like the Dahomey, in remembrance of all those unknown intellectual ancestors whom I may slight in the temporary writing of a preface, but who once gave of their substance and excellence in shaping this manuscript, however devious and unknown the process.

WILLIAM J. GOODE

*Columbia University*
*September 1, 1950*

# INTRODUCTION

T HE READER holds in his hands a rather unusual book—one on the theory of religion by a contemporary social scientist. In general the present generation of social scientists appears to be neglecting the subject. A recent textbook on social psychology, for instance, contains in the index not even a reference to religion, ritual, the church, or the sacred.[1] Linton's well known *Study of Man*, although attempting a general synthesis of ethnographic materials rich in description of religious phenomena, has no explicit treatment of the subject, and the same can be said for several textbooks in sociology. Although Professor Goode's bibliography shows there are exceptions, it is especially on the systematic level—the theory of religion as a social phenomenon—that little work is being done. It was this impression of current disinterest in the social theory of religion, despite many classical treatments in past generations, that led Professor Goode several years ago to regard the subject as a challenging one. I feel now that he has admirably borne out this hunch by making a substantial contribution toward filling the gap.

Perhaps contemporary social scientists are rebelling against the former generation's preoccupation with religious studies. Or possibly they are reflecting the general secularism of our time—which, however, is often exaggerated except for the secularism of the social scientists themselves. In addition, these contemporary analysts, masters of the slide rule and the contingency coefficient, may be encountering difficulty in understanding religion. Not only is the subject one which the public hates to see studied in a neutral spirit, but one that is also intrinsically refractory to scientific comprehension.

Social theory is at its best when it operates within the assumption of rationality—as does economics, the most advanced. It is at its next best when, often in the spirit of debunking, it is demonstrating the influence

[1] Theodore M. Newcomb, *Social Psychology* (New York: Dryden Press, 1950).

11

of nonrational factors on supposedly rational behavior. It is at its worst when trying to explain nonrational behavior itself. When required to produce such an explanation, it tends either to fall back upon a biological *ex machina* (instincts and urges) or to gravitate into a falsely rationalistic position, saying in effect that religious behavior is an *attempt* to be rational or that it is rational within its assumptions. Indeed, still influenced by the preoccupations of philosophy, social theory has a sterile tendency to view religion primarily from a cognitive standpoint. The question then becomes, "Do religious ideas represent reality?" Since they obviously do not do so directly, as do scientific ideas, then a search is made for some indirect way in which they may do so, resulting in some such bizarre view as that they "represent" society or a "higher reality." If the question is answered in the negative, then the problem is how human beings happen to fall into such errors. How do they come to believe in souls, gods, and incantations? Here again the answer is given in terms of the inquiring mind, the scientific mind, which is misled by some of the apparent phenomena of nature.

Actually, whether or not religious ideas are true is probably the least important question for social science. Religious behavior includes many things besides statements of purported fact. Much more important for social science is the role of ritual and belief, of the clergy and the church, of symbols and taboos, in the social system. It is this sort of problem to which the author of the present volume has addressed himself. As he says, religious action takes place and has concrete effects in this world, even though many of its ideas are directed to another. He has thus addressed himself to an empirical rather than a metaphysical problem; and accordingly he has gone for his answers to the first-hand reports of field research.

Having undertaken to work out a theory of the social role of religion based on first-hand observations reported in the scientific literature, the author has several alternatives open to him. He could have elected to draw on descriptions of primitive societies generally. In the past, in the days of Tylor and Spencer, of Sumner and Keller and Radin and Lowie, this piecemeal comparative approach could pass muster. The ethnographic literature was culled for illustrations of principles intuitively judged to be generally valid. Now, however, comparative study has grown more methodologically sophisticated. If one draws upon data from many societies, one must treat them systematically and statistically, as Murdock has done in his book on *Social Structure*. One can thus discover the degree to which carefully formulated hypotheses hold true in the universe of primitive societies. But one can take an entirely different tack and elect to study a few societies in great detail. Such a case approach has the advantage of delineating the *system* of relationships as they appear concretely, and thus helps one in formulating hypotheses that may ultimately be tested on the broader statistical canvass. This is the alternative the author has chosen. He wisely limits himself to a detailed analysis of five diverse primitive societies.

In approaching the data of his five societies, Professor Goode has necessarily had a frame of reference in mind. As Appendix II demonstrates, he has been far from ignorant of past thought on the subject. Indeed, his knowledge of the theory of religion is what gives him his right to undertake the task in question. There are endless descriptions of primitive religion, but there are few present-day theoretical formulations based on the better field reports. No new formulation would be worthy of the name which ignored either the past theory or the first-hand descriptions. It should be emphasized, however, that scientific theory is not loose speculation. This is doubtless why Professor Goode explicitly sets forth at the start the kind of frame of reference he is using—what has come to be called a functional, or structural-functional, approach.

Unfortunately, social science is still so immature that a label always runs the danger of becoming more confusing than enlightening. In sociology and social anthropology the term "functional" has come to be applied to a presumed school or coterie of scholars who are assumed to be on one side of the fence on a number of issues. As thus used, however, the term is misleading, for the conception of great issues which can split a field of inquiry into opposing camps is a notion applicable to scholasticism and philosophy, not to science. When used merely as a name for a conceptual framework, one is not sure whether the term describes the kinds of questions one asks about reality, the methods used in testing one's propositions, or the nature of the results one claims to find. My opinion is that the sole difference between a functionalist and a non-functionalist lies in the kind of scientific question raised. So far as method is concerned, any difference is solely due to the opportunities and limitations set by the questions pursued. In fact, anyone who scientifically studies living phenomena as wholes is using a functional type of analysis. The physiologist, the ecologist, the economist—these are all functionalists. But any particular kind of question will generally require techniques to answer that are different from those required by other kinds of questions. It is not a case of one technique being necessarily better or worse than another in a general sense. The technique cannot be judged at all (apart from logical consistency or mathematical adequacy) until the question it is designed to answer is known.

The author of the present volume has characterized the functional approach in ethnography in terms of its characteristic emphases (i.e. kinds of scientific questions). Functionalism, he points out, is not interested in the history of culture *per se*. This is certainly true, but it does not follow that the functionalists are to be damned for their disinterest or that they can damn the cultural historians for their predilection. There must be specialization in science. The poorest scientist is the one who tries to answer all questions at once. An interest in cultural history is just as legitimate as an interest in family interaction. Surely, however, the various questions asked of reality are not entirely independent of one another. To say that the functionalist is not interested in history *per se* does not mean that he fails to use changes in time as a means of understanding social organization. It means that he does not stop when he has answered the historical question, and does not subordinate his other questions to that one, just as the historian whose attention is focused on change, does not stop when he has answered a question about social organization at a given moment. The difference is a matter of what receives primacy in the intellectual quest, not a matter of mutual exclusion. It is strange to find social scientists implicitly assuming that everyone should be interested in the same kind of question, and forming schools of opinion each extolling its particular brand. Surely there is room for as many varieties of social scientist as there are questions to be asked about social reality.

It is also pointed out that functionalism puts greater emphasis upon social interaction and informal social behavior than upon technology, artifacts, or external rituals. Again, this is a matter of what one wants to know. No one would want to confine all study of culture to an investigation of techniques and artifacts, but on the other hand no one would want to exclude these important phenomena from study. Rituals may be studied in terms of their "meaning," their esthetic form, or their geographical distribution; and until an overarching question is agreed upon for which the study of rituals is purely subsidiary, there is no way in which one of these approaches can be judged to be better or more important than the others.

Professor Goode says further that the functionalist puts "greater emphasis upon the society as a unitary process." Here, I think, he puts his finger on the master-question that the so-called functionalist school pursues. It is the question of how societies operate as wholes, as going concerns. It immediately leads to other questions: What are the necessary conditions for the existence of any human society, no matter what its specific form? What are the main types of society, and what are the special requirements for the existence of each type? What contributions do the major institutional structures of a society make, both negatively and positively, toward its maintenance? Professor Goode regards these questions as too difficult for present research designs to solve. Perhaps so, but this does not justify our ignoring them, and he does not actually do so. Scientific progress is not made by forgetting important questions because they seem insoluble by present techniques, but rather by supplying tentative answers on the basis of logic and fragmentary induction in the hope that these answers themselves will suggest better procedures. As he says, "We cannot retreat to a mere recording of data."

Although I find the so-called functionalist type of question more intriguing than most other types, I should like to stress my opinion that it has no special legitimacy or importance as against other kinds of social science questions. In fact, I would agree with our author that the functionalist type is extremely difficult to answer. To many hard-boiled critics it reasonably seems like a will'-o-the-wisp. Let us then approach the knotty problem of method as exhibited by the handling of religion in the present volume.

The guiding question behind all the others seems to be this, "What is it that religion does for human societies?" Since every society seems to have something called religion, its presence can hardly be dismissed as a sociological accident. If, given the major conditions of human social life as known up to now, religion made no contribution to societal survival or was not inextricably attached to something that did contribute to survival, one would expect that social systems and cultures would long since have evolved without it. There need be no assumption that religion is entirely adaptive, that its role is identical in all types of society, or that in some distant future its functions might not be instrumented by some other kind of cultural structure. There is simply a good *prima facie* case for asking a question about its functions and trying to answer the question scientifically.

To this guiding question Professor Goode gives a theoretical answer. He says in effect that, granted the basic cultural and biosocial character of human society, with the consequent necessity of communicative interaction and agreement on group goals, religion can and does play a unifying role. It helps to widen the meaning and strengthen the apparent reality of common values among its believers, and to motivate behavior favorable to these values. It thus helps to avoid the social chaos that would result from a completely utilitarian attitude on the part of the societal members. The author does not imply that religion unerringly does this, that it does nothing else, that it can be studied only from this point of view, or that every element in any particular religion is always positively functional.[2] Obviously, the concrete manifestations of religion vary greatly from one culture to another. It is the repeated elements for which the assumption of direct functionality seems most plausible. A functional explanation of a particular rite or belief is far-fetched, because many different rites or beliefs might well perform the same function, so that the explanation of this particular one is left indeterminate. Such, however, is the character of all scientific explanation: it cannot account completely for the concrete and therefore unique case.

So far I have stated what seems to be the author's theoretical answer to his guiding question. His main emphasis, however, is on his empirical materials. For evidence of the social role of religion he has painstakingly pointed out the complex interrelations actually subsisting between the religious and the other aspects of the four societies. Since the number of relationships is limitless, he has, in accordance with his guiding principles, selected for special attention the ones which, negatively or positively, bear on the problem of consensus, the problem of order, in social organization. In Chapters VII-X, for example, dealing with religion in relation to economic and political behavior, the effort is primarily to inquire whether religion operates to protect the consensus, the ethical and institutional structure, while nevertheless permitting the necessary functions of economic exchange and political authority. He finds that not only is economic activity expended in part on religious ends, but that the religious system helps to maintain the institutions that regulate and motivate economic behavior. Thus, with reference to the Manus,

It is evident that in this society of intense interest in economic affairs the religious pattern nevertheless helps to motivate and shape such action. Far from being merely a cold-blooded compact between the personal deity and the individual, privately made and broken, the relationship with Sir Ghost actually is in the nature of a covenant, moral in nature and publicly sanctioned and supported. Sir Ghost in turn is not merely the helper of the Manus, but insists on the other hand that the individual accept and live up to the demands of various economic obligations, by husbanding his resources, by allocating his wealth to the proper channels instead of using it selfishly or short-sightedly, and by producing energetically so as to make his payments when they are required. Sir Ghost even initiates demands of a productive nature by his desire for recognition on this plane. He further helps to motivate and keep to the mark any who would fail to recognize the important ceremonial events in the life of the individual and the family.

---

[2] One must state these obvious qualifications, because there is a tendency to attribute unrealistic assumptions to those who have tried to answer functional questions. An example is that of Robert K. Merton, *Social Theory and Social Structure* (Glencoe, Ill.: Free Press, 1949), pp. 21-81.

Similarly, he finds that the support given the political system by the religious is not merely explicit but also implicit and symbolic, not simply one-sided but mutual. When the two systems "are not identified in the same personnel, there are institutional patterns for avoiding conflict." The society, which is "not a mere aggregation or addition of several hypothetical 'individuals,' . . . has manifest and latent aims of its own, and these must possess some sort of compatibility if the group is to continue as a society." Clearly there is the commanding idea in this analysis that there are certain functions that any human society requires, that each has some structure by which the functions are performed, and that, since each function is indispensable, there has to be some balance, some mutual adjustment, between the structures that carry out the functions.

The value of such a conceptual framework is the direction it gives to inquiry and the chance it offers to use empirical investigation for genuine scientific development. The controlling ideas remain trivial until they are demonstrated and added to by working through the factual details, where new discoveries emerge. The author's phrase, "interlocking details" vividly describes the nub of his effort. In finding and setting forth these interlocking details in five different societies he carries the functional analysis of religion further than, to my knowledge, it has been carried before, although the same basic approach has been used many times before. The book could have been organized in a different way. It could have had chapters on religious belief, ritual, symbolism, magic, etc. But the organization adopted, where the central discussion concerns the relationship between religion and the other major aspects of society (economic, political, and familial) is, to my mind, the best; because the functional importance of the main structures involved hardly needs arguing. If in the face of the other major structures religion retains a separate place, being no more dependent on them than they on it, the argument for its functional role in the social system is hard to deny.

With the central discussion flanked by introductory chapters on the general theory of religions and by extremely valuable appendices on types of religious systems and types of past theory, the volume represents a rare and solid contribution to contemporary social science. It should fulfil the author's hope that, in addition to further work on primitive religion, it will stimulate systematic research on the strange role of religion in urban-industrial society.

KINGSLEY DAVIS

# 1. RELIGION AS AN OBJECT OF SCIENTIFIC STUDY

Has social progress moved us beyond religion? Does scientific knowledge make all religion useless?

These questions could have been answered easily by the heralds of the new era in the late 19th Century. It was an epoch which, except for a disgruntled few, believed man was moving forward in all important ways. Men no longer looked back to a Golden Age. Forward lay Utopia.

Science was coming into its own. Man's problems were to be solved by the magic of experimentation. This stage would not come about immediately, but progress was inevitable. Disease, poverty, crime, illiteracy, and ugliness would disappear along with the jungle and desert, unexploited ores and primitive men, the ox and the manual laborer.

All these material gains, spoke the seers, would come from science. But they were as nothing compared to the unfettering of the human mind. Superstition could not withstand the attacks of scientific truth as it had stubbornly resisted the arguments of reason. Magic, too, would weaken and die. Then religion, that last, great edifice of systematic irrationality, would crumble.

There seemed, indeed, ample evidence that this destruction was under way. The violent controversy which centered about evolution, after the publication of Darwin's *The Origin of Species* in 1859, was part of a relentless conflict between the scientific forces and the religious. In that conflict, the religious forces consistently lost ground. Where dogma asserted an empirical fact—the world was created 4004 B.C., at nine o'clock in the morning—science demonstrated its error. Where doctrine asserted a metaphysical principle—man has an eternal soul—science shrugged at the trivial question. Where the church pointed to its past, science put tools in the hands of the young, and bade them go forward into the future. The age was becoming more secular, and paid its tithes as only a rational act calculated to prove its standing as a respectable citizen.

Furthermore, it was not merely the *facts* of science which controverted the assertions of theology. The *temper* of science was, as it is, opposed to religion. Those who are trained thoroughly in the one usually find the other somewhat less congenial. Intuition and faith are, in attitude, to be set against empirical experiment. The search for further religious truth based upon the past is different from the systematic scepticism of science. Moreover, the questions which are so crucial for the religious man—his relationship to his God, the state of his soul, the meaning of sin—must be considered scientifically irrelevant, since science has no techniques for answering them.

Yet even the optimist among atheists must admit considerable evidence that religion has not lost its hold on men's minds. Church membership in the United States shows no signs of dropping to a zero point, but is rather keeping rough pace with population growth. The many revolutions in Latin America which were anti-clerical have not succeeded in destroying the Catholic Church. In "Protestant America," the Catholic Church is, indeed, sometimes accused of having far too much influence. Even the materialism of Communism has had difficulty in Europe, when it has battled with religion. There are strong forces in Israel which press toward orthodoxy. And many intellectuals and artists show an increasing concern with religious matters. Indeed, religion has become "box-office" along with sex, so that a number of novels and films on religious themes have scored popular successes.

Furthermore—and here we approach more closely to the subject of this book—although Western science did manage to destroy the religions of some primitive tribes, it managed to do so by destroying the tribes themselves. Perhaps, if we continue our present increase in destructive efficiency, Western science will destroy all religion, by the simple act of destroying all men.

However, the past century was like others in that there were many currents of thought other than the dominant ones. Occupied with the thought mold of evolution, analysts of religion in the latter half of the 19th Century sought to determine the *origin* of religion. Some of them looked for its origin in the spectacular phenomena of nature, such as storms, the sun, the sea, or powerful animals. Others dealt with the dreams of men, in which the dead reappeared. Still others decided that tricks of language were important in the development of religion.

These theories can be studied later. For our purposes, what is significant is that most of them tried to find the origins of religion in individual experiences. Furthermore, religions seemed to be cognitive patterns, ideas used prior to the development of science. Religion could also be looked upon as a tool for manipulating superstitious people.

Yet there were other currents of thought which did not view religious action in such a simple light. Even Edward B. Tylor, whose main ideas on religion could be classed as individualistic and rationalistic, was cautious enough to recognize that *every* primitive society seemed to have a religious system, and that all claims to the contrary were eventually seen to be false. In addition, men like William Robertson Smith, Émile Durkheim, Max Weber, or Lucien Levy-Bruhl began to see religious action as a *social* phenomenon.

Cautious anthropologists and sociologists began to reject the piece-meal methods of proof used by the evolutionists, and gradually moved away from any consideration of ultimate origins at all. The question seemed rather to be: What is the importance of religion in modern societies?

It must be confessed that the sociologist still has no answer to this question. Social historians have indicated how religions have been of importance *in the past,* by showing the relationship between ascetic Protestantism and the development of capitalism, or the same religious movements and the development of technology and science. Yet the systematics of religious values in modern Western European life are still unexplored, in the main.

Failing that close analysis, the sociologist has for the most part simply taken from the anthropologist the easy answer: Religion is very important. This answer, however, is one which would be given to any question about any element in the society, if we were to accept a thorogoing functionalism. That it has not gone beyond the general statement that religion helps to support the ultimate values of a society is perhaps due to the same lack of interest in the subject, so characteristic of the past generation.

It is hoped that the present study will be the precursor of many empirical investigations of religious action. Perhaps the growing interest in religion on the part of those laymen, intellectuals, and literati who look for some kind of faith, will also stimulate scientific interest.

This study can only be a precursor, however, since it will deal entirely with primitive tribes, not modern society. No apologies need be made for this restriction. It is possible that a sketch of the broad ways by which religion intertwines with other aspects of social life will yield guide lines for research in "civilized" societies. Perhaps the complexities of secular life are more easily seen, once the complex interrelationships in primitive life have been described. In any event, it seems correct to state that we must begin once more to take up the task of such analysis, instead of letting our assertions about religion become obvious clichés.

*What this study does not attempt to do.* Every study must be assessed in its own terms. All investigations are restricted in aim, if they are to accomplish anything. This is no exception. However, it is only fair to outline such restrictions for the reader. Furthermore, it is necessary to state positively its goals, as well as the framework within which analysis is to proceed. Let us first note what the following study does *not* attempt to do.

*What is the origin of religion?* First of all, it is not a new attempt to probe the "origins" of religion. Whether the beginnings of religion arise from the ultimate revelations of some Divine Being, or from an apocolyptic experience, will not be considered relevant. Most anthropologists would accept this position, but its basis needs to be restated.

In spite of the advances in archeological discoveries, there are no techniques by which the detailed social interaction of bygone non-literate societies can be resurrected. We can frequently study in detail the technology of such a society, if there are sufficient artifacts. We can learn how they made their pottery, wove their cloth, or killed wild animals. If we study further, we can sometimes infer that they did some trading, since we find objects or substances not indigenous to the area, from which we guess that they must have had some contact with other groups.

Nevertheless, these are but the crudest elements necessary to analyze social action. Even if we find pottery figurines which seem to have been gods, we do not learn from their physical existence what was their social meaning. Whether they were indeed divine, or merely personal magic, or dolls, will remain at best a matter of surmise, unless we have some written records. Without the latter, we can never know their legends, their "theology," their rituals and chants. We can know little about the range of the divine beings, or who were the religious practitioners. It will be impossible to discover who were the dissidents and who were the faithful. Inevitably and forever, we are barred from obtaining the needed data for non-literate tribes which have disappeared.

Even when we can make intelligent guesses about these matters, we are not even close to a knowledge of a phenomenon which perhaps appeared with the very first men. To make a surmise about even the religion of a Neolithic tribe is to fall far short of an analysis of religion still earlier. And to speculate about how, under what conditions, man began to believe in divine beings nearly a million years ago must remain sheer speculation.

*Which religion is the right one?* A further task which this study does not attempt is that of "proving" any one religion to be "incorrect." Science has no techniques for demonstrating any such assertion, now or in the future. Science can describe the religious beliefs of a group. It may also discover the *intensity* of these beliefs, for groups or for individuals. Science can show whether, and how, such beliefs influence action. The process by which the child comes to hold such beliefs can also be the object of scientific analysis. Or, under some conditions, the gradual changes in beliefs over several generations.

It is clear, however, that these are different tasks from that of demonstrating the "truth" of a given theology. Science can only measure or describe empirical phenomena. It has no way of weighing the soul, or describing the color or smell of a divine revelation. It cannot measure the height of a Divine Being. It cannot even challenge its existence, for there are no empirical techniques to prove the nonexistence of nonempirical phenomena. It must, rather, maintain an agnostic attitude toward such phenomena, and admit the irrelevance of its techniques to such an investigation.

*Is religion "good?"* Nor is this treatise to be a justification or indictment of religion, or even an "impartial weighing of good and bad." Again, science can present facts and structures of facts; it cannot answer the moral question. If by the reader's values certain actions are good—or bad— that judgment is his own concern. Science can not play prophet and claim empirical truth for its domain.

This is not the place for a detailed analysis of the complex relationships between values and scientific action. Such relationships exist, however, even if one accepts the extreme relativistic position taken here, that there is a fundamental distinction between scientific judgments and value judgments. The former type of judgment, to put it roughly, tells us *what is,* and can be proved or disproved empirically. The value judgment tells us what *ought to be,* and can not be proved or disproved empirically. Granting such a distinction, at least a few of the relationships between the two can be mentioned briefly and dogmatically:

1. The ultimate basis of all science is a group of essentially unprovable propositions about the existence of the physical world, its relationship to sense phenomena, the criteria for validity, and so on. These propositions are acts of will and of sentiment, i.e., expressions of value, rather than verifiable descriptions.

2. The motives which impel a society, group, or individual toward science at all, or toward a particular field, are basically value judgments.

3. The decision that a given problem in science is important is value judgmental.

4. Within science itself, the scientist accepts an entire "ethic of science," which is again an expression of sentiment.

5. Science is a tool by which values may be achieved, or by which the concomitant consequences of such achievement may be measured, or by which alternative methods of achievement may be developed.

6. Science can analyze the logical relationships between values: e.g., if one accepts a given value, must one accept other values also? Or, given two values, do they stand in contradiction to one another?

7. Science can take values as its object of study (as do the social sciences).

This list is merely an outline, but each relationship is different, while no one of them allows the demonstration that a given set of values, or religion, is "good" or "bad." That must be a decision based upon the reader's values on the one hand, and the data which are congruent or conflicting with those values, on the other.

In any event, this study is an empirical analysis, with the assumption that within such a limitation there are no techniques by which one can demonstrate that religion is "good" or "bad."

*What is a primitive tribe?* This study further limits itself to an analysis of religious life in certain primitive tribes. The term "primitive" is unfortunate, for it suggests the notion of "backward" societies, or those somehow undeveloped along some evolutionary scale. However, for most anthropologists such a unilinear evolutionary scale is not assumed and is not assumed in the present analysis.

Sometimes, the term "nonliterate" is used instead, since these societies usually do not have a widely used written language. The term, "savage," is of course considered too invidious to be applied.

Societies generally classed as "primitive" generally have a technology which is less developed than "nonprimitive" technologies. Usually, also, they are isolated, both physically and socially, from the societies we call "civilizations," and in this characteristic can be distinguished, in the main, from peasant groups. Frequently, they seem to have a greater social integration. That is, there are few sub-groups which can be called "alien," "marginal," or "dissident." In vaguer terminology, they are thought to be "simpler, more harmonious." They are contrasted with urban societies, and not infrequently one detects in descriptions of the primitives some of the nostalgia which the sociologist may express when discussing rural social behavior.

Until anthropologists began to investigate modern urban society, it was possible in desperation to define primitive societies as those with which the professional anthropologist concerned himself.

Although these statements may suggest that the anthropologist does not know how to define his object of study, they really mean that there is no simple line to be drawn which divides all societies into one or the other, primitive or non-primitive, rural or urban, folk or civilized. Rather, one may think of societies as ranging along some kind of "rural-urban" continuum, or scale, from the urban civilizations of Western Europe as one extreme, to the societies which are most isolated geographically and socially, least developed technologically, most integrated socially, with the smallest populations, at the other extreme. All of us would prefer, naturally a set of neat categories, mutually exclusive as well as exhaustive, but this is merely another example of objects which do not easily divide. Perhaps a different mode of classification can be developed with the desired precision, at some later time. That time is not now, and we must work with what we have.

In any event, this restriction to primitive societies suggests that the conclusions of the present study are not assumed to hold for all societies. Certainly some of them do, and many of them would be true, with some qualifications. The assumption *is* made that the broad patterns of social interaction are quite similar for both ends of the continuum. However, the extent to which the conclusions of this study are applicable to the religions of nonprimitive societies is a subject for later investigation, and therefore will not concern us here.

# 2. SOCIOLOGY AND SOCIAL BEHAVIOR

T HE PRECEDING CHAPTER suggested that the subject of religion is of some importance for a science of social action, and indicated some of the limitations of the present study. This chapter will explore further the positive approach to be used in the investigation. That approach may be characterized as *sociological, functional, and comparative*. Although some redundancy may be contained in such a characterization, these terms can be separately discussed.

Briefly, a sociological approach analyzes human action to the extent that it can be understood in terms of common-value integration.[1] Like most definitions of any broad area of study, this has its weaknesses, but it furnishes a convenient basis for exposition. Actually, the formulation suggests several propositions. Two major statements may, however, be singled out for emphasis: A. Sociology deals with value-motivated action; and B. The sociological aspects of action constitute only one of many possible aspects of the universe which are worthy of study. Let us look at each of these in turn.

It is the conclusion from an immense body of data that the social action of men cannot be adequately explained either by (1) assuming that they spend their time rationally calculating how to reach their goals, or by (2) assuming they are impelled mechanically by a group of fixed biological drives. Now, both these statements are very complex. The classical schools of thought which viewed man as seeking pleasure and avoiding pain, while driven by individual motives, have not been supported by the studies of the past half-century.[2] These have rather indicated that the *motives themselves* are of social origin.[3] Furthermore, the decisions and the means are also structured by the values of the society, so that the individual is not entirely free to calculate rationally. In addition, the values and goals of any one individual are not random, but are integrated with those of other members of the society.[4] Finally, these values, while occurring as part of the individual's emotions and senti-ments, usually function so as to contribute somewhat to the continued existence of the society—the reproduction and socialization of children, the production and distribution of food, and so on.

That hedonistic view, which gradually lost ground in the face of sociological investigation, was empirically much more difficult to refute than the view of man as obeying fixed biological patterns. As to the latter, there was a strong belief in "instinct" only a generation ago, but it represented a brief fad, and did not have many followers among social thinkers who looked beyond their own society.[5] The idea of "race" as a determinant of human behavior belongs in the same category.[6] The so-ciologist and anthropologist look upon both these notions as typical of a bygone era of thought, almost as superstitions. The body of data refuting them is vast and incontrovertible, and may be stated in somewhat this form:

1. No social pattern has been found which seems identical with the "instincts" of lower animals.

2. Every biological drive is conditioned and structured more or less by the culture in which the human being is reared.

3. No human being is born with values; he must acquire them by a socialization process in which other human beings must figure.

4. Any division of human beings into "races" or biological "types" is extremely difficult.

5. Even when such a division has been made, it is made solely on the basis of biological characteristics, and no conclusions about the culture can be drawn from these characteristics.

6. So far as the available evidence indicates, any race or biological type can acquire any culture.

This body of evidence refuting a biological determinism in social action ramifies greatly beyond these simple statements. It is clear, for example, that an I.Q. score can be affected greatly by social experience,[7] and the suggestive studies of psychosomatic phenomena almost assert a social determinism of biological phenomena.[8] However, we need not pursue these ramifications, since we are only concerned with the type of approach labeled "sociological."

Sociology, then deals with values and structures of values, the modes of acquiring them, their succession and history over generations, and their effects upon human action. However, let us return to statement (B), that there are many other aspects to human behavior other than the sociological.[8a] This, again, is a fairly complex statement which can be only briefly treated here.

Almost any object or phenomenon can be dealt with from a great variety of viewpoints. A chair, for example, may be looked at as the product of a *technological process*. It may also be seen as an item of importance in *economic exchange*. The chair may also happen to be a throne, and thus be analyzed from a *political* point of view. We may look at it as an item of *sociological* interest, as when we attempt to study the social effects of housing, the changes in furniture styles as a result of changing social patterns, etc.

At the same time, the chair happens to be made of organic substance, and can be analyzed both *biologically* (its cellular structure) and *chemically*. That it can be viewed as mass, or as a group of molecules, or even energy, must also be obvious. In any event, we see that such a prosaic object has many aspects which can be investigated. Each such aspect may be considered by someone to be worthy of study. On the other hand, it must be equally clear that any given investigation must restrict itself to a limited aspect, if it is to be fruitful.

If the example of a chair seems too prosaic, we might point out that a murder can also be investigated from various points of view: The man murdered may have been of political consequence, or a series of such murders may be investigated from this point of view, that of power distribution. Murders, or this murder, can be investigated as an economic phenomenon, or as a sociological phenomenon. That it has biological consequences and ramifications surely goes without saying, as would be true of its chemical after effects.

Of course, no scientist feels that by describing one aspect of a total, complex phenomenon he has exhausted its importance. The technique of *abstraction,* by which we abstract only part of a concrete process for our study, never exhausts reality. It is thus a mere conversational gambit to say that "the human body is just a group of protons and electrons, or a few chemicals worth twenty-one cents." Such a statement is the kind of part-truth embodied in the statement that "marriage is just a way of satisfying the sex urge," or "water is just hydrogen and oxygen."

All such statements fail to recognize the totality of any process or phenomenon. Any one abstract science analyzes only part of it. Furthermore, it is equally absurd to insist that the sociological (or political, or economic, or chemical) aspects are the most important. Such an assertion is like claiming that the hydrogen which goes to make up water is "more important" that the oxygen, or that viewing water as an energy concentration is "more important" than viewing it as a chemical.

We thus insist upon the concrete totality of any process or object, while pointing out that it can be profitably studied from many points of view, each of which is partial, an abstraction which by its very narrowness leads to carefully grounded facts. Every science must deal with its objects from its own limited point of view. Indeed, this recognition of the qualitatively different phenomena or aspects to be seen at different "levels" is so well known in the study of scientific method, that it possesses a specific label: We call these "emergent levels," and the different phenomena (water, as distinct from hydrogen and oxygen) "emergent phenomena."

This, then, is a *sociological* study of religious action among certain primitive societies. The common values which motivate men toward specific religious activity will therefore be the focus of our analysis. Since, however, this action is never self-enclosed, but affects other spheres of the social life, we must indicate how such action interrelates, or is integrated, with other activities. A study could be made of the cooking practices in religious action, or of the dances, or even of the physiological changes occurring in the bodies of the participants. The present study, instead, attempts to relate the religious values and actions to various aspects of social life.

This investigation is also a *functional* analysis. Since most social research in this generation is called functional, the weaknesses of this form of analysis must be at least suggested.[9]

If the above meaning of *sociological* be accepted, it is redundant to state that this study is also *functional*. There is, indeed, hardly a single extended, modern sociological report which is not also functional in orientation. Yet the discussions of this term have been so varied in focus and polemic in tone, that some explanatory comment is in order. In spite of the intense concentration in American sociology upon techniques of research, there exists no codification of the meaning, application, and method of proof involved in functionalism. As a consequence, we must steer a course between the book-length treatment it deserves, and the necessarily cryptic sentence announcing that this treatise is functionalist in approach.

Let us begin with a formulation whose core meaning is generally accepted by those who label themselves "functionalists." Then we can proceed to a formulation which is closer to actual practice, as well as to the meaning implicit in this study. Since the term *function,* as the careful reader will know, has as its correlate the term *structure,* we use a definition containing both: "On the societal level we apply the term *structure* to the relationships between the constituent individuals and acts, and the term *function* to the contribution which each relationship makes to the maintenance of the entire society."[10] Assuming that the society is a functioning whole, a structural analysis would indicate its elements and their relationships to one another; a functional analysis would see these in action, as they contribute to that on-going unity.

A systematic exposition of this approach would involve most of the basic problems which modern social science faces. Consequently, we shall have to note problems in passing, rather than solutions. Nor is this situation helped by the fact that many discussions of functionalism have sometimes done little more than treat these two questions: 1. What does functionalism "really" mean? and 2. Who introduced it first?—instead of the more crucial queries: 1. What are we doing when we analyze functionally? and 2. Upon what grounds does the validity of functional analysis rest?

Answers to the first two can be given, although they are likely to seem unsatisfactory to some who have contributed to these discussions. Functionalism "really" means whatever its users care to have it mean, and at the present time it "really" means half a dozen disparate and incongruous things. Furthermore, no amount of linguistic skill or weaving of snythetic and eclectic formulations will evade the basic problem: What are we doing? It is, after all, only when we can agree upon a specific referent, that we can end any given state of conceptual confusion. This process of conceptual clarification is difficult, but surely we cannot avoid it longer. That the author does not attempt to state dogmatically what functionalism really is, derives from his conviction that the process of conceptual clarification is a group process, not the result of individual fiat.

As to the second question in the first set of questions, the first functionalist was very likely the first man who ever thought systematically and somewhat objectively about human society. As a mode of thought, functionalism dates from the appearance of the first wise man. Granted, it did not receive a label until the past generation, but man also required several hundreds of millenia before learning that he speaks prose. Every serious social analyst in the history of human thought has at times used functional analysis. However, since the turn of the century we have accepted some of the implications of the biological analogy by using the labels self-consciously (anatomy and physiology, or structure and function). This turn of events is fruitful. The awareness leads us to examine critically our position, and to see just how we can proceed to exploit it more fully.

In spite of the ancient history of functional analysis, its self-conscious application has meant several differences of emphasis as against earlier work. These differences of emphasis may be seen most clearly by comparing a standard ethnographic report from American anthropology at the turn of the century with a report from the Malinowski "school" a generation later. Allowing for individual variation, and remembering that we are speaking of a varying *emphasis,* not a radical divergence, the following differences seem to be present:[11]

1. Functional analysis has paid less attention to the history of the society, or to social change.

2. There is greater emphasis upon social interaction than upon technology, artifacts, or rituals as seen by the outsider.

3. There is more reporting of informal social behavior.

4. There is greater emphasis upon the *meaning* of rituals, symbols, objects, from the standpoint of the believer.

5. There is less attempt, as a consequence, to impute to the primitive the feelings, knowledge, and beliefs of the Western European.

6. There is greater emphasis upon the society as a unitary process.

7. There is greater emphasis upon the interconnections which are not clearly seen by the tribal members.

The reference is specifically to social anthropology, but to apply these differences of emphasis to other fields (the sociological economics of Karl Marx or Thorstein Veblen, the sociology of Emile Durkheim, the social history of Charles A. Beard, Freudian, Gestalt, or indeed any modern psychology, etc.) would require only slight emendations of dates and wording.

Granting that these statements roughly characterize the differences in emphasis to be found in functional analysis, the non-technical reader may ask a question not usually asked by the specialist: Just how does all this relate to the contribution of a societal element to the continued existence of the society? In terms of these differences, then, we can almost redefine functionalism: It is the attempt to *investigate the interrelationships of social action.*[12]

This formulation seems: A. to describe more accurately the activities of modern functionalists; B. to avoid some of the errors and dubious assumptions implicit in much of functionalism; and C. to be more appropriate to our available techniques and theory.

The first of these three propositions is perhaps the most difficult of proof, and no attempt will be made to demonstrate it adequately. However, a rereading of perhaps the most radically functionalist group in modern anthropology, the Malinowski group, suggests that the preoccupation is much less with the maintenance of the society than with the manner by which all sorts of apparently disparate social actions relate to one another. Moreover, when we leave such a special group, and study the researches of Veblen, Marx, Beard, George Herbert Mead, John Dewey, etc., we see that the special problem of societal continuance is not ordinarily the focus. Even Malinowski does not often attempt to tie closely a social pattern and the maintenance of the society. For the most part, he is carefully tracing out the remote connections between various patterns of social behavior.

The claim can be made, furthermore, that had this problem of societal maintenance been faced systematically, some of the ambiguities and dubious assumptions implicit in functionalism would have been avoided. Their continued existence suggests that functionalism was not focussing on this specific problem, but on that of describing the interrelationships between various social patterns.[12a]

Merton has pointed out three such dubious assumptions:[13] 1. That every element in the society is integrated with every other (the assumption of complete functional unity); 2. That every element has a positive function (universal functionalism); and 3. That every item (or *function*, another ambiguity) is indispensable to the society.

It is possible to subsume the second assumption under the third, but that these assumptions are widespread cannot be denied. However, once we see that these assumptions are implicit in much of functional analysis, it is clear that the functionalist has not been investigating the extent to which given behavior contributes to the continued existence of the society. For, if every part of the society hangs together, and every part is indispensable, the investigation is over before it has started.

We need not accept Merton's statement that these are *assumptions*. Even as *themes*, they are conspicuous by the absence of any demonstrated articulation between any given element and its presumed final outcome, the maintenance of the society. For it is clear that we have only to apply ingenuity to see that *any* detail of our culture *can* be construed as making its contribution, from tipping our hats to ladies, to stopping for traffic lights. We must have, however, not only this articulation, this detailed statement of the *steps* by which this effect occurs, but a statement of the *extent* of this contribution, both negative and positive.

It is clear that the revised formulation suggested by the author need not involve these assumptions. However, let us explore this matter of assumptions somewhat further, in order to see their relevance more clearly. In failing to accept the problem of maintenance, most functionalists have failed to analyze *disfunction*, or *negative function*, i.e., the extent to which a given activity contributes to the downfall, or *anomie*, of a society. Since the functionalist is investigating these matters from the viewpoint of the actor, we have a number of possible arrangements of data which have not usually been tabulated. These can be diagrammed as follows:

| POSITIVE FUNCTION | | NEGATIVE FUNCTION | | IRRELEVANT | |
|---|---|---|---|---|---|
| Manifest | Latent | Manifest | Latent | Manifest | Latent |

Functional anthropologists have concentrated upon those *positive functions* which are *not usually known* to the members of the society, i.e., the positive, latent functions. The rebels and debunkers among modern economists and historians have concentrated upon the *negative latent functions*. It is clear that much exploration remains to be done among the remaining cells.

A further ambiguity should be mentioned in passing. The phrase "continuance of the society" fails to make explicit whether this particular society, in all its details, is meant, or *any* society. This is an important distinction, since, with reference to religious action at least, there are many activities which help to continue the existence of this particular organization of statuses, power distribution, economic wealth, and so on. There are also pressures toward variation. The claim can be made, however, that this organization need not be maintained at all, that an entirely different type of society is possible. Then we must ask the final question: What are the requirements for the continued existence of any society? If these activities maintain this society as it now exists, but do not serve the requirements of societies in general as well as other activities might, the activities cannot be considered completely positive in their effects. Functional analysts have not ordinarily probed this ambiguity, or weighed both positive and negative results.[14]

The defense may be made that such a subtle analysis is too difficult for social research at the present time, that in the complexities of social action we cannot be certain that a given element maintains this society, or society in general. This would be especially true for many of our minor actions. The author accepts such a statement, and it is for that reason that he has suggested the amended definition of functionalism: our techniques and theory have not developed far enough to be able to handle the problem. A more modest approach would seem to be indicated. Perhaps we should for a while confine our empirical researches to the causal interrelationships between various behavior patterns within the society. We can then learn which patterns are less, or more, connected with one another, and how they are related. With an increasing body of such data, we can discover which groups of patterns are more closely connected than others, as against others which are more peripheral. Our present research tools seem as yet incapable of solving the research design problems needed to demonstrate exactly what are the requirements for societal maintenance, or what are the alternative activities which can have such functions. The approach suggested is that we become skeptical of even the causal inter-relationships, and especially their societal contribution, until we can demonstrate clearly the steps of the causal process. Each attempt at demonstration, including the present one, is worthy of consideration as an approximation, but we must be aware of our own limitations.

If the above statement is a brief outline of what functional analysis is trying to do, the answer to the second crucial question becomes difficult: What are the grounds for the validity of functional analysis?

We must face the fact that a given functional analysis in sociology, like that in economics, history, psychiatry, psychoanalysis, or Gestalt psychology, is often in the scientifically weak position of being rejected because the reader "simply does not see" the relationships or patterns which are claimed to be present. This position is called scientifically weak because one of the basic criteria of good research is that all who are adequately trained can test or repeat the data, reasoning, and conclusions offered. If then, the patterns "cannot be seen" by the scientific audience, our techniques are to be considered inadequate. As is frequently the case in the development of any science, however, major propositions are often presented long before really satisfactory tests have been achieved.[15] We are forced in this case, also, to deal with analytic problems for which our techniques are not wholly adequate. Let us briefly examine the claims to validity which functionalism makes.

These claims are ultimately based on a particular conception of the nature of societies and social action. This conception has a great deal of empirical support, and is widely accepted by social analysts. Although some elements in this view of social behavior have already been sketched, under the term *sociological*, they can profitably be repeated. A basic element in this view is that a society is not merely an aggregate of discrete individuals. Rather, it has a structure of its own, just as an organism has such a structure. In both cases, the whole possesses characteristics which are to be found in none of its parts. The society has "ends," "goals," and unitary activities which will not always be those of a given individual. As a consequence, the society may continue to exist even though a given individual dies, just as it may generally be prosperous and healthy while given individuals are unhappy or sickly.

However, these societal needs, whatever they may be, cannot be achieved without the work of individuals. Naturally, then, many subsidiary and seemingly individual ends must be achieved in order that the larger needs be met. That is, they must be *integrated*. Further, the ordinarily predictable ignorance of men about the ultimate effects of their actions would mean that many actions aid in the attainment of societal ends, without the individual being specifically concerned about them. For example, we can accept the proposition that the society requires that a new generation be procreated as well as socialized, fed as well as trained. Yet the individual may be conscious of only his own desires for a mate and children, his love of children, his pleasure in rearing them, and so on. The former are latent; the latter are manifest.

Whether we believe that the task of functional analysis is to note how social action preserves the society, or merely to note how behavior patterns relate to one another, the above propositions will be acceptable. In either case, as noted previously, a given activity may be negatively or positively functional for another activity, or its effects may be so minute as to be considered almost irrelevant. Further, the individual may be aware of this (manifest) relationship, or he may not know of it (latent). Indeed, we may add a further dimension, by suggesting that in some cases he *desires* the results, while in others he will not like part of the consequences.

These are mere categories of data, however. When we attempt to apply them to actual behavior, we note that there is a *wide variation in the certainty with which we can assert such relationships*. Although functionalists in anthropology and sociology have concentrated upon the positive latent functions, and reformers and debunkers have concentrated upon negative latent functions, neither has the advantage in the matter of certainty. This statement is valid for either of the two definitions of functionalism used here. Let us look more closely at this range of certainty.

Perhaps the most obvious and certain propositions are those which relate to technology or biology. Some of these may be known to the actor. For example, a group may have definite knowledge about fishing or yam growing, applying this knowledge in order to eat. Then the functional proposition has a fairly high validity: These activities function to produce the group's food supply, or function thereby to preserve the society. Such a truism is based on our technical knowledge of fish and yams. We can test this empirical knowledge, and its relationship to food production. We can also learn that in some cases their techniques are negatively functional, since some activities (destroying cover crops, digging or plowing so as to permit erosion, allowing herds to increase to the point of destroying grazing lands, using fish poisons which kill more fish than are replaced by natural increase, etc.) may actually *reduce* the food potential, and finally endanger the society.

An equally obvious example may be chosen from one of the societies analyzed in this study, Tikopia. In this Polynesian group the practice of bathing very often is of undoubted importance in the reduction of disease. We may state, therefore, that this activity functions to preserve the society, or is positively functional with respect to any of the major activities requiring healthy individuals, from gardening and fishing, to ritual activities. However, it is equally clear that the Tikopia are not conscious of a germ theory and its relationship to cleanliness. This result, consequently, may be called a *latent positive* function of bathing. That is, the reduction of disease is not a conscious end, while in the case of gardening techniques, the growing of yams *is* a conscious end.

Although these examples may seem too obvious to be questioned, their logical structure corresponds to that of more subtle functional propositions. In all such statements, we seem to have these elements: A. Some fairly acceptable empirical knowledge of a generalized type; B. An implicit recognition of the specific *conditions* (social or physical) to be found in the society; and C. The application of these generalized relationships to the specific, observed relationships in the society. Thus, we know something about the results of various techniques of growing yams. In a given society, we note the conditions to be met, such as work organizations, climate, soil, food requirements, etc. Then we usually apply these facts in a fairly commonsense fashion to, say, the observations we have made of yam yield, food consumption and distribution, etc., in the society, to see the effects of the behavior pattern.

However, when we move from such obvious statements into more purely social relationships, our feeling of certainty fades somewhat. For example, we may assert that the Manus' former custom of capturing foreign women for rape and prostitution helped to reduce general intrasociety sexual competition as well as specific conflicts about adultery and fornication. This may be the opinion of the Manus men and may be that of the anthropologist, as well.[16] This functional relationship is based on the notion that under certain conditions the lack of libidinal outlets may lead to various conflicts and certain types of competition. Manus life is very inhibited in sexual matters, and one may find Manus men who think fondly of the old times when they had access to these captured foreign women. We can make specific observations about present conflicts over adultery and fornication. The final conclusion, that the former custom did in fact reduce these conflicts, states the apparent resultant of these factors.

A direct test of such conclusions seems difficult, and perhaps our techniques for demonstration are not yet adequate. Let us note a similar case. If an individual male is not considered an adult until he is also a gardener of yams, we will ordinarily state that this belief functions to continue the behavior pattern of yam growing (and, ultimately, to preserve the society by producing its food). For the young man will also be reared to believe that he must become a gardener before being considered an adult. He will, in addition, be motivated to desire adulthood, with its wider privileges. He will also be given the necessary technical training, formally or informally. The result will be that he will desire to cultivate yams, doing so if not hindered, and the yam gardening complex will continue.[17]

Here, of course, we are basing the conclusion upon fairly established data concerning the process of socialization and motivation. Given the conditions of the particular society, the data seem applicable, and the final conclusion seems reasonable enough. However, to this writer, we have not adequately tested this conclusion, and we must wait for better tools before we can do so. Yet we cannot retreat to a mere recording of data. It is only by attempting to organize and relate data that we can formulate propositions which can be tested. At least the definite statement of propositions of functional relationships can stimulate the development of better techniques as well as the criticisms of existing techniques. Until that time, however, we must go as far as the data permit. For it is clear that only by making explicit our conclusions and our reasoning, can these weaknesses be exposed and eliminated.

# 3. A SOCIOLOGICAL THEORY OF RELIGIOUS ACTION

THE GENERAL SOCIOLOGICAL APPROACH which was outlined in the preceding pages may also be used to interpret religious action. However, its application requires a closer view of the relationship between the individual and his society.

Just as the analysis of a society can only be done by observing individuals, so the "work of the society" can be done only through individuals. We have already noted the truism, that human beings consciously attempt to achieve their goals, but that in doing so they also help to meet the needs of the society, and in general conform to the rules of the society. This integration between the action patterns of the individual and those of his society occurs through the socialization process. For we inculcate in the growing child the values of the society, to such an extent that it is fruitful to think of "the individual" as an abstraction, the mirror image—whether distorted, imperfectly reflecting, or tiny—of the society itself. Since, in a metaphorical sense, we place the society inside the child, it is not surprising that the normal adult's action patterns integrate with those of the larger unit, the society.

This result of the socialization process is, naturally, well known, even though we may not understand its mechanisms in detail. The process, in turn, is based upon an equally truistic fact, that man is the only animal with a culture.

However, like so many truisms, this requires closer examination. It is an implicit assumption of parlor psychology that man is "just an animal with a culture." In this view, which may also be found in more sophisticated circles, society plays the role of a repressive force. The natural drives of the animal are forced to exhibit themselves with less intensity. The socialization process simply places a thin veneer over the animal urges, one which can easily crack under stress. The cultural acquisitions —political and economic institutions, religious beliefs, marital customs, etc.—are seen as a sort of superstructure built on a fleshy foundation. Or, put differently, the plastic infant is forced into a rigid mould by the power of the society. Not all who accept such assumptions would take the further step, that these cultural elements are in some sense "less real," or less valid, than the biological, but those familiar with this conception will know that many do take that step.

Such a conception of the relationship between the biological and the social aspects of human behavior fails to recognize the qualitative differences between man's adjustment to the external world, and that of other animals. Man is not part animal and part human being, in whatever proportions one may select. His adjustment to the external world or to his own biological urges, is *always mediated through a cultural structure.* The only time that man faces the natural world as an animal is at birth.

One may differently express this fundamental relationship between the biological potential and the social reality of human behavior, by insisting that the human animal reared apart from social contacts is not simply a wild, savage, human being. He will not be a human being at all.[1] This is true of no other animal. Even the chimpanzee reared apart from other chimps grows to be a quite ordinary chimp. He may have to fight on entering a new chimp grouping, but so may the chimp reared with other chimps. The usual processes of maturation and individual learning do not cause a radically different type of adult animal. This, of course, is another way of saying that there is no chimpanzee culture. It is seen that this view does not deny the importance of biological drives. Rather, it insists that no amount of biological analysis will suffice to explain the social behavior of man, that the *social is the emergent level at which we must attempt to understand human action,* and that analogies from animal behavior invariably miss the point.

A more concise way of putting this is to say that in human beings (A) the biological drives are shaped, channelized, or changed by the culture in which the individual is reared; and that (B) the values of the society are themselves tied to biological reactions. As to the first of these relationships, the society does not prevent the satisfaction of such drives as sex, hunger, etc. Rather, they are given legitimate channels of expression. These channels vary from one society to another, but are always to be found. The result is that the adult will simply be unable to eat certain foods which are nourishing, and which are eaten by other groups. His rejection is not intellectual at all. He will be revolted *physically* by such foods, as a result of this shaping process. Similarly, certain sexual situations, or certain members of the opposite sex, are not seen as possible outlets for his sexual drive. Furthermore, the satisfactions within acceptable outlets serve to reinforce the importance of the outlets.

As to the second relationship (B), many norms of the society are not mere channels for an existing or potential biological drive. Yet they must be grounded in physiological reactions, such as those of ductless glands and the autonomic nervous system. When we have violated a moral rule, and are conscience-stricken as a result, actual physiological reactions occur. We may blush when embarrassed. The feeling of religious exaltation derives, naturally, from our social participation, but the feeling is also grounded in such physiological reactions. In short, the individual comes to react emotionally toward various objects and situations which had no such biological relationship before the socialization process. The nature of this relationship on the physiological level needs considerable analysis, but its existence cannot be doubted.

This holistic view, then, views social norms as the determinants of human behavior, remembering that any norm has its cultural as well as its biological *origins,* its cultural and biological *aspects.*

Such a statement of the relationship between the biological potential and the culture does not, however, indicate the importance of *integration between the various values in the culture.* That these values do have many interrelationships, that they constitute a pattern, is observable. Let us look briefly at this integration.

It is clear that when we analyze the abstraction, a single "act," we see several elements.[2] There is an actor, a person, who desires an end. The end, in turn, is attainable by certain means within the situation. Viewed in this fashion, we see an essentially *technological* process, in which the individual adjusts the available means to the given situation in order to reach the goal desired.

However, when the individual contemplates more than one act, or more than one goal, a further adjustment is required. Some integration is forced upon him. He must make a choice. For there is a scarcity of time, energy, materials, skills, or some other element. Some ends will forbid others. Perhaps the ends can not be achieved at the same time. Some type of choice, then, is required. This level of action integration may be called the *economic,* for here we see the classical economic problem: the allocation of scarce resources to alternate ends.

Both these adjustments, at least abstractly viewed, can exist within the action system of a single individual. The entrance of another person, another action system, introduces a new factor. Existence of both within the same "social space" requires a further integration. The second person can be used. He may be coerced, dominated, or manipulated, in order that the two action patterns may not be in conflict.[3] Many types of integration are possible at this essentially *political* level of adjustment, where power over others becomes an issue.

Nevertheless, a society cannot exist on such a basis. An individual who obeys the rule because it is the simplest way to obtain his goal will disobey it for the same reason. The individual who is law abiding only because the policeman restrains him will break the law when the threat is removed. No one has more powerfully analyzed the impossibility of a social system based on rational means-ends action than has Thomas Hobbes in *The Leviathan*, but the observation has an ancient history, woven deeply into folk wisdom.

We recognize this impossibility when we rear our children. True enough, we often preach to them the advantages of being good. But our most telling argument can never be that "crime does not pay very much." Rather: crime is *bad*. We attempt to develop the necessary restraints *within* the child. He must refrain from evil, not merely avoid being caught.

An integration based on technical efficiency alone, or economic rationality, or political power, can therefore not be sufficient. There must be an integration through *common* values, some of which will be *group* values. Social behavior can not occur at random. Its patterned character is seen in the fact that we are able to understand the behavior of others, that we are moved emotionally by similar situations, that we are able to predict human action.

Note that reference is made to *group* values, as one type of common value. The distinction is useful, since many goals are desired by most members of a group—therefore *common* to those members—without being groupal goals. Indeed, many common goals create considerable conflict. Perhaps all wish to be leaders, or to be wealthy. Not all can be the belle of the ball, but the goal may be common to the group. Other value structures must allay this possible conflict. Many common goals, such as marrying and having children, are open to most of the society, and help to pattern and integrate social action somewhat.

On the other hand, there are values which focus on the group as such. In a nationalist era such as the present, most of us have in common some deeply felt emotions concerning the survival of our own country. The symbols of that larger group can, at times, move us powerfully, even to the extent of sacrificing our own lives for it. In more religious epochs, individuals may feel such emotions for their religious group. Of a more trivial character, perhaps, are those group values which undergraduates come to feel for their university and its continuing life.

The integrative character of such ultimate values is a matter of common observation, and we implicitly agree in action upon their integrative function, when we call upon such values in an effort to arouse the group to action. Such values may also furnish reference points, or criteria, for judging individual action. Certain ultimate, common values may serve the same function. However, since these groupal values also define the major foci of action, they give significance and meaning to minor activities of the group. We expect, then, that all groups will have some groupal values held in common by the members of the group.

These ultimate values are most powerful, of course, in moments of crisis, when the group is threatened. However, it is likely that periodic activities with almost a ritual character will help to reaffirm those values. In addition, there are likely to be groupal activities of a less emotionalized character which also reaffirm the group's existence by requiring shared action. Moreover, the group is likely to have various symbols which serve to indicate unity and importance, as against any particular member.

It must be remembered that such statements do not imply the "goodness" of such integration. Nor is there any assumption that integration within one group necessarily leads to happiness, or to lack of conflict with other groups. Indeed, it must be rather clear that highly integrated sub-groups within a society will inevitably conflict, unless there is a still more ultimate set of group values which can reduce their importance. All that is implied in the foregoing statements is that a major factor in the integration of individual action systems is a system of ultimate, groupal values, and that no society can continue to exist without such values.

It is clear that we have left the realm of biological drives. We are speaking of value interrelationships. If there is a religious "drive," a nationalist "hunger," the physiologist has not been able to discover it. We must, rather, accept the reality of social factors, the importance of value elements, to the society itself, and only derivatively to any given individual. Such values are no less powerful, merely because they do not originate in specific physiological mechanisms. And, as noted before, they are deeply rooted in physiological reactions through the process of socialization.

A further point of clarification needs to be added. To insist that such groupal values are necessary for the continued existence of a society does not mean that they are alone sufficient. Obviously, many other needs must also be met. Moreover, since any society has several such groupal values—survival or success in war, ritual observances and the approval of the gods, the succession to kingship—they may come into conflict. And, under certain conditions, holding rigidly to one set, such as ritual observances, may actually help to destroy the society. A high level of integration, in short, does not necessarily mean flexibility in adjustment.

Whether all societies must possess a religious system as part of its groupal value system may be doubted by some. It is certain that all societies have had a religious system, and it is possible in view of the increasing idolatry of Stalin, to maintain that even Soviet Russia is trying to develop one. In any event, we are on safe grounds in asserting that all primitive societies have a religious system.

This ubiquity, coupled with the lack of any demonstrable physiological "drive" of a religious nature, suggests that religion in primitive societies is of great social importance.[4] Previous discussion has indicated that its beliefs and rituals are social phenomena, and passed on from one generation to the next through the socialization process. In conformity with the social character of religious behavior, we may also note that the relationship between the gods and man is thought of as a social one.

That the sphere of religion is one of ultimate groupal values suggests, moreover, that it usually approves action which is in conformity with existing custom, and that individuals are motivated by such values to devote their energies to what is believed to be the welfare of the society.

To speak of ultimate groupal values implies a distinction which is fundamental to any analysis of religion, that between the *sacred* and the *profane*.[5] In addition, the previous discussion has emphasized religious behavior, or action, indicating that some distinction must be made between *ritual* and *belief*.

Several of these propositions, basic to the present study, deserve some attention. Let us begin with the social character of gods in their relationship to man.

The statement that the religious entities, or gods, are like men cannot be called a wholly original discovery, for it has been repeated by one philosopher or another since Xenophanes, some two and one-half millennia ago. Yet, like many earlier insights, it requires some modification to fit the facts, and the modification most pertinent is sociological. For the sacred entities are not always anthropomorphic. They do not always have arms or legs, or other ordinary physical attributes of man, and no images may be made of them. They are, rather, "anthroposocial." The gods can *perceive*, even though specific sensory organs may not be attributed to some of them.[6] This is true even of the high gods, who may not be particularly interested in man (if certain interpretations can be accepted) but who at certain crises will perceive what man is doing. Or, they will receive messages from other gods, or from man. This does not mean that they are omniscient or omnipotent. Nevertheless, their perception will be very efficient with respect to evil or to moral violations.[7]

Thus, one may say that the gods are "socialized." They are intellectually and emotionally aware of what the tribe considers good and evil. Indeed, the order is usually reversed in the opinion of the society, for the definitions of good and evil are thought of as coming originally from such religious entities.

Further, the gods show their social personalities by being interested in the general welfare of the group.[8] This becomes explicit in the Tikopia ritual, with its resounding appeal for "the good of the land." Thus, the ritual formula recited during the oiling and scenting of the center post at Somosomo (no longer recited):

> "Thou, Ancestor!
> I eat ten times thy excrement
> Turn thou Mapusia to thy post
>      which is being anointed
> Anointed for welfare
> Untold welfare for thy crown of the land."[9]

This interest in the general welfare of the group may be looked at more closely, as exhibiting the type of social relationship which exists between gods and men. Religious rituals continually ask for spiritual and physical favors from such entities. However, the petition is rarely thought of in only contractual terms. The assumption is made, rather, that the spiritual powers are generally more interested in sending good things than in sending bad ones, if good relationships between gods and men continue. This assumption does not exclude a Trickster God, who may play whimsical or cruel jokes on men.[10] Nor does it deny the existence of a vengeful Jahweh, or an evil Loki or even Satan. Nevertheless, we can no longer accept the once prevalent belief that primitive man, unlike the enlightened and civilized Western European, lives in constant terror of the black forces which surround him. Instead, we must see that primitive gods have somewhat the same idea of what is good as has the tribe, and they are moreover able to send good things to the tribe when needed. Friendly relations are maintained so far as possible, even though the emotional closeness between gods and men is variable. It is moreover clear that societies generally believe that they succeed, for it is evident that good fortune, not bad, is taken for granted. So long, briefly, as the group is living according to precept, the general action of the spiritual entities is expected to be beneficial, not inimical.[11]

Their social character is further seen in that they desire ritual recognition, and can be supplicated and moved. They are not deaf to the pleas of men who approach them with proper gifts, attitudes, and ritual observances. Of course, as in the case with powerful human beings, the supplicant can not be certain that his plea will be granted, but there is the expectation of response of some kind. The attitude is not simply that of the engineer, manipulating an impersonal, physical situation, or that of the contractor, offering a return for favors received.[12] It is that of deference offered to a personage on whose good will the supplicant's goals depend.

A distinction between the *sacred* and the *profane* has been mentioned as fundamental to an analysis of religion. It is, indeed, the distinction on which there is general agreement between opposed theorists. Religious behavior is set off from other complexes by a particular emotional set, an *attitude*, of the participants. This is sometimes designated as awe or reverence. Such an attitude does not, of course, exclude the possibility of fear. Nevertheless, the adherents of a religion are not, strictly speaking, merely fearful of their gods. There is respect mingled in the emotion. This feeling that there is something sacred, which is powerful, seems to be universal for all primitive religions. The attitude, then, sets off the "holy" from the "common" (W. Robertson Smith), the "sacred" from the "profane" (Émile Durkheim), the *charismatisch* from the *alltäglich* (Max Weber).

The intensity of the emotion will vary in different societies, for some are certainly more secular than others. The emotion, moreover, does not appear at random, but in specified situations.[13] It is not characteristic of an everyday, utilitarian set of circumstances, but is set apart, surrounded with tabus, and called forth by definitely limited occasions. In fact, Durkheim found it difficult to characterize the religious complex except in terms of this set-apart attitude.

Since the emphasis in this study is on religious action, perhaps we should select a situation, for brief analysis, from one of the societies being considered. It is when we observe a rite in progress that we see these characteristics of the sacred, such as being set apart, imbued with emotion, having deep significance, being fixed in its elements (traditionalized), and so on. Of course, these qualities of the sacred will be discussed more extensively later on.

A case may be chosen from the many observed in the Tikopia rituals. As a part of the "work" of Somosomo, the women had to plait the sacred mats which figure so often in gifts and in the refurbishing of Tikopia temples. Let us look at the situation as a going process:

The plaiting of the sacred mats was a rite of importance. The women who sat down to plait were supposed to do so in Ama [Ama: an undiscussed symbolism; it is that part of the temple site towards the coast, not toward the sacred place of Uta. It is also the port side of the canoe, to which the out-rigger is attached and from which fish are not taken; it is thus the left side in Somosomo. It is opposed to *katea*, though the Tikopia have ordinary words for "right" and "left"], though they sometimes placed themselves further forward. Moreover, they had to turn their backs to the sea coast, not to the lake. The reason for this was that by following the latter course they would be showing disrespect to the sacred district of Uta, which lay on the farther shore. This is a point on which the elders in charge were insistent. In my presence Pa Rarovi called out to the women as they were standing up to prepare their leaf, "Your backs, do not turn them to Uta," as a warning. When the actual plaiting began the taboo of silence was imposed: the women might not speak to each other, nor the men to them. This rule was not absolute—one woman asked another about a technical detail of the plait-ing, for instance, and when a light shower of rain came on the elders called out to the women to go on working. But this latter was due again to the sacredness of the task; it could not be laid down because of mere weather conditions. All ordinary conversation, however, was barred. Nor might the workers be approached by anyone else. A boy, grandson of the chief, when about to cross the *marae* [open space used for religious rites] was told to go inland, by the hedge, and not to go near the women. The *marae* as a whole was in fact taboo during the progress of the "work" there. During the clearing operations a lad came along the path carrying a food bowl and taro grater. He was at once stopped and rebuked for not proceeding by an alternative route [i.e., a *secular* route] which ran some hundred yards or more inland and avoided the glade altogether. On his protestations of ignorance, however, and after a good talking to by the older men, he was at last allowed to go past. The *tapu* extended also to all details of the sacred work. Thus the women on their return with the coconut fronds from Materetoro expressed their indignation at another, not a participant, who had bathed that morning near the spot where the fronds lay. "No one should go near when the Work is in progress," was the comment passed.

As is customary in Tikopia ritual of this type where several different groups were concerned, a definite precedence was observed. For this plaiting of the mats each woman had her place, the seating order being as follows: at the head of the row, nearest to the stone of the Atua Fafine [goddess-protector of women], sat the woman of the "house" of Kafika; next to her was the woman of Rarovi, then the women of Tavi of Fangarere, and lastly, in former days, of Porima.[14]

Perhaps the primary point to be noted, in this discussion of the sacred, is that even such a minor section of a religious ceremony is important. No such care would be ordinarily necessary for the plaiting of mats.

Plaiting is a common enough activity, and is usually done without such precautions. Here, however, the activity is no longer casual. It is part of ritual, and the mats are destined for the use of the temple, to pay honor to the gods.

Further, the activity is carefully stereotyped. The location of one woman with respect to another, and their position with reference to the temple and sea are definite and fixed, and the same is true for the duration of the activity. It cannot be easily interrupted. As against the usual chatter during plaiting, silence is imposed. The stereotyping is not based on the demands of efficiency. If the "function" of the weaving were only the production of mats, it is unlikely that these ritual demands would be made. The basis is, rather, tradition, and violations of tradition, in favor of efficiency, are not acceptable.

Indeed we may phrase this relationship differently, by saying that these various differences from the ordinary plaiting situation serve to shift emphasis from the obviously productive nature of the activity to its religious significance. The external differences (silence, specified positions, exclusion of other nonsacred activities, insistence on completion in spite of rain, etc.) act as material *symbols* of the religious importance of the activity.

Although this ritual section does not involve any direct communication with the gods, and none of the higher officiants participate, some emotional elements are seen. For example, indignation is shown merely because someone has bathed near the work. An intrusion of the secular, or profane, into the sacred has occurred. This is likewise true in the case of the boy who came too close to the work area. One would expect, of course, still stronger emotions to be shown in major rituals.

The distinction between sacred and profane may be seen in another example, taken this time from Dahomey. The Dahomeans are more sceptical and rationalistic than the Tikopia, as can be seen in more detail in Appendix II as well as in the following chapter. Their rituals are more complex than those of Tikopia, and more formally controlled. They may even postpone a ritual section because of threatening rain. Let us look, however, at part of the rite of emergence from the cult-house, after initiation, in order to see some of the same elements as those noted in the Tikopia excerpt:

"A feeling of tension and great excitement could be sensed as the procession started. First came the old woman with her rattle, a gourd with seeds inside and a braided mesh to which some cauries were attached over it. Following her came a priestess—not a candidate, who carried a white enameled basin on her head in which rested an object covered over with crimson cloth of the

same color as the cloths worn by the candidates. This was the representation of
the deity itself; the most sacred object of the cult, which might be unveiled
only before the initiate in the darkness of the temple. Following single file
came the novices . . . On the heads of the man, and of the woman who immediately followed him, were small red pots, covered and ornamented with
strands of cauries and blue, white and black beads which hung from them.
Each of these two persons also held three [a number figuring often in
Dahomean rituals] strands of cauries in his mouth. The eleven who followed
likewise carried pots on their heads, and in the case of all thirteen, these pots
rested on chaplets of cauries which took the place of the rolled cloths used by
burden carriers to steady their loads. Each of the following eleven carried one
strand of cauries in the mouth; in all these cases, the cauries were to prevent
the candidates from speaking [sacred imposition of silence]. Though there
was no opportunity to examine them, it was stated that each string contained
the sacred number of forty-one cauries . . ."[15]

Again we see the emotion of ritual. The traditionalized details are once
more apparent: homogeneity of color, covering of the sacred objects,
specification of the number of caury strands, the order of procession, the
use of caury chaplets instead of ordinary rolled cloths, the imposition
of silence on the candidates, etc. The carrying of a burden on the
head, a secular activity in Dahomey, becomes sacred here.

The sacred character of religious activity may also be marked by the
use of *sacred words*, either specialized words or ordinary words with a
sacred meaning. The cult training procedure in Dahomey, for example,
includes a prohibition on speaking Fɔ on emergence. The initiate must
speak Nago, or Peda, or Porto Novo, etc., and only gradually is he
allowed to speak the Dahomean (secular, ordinary) language again.
Such an extreme elaboration would, of course, be rare, but one would
expect to find nonsecular words in any religious system. A few noted at
random from Tikopia might include:[16]

| SACRED | | SECULAR |
|---|---|---|
| raorao | calm | Ngaio |
| kasoa tapu | wind | matangi |
| rau vati | foliage | rau rakau |
| urufenua | breadfruit | mai |
| matauri | adze | faingata |
| uaroro | coconut | niu |

Since the immediate effort here is not to prove any theory, but merely
to make clear the meaning and use of certain conceptual distinction, in
particular that between the sacred and the secular, such illustrations may
suffice. It becomes clear that it is not the object, or word, or gesture which

is the source of the sacred. *These vary almost infinitely. What is constant is the imputation of religious significance,* or a relationship to the gods, or some definition of the object as charged with sacred power. This fact only documents again the weakness of individualistic theories of religions, which seek to understand the sacred as derivable from particular objects or experiences (See Appendix III). For no object, phenomenon, or experience is intrinsically sacred. It is rather by virtue of the relationship of the object to the society that it is imbued with sacredness, made symbolic and charged with meaning. It becomes more than merely an object, or a word, or gesture, or an experience; it rather implies and evokes the feeling and presence of sacred powers.

The sacred, then, is intrinsic to both *belief and ritual.* One must take account of the distinction between these two. *It is the beliefs, the system of religious ideas, which define the meaning of the ritual.* The ritual, in turn, becomes the material symbol of what is embodied in the beliefs. For it consists in the manipulation of sacred things, sacred gestures, or sacred words. This active orientation has nevertheless a symbolic character, since it is by this manipulation that the believer feels he is having an effect on the concrete and spiritual worlds. "Religious ideas may be held to constitute systems of symbolic representations of sacred entities,"[17] but the ritual embodies active attitudes as well, not merely a cognitive acceptance. Religion is not, therefore, merely philosophy; it requires action.

Although such ritual activities are *means,* by virtue of their stereotyped, symbolic character they become *ends* as well, as is frequently the case in social behavior. They are assumed to have some efficacy in dealing with sacred entities, but they must be carried out because of their sacred character, and thus have the immediacy and importance of ends, also.

Since the rituals are thus techniques for entering into, continuing, or reasserting social relationships with the gods, the beliefs embodied in such rituals have a meaning far beyond the immediate act or its supposed end. For it is thereby that man is able to deny the blindness and impersonality of the cosmos. Instead, he has fundamental, meaningful relationships with all that exists and happens, through his social relationships with the gods. This is easily seen even in our own culture, which emphasizes empirical causation more than any other. For we find a merely causal explanation of personal or social disaster not at all emotionally satisfactory. The "Why?" which we ask is not a demand for rational cause, but a desire for meaning.[18] Without inquiring now into the further ramifications of religious significance, we can at least note this interrelationship between the belief embedded in ritual, and the meaning of the universe which the believer derives from his social relationship to the gods.

As will be seen later, for the purposes of the present study the rituals, or *the broad actional demands of the religious system,* are of crucial technical significance. They represent the actional link between religion and the physical or social worlds. It is through the study of such actional demands that we see that *religion is action,* and *occurs in this world,* as well as being defined by beliefs. Through such demands, then, we can discern and test the interrelationships, or functions, of religion with respect to other spheres of social behavior.

As a final distinction to be made, let us discuss that between *magic* and *religion.* This distinction has been made, using different criteria, by several generations of social analysts, and is to be found in lay thought as well. It will be the aim of the present exposition to integrate these bases so as to understand better the relationships between these two complexes.

The traditional distinction between magic and religion has gradually assumed conceptual clarity in anthropological literature during the past three decades. The present discussion centers on that distinction and the implications of it for a better understanding of primitive society.

This theoretical clarity has emerged slowly because of concrete similarities in the phenomena, and the consequent conceptual difficulty of cleaving through such apparent similarities.

*Similarities.* The rather close similarities to be observed in the concrete phenomena stem, naturally, from their relationship to the supernatural. They are (1) both *concerned with the nonempirical.* They refer to a realm beyond that of the "logico-experimental," to the nonmeasurable, the intangible, where the nonbeliever "cannot see" those elements which are real enough to the faithful. Thus, (2) they both stand in somewhat the *same relationship to Western science,* which itself has imposed this distinction on the primitive. To the primitive society, of course, such a distinction is impossible: the supernatural is as real as what we call the empirical, and the world does not stop at the borderline of the Western scientist's senses.[19]

Further, (3) both are pervasively *symbolic.* That is, objects which may be ordinary in one situation are endowed with religious or magical significance in another: they *stand* for something else, such as a magical force, an idea, an occurrence, etc.[20] Thus suggests another similarity: (4) they both deal with nonhuman forces, sometimes called the sacred.[21]

A systematic symbolism suggest, (5) however, a *ritual system,* and this, too, is common to both, the rituals frequently functioning as external representations of the supernatural. As to the things or forces symbolized in the rituals, both systems (6) contain many "anthropopsychic" entities. That is, the entities are dealt with frequently as though they had mentalities like the members of the society: they can be threatened, cajoled, or addressed; they may be whimsical, moody, or vain; their definition of who is worthy to approach is similar, etc. Now, as to practitioners, (7) there is usually a specialized (a) *set of skills,* and (b) *a select group* holding those skills, for dealing with such forces.

In spite of such similarities, however, anthropologists have been working toward a distinction based upon a number of characteristics. Part of this distinction goes back to Tylor's idea that magic is a pseudoscience based on an inaccurate association of ideas, divination being a "sincere but fallacious system of philosophy."[23] From this notion, several other characteristics emerge. One, naturally, is the instrumental nature of magic, meaning that it can be used for either good or evil.[24] Malinowski and his student Ian Hogbin have both pointed to this use of sorcery in the Trobriands and in Ontong Java. There is thus an implicit acceptance of the impersonality of magic.

This instrumental and impersonal nature of magic suggests an emphasis on *personal* ends, not *groupal* ends. Reasoning from this, it would seem likely that there might be fewer cult activities in the case of magic, and thus a simpler structure, than in religion. "As a general rule," this may not be far wrong. However, under conditions which have been generalized as hypotheses, a complex cult development seems to be possible.[25]

Lowie has qualified somewhat the notion of impersonality, and the attitude of control, presumed to be held by the magician.[26] In his discussion, Lowie agrees that this "roughly" describes the "more or less prevalent character of individual reactions."[27] Nevertheless, he suggests that this is not at all a universal reaction. Even in the religious situation, one may find the Winnebago practitioner "compelling" the spirits (following Radin), in spite of reverence. Malinowski, in his treatment of the "origin" of magic (almost in biological terms, in the "primal situation"), emphasizes the emotional nature of the magical situation, and of course there may be respect, if not reverence, for the magical apparatus and formulas.[28] Nevertheless, both in his earlier and later treatments, Milinowski adheres in his descriptions to the conception of magic as prosaic, without humility or reverence for the most part. Evans-Pritchard, who also notes that there may be emotion in the magical situation when the disease is serious, follows this conception of "ordering" the magical forces, calmly, "just as he would tell a boy were he dispatching him on an errand."[29]

Yet the magician clearly has more than a craftsman's attitudes toward his apparatus and beliefs.[30] For this reason, Lowie, seconded later by Radin, suggests that we should expect some overlapping between magic and religion.[31] Little change in the one would be required to convert it to the other.[32] Marett, Goldweiser, and others express ideas close to this. Herskovits goes further, claiming that "magic is regarded as an integral part of the Dahomean religious system."[33] Warner, similarly, maintains that ". . . the essential nature of magic and ritual is the same . . . at least in Murngin society."[34] In Firth's Tikopia, the magical and religious practitioner are the same.[35]

Such a brief discussion suggests several propositions: A. A distinction between magic and religion has generally been made in anthropological literature; B. The distinction seems to be based on several concrete criteria; C. There is rough agreement on these criteria; and D. There is no sharp concrete line to be drawn between the two.

The corollary of these propositions is that magic and religion can be distinguished through the use of a theoretical tool, the polar ideal type concept.[36] Such a conceptual device is widespread in the social sciences, and in some form occurs in all anthropological generalization, whether consciously or not. In its application one accepts the idea that any given magical or religious system is concretely not to be found at either extreme, theoretical pole, but somewhere between the two. If the conceptual "exaggerations" constituting the poles are useful, such systems will fall near one or the other of the two. This is, of course, always an approximation, as the application of any scientific concept to concrete situations will be: the unique situation or phenomenon rarely, if ever, equates with the conceptual description or theoretical formulation of any science. Further, the decision as toward which pole a supernatural system falls requires *several* characteristics, each of which is a variable running between two opposing or antithetical forms.

A spatial representation of such a result is possible:[37]

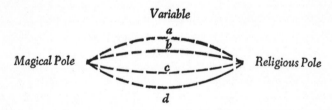

## THE DISTINCTION

The characteristics most prominently emerging in anthropological writings as theoretical aids in distinguishing these two complexes seem to be the following:

1. *Concrete specificity of goal* relates most closely to the magical complex. This overlaps toward the religious goal more than most characteristics, since religious rewards are usually to be found in this world. However, religious goals do lean more heavily in the direction of "general welfare," "health," "good weather," and eschatological occurrences.

2. The *manipulative attitude* is to be found most strongly at the magical pole, as against the supplicative, propitiatory, or cajoling, at the religious pole.

3. The *professional-client relationship* is ideally-theoretically to be found in the magical complex. The shepherd-flock, or prophet-follower, is more likely in the religious.

4. *Individual ends* are more frequently to be found toward the magical end of this continuum, as against groupal ends toward the other.[38]

5. The magical practitioner or his "customer" *goes through his activities as a private individual,* or individuals, functioning much less as groups. At the religious extreme pole, groups carry them out, or representatives of groups.

6. With regard to the process of achieving the goal, in case of magical failure, there is more likely to be a *substitution or introduction of other techniques.* Stronger magic will be used, or magic to offset the counter-magic of enemies, or even a different magician.[39] Since much of religious activity is less specifically instrumental, is concerned more with the intrinsic meaning of the ritual, and is expected to achieve concrete goals indirectly, by maintaining the proper continuing relationship with the gods, such a substitution is far rarer in the area of the religious pole.

7. Although the practitioner may feel cautious in handling such powerful forces, a *lesser degree of emotion* is expected at the magical end of this continuum. This may be described as *impersonality.* At the religious end, one expects a greater degree of emotion, possibly awe or worship.

8. The *practitioner decides whether* the process is to start at all, toward the magical pole. Toward the religious, the ritual *must* be carried out. That it must be done is part of the structure of the universe.

9. Similarly, the *practitioner decides when* the process is to start, in the case of magic, more often than in the case of religion. Toward the latter end of the continuum, the time relationships of rituals are fairly fixed, within rough limits, even when not calendrical.

10. Defined as instrumental by the society, magic is thought of as at least *potentially directed against the society,* or a major accepted group within it, or a respected individual in good repute with the gods. Re-

ligious rituals are not thought of as even potentially directed against the society or such respected people.

11. As a final, ideally distinguishing characteristic, magic is *used only instrumentally*, i.e., *for goals*. The religious complex may be used for goals, but at its ideal pole, the practices are ends in themselves.

Such a set of ideal-typical criteria is sufficient to set apart the extreme poles, and it seems likely that a given magical or religious complex will fall fairly definitely toward one pole or the other, although of course no such concrete complex will be found exactly at either extreme.

The theory of religion which has been sketched in this chapter properly issues in more specific propositions which can be tested, in at least a rough form, through the study of the data in the following chapters. It will aid clarity, then, to outline some of these concrete generalizations, even though their full meaning will become apparent only by applying them to actual religious behavior.

These concrete propositions are as follows:

1. Human societies distinguish between secular and sacred things, as defined by the group attitudes in the society.

2. These sacred things include various objects, among which are to be found natural forces and animals, or inanimate objects, deities, acts, areas, words, gestures, etc.

3. The socialization process, which sometimes includes specific cult training as well, inculcates knowledge of and respect for the sacred.

4. Conformity with religious prescriptions will usually give support to other institutions and to common, or groupal, goals, due to the integration of the society at the common value level.

5. The religious practitioners gain certain advantages from their relationship to the sacred, such as prestige, power, and goods.

6. The supernatural entities, or gods, are not always held to have bodies like men, but their values, attitudes, perception, and thought are "anthropo-social." That is, their "personalities" are like those of members of the society. This is evidenced by these facts:

a. The deities take notice of man's actions;

b. The deities act broadly to further man's welfare, such welfare conforming closely to the society's desires;

c. The deities desire human attention, and are pleased by honor paid to them, as well as displeased by neglect;

d. The deities usually punish men for not acting in accordance with the rules of the society, such punishment usually occurring in this world;

e. The deities are not invariably "good," for they may also have "moods," and some are whimsical or destructive at times;

f. The relationships between deities and men, and among deities, are also conceived in such social terms, in that there will be communication, promises, reminders, approval, and perhaps even threats.

7. There is a body of religious belief common to the society, which may not always be developed into a "doctrine," but which constitutes the *meaning of ritual*. These beliefs treat of the origin and nature of the deities, and their relationships to men, punishment, the nature of human souls and their destiny, etc., and impute order and sense to the world.

8. Religious rituals make many actional demands upon men, and thus form the link between religion and other spheres of action, so that one can observe the concrete interrelationships of the religious system with other social action: by diverting, increasing, or decreasing production, distribution, and consumption; and shifting or strengthening the political structure.

9. The sacredness of objects and of rituals is based upon their *symbolic* character, as representative of the will or action of the deities, or as objective embodiments of religious belief.

10. Rituals are not thought of as contractual in character, but they will contain frequent requests for favors.

11. Magic and religion are not dichotomies, but represent a continuum, and are distinguished only ideal-typically.

With the general sociological approach in mind as well as these concrete propositions, let us now look at the religious systems under our scrutiny, Dahomey, Manus, Tikopia, Zuñi, and Murngin.[40]

# 4. STRUCTURE OF THE RELIGIOUS SYSTEMS

IN ORDER to keep clearly in mind the general focus of the present study, it is useful to sketch briefly the essential elements of the religions involved. Some points can be only suggested whose more detailed treatment is more relevant elsewhere. Such an outline of the religious structure, furthermore, allows some clarification of the theoretical formulation in the preceding chapter.

## DAHOMEY

The Dahomean system is composed of several sub-systems, and seems complex enough to require an extended treatment.[1] As the Herskovits's point out, the organization of the Dahomean gods is a reflection of the organization of the society, though in a somewhat rough fashion. This includes the idea of reigning over a kingdom, and of a hierarchy of organization influencing all aspects of the social and economic life. The apex of this organization is embodied in a kind of Sky-God, who has divided the universe, and has given her possessions, including many special powers, to her sons. "The method of passing on her possessions, and the autonomy enjoyed by the owners of what had been given them as their portion, follow Dehomean practice in the everyday world."[2] The specialization is of the same cloth, since the Dahomean god is like the Dahomean in that he does not perform all tasks. Rather, his powers are definitely limited. There are, instead, *groups of deities,* organized into a sort of pantheon under a pantheon head. This group comes to be the focus of what is essentially a church, even in an ordinary sense, since the given Dahomean—even a priest—will not know all the practices and beliefs of other pantheons than his own.

There is also an arch-individualist, the trickster, to be found in the system. Every pantheon has such a trickster, though he is a rather earthy one. Usually, he is the youngest member, always a younger one, who outwits the older, more powerful gods. This fits the Dahomean notion of the youngest child being the spoiled, whimsical, bright child.

Besides these Great Gods, the pantheons with pantheon heads, there are ancestral cults, which are of more immediate importance for the daily life of the Dahomean than the cult of the Great Gods. Nevertheless, since the latter have religious devotees, they do figure in the daily lives of such worshippers. Furthermore, they are "public gods," by virtue of the protection and nourishment they furnish to the kingdom. The ancestral cult, however, does represent a step closer to earth, and is linked to the cult of the public gods through the cult of the spirits which "represent the first offspring of the supernatural founders of the thirty of forty sibs.[3] These founders have the rank of the Great Gods, in the case of the more important sibs.

Included with the main ancestral and public deities there are some lesser gods. These do not have the immediate daily importance of the former, though they follow them in ceremonial. They originate in the chief pantheons. However, they are actually on the earth, since they were sent here to live among men, sometimes mating with men to produce semi-divine spirits who people the earth. These are different from, though closely related to, the personal deities and forces, destiny and the control of fate, which are part of the daily acting foundation of organized religion. This, it is maintained, also includes magic, and the serpent who brings wealth. The genuine fetish is found only in magic.

It becomes clear, then, that we are dealing with an extremely complex, formal religious system. This is the more apparent when we examine the Sky-God, Mawu. This deity is mentioned as having ultimate control of the universe, but its nature is variously explained and often is not clear. Those who are directly related to this cult will speak of this god as Mawu-Lisa. This relates Mawu with the other chief member of this pantheon, Lisa.[4] The usual statement is that Mawu is female and reigns over the moon, while Lisa is male with dominion over the sun. However, to some, Mawu is androgynous and Lisa is the son of Mawu. Or, another version, they are two beings in one. Or, still another one, Mawu is male. Or, that Lisa is the grandmother of the trickster.[5]

This confusion would be incomprehensible if Mawu, or some other god, were understood to be the sole, unique creator, before all things. Actually, other forces play a part as coexistent or coeval entities. For example, Aido Hwedo the serpent is the god responsible for thunderbolts and is the support for the earth. It is also the personification of the gods unknown to the Dahomeans but preceding those which first figure in

Dahomean tradition. Actually, the Dahomean mythology begins with
conflict among the deities, especially with fraternal jealousies.

Nevertheless, in spite of an apparent lack of crystallization—or perhaps it is crystallization in many directions—Mawu is certainly the
symbol[6] of the founder of the family of deities, for it is from her (him)
that their power came. Herskovits and Herskovits sum it up in this
manner:

It is Mawu as parent of the other gods, who gave them their power. It is
Mawu who, according to the diviners of Destiny, holds the formulae for the
creation of man and matter. It is Mawu who sent the art of divination to
earth so that man might know how to appease the anger and thwart the ill
intentions of the reigning pantheon heads, Mawu's children. It is Mawu who
gave her favorite son, the trickster Legba, to man to help him circumvent
Fate. Most important of all, it is Mawu who, though she divided her kingdom
among her children, the other Great Gods, and gave each autonomous rule
over his own domain, has yet withheld from all of them the knowledge of
how to create, so that the ultimate destiny of the Universe is still in her
hands. When her children punish and destroy, she can create anew.[7]

This is true, even though Mawu is but one more god important to
the welfare of the nation. Mawu is not supplicated in prayers, unless the
Dahomean in question is a cult-member of the Sky pantheon.

All this, however, is but the grossest part of the Dahomean religious
framework. Some more detailed facts of the system must be brought in,
to keep more firmly in mind the general locus of later discussions. Perhaps the most immediate attention should be given to the Great Gods,
the pantheons of Sky, Thunder, and Earth.

The worship of the Sky is a cult, with priests, initiates—"wives" of
the gods—periods of initiation and training, long and complex rituals.
It is "highly stylized" and closely related to the monarchy, becoming
almost like a state religion.[8] The chief groups of temples for the Sky
deities, and the cult houses of seclusion for initiates during their training,
are located in the palace enclosure. There is considerable pageantry in
the rites of the Sky pantheon, and their funeral finery is often referred
to in Dahomean conversation and in travelers' reports.

Interestingly enough, in this Mawu-Lisa cult neither Mawu nor
Lisa is the world-creator, but Nana Buluku. Nana Buluku has her (his)
seat of worship northwest of Abomey, where homage is paid to her by
representatives of each Sky God temple. However, she is not the center
of the cult, which is rather occupied by Mawu and Lisa. Mawu is
thought generally to be gentle and forgiving, while Lisa, the male and

the sun, is robust and ruthless. "In Mawu is concentrated the wisdom of the world, and in Lisa its strength."[9]

There is neither space nor occasion for outlining the powers of all the gods of the pantheon under discussion. To Mawu and Lisa, the twin son and daughter of Nana Buluku, were born many children, the androgynous Sogbo, the twins Sagbata, the twins Agbe, Gu, Agε, Dji, Wεte, Mεdje, Loko, and others. Since Sogbo, Sagbata, and Agbe do not form part of the Sky pantheon,[10] but are rather the focus of the pantheons of the Thunder, Earth, and Sea respectively, it is Gu who is first after Mawu and Lisa. His close relationship to the monarchy, which is supposed to have introduced the Mawu-Lisa cult into Dahomey, is seen in his character[11] as the deity of war and of metal. More specifically,

. . . he was not created in the shape of a living being. His trunk was of stone, and from it projected a blade of metal; some say that this blade was once stone, too. Gu was charged by Mawu to make the earth habitable for man. It is Gu who gave tools so that man might build shelters, and hoe the ground, cut down trees for firewood, make boats and implements, and triumph over enemies—the words of a Dahomean priest were, "Thanks to Gu, one can cut off heads."[12]

It would not be profitable to delineate similarly the rest of the gods in the pantheon, except to note that they all have specific tasks to accomplish, that two of them, males, are guardians of Lisa's possessions while two females perform the same function for Mawu, and that there is a Lεgba, a personal spirit of the type figuring widely in the Dahomean world-view.

Though this pantheon is associated with the monarchy, and its constituents are powerful, it is not a "popular" religion. Both the Thunder and Earth pantheons have more cult-members. The Earth-cult, focussing in Sagbata, is not dominated, as one might ordinarily expect, by the conception of the "fertile mother." Sagbata is the symbol of the first son[13] of Mawu and Lisa, and not an individual god at all in this pantheon. Thus the interesting overlapping of deities occurs here, which Müller made so much of at an earlier period with respect to the Indo-Germanic languages. This, however, is not the same deity under different names in different cultures, but within the same culture. The Tikopia, likewise, will be found to have such a pattern, as also the Murngin. In this cult, the God of Thunder (Sogbo) is called Xevioso, and is the younger brother of Sagbata.

In order to depict better the relationship which ideally holds between these cults, and to make the type of religion clearer, it might be useful to depart from brevity by quoting the Herskovits' abstract of the usual myth relating the two:

When a son was to be chosen to rule the earth, Xevioso wished to come. Mawu, however, said that since the Earth was too far from the sky, it was better that the oldest son, Sagbata, go there. In sending Sagbata, Mawu told him to take all the possessions he could carry with him to the kingdom below, but made it a condition that, once gone, he should never again return to the sky. Sagbata (who actually represents a pair of twins, from the mating of whom came all the other members of the Sagbata pantheon), was greedy, and tried to take everything. The wealth he carried was so great that he could not find a place for fire and water, and, thinking them of slight importance did not trouble about them. These two elements thereupon became the portion of Xevioso. Xevioso, resenting the greed of his brother, withheld water from the earth, so that the inhabitants, who had welcomed the new king who came to them with great riches, became discontented, for on earth there was no rain and nothing grew. Famine was everywhere. In desperation, Sagbata called his younger brother, Lɛgba, the favorite of Mawu, and the one possessed of the greatest cunning. Lɛgba, who had connived with Xevioso in his plan for vengeance, but who realized that the quarrel between the brothers must be kept from the knowledge of Mawu, decided at last to occupy himself with reconciliation, and this he achieved. Today the two brothers work together to feed mankind, and they share the rights of meting out supreme justice; Xevioso with fire and thunderbolts, Sagbata with smallpox and other skin diseases.[14]

As a consequence, Sagbata "is the greatest king on earth and it was because the kings of Dahomey felt that 'two kings cannot rule the same city,' that in every Dahomean town the temples of the Earth Gods are always outside the limits of the settlement proper."[15] Sagbata has the power of life and death over his subjects, just as has any king. As he gives man the bounty of his grain for life, so he can send grain-like eruptions of the skin, such as the terrible small-pox.[16] This relates in a neat fashion his power as ruler to his specific character as Earth. This cult, like Mawu-Lisa, also has a large number of gods, supposedly born of an androgynous Mawu-Lisa, with Lɛgba as the youngest again.

The third great group of public deities is the Thunder pantheon, Xevioso. Within it is a related group of gods who rule the sea. The priests of this cult *do not, however, call the world-Creator Mawu, but Sogbo*. This Sogbo had a son, Agbe, who was to rule the world. To do this, he descended from the sky, and created the sea for himself, while Sogbo rules the much larger realm of the sky, which has far more inhabitants than the earth. Since Sogbo did not tell Agbe how to cause rain to fall, he must first make water rise from the sea. To the Xevioso priests, the

sun is the eyes of Agbe, who corresponds to Lisa. He remains in contact
with Sogbo, since the sea and sky touch each other. Sogbo does not, however, tell him all her secrets. He cannot create anything, or make the
earth bear its fruits.[17] In this pantheon, also, there are many beings,
with specialized abilities and characters. The youngest in this pantheon
is a female, Aflɛketɛ, who is somewhat like Lɛgba, dancing like him in
rituals. She is a persistent gossip, and has great power by virtue of her
knowledge of her father's secrets. She is the daughter of Agbe, while
Sogbo's youngest is Gbade, more robust, but paralleling Aflɛketɛ's personality.

In this brief summary of the general structure of Dahomean religion,
the ancestral cult figures next in importance, though the importance is
overlapping in nature. For some gods of the pantheons are somewhat
neglected, while the cults of the sib founders are widely worshipped.
Though the *Tɔhwiyo* do not constitute all of the ancestral worship of the
Dahomeans, they occupy a central position, and deserve some mention.
These are the *founders of the Dahomean sibs*, figuring as elements of an
essentially totemic system of belief.[18]

These founders of the Dahomean sibs are the immediate children of a
supernatural animal and a human being. The supernatural animal is
respected, and there are usually various *su* connected with the animal,
i.e., essentially tabus. But it is the offspring who are the genuine Tɔhwiyo. These were not at first precisely like human beings, but became
human through several generations. Their background is somewhat as
follows. After man had started on earth, there were few men, and they
did not live well. Even after Gu had come to give tools to man, or Lisa
(depending on the myth), this was true. On the visits of Gu and Lisa
to the earth, they mated, thus beginning the first families. After this,
however, Fa (the Dahomean system of divination), or Destiny, was
preached by the sons of Fate (Gbadu), and it was revealed that supernatural beings would come to begin families on earth. Those families
already settled thus came to have no ancestral cult, for their Tɔhwiyo is
Lisa himself.

The other families were created by supernatural beings which came
from rivers, trees, mountains, from the earth, from the sky, from plants.
One was founded by a horse, another by a peanut, still another by a pig.
In each case, one of these beings mated with a human being, male or
female. It was from the supernatural being that the *su*, or prohibitions
and injunctions, came, as well as other sib secrets, though later *su* were
added by later members. The necessity for secrecy regarding origins is
characteristic of the sib myth.

The Tɔhwiyo have tremendous importance in the daily life of the Dahomeans and, like the secular institutions governing daily activities, have the power to punish or reward. These have essentially the powers of a king, and can condemn a sib member to death if he commits grave offenses. Infidelity, for example, is punished through the wife by killing her, or, if the husband knowingly fails to seek redress, through the husband by killing him. The Tɔhwiyo can call back all women of the sib married to another sib when a grave conflict occurs between the two sibs. This is done through the head of the sib, who thereby divorces these women from their husbands. Moreover, it is by the Tɔhwiyo that a sib member swears in the native court, not by the various pantheons. The yearly dance for the Tɔhwiyo will not be so named, but will be announced as a dance for the Vodun,[19] or gods. All the siblings of the various cults will dance, but one of them impersonates the Tɔhwiyo, and dances and dresses differently. Some of the Tɔhwiyo of important sibs will have temples, and initiates to dance before the temples, just as do the great gods.

Included in the Tɔhwiyo are the *tovodun* (deified ancestors); *tɔxɔsu* (the abnormally born); and Dambala (Dambada) Hwedo. These latter symbolize the unknown but powerful ancestors who have entered certain large trees, and mountains. The tovodun are ruled by the royal Tɔhwiyo; the tɔxɔsu are ruled, still following the pattern of legitimate power, by the royal abnormally born. Only the royal princes and their children, and the Adja sib (which claims Lisa or Agε as founder), do not have temples for their deified ancestors.

The princes do not belong to one of the pantheons, since they are too divine to be servants. They are not even permitted to be cult members of the royal Tɔhwiyo. Their mode of organized religion is ancestor worship, including the Tɔhwiyo, the Nεsuxwe who are the princely dead, and the princely Tɔxɔsu. A prince will dance for the princely dead, but not as servant. He is rather representing the particular ancestor, whose soul enters the prince's body for the duration of the ceremony.

The link between the living and the dead is maintained by the eldest male and female of a given sib. Both have great authority, for they are spokesmen between the ancestors and men. Ancestors, like other deities, must be consulted on important matters. This couple seats a man on the ancestral stool when he inherits his father's title and property. A man must always make ritual contributions to the funeral of the wife's mother or father, else divorce becomes almost inevitable. It is an insult to the sacred ancestors. It would then follow that sacrifices must be made to the ancestors, whose names must be known and called out. There are ceremonies wherein the important ancestors are impersonated in dances, but these occur rarely, once in three to five years. No names may be omitted, under penalty of the ancestor's wrath.

As noted above, it is widely thought that there were deities existing before the time of Mawu. The Dahomeans think that any god is apt to have antecedents, and to be unknown. Thus Dambada (Damabala) Hwedo, as the oldest unknown ancestor of each sib, symbolizes all those of a sib whose souls were lost to the sib without an effigy burial, before the ancestral cult was fully established. This kind of loss is carefully avoided now. The strong souls entered great trees or mountains, while lesser souls entered lesser trees. The former will perpetrate evil if they are angered, and the latter can be used by those who know how to use them. One way of angering any of these spirits is to omit their ceremonial due. No one who has once been a sib member should be lost. It is highly dangerous to any Dahomean if ceremonially the member is lost. If the spirits of the family dead are not ceremonially respected—the Tɔhwiyo, Dambada Hwedo, Tɔxɔsu, and Tovodun—the Dahomean knows that his life in this world will not be stable or happy.

Dan, the serpent, and Lɛgba occupy curious positions with respect to terminology and cult, as does Mawu. *Mawu* is the general term for deity, and this becomes a symbol of the supernatural world, while it is also the name of one member of the Sky pantheon. Somehow similarly, Lɛgba is a particular member of certain pantheons, and thus may have some individual vowed to him. But his cult is simpler and broader in base, since every offering that is given to any deity is accompanied by a gift to Lɛgba, who is the messenger of the gods. Lɛgba is tied closely to *Fa*, or Fate, since it is Lɛgba who carries the information from the gods as to what will happen, and he also can intervene. Dan, also, is the object of a rather localized worship,[20] but is more important as a general force or principle, that of life, mobility, force, dynamics, fortune, incarnate in or as a vodun or god.[21]

Mawu has still another function, as Segbo-Segbo, or Mawusɛ, the keeper of souls, for all souls come from her. Dahomeans have three souls. Besides these, there is a non-corporeal manifestation of one of them as well as an ancestral spirit.[22] This ancestral spirit, *djɔtɔ*, is often the pattern after which the Dahomean's body is formed, so that individuals can tell by the face who his particular guardian is. Before it actually becomes a djɔtɔ, however, it has to find the clay from which Mawu can form a new Dahomean. At this stage it is called *sɛmɛkɔkanto*. Besides the *sɛmɛkɔkanto*, the second soul is *sɛmɛdon*, and third is *sɛlidon*.[23] Herskovits expresses the relationship in this manner:

If, reinterpreted the terms of western world concepts, the sɛmɛkɔkanto is thought of as the biological forces which form the individual, and the sɛmɛdon as his personality, then the sɛlidɔn may be conceived as his intellect and intuition, for in Dahomean explanation it is this soul which is the inner voice that tells a person to do something or not to do it, who dictates spontaneous questions and who makes it possible for man to tell, without being able to explain why, the presence of danger, or to sense that it is wise or unwise to say or do something on a given occasion. The sɛlidɔn is held to be the soul that at death returns to bear witness against the sɛmɛdon if the latter attempts to falsify the record of the conduct on earth of the human body both souls had actuated in life. If Mawu (Segbo) is very displeased with an individual, however, the lidɔn of that person is recalled and premature death ensues.[24]

# MANUS

The lagoon-dwelling Manus are fishers and traders, having almost no land, manufacturing little[25] for trade, and obtaining their food and goods requirements by fishing, marine transportation, and trade. Basically middlemen in a money economy (dogs' teeth and strings of shells), their daily lives are enmeshed in business, exchange, and contract. Their business relationships have become so complex that the important planning is concentrated in the hands of a few, who direct the activities of young, dependent relatives.[26] Their system of exchanges includes three separate types: (1) daily marketing with the land-dwelling Usiai; (2) affinal exchanges, binding villages and validating births, marriages, deaths, etc., as well as acting as distributive agency for foreign products; and (3) trade partnerships with distant tribes, involving large objects such as turtle, dugong, carved beds, etc.[27] Barter is characteristic of the first type, used partly in order to insist on obtaining a particular Usiai product, and not merely its monetary equivalent.

The religious system of the self-seeking Manus seems at first glance to be extremely individualistic, and it is not until many of its characteristics and relationships have been taken into account that its integrative nature is apparent. The system is highly individualistic in that the sacred entity worshipped is the spirit of one person, usually the father, though sometimes it may be the son, or brother, or one who stood in the mother's brother-sister's relationship.[28] The dwelling place of this spirit is the man's house, and its concrete manifestation is the skull of the dead person. Placed in a carved wooden bowl above the inside of the front entry, the skull is the focus of the spirit's power, which stands watch over the house and "supervises the morals of its people."[29]

The Manus male calls this spirit Sir Ghost, to distinguish it from the ghosts of other individuals. He expects Sir Ghost to prevent accidents, prolong his life, and bring him wealth.[30] The household, sometimes several of them,[31] is also to be guarded, and its moral derelictions severely punished.

Clearly, Sir Ghost must fail in its task. Inevitably, there will be accidents and its "ward" must die. Not everyone will be wealthy. When the ward finally dies, there is final proof of the failure of Sir Ghost to protect, and the son of the ward casts out Sir Ghost (i.e., the skull), so that Sir Ghost no longer has anyone to honor it.[32] The ward may have threatened to do this many times during his lifetime. Neglected, Sir Ghost wanders on the sea between the villages, being a slight danger to sea voyages. Finally, however, Sir Ghost becomes a sea-slug. Since Manus die early,[33] by the time a man reaches adulthood and establishes his own household he will usually obtain protection from his own father, who may have died by this time.

Sir Ghost is not, however, Sir Ghost to other people or families. It is only a ghost, and as such is thought to be malicious. Sir Ghost hurts those under his care only when there has been a breach of the moral code; *ghosts* will hurt anyone. A man will thus feel that he has some control or method or persuasion against his Sir Ghost; against ghosts, however, he can only ask his Sir Ghost to protect him.

Punishment or hurt is accomplished by taking a man's soul stuff. There is soul stuff in every mortal. This *mwelolo* is divisible, and its absence means the death of the individual.[34] Even a small piece of a man's soul stuff will inevitably result in death. It is assumed that

. . . several different angry ghosts can, and often do, each possess a piece of the same mortal's soul stuff. How sick that mortal becomes under the treatment depends on how much of his soul stuff is kidnapped in this way, how far away from him it is taken, whether or not when taken away it is hacked or treated violently by the kidnapping ghost, and finally upon how long a time any piece of it is kept. Recovery from sickness is due to the kidnapping ghost or ghosts returning the soul stuff in response to mortal measures. Death is due to relentlessness on the part of the ghosts.[35]

Sir Ghost must never be guilty of such maliciousness, but must instead watch over his ward, accompanying him wherever he goes.[36]

It is believed that Sir Ghost does not act maliciously, and that most of any household illnesses are caused by Sir Ghost, punishing for moral derelictions.[37] For such punishment, Sir Ghost is not normally scolded if it is a temporary withholding of soul stuff, to be returned to the member of the ward's household when confession and expiation are made. This is Sir Ghost's proper sphere of action. Even in ordinary sickness which is laid to ghostly malice, Sir Ghost is not blamed severely for lack of concern for those under his care. The excuse can be made that there are too many for him to be able to watch all simultaneously. However, when ghostly death occurs Sir Ghost is berated and even suspected somewhat of complicity.[38]

Up to this point in the discussion the individualistic nature of this system of belief has been emphasized. It becomes *public* in nature through the diviners (men) and mediums (women). Any male may speak to his Sir Ghost, but to receive communications from the other world diviners or medium are necessary. Since permission to receive communications comes from the other plane, in effect permission is obtained from one of the existing diviners or mediums.[39] The diviner can obtain an answer of only "yes" or "no," using two short pieces of bone attached to a string and thrown astride his shoulder so that one falls on the chest, the other on his back. An itching feeling on the left side of the back means "yes," on the right side "no." It is the man's Sir Ghost who gives this answer, to whatever questions the man propounds.

A medium must obtain her power from the Sir Ghost of her house. She must also have given birth to a male child who died in infancy or childhood, and she must pay an established medium a fee for consecrating both the child's ghost and the novice. The child's ghost comes to act as intermediary on the other plane, going to ask other ghosts why someone has fallen ill, or asking someone's Sir Ghost why it has punished its ward or someone in ward's household. This communication takes place by means of whistles, given by the ghost through the medium's mouth without any special meaning given to any whistle. The medium merely says what occurs to her.[40]

If these oracles were to speak only in private to a man, or only to his household, informing them of the source of their misfortune, it is conceivable that this system of action would have comparatively little effect on the moral system. If someone were being punished for a transgression, no public sentiment would be roused against it, and a magical system of defense might be created against both ghostly and Sir Ghostly action. We may see the public nature of the system as it relates to the prime offense in Manus society, loose sexual conduct.

Such conduct includes almost any sexual situation outside the marital relationship, not merely sexual intercourse, but even accidentally seeing someone of the opposite sex exposed during sleep or in a fall from a house, or obscenity between husband and wife. This, of course, is aside from breaches of prescribed conduct such as failure to pay economic obligations on time, or disobedience, or not keeping the house of ward and Sir Ghost in good repair.[41]

The result of such loose sexual conduct is illness. This may occur in the house of the youth in question, or of the girl, or the house in which the offense occurred. In each case it is the Sir Ghost of each house in question which causes the illness. The illness, in turn, may attack anyone of any of the three houses.[42] This point is highly important, since it functions to interest everyone in the society in the transgressions of anyone else. No one can be sure of safety through his own innocence. As a consequence, "the moment such an illness occurs the community is all suspicion. If the oracles have anything to go upon, and being older puritanical persons they are likely to have, they oracularly make the charge."[43] That is, a diviner may remember having seen someone slip out of a house furtively a few days before a member of that house became ill, and therefore ask his Sir Ghost (through the bones) whether the cause of the illness is sexual sin. Since both question and answer are public knowledge, there is no hiding from the charge of the oracle. The guilty ones must confess in spite of the shame involved, else the ill person may die. If there is no confession, the public suspicion is that the ones charged have in effect murdered the one who died. After confession, expiatory payments to the ghosts are in order: to the ghost or ghosts of the house of the girl's betrothed, paid by the girl's kin; to those of the boy's betrothed, paid by the boy's kin; and to those of the house in which the offense occurred. No possibility of such conduct exists between the betrothed couple, since there is strict avoidance between them. The payments are objectively made, of course, to the kin in question, although the interpretation is that they are payments to ghosts.[44] Once such a payment is made, the sin is wiped out, and subsequent illness must be due to other causes.

The situation is, of course, more delicate when the illness is serious. If the oracular charge of sin within the family were to be maintained, many kinship ties would be strained by the constant suspicion of murder. Consequently, when death seems to be approaching, *ghostly* malice is charged.[45] The burden of death is consequently shifted to outsiders, releasing the kin of the dying or dead person as well as their Sir Ghost or Sir Ghosts.[46] The puritan Manus do not accept this shift of burden for long, however, and of course the kin of the ghost accused protest in any event. Those who have been dead for a long while, or their kin, are assumed to have sinned, whatever the discretion of the medium or diviner near the time of death.[47]

Of course, other misfortunes may result besides illness, just as the other causes are operative besides sexual laxity. Fishing may be poor, so that a seance must be held to ascertain which ghost has taken the soul stuff of the fishing gear. It may be that no breach of the social regulations is found by the questions of the diviner or the conversations of the medium, not even a failure in economic obligations. The oracle may then discover that a breach has occurred with respect to the other world, e.g., a lack of exchanges in honor of Sir Ghost marrying, a fact which underscores the anthroposocial conception of Sir Ghost. For he is thought to marry, have children, and otherwise carry on social affairs there as he did here, with somewhat the same social position.[48]

This system of oracular charge, confession, expiation, and cleansing does not hold, however, for the deaths of infants, a fact which helps to strengthen it where infant mortality is high.[49] Instead, black magic is assumed to be the cause, thus opening the possibility of exorcism, an affair without the shame and embarrassment of confession in adult life. Most of this magic originally came from outside Manus, and is perhaps constantly being renewed.[50] Most of these infant or child deaths are caused by persons who stand in a kinship relationship to the mother.[51] The possibility of such magical power being applied is so completely accepted, that if a newly born infant seems to cry very much, it will be exorcized by a magician not on good terms with the family—this process amounting almost to a *rite de passage*. This type of magic is called magic of pregnancy, but it is evident that the religious system does not allow much recognition of magic being directed against innocent adults. Their deaths can be imputed to sin, whereas infants could not transgress the social rules in such a fashion. They simply remain for the most part outside the pattern of sin and expiation. This reduces the probing of conscience necessary, confining it to adult sickness.[52]

This magic of pregnancy is not so much a part of the system of enforcing conformity as it is a pattern which makes that system work more smoothly by giving it less work to do. The magic of property protection, however, common to Oceanic peoples in general, works closely with the system of enforcing the law and morality of the society. For the Manus, as would be expected of a group with such a high respect for property, think that thievery is a scandalous offense.[53] This "cult" of *sorosor* therefore calls for a twofold action, one directed toward the spell or magical activity, and one directed toward expiating the transgression. This type of magic is not, of course, a true cult, since there are no established forms or general practices, all magical powers having been acquired from outside Manus society.

The only type of genuine Manus "magic" is not really typical of magical practices elsewhere, since it is a power held by children of a set of sisters, transmitted to the men as far as one generation in that line, but always through the sisters of those men, never through the men themselves. As is clear in a patrilineal society, it is the children of brothers who inherit, whether it is house sites or the privileges of the gens, while the children of sisters are scattered through the whole society, wherever the women have married. However, in Manus society the children of sister can curse or bless the children of brother by causing barrenness, and stillbirths, or the early deaths of the children born to their wives. This is rarely done.[54] This power extends to bestowing fertility, controlling the sex of children, or to spacing children. It is this descent group, "an unbroken female descent line of which the female children-of-sister represent one generation," which releases a given individual from segregation at life crises, "such as ear-piercing, first menstruation, before marriage, after first child bearing, after the death of a husband in the case of a woman, and after ear-piercing in the case of a man."[55] This "blessing" is, then, part of the ceremonial of life crises which consist essentially of segregation with ritual precautions, followed by such a release with the invoking of the ghosts. These children of sister invoke such ghosts by reciting the males of the male line for several generations back, then the female ghosts of the female line. The invocation is supposed to work in a more or less automatic fashion. This power, whether destructive or beneficent, is open and public in nature.

From the point of view of Western society, such a system seems simple and harsh. It emphasizes a strict sexual and economic morality, a rigid punishment, public admission of guilt and public expiation, and close relationship with a Sir Ghost which is interested in turn in maintaining impersonally the social rules. The magical system, also without elaboration, is partly incorporated in this system, and partly takes away some strain by giving it fewer moral cases to decide.

# TIKOPIA

Complexities of another order than in Dahomey are to be found in the religious system of Tikopia. Though entire interest is not centered in totemism, it is clearly to be found in Tikopia.[56] Or, "there is a peculiar association between certain animal and plant species and the religious interests of the people. This association is stated by most writers in terms of a native belief that the animals and plants are used by deities as a form of visible incarnation."[57] Since this is a very small society, on a tiny, isolated island, we would expect to find a rather complete integration on the one hand between the religious system and the social structure in general.[58] There are four large patrilineal kinship groups, each governed by a chief. This chief is also the religious head of his kinship group. Performing the principal ceremonials, he is very close to the gods, at times being divine himself. These deities include the spirits of the chief's ancestors, the dead clan chiefs in order of precedence, headed by a number of major deities who have never lived on earth as men. These chiefs have assistants in their religious activities, a small number of elders, holding rank by their position as important family heads.

The deities are of varying rank and significance, and are divided among the chiefs, so that each chief has a ranking deity as his main god. The highest of all the deities "in point of power is a deity of the culture-hero type, who lived in Tikopia as a man and chief of surpassing size and strength, instituted a number of customs and performed some remarkable feats. After this he was killed by a mortal man, and going, without doing violence to his slayer, to the abode of the great *atua* deities, induced them thereby to hand over to him their *mana*, their supernatural power, by means of which he attained supremacy among them."[59] This deity is the principal *atua* of the chief of the Kafika clan, who is also the principal chief of the island. However, the same deity, under different names, figures in the pantheons of other clans also. Nevertheless, their control over or influence on this deity is less than that of the Kafika chief. The same pattern of using different names for the same deity is followed in the case of other deities. Thus there is an interlocking system of deities, in which all have a common interest, and no one group achieves a complete dominance in such matters, since some degree of closeness is implied in the use of a different name for the particular clan.

The term *atua* applies for the most part to supernatural objects, of human or non-human characteristics. In this sense, it is used to indicate: 1. Particular supernatural entities as spirits of the dead, ancestors, and principal gods who were never men. These have a particular personality, names, often a particular appearance. 2. Supernatural beings of the "wandering ghost" type, with a personality but no name, and without continuity in the social structure. 3. Sacred objects, associated with supernatural forces or imbued with supernormal characteristics—stones, trees, weapons.[60] It must be emphasized, in discussing this as totemism, that these material objects, such as taro, yam, coconut, and breadfruit, *are not the atua themselves*, but are rather *symbols* of a supernatural being. This is contrary to Rivers' treatment of totemism in Tikopia.[61] The actions which Rivers thought of as characterizing the object were really typical of the *atua* symbolized.

The focus of ceremonial attention in Tikopia is the series of rites which are known as the Work of the Gods.[62] There are several main divisions: "a symbolic act to initiate the cycle; a resacralisation of canoes; a re-consecration of temples; a series of harvest and planting rites for the yam; a sacred dance festival; several memorial rites on the sites of vanished temples; and in the trade wind season, the ritual manufacture of turmeric.[63] The central god of Kafika is supposed to have begun the ritual cycle, though other gods and groups are brought into the ceremonies. The ceremonials are a "perpetuation, to native ideas, of the work of the culture-hero of Kafika." They thus become the ceremonial focus in terms of production and work, and are so much the scene of high dramatic movements and exotic dances that the Tikopia look forward eagerly to the Throwing of the Firestick, the beginning rite.

Not only the ritual itself, but other religious knowledge, is considered to be the property of the chiefs and elders. This holds especially for the various names of the gods. It is not true that other individuals do not have much of this knowledge, merely that traditionally they are not supposed to have it, and are not allowed to discuss it. The most typical feature of the Tikopia ritual, the *kava*, is performed by the *ariki* (chief) or elder, who alone will know the formula to be recited. The recitation is made along a *kava* plant without leaves, held up in one hand by the elder or chief. This ceremony is an integral part of numerous larger rituals. Following the actual recitation, offerings of food are set out for the gods concerned, while a bowl of *kava* is being prepared. "Cups of this are then carried to the *ariki*, who pours out libations to his deities with appropriate invocations dealing with canoes, fish, taro, breadfruit, recovery from disease, etc., according to the circumstances. The whole ritual is of a very formal nature, each act being very carefully defined in place and time, with minute observance of detail according to traditional usage. Only the chief or elder may recite the *kava* formulae; his relatives and clansmen are in attendance to assist in preparing food, and to show to the *atua* a proper recognition of the importance of the occasion."[64]

One element of totemism, not of basic significance for the religion, relates interestingly to the phenomenon of possession. The association of clans with animals and plants has as its basis in belief the idea that *atua* can enter objects, animals, etc., for their own purposes. Thus, if a crab shows an abnormal interest in human beings, it will be suspected of harboring an *atua*, for the moment at least. But an *atua* does not appear only in lower animals, or plants. They may also possess men. To be possessed by ancestors or even higher deities is very typical in the Tikopia religious pattern. In fact, each chief has a particular medium, acting more or less as a line of communication between the forebears of principal *atua* and the chief, enabling the chief to converse "directly" with them. Firth says further of these *tauratua,* that they

function only at certain important religious ceremonies, or when the chief is desirous of receiving information on any serious issue. There are a host of minor mediums, *vaka atua,* vessels of the gods, who are possessed by deities of lesser importance, and by ancestors not long dead. These people are called in on occasions of sickness, loss at sea, storms or other critical times, pass into a light trance, and converse freely with the household in deep jerky tones, purporting to be the voice of the actual spirit. The phenomena are apparently those of auto-hypnosis, and the medium retains but an imperfect recollection of the conversation in which he has taken a leading part. The medium often receives food and betel-nut in return for his services, but there is little if any conscious fraud. It is worthy of note that many persons who have become mediums have displayed prior symptoms of a coma or mild periodic insanity.[65]

Man's spiritual counterpart does not leave his dead body until five days after death, in Tikopia. Meanwhile, as is customary with almost all the principal rituals and ceremonies, there are heavy exchanges of gifts. Such exchanges, in which there is almost no profit, except for the one case of ceremonial acknowledgment of chieftainship at certain times, involve both food of various kinds and bark-cloths. They serve the important function of maintaining an extremely close integration of the social structure, emphasizing the clan and family lines and their bonds to other groups. When on the fifth day food and bark-cloth are set out in the house near the grave, the ancestors of the dead man are thought to descend for this spiritual counterpart and the gifts (in essence). Both are carried off to the spirit world.

These gifts have a particular purpose in *Rangi,* the spirit world. When the individual arrives in this world he must pay his respects to his family and clan *atua.* There are such *Rangi* for different clans, and some *atua* other than the principal ones have *Rangi* of their own. After paying his respects, the individual has to be cleansed from the taint of mortality, and does so by being immersed in a pool for five days, after which all traces of his mundane character have vanished. This phase is under the care of the deity of his mother's family, i.e., the mother's brother again plays a part in this world. If the man was of high rank during his stay in the world, this deity places a branch of an aromatic shrub at the back of his waist-cloth. This *vave* is implicative of power, speed, movement, the supreme deity having considerable *vave.* There is some difference of opinion as to what the *atua* do in this spirit world, but there is unanimous agreement in maintaining that they dance a great deal. Also, the *atua* may become aged, the remedy being immersion again into the cleansing pool.

It is seen, then, that this "secondary" totemism plays a somewhat peripheral part in the Tikopia religion, particularly with respect to animal species. As noted, there are rites to promote the fertility of the plant foods, but no such particular ceremonies exist for the animals, no offerings are made, and little attention is given them. This follows from the conception of an *atua* entering an animal for a while, which in the Tikopia mind effectually dissociates the two, for ritual functions. On the other hand, much of the ritual converges on one of the chief food plants, the yam. According to a myth, this plant came under the control of the Ariki Kafika, while the Ariki Tafua received control over the coconut, the Ariki Taumako over the taro, and the Ariki Fangarere over the breadfruit.[66] Each chief thus has a set of rites for his plant. However, the yam is associated with Atua i Kafika, the supreme deity, being considered his "body," and is also an important food in its own right, since it can be stored for long periods. Thus there is an elaborate set of ceremonies functioning as fertility rites, in which the interest of the whole island centers. The Ariki Kafika is the center of attention, consequently, though it must be emphasized that anyone on the island may eat or grow any of these plant foods.

# ZUÑI

The Zuñi of New Mexico are town dwellers and so have been for centuries,[67] although their sources of food are mainly agriculture and stock raising.[68] The greater part of this country is arid, and dry cultivation is required. Sheep are the most important stock, and were originally obtained from the Spaniards. They are now the chief cash crop. The work of both herding and crop raising is done by Zuñi men.[69]

The social structure found in this society is highly cohesive and solidary, as might be judged from the fact that it has survived the impact of four centuries of contact with Western civilization. The main types of organization within the society, according to Kroeber—he calls them "planes of systematization"—are the clans, fraternities, priesthoods, and kivas, and to a lesser degree the gaming parties.[70] Bunzel does not deviate significantly from this when she names as the main groups, "the households, kinship groups, clans, tribal and special secret societies, and cult groups."[71] The household, kinship, and clan affiliations are, of course, fixed by birth. However, whether the relationship to a group is fixed by birth or not, a man will belong to many social groups. Most of his daily activities revolve about group functions, a general statement which has often been made about the entire Pueblo area. These group loyalties do not, as might be supposed, tend to divide the society, since they cut across each other at many junctures. That is, to follow Kroeber's interesting suggestion, kin A does not separate from the society with its own local group, society, kiva, etc., since kin A is likely to be associated with society C, or even more probably with no particular society, with clan D, and with priesthood B. This point relates to what was termed the "organizational complexity" of Zuñi ritual, discussed in Appendix I. A given ritual seems to be even more complex than it really is, since different parts of it are performed by different groups.

Within this complex of social organization, the family or house is the center of the individual's life, while the clan is important above all for ceremonial activities.[72] The blood ties, whether through a male or a female relative, evoke loyal and affectionate sentiments. The house itself is a sort of stable channel through which generation after generation of such blood relations flow. The ownership of this house on the part of the woman gives them some eminence, and is a strong basis for Zuñi matrilineality. "But kinship is thoroughly and equally bilateral."[73] The clan is, of course, maternal, and has a totemic name, although there is no belief that its members descended from the naming object or animal. There are no clan food taboos. Ordinarily, an individual does not marry into either his father's or his mother's clan. However, there is no specific authority within the household for the enforcement of an order. Some definiteness of decision may be reached at times when a man in the household conflicts with the female members, for it is possible for them to present a united front, forcing the man to withdraw. If he leaves the household, his male successor is responsible for the care of his children, though this does not affect their blood relationship. However, adoption is frequent, and there is stretching of kinship to include affinal relationships.

At puberty, each male Zuñi is initiated into the kachina or mask dance society.[74] This is, then, a tribal cult. However, the restricted ceremonial groups taken as a whole also include a large proportion of the tribe. These include the twelve medicine societies, the priesthoods who control rain, the war society, and many minor groups which have for the most part the task of caring for sacred objects.

The Zuñi ceremonial activities do not center about the fate of the human soul, although its characteristics are relevant to cult activity.

Man's spiritual substance is related to intelligence as well as emotions. It is also associated with the breath, which is the symbol of life. Sacred entities communicate with men by means of the breath, and inhaling becomes part of ritual acts, since the participants inhale from sacred objects as well as from chants (at the conclusion of the chant or prayer).[75] During severe sickness the soul can leave the body. After death it does so, though there is considerable variation in Zuñi belief regarding the soul after death. Generally, however, human souls are believed to go elsewhere.

Nevertheless, this soul does not occupy the center of Zuñi attention. There is no cosmic struggle of good against evil in the soul, or a conflict between human souls and the gods, or even a deeply personal relationship between the individual and a powerful god. Instead, the collective human forces come into contact with the collective sacred entities, with great color but with "no single bit of religious feeling equal in intensity and exaltation to the usual vision quest of the North American Indian."[76]

Although Zuñi religious feeling may possibly lack the spectacular intensity of the Plains Indians, there is no denying its broad base and pervasiveness. The fundamental element on which rests all Zuñi religious or ceremonial activity is the worship of the old one, the ancients or ancestors. This is not, strictly speaking, ancestor worship, since a given person's ancestors do not figure as such. Further, they are the same for all, "regardless of age, sex, or affiliation with special cults."[77] All ceremonies include the *alacinawe*, whose special offering is food. They are to guide and protect mankind, as well as bring the blessing of rain.[78] The favors for which Zuñi pray and make offerings are given by the *alacinawe*, but the feeling toward them is not entirely trustful. For the dead still love the living, and the recent dead especially may wish to attract them to the realm of the dead. To prevent the effects of such an attraction, rites of separation cut off the recent dead from the living.

Although this element of the Zuñi religious structure figures in all ritual activities, it does not actually constitute an esoteric cult. Actually, any individual may have direct access to the ancestors, and there are perhaps no sacred places for them.

However, against this background stand the six major esoteric cults. Each has a priesthood, secret ritual, a special group of sacred entities, a calendrical organization of rituals, and permanent possession of fetishistic power.[79] They are: "1. the cult of the Sun; 2. the cult of the Uwanami; 3. the cult of the kachinas; 4. the cult of the priests of the kachinas (a distinct but closely related cult); 5. the cult of the Gods of War; 6. the cult of the Beast Gods."[80]

*Rain Spirits.* The central place of the sun is suggested by its character as the source of all life. Its association with the moon is not, however, considered a mating union. It is worshipped daily at sunrise, when corn meal is offered in a morning ritual. The sun's chief priest is *pekwin*, who is the priestly leader of all Zuñi, having final responsibility for the tribal welfare. His tasks, therefore, extend beyond the worship of the sun. He is the highest priest and installs other priests, appoints persons to certain offices, and puts up altars for joint ceremonies. He is also the keeper of the calendar, and is supposed to see that the time of the solstices, when great public rituals are held for the sun, coincide with the full moon. He further initiates the public ceremonies in the winter.

The rain spirits, or *Uwanami*, share the sun's position, a fact which is underscored by the aridity of the region. These spirits have attributes which symbolically suggest water, such as their domicile in all the earthly waters, within houses of cumulus clouds, their having a breath of mist, and frogs as children, etc. Their worship has been elaborated to the extent of having at least twelve priesthoods.[81] A Zuñi family may be connected matrilineally with a priesthood, since a matrilineal family group possesses the house in which the group fetish is guarded.[82] Membership is generally passed down matrilineally.

The rain priests are holy and must therefore avoid worldly affairs or strife. They do not hold public ceremonies of their own, although they hold a series of important summer retreats, the immediate purpose of which is to obtain rain. These begin toward the end of June and last into September, the entire rainy season.[83] At this time, prayer sticks are made before each retreat and are placed in the sacred spring. The members do not leave the ceremonial room at all during each retreat, meals being brought in by a woman of the house. Any group will be censured if it does not obtain rain during its retreat, the charge usually being that someone in the group has disobeyed ritual prescriptions. Although there are also corn fetishes, these retreats emphasize the rain-making function, which is the more important.

*Kachinas.* All Zuñi males belong to this important cult, and participate in its ceremonies, which pays respect to a group of Zuñi supernaturals by impersonating them in spectacular dances.[84] These spirits are not completely identified with the dead, although mortals go to kachina village at death and become part of the supernatural group. The masks used in the dances are very sacred, and are surrounded by a number of rigid taboos.

Although kachina dancing is a rain-making ceremony, its spirits are not extremely forbidding or awesome. They like dancing, pretty clothing, and feathers. The folk tales[85] describe them at their home, which is very like Zuñi, "scrambling for their feathers at the solstices, quarreling amiably among themselves, meddling in one another's affairs."[86] Their forbidding character is observed in a few situations, mostly those in which someone has violated their sanctity.

Besides the ancient and permanent masks, which are supposed to be the original masks and are therefore tribal property, there are individual masks. These are made by an individual, and without a mask no one can come back to visit Zuñi after death. Although they are expensive, a man will acquire one as soon as he can afford it. The initiation ceremonies take place in two stages. The first does not admit the child (between five and nine years old) to the mysteries, for he is still not told that men are impersonating the spirits. He is rather whipped and filled with awe, so as to accept the kachinas completely as genuine supernaturals. He is not told that they are men until he is older (between ten and fourteen years, depending on his maturity).[87] At this later stage, which is sometimes delayed by the absence of children in schools until eighteen or nineteen years of age, the youth learns the secrets of the cult. Nevertheless, the earlier stage is important, for it links the child to the spirits, and thus helps to safeguard the child. Bunzel compares this earlier stage to Christian baptism, "which tentatively admits the child to the congregation of the elect until, having reached the age of understanding, he establishes his relations with the supernatural by voluntarily partaking of communion.[88]

*Kachina Priests.* The existence of this cult interestingly emphasizes the "human" or "Zuñi" character of kachina village, for just as in Zuñi a priestly hierarchy rules the village, so in kachina village. This is also an impersonating cult, using masks for that purpose and thereby gaining control over the supernatural. However, the masks represent definite individuals with specific personalities, unlike the kachina cult, and its times of appearance as well as its membership are independent of the latter cult. Each individual kachina priest has a permanent mask, like the permanent masks of the ordinary kachina cult, which is tribal property and used only in the specific ritual which it is that individual's unique right to perform. Further, for each there is a cult group, ritual, prayers, etc. Although these supernatural priests are like other Zuñi spirits in that they bring rain, their more special power is the granting of fertility.

Among these supernaturals are the mocking, grotesque, and obscene Koyemshi, or clowns. They are powerful but loved, and undergo rigid taboos, among which is the absolute prescription on removing their masks, sleeping, speaking, eating, drinking, or sexual intercourse from

sundown to midnight of the following day at the end of their ceremonies.
Another of these supernaturals is Pantiwa, who is chief of the masked
gods in Kachina village, and who is kindly, beautiful, dignified, and
attractive to mortal maidens. It is he who leaves the feathered sticks
which are given to those who are to impersonate the spirits in November.[89]

After the immediate appointment of the impersonators, prayer sticks
are planted at full moon each month, at distant sacred places.[90] The
ritual duties accelerate as November approaches, and before the great
and expensive public ceremony each group holds a retreat.[91]

*War Gods' Cult.* The Bow Priests have been gradually disappearing,
as must be obvious from the requirement that membership be restricted
to those who have killed an enemy.[92] They are the keepers of the
(religious) peace, and leaders in time of war. They used to protect all
Zuñi against witchcraft. They prevent desecration, and carry out the
orders of the priestly hierarchy. Their chief ceremonies take place at the
time of the winter solstice, and there are no War Gods ceremonies at the
summer solstice. They do participate in the summer retreat, however.

*Beast Gods.* This cult is composed of the medicine societies, possessed of much secret ritual and medical knowledge. The beast gods are
the beasts of prey but also of long life, the source of both healing and
destructive magic. Each society composing the cult practices some spe-
cialty, besides general medicine.

Entering the cult is usually the result of sickness.[93] That is, the
members of a society are brought in to cure a sick person. However, he
need not join. Instead, the individual official may simply be paid and
the patient is "given" as a member of his family. The initiation is long
and elaborate, as well as expensive.

All members of the cult plant prayer sticks each month at full moon,
though not at the same place, offered to the ancients, the kachinas, and
the beast gods. However, the chief ceremonies are in fall and winter,
while during the summer the drums must not be beaten at all. The
winter solstice ceremonies are the most important, at which time the
great retreat begins. Female members may go home at this time, returning during the day, and even ordinary male members may visit their
homes. The officers must, on the other hand, observe rigidly the requirements of retreat. This four-day period is utilized in making prayer sticks
and preparing in general for the great ritual of the final night. This is a
public ceremony to which sick people may go for curing, since those who
are able to impersonate the bear (the oldest and most learned) can see the
sickness in anyone. This is a ceremony of great excitement.[94]

The Zuñi religious life is thus seen to be closely tied to a calendar of activities, according to which the year is really two periods, revolving about the winter and summer solstices. The winter ceremonies are perhaps less intense than the summer, at least with respect to rain making, since the problem is pressing at the latter time. Religious activity is also observed to be highly collective, with little or no room for personal crises or struggles. The individual enters a cult group for protection and is never a lonely individual in quest of his personal conception of the sacred. The ceremonies and cult groups have such a complexity that one man will belong to many groups, while different groups of spirits are understood to have an interest in other ceremonies than their own. The attention of the society is oriented toward cult activities rather than secular tasks, and this is especially true of the men, who hold the highest offices. Prestige and power are thus attached to the priesthood, and not to the civil officials who deal with outsiders. Although much of the religious activity is public, with a real display of sacred paraphernalia, including the sacred impersonating masks, there is a vast amount of secret ritual and knowledge which is still unknown to non-Zuñi. Nevertheless, there is no evidence to suggest that this added knowledge would change the broad outlines of the religious system as it has been described up to the present time.

# MURNGIN

The Western world has long been interested in the Australian aborigines, and the Murngin[95] are no exception. They are "an exogamic patrilineal group averaging forty or fifty individuals who possess a common territory which averages 360 square miles. This group possesses one or more sacred totemic water holes, formed by a creator totem, in which the whole of the tribal life is focused. All members of the clan are born from this water hole, and all go back to it at death. In it the totem's spirits live with the mythological ancestor, the souls of the dead, and the unborn children. The male members of the clan who can be the permanent occupants of the group's land possess totemic emblems in common."[96] The clan is exogamous, since it belongs to a moiety, whose opposite moiety contains the eligible partners. Since the groups of clans do not function as a tribe, war-making is given over to the clan itself, which rarely fights as a group. Rather, there are eternal feuds with other clans (never within the clan), leading to ambushes and occasional killings.

Being wandering groups, territory is very important, and it is linked to a clan by tradition and myth, not by force of arms. Since the territory is a dry region for six or seven months of the year, water and water holes figure largely in tribal life. Further, since this is tied closely to the abundance or lack of food, one might expect some reflection of it in the social patterns. And, indeed, water is a chief symbol of a clan's spiritual life. This figures even more definitely in the metaphor of the totemic well, and the actual existence of sacred water holes. It is below the waters of a clan water hole, further, that the clan totems lie, as well as the "old mythological ancestors who lived in the time of the activities of the totems on earth in the great mythological days when the world was made and named."[97]

It is from this clan water hole, moreover, that the spirit of a child to be born actually comes. There it has the appearance of a small fish. This spirit informs the father of the child, by coming to him and asking him to point out its mother. After the mother has been pointed out, the spirit child enters the vagina. If the child dies while still a baby, it will return to the well, where the totemic spirit lies which is in the higher totemic emblem (also kept in the mud of the water hole). The child will remain a fish a while longer. At some later time the father will again have some peculiar experience which will be interpreted as a message from the supernatural, that a child is to be born. This message and this conception of birth overshadow an actual knowledge, of the old men at least, that seminal fluid has some importance for conception.[98] Likewise, the physiological facts of death loom less large than the important fact that when a man dies he goes to the very sacred totemic wells (narra).

It is the man's marikmo (paternal grandfather) who takes him to the narra well, whence he never returns. As part of the process of sending his spirit back to the well, a Murngin will dance his death dance if severely wounded, thus symbolizing the ceremonies which would accompany his death. Even though the water in the well be clear, it is assumed that the man (i.e., his spirit) is really there, far below with his totemic emblem, totem, and his marikmo. This is also true for women. It is assumed that death has occurred before it actually does.

The extremely complex system of seventy-one types of relatives is further complicated by the system of age grading. These stages are related to physical age levels for the men, though it must be emphasized here, as is true for such classifications generally in human societies, that purely social factors have at least an equal importance in determining age grade status. Furthermore, status in the age grades is tied closely to family position. Since a man passes through a definite series of phases during his lifetime, at any given period his ritual status is closely related to his ordinary status, though they have slightly different criteria.[99]

As is true of socialization generally, little children begin to play out their later statuses long before they are actually attained. Boys remain with their families of orientation until circumcision at about six to eight years of age, then leave for the unmarried men's camp. It is here that they are to learn the proper ways of acting toward women, and they remain there as growing boys until they are finally recognized as simply unmarried men. When they marry, they leave this camp and enter the general camp. During the stay in the young men's camp, they are instructed in totemic emblems, tribal mythology, tradition, etc. by the oldest man in camp. This is merely one phase of the whole process of a man's life, by which he becomes more and more sacred while passing through the various statuses and acquiring definite privileges. Succinctly,

Age grading in Murngin societies is highly ritualistic and controls a man's religious life far more than it does his ordinary daily existence. A man's religious knowledge and his understanding of the sacred totemic lore, with the associated myths and rituals, are dependent upon how far he has been initiated into the sacred mysteries. The initiations elevate him from a lower and more profane existence to a higher and more sacred plane and mark his transition from one age grade to a higher and older one. Age grading, then, controls the degree of sacred participation a man has within the community.[100]

It is by virtue of this system of graded statuses that the older men maintain a rather complete dominance over the younger men. They are "the final repositories of all the sacred knowledge which can be obtained only by their willingness to initiate the younger men of the lower ranks into their own group." The society is class-mobile, but the mobility occurs through narrow portals guarded by sacred rituals and individuals. The power is thus two-fold, the possibility of preventing the attainment of a higher status, and the very real supernatural forces with which the old men are identified. The religious forces themselves will be used to effect discipline, evil things occurring to the disobedient, such as receiving no help in need or remaining childless, or being left without ancestors to accompany him to the totemic water hole when he is killed.

This phenomenon of age grading, then, can be looked at as a whole, in the manner of the Murngin. That is, the individual's life is a *social unity*. It is a religious phenomenon, in which the individual begins in a sacred place and ends there. An individual begins as an unborn spirit existing with the totemic clan spirits, totemic mythological ancestors, the ancient clan dead, and those recently died. There he is under the control of his ancestors and totem, and he will not proceed to the world of the living unless his parents act properly. The father has a religious experience announcing the child, and himself is rid of ritualistic tabus by the birth of the child, thus placing him definitely in the older men's group. When an old man, the individual sees the most secret and sacred of totems, learning the ultimate mysteries of life in this manner.

When he dies, he assumes still another status, continuing to have a social personality as long as he is remembered. He will finally become only an undifferentiated element in a long line of clan ancestors, being absorbed in the sacredness of the clan well. This is less directly true of the woman, whose spirituality is much less clear-cut, though she does participate somewhat in the totemic rituals, comes from the same hole, has a number of sacred totemic names (unknown to her), and also returns to the clan hole.

The totemistic pattern consists in a ritual relationship between clan members and certain species of plants and animals, this connection being expressed in myth and ritual. Warner found two great types of rituals, the Wawilak and the Djunkgao. These in turn include sub-ceremonies.[101] The Wawilak includes four fundamental ceremonies,

. . . the Djunkguan, Gunabibi, Ulmark, and Marndiella. (The Liaalaomir and certain Dua clan ceremonies and certain *garma* (low totem) rituals . . . seem to be related to the fundamental Wawilak myth). The Djunkgao rituals in Murngin thought form a separate myth-ritual constellation with another fundamental myth—the Djunkgao Sisters (as opposed to the Wawilak woman) myth—and comprise two major ceremonies, the Dua Narra and the Yiritja Narra. Other important but less elaborated myth and ritual groupings . . .

are also found among the Murngin.[102]

The two main cycles have a slightly different orientation. The Wawilak Myth Cycle of ceremonies is centered in the main in the rites of passage of the individual, and are very elaborate, extending over several months. The Narra rituals of the Djunkgao Myth Cyclo, again long and elaborate, are rather oriented more immediately "toward totemic behavior as it centers around the totemic well."[103] Since these are all based on assumptions of the effect of human ritual upon natural phenomena, Warner calls both these ceremonies and "expression of the social logics (usually illogical thinking, if observed as the mental behavior of an individual) of the people as they are focused on the problem of adapting nature to man."[104]

As hinted before, the Murngin ritual and social organization is closely tied to the geographical or climatic pattern. The alternation between wet and dry seasons is also connected closely to the Wawilak myth, for the inundation of the flat coastal areas is considered analogous to the swallowing of the Wawilak sisters. They had copulated incestuously with their own clansmen, and the older sister had carelessly dropped some menstrual blood in the sacred python pool. The ceremonies, which must be carried out because of this original episode of sin, help man prevent the coming of the dry season of plenty caused by the fructifying waters. The snake, Yurlunggur (or Nuit), symbolizes the wet season. In the myth, he swallows the women and the children, then regurgitates them. Likewise, he swallows the dry season, then vomits it up again. The women in the ceremonies usually are the unclean elements, with the snake played by men. On a much deeper level, "the man's age grade is a snake and purifying element, the sociological women's group is the unclean group. The male snake-group in the act of swallowing the unclean group "swallows" the initiates into the ritually pure masculine age grade, and at the same time the whole ritual purifies the whole group or tribe."[105]

Though the two myth constellations are slightly different in concrete content, there are fundamental similarities. The Wawilak myth describes the wanderings of the Wongar sisters, who name animals, places, wells, of the clans as they go northwards. The Djunkgao myth has two sisters go by water and by land, doing the same thing. The rule of clan exogamy is broken by both. The Wawilak adds the element of menstrual uncleanliness. They are similar again, however, in that the women turn over to the men the ritual objects and mysteries, and acknowledge their subordination. The Djunkgao lose the totems, and the men steal the rituals. The Wawilak tell the men how to perform the rituals. The Djunkgao (Narra) ceremonies center their interest more on the "individual clan wells, on their clan totems, and on the process of purifying the clan of its uncleanliness."[106] The Wawilak emphasize one well, and use different symbols. The incestuous uncleanliness in each case resulted in the seasonal cycle and reproduction, while purification is called for in each case. This cleansing is done symbolically by the Murngin in the ritual of community baptism. Interwoven are numerous elements of myth and symbol which even more closely relate the myth to the ritual, the phenomena of nature to the myth and ritual, and the social organization to the ritual. Obviously, the complexities of this immense group of rituals and myths cannot be reproduced here, since only the grosser elements are being outlined. The same proposition holds for the elaborate Murngin funeral ritual, which, as noted above, is part of the whole cycle through which the individual passes. The ceremony ritualizes the relationship of the soul[107] and the mourning kin to the sacred and the dead.

In this section, no effort has been made to present in detail even a minor part of the details necessary for later exposition. However, the theoretical formulations already presented take on more clarity when these sketches are borne in mind. Further, these materials have a further general function, since even those who are familiar with some ethnological data may not be familiar with the larger structure presented. Moreover, some points have been suggested which might be otherwise occasionally slighted. Let us now look at the concrete interrelationships of these religious systems with other aspects and areas of behavior in the societies.

# 5. RELIGIOUS AND ECONOMIC ACTION

THE ECONOMIC and sociological aspects of human action were discussed in Chapters II and III, as different levels of integration and emergence.[1] Economic action, it was maintained, enters or could enter without any other person being involved, since the allocation of scarce means for given wants is found in any individual's action system.[2] That is, "an economic element enters in only in so far as the comparative scarcity of alternative means to a given end becomes relevant to the choice between them."[3] This fact limits an economic discussion in several directions. The technological thereby becomes peripheral. For this would involve the concept of "efficiency," not that of "cost." One need not analyze in detail the technical efficiency of one type of fishing, or of baiting hooks, or of the tools used, or the methods of manufacturing in a given society. A study of techniques is not a study of economics.[4]

This problem of economic choice assumes the ends to be achieved. Classical economics would have fallen into a hopeless morass of complex problems had it not generally attempted to exclude the problem of *how* ends are set at all, or of the source of goals.[5] One important proposition which is implied by this fact, however, is that the economic analyst cannot then claim that the ends which a given society strives for are "irrational."[6] Since in an absolute sense, and without any value judgments, all goals are "irrational," or at least non-rational, the category itself has to be abandoned. Also abandoned is the claim that a given economic pattern is "irrational" because it does not strive for a maximum monetary return. Rationality may enter as a concept, *when the choice of allocation is made*, the judgment being made on the basis of available means, overabundance or insufficiency of means allocated for a given end, allocation of scarce means to immediate ends because of lack of foresight and inability to think of important goals (in the person's own value system) in a future period, etc. Consequently, a maximum monetary reward may actually be "irrational," since in many societies the currency would have only a curiosity value.[7] It is only in societies where a maximizing of money means at the same time the greatest increase in means that a failure to work for the highest reward can be classed as irrational. And, even then, if the values one holds highest are not to be achieved with money, such a pattern of action could not be classed as irrational.[8] Actually, the use of a price system allows values to be expressed in terms of one factor alone: money.[9] In a complex society, Firth remarks, "the existence of a price mechanism allows of an adjustment between supply and demand, by giving indices to producers and consumers of the pressure of wants and the level at which they can be satisfied."[10] Furthermore, it is evident that "the existence of some standards of measurement and some mechanisms of control of supply and demand are necessary for the operation of any economic system."[11] Consequently, the lack of the price system in the economic systems of some primitive societies will mean other features: "(1) Multiple standards of evaluation, particularly when services are measured against goods. (2) The absence of any fine adjustment of supply to demand on a large scale even if market conditions obtain. (3) A tendency to work for things directly and not for the medium by which they are procured."[12]

Because of the general latter-day extension of information about other societies, no effort need be spent in destroying common misconceptions of the primitive man, held so dear and so long by the orthodox economists. Over a decade ago, Firth found it necessary to spend some time pointing out, for example, that Seligman had presented many preconceived notions of "primitive" man in his economic discussions, particularly the assumption that in a self-sufficient economy there is no necessity of barter or exchange.[13] This is no longer necessary. Nor is it necessary to devote attention to a refutation of some unilinear plan of social or economic evolution, such as "collector to hunter to herdsman to agriculturist."[14]

Anthropology is indebted to Firth, trained as an economist, for a clearer understanding of the theoretical problems of analyzing the economic system of primitive tribes, just as economics may well be indebted. Being competent in both fields, he is not guilty of maintaining that the "mentality of the primitive" is incapable of seeing his own advantage,[15] or of maintaining, as does Warner, that a primitive tribe has no separate economic structure, being dependent on other social institutions to regulate economic processes.[16]

# DAHOMEY

There is a genuine market economy which exists in Dahomey, and one may well expect that the effects of religious beliefs and practices would, if there are any such effects, be subtle and difficult to trace.[17] The earliest literature gives evidence that this society is highly competitive, suggesting patterns of sharp competition and hard bargaining. The sloth which, in the folk philosophy of America, is supposed to characterize the Negro is not part of Dahomey. There is an ideal of hard work, reflected in the saying, "Every Dahomean man must know three things well: How to cut a field, how to build a wall, and how to roof a house."[18] Since the king and his court did not work at ordinary labor, this means that a considerable surplus had to be made[19] for their support, in turn creating the possibility of even "international" trade. Further, a high degree of specialization developed, as well as of secularization and rationalization of techniques in production and distribution. This suggests, moreover, a proposition which has already been noted, that the priests would receive payment for their activities, and in the case of such a type of society we would not expect the recipients to redistribute much of it.

Dahomey is principally an agricultural community, while raising animals and hunting are secondary. The products are sold in the markets as well as consumed at home. Small domesticated animals such as sheep, goats, chickens, and pigs are also raised. All these play some part in the ceremonies of sacrifice so characteristic of this society. The pig is even "one of the totemic animals 'respected' by one and perhaps two Dahomean sibs."[20] Hunting is tied closely to the supernatural. It is peculiarly the woods where the supernaturals are found who give *gbo* to man, who aid him in finding various kinds of magic for his problems of sickness, love, death, and so forth. There are ritual restrictions even on the wife, and hunting success calls for a sacrifice. As in many other agricultural communities, there is a close association of fertility with the deities, either personal, localized gods, or public ones, more broadly worshipped. This association is not confined, however, merely to the planting of the crops, but extends to the steps taken to prevent a swarm of locusts from attacking the crops, the selection of the plot of land to be farmed, when to abandon a field of low yield, and so on.

Without now attempting to generalize from the data, it might be profitable to take a synoptic view of many of the types and phases of production at which the calculating Dahomean feels it necessary to bring in the supernatural as an aid in his production. As in the case of Tikopia, it will be seen that this may take the place of fuller scientific knowledge, and in many cases would certainly prevent the individual from investigating further the causal sequences which he is trying to influence by means of the deities or magical forces he knows. Furthermore, it will also be seen to what extent energy is diverted from purely technical affairs to the non-empirical. This is an economic shift in the broadest sense. Let us note a few of these allocations of scarce goods.[21]

### CULTIVATION

a. Selection of the site by divination.

b. Confirmation of a favorable answer by sacrifice.

c. Determination of the divinity guarding field.

d. If Dambada Hwedo (ancestral deity, of unknown ancestors) is the guardian, discovery of his tree of residence, where a minor shrine begins.

e. If there is success, this deity may be "established."

f. If locusts appear, royal diviners discover which sacrifice will divert the swarm—usually a scapegoat.

g. Supernatural sanctions prevent work on one day, Mioxi, of the four-day week.

### HARVEST CEREMONIES

a. Harvested millet is ground into flour and mixed with water, then this is sprinkled over the ancestral shrines.

b. Divination to discover whether strong drink or animals should be sacrificed at the shrines.

c. For yams, there are three variations:

  (1) Diviner: Must offer kola nuts, drinks, kids, pigeons, chickens, new yams, etc. (To Gbadu or Fa); the morning after, the yam is made into a dish given to those who have completed their Fa, then songs are sung, with gongs accompanying.

  (2) Followers of Sky, Earth, and Thunder and of loko tree (where Dambada Hwedo lives): yams are cut for the deity, his followers, Lɛgba; and beans and two chickens are offered.

  (3) Women of compound: offerings to Yalode and Tokpedun (final "n" not nasalized), in forms of shells, ram, three white chickens, cornmeal dumplings, new yams; several stews are made for feasts, festival continuing for four days.

### HUNTING

a. Supernatural sanction in many phases of hunter's life.

b. Renewal of hunting powers by chief priest of Adjagbwa.

c. Certain animals possess supernatural powers, and are related to men as totemic ancestors; they must be killed by special techniques of magic, and honored afterwards by those who may kill them.

### IRONWORKING

a. Certain days are sacred to the god of iron, Gu.
b. Anvil must be consecrated, involving religious ceremonial.
c. Altars for ancestors.

### WEAVING

a. Funeral cloths woven as funeral offerings.

### POTTERY

a. Ceremonial pottery for serpent cult, twin cult, for Earth deities, as well as others.

### WOODCARVING

a. Making of statuettes for temples or magic house guards.

### CLOTH SEWING

a. Dressing of the gods, and people on ceremonial occasions.

### GRAVE DIGGING

a. Washing of corpse, dressing, burying it, and digging grave.

It is clearly seen how even in a society which carefully calculates probable rainfall, the time of planting, the fertility of the soil, crop rotation, the proper techniques for working iron, the proper "mix" for the pottery clay, the intricacies of demand and supply in a time of drought, and which understands the technical requirements for many types of difficult production, nevertheless does not rely on such secular knowledge alone, but pays great attention to the supernatural. Even though many of these phases are tied to magical rites, it must be remembered that in Dahomey the relationship between these and the central religious focus is intimate. Moreover, the larger part of these are elements in the broad area of the religious.

Several suggestive propositions may be formulated. One is, that the economic level is likely to interact with the religious sphere at points where the *various occupations become socially significant in other than market terms.* This is but a general way of stating that the religious complex will make use of economic elements, particularly the productive aspects, for ceremonials and sacred objects. Further, the various occupations will call on the supernatural for aid, or will in turn aid the realm of the supernatural. This is, again, but a different case of the more general proposition that the deities are interested in the handiwork of man. In terms of functional relationships, this parallels some patterns in Tikopia, since religious motivations play a large part in determining *what* will be produced: altars, shrouds for the dead, urns for *aizan*, statuettes for house or temple. Further, they furnish an incentive to perform the work[22] demanded, since the favor of the gods can be kept only by continuing the offerings. Moreover, some productional ends are necessary for the peripherally religious activities of the diviner, since chickens are usually necessary, as well as other sacrifices. Most of these practices rather divert attention from the technological aspects of production, and therefore in terms of both knowledge and energy do not lead to increased production, but a *less* efficient utilization of resources, granted the ends desired.[23]

Though we must think of the Dahomean market as a secular pattern of exchange, it is not possible to consider it merely in terms of profit. Actually, ". . . more than an economic significance attaches to this institution, for the market place is also a center for social activities and a place where religious rites are held."[24] The particular market which is held by tradition to have been the first established on any particular day of the week gives its name to that day,[25] the first Mioxi market being at Kana. It is believed that on this day "the deities do their own marketing," and as a consequence this day is poor for agriculture, as was noted above. Another proposition follows in Dahomean thought, that religious ceremonials are not to begin on this day. This would be both futile and discourteous.[26] One may instead make offerings to Destiny (Fa). Adokwi (the second day) is auspicious for agriculture or hunting, but not for ceremonies for the dead or for funerals. It follows, then, that one should not begin ancestral rites on such a day. It is the third day that is auspicious for beginning any venture, even more so than the fourth day. Thus we see another economic shift, demanded by sacred prescription.

Likewise, the establishment of a market, though to the Western mind a purely secular affair, requires some assurance that the future of the market will be prosperous. This assurance must come from the deities.[27] It is here that the *aizan* again appears, as the protector of human beings, whether placed in front of gates, houses, city entrances, markets or any other place where people pass. These amount to local guardians, particularized in this case by including in the mound some earth from seven of the important markets, as well as a bit of every commodity to be sold.[28] Here, again, the diviner must be used to consult fate about the future of the market before making the venture.

The *aizan* of the market is not, however, merely a magical object of an entirely secular import. When the cult-initiates are brought from their long period of training in the cult house, one of the three places to which they are taken is symbolically, the market place.

Later, as *agǫmasi*, a rank intermediate between the novitiates and those who have completed the training for membership in the cult-group, they beg alms and demand gifts from the sellers and buyers in the market places. As soon as twins are able to walk, it is prescribed that they must be presented to the spirit of the market. When the *loko* deity "comes to the head" (ritual possession) of a person who has gone through the initiatory rites the new follower of the deity is taken, to the accompaniment of the beating of drums, to the *aizan* of the market. When a child is born whom a diviner declares to be the reincarnation of the first human offspring of the supernatural founder of the sib, the *tɔhwiyo*, the elaborate ceremony which releases the mother from the taboos imposed upon her as a "wife of the *tɔhwiyo*" have (sic) largely to do with announcing that fact to the *aizan*, and asking it, as one of the most powerful spirits, to notify all the others (sic) powers that this woman has earned her release by the performance of the duties laid upon her.[29]

It thus becomes clear that the secular character of a market place does not entirely dominate the transactions which take place there, but that rather the social significance of the market place in turn makes it the locus of important rites; and further, that these rites are partly related directly to market and exchange, but more preponderantly to other values and ideas. These, in turn, gain some added importance by taking place where public recognition is given to the events. Thus in the cases mentioned above, a new religious state is made known by rite and by open presentation. Since the Dahomean is very cognizant of the occurrences in the market place, an important socio-religious function is attained by relating them to a seemingly economic context. This does not mean at all that the market place then becomes only the locus of religious rites. It would rather seem that those mentioned instead derive much of their social, if not their religious, significance from the place chosen, and not *vice versa*.

In these markets, many objects of supernatural import are sold, thus indicating once more the high degree of secularism in this culture.[30] Besides the sleeping and doorway mats, there are mats used in the ceremonies for deities. The altars are also sold in the market. They resemble rods with inverted candle snuffers on them, used for ancestral shrines. All the materials for magical charms are to be found in the market as well, including herbs, leaves, creepers, pelt fragments from felines, skulls of monkeys, etc.[31] The pottery, too, which is used for twins, that for the snake deities, as well as the "whitened, elaborately decorated pottery for the cult of the founder of the royal sib," is found.[32]

These objects, however, follow the general rules of the market with respect to that type of product, and do not call for a special type of handling, or different system of pricing. Though profit is an aim in the Dahomean market, there are different methods of pricing. Retail prices are set daily in the case of pottery, which is sold by both makers and middlemen (actually, women). Palm oil prices are dependent on the price of a basket of palm nuts, and are thus fixed. Trade societies, on the other hand, fix prices for the coastal cities.[33] Foodstuffs are priced by the first seller, without any of the expected underselling.[34] Actually, it appears that everyone sells his stock completely anyway, so that undercutting would simply reduce profits. Cloth is priced by the individual who designs a new style, but it is done by bringing in his fellow craftsmen for confirmation. Blacksmiths actually do follow a system of open competition, as is true of brass and silverworkers, and those who work in appliques. Thus it is that traditionalized or traditionally calculated prices characterize the Dahomean market, while stiff competition is not common. Further, objects which will be sacred in a ritual context are sold according to the system of pricing holding in that type of commodity, such as iron, cloth, pottery, etc.

The "cost" of worship in Dahomey is much more definite and is much greater than in Tikopia, by virtue of the simple fact that there is a priesthood. That is, there is a separate large profession which cultivates relationships with the deities, intercedes with them for human beings, and finds out their will, while not taking part in production. This is, of course, only one more aspect of the specialization of occupational function found in Dahomey. Another fact is highly influential here, the love of display and pageantry in Dahomey, exemplified in the earlier reports of the royal court and ceremonies, and still carried on to a lesser extent in religious and secular ritual. "Conspicuous consumption" has its place in the religious sphere as in the action system of the ordinary individual, and in few places is it so clearly shown as in the rituals of Dahomey.

The motivation for such expensive outlays in the realm of the religious is clear, and has been pointed out at several stages in the discussion. It is only thus that the favor of the gods can be kept. It is not so much a question of *buying* the favor of the gods as it is that the economic outlays indicate an inner attitude of respect, awe, and devotion. This is exemplified, as a case in point, by the cyclical ceremonies in honor of the ancestors. Most of the attention given in the cult of the ancestors is not costly or elaborate. An offering or sacrifice of no more than a few beans, some corn meal, or even a chicken, may be sufficient for the daily problems and crises facing the Dahomean.

On the other hand, the greater ceremonies are not so easily satisfied by such offerings. It may be put in this fashion:

Yet these humble approaches to the deified ancestors, without the more elaborate cyclical rituals . . . would be insufficient to insure the protection they give their descendents. Like the human creatures they fundamentally are, the ancestors are held to love display and ceremonial, and they would resent a role of oblivion in the daily round of life. They would be angered by failure of the members of their sib to consummate the "customs" which publicly glorify their deeds while on earth, and bring them back to the world of the living for several days of enjoyment among their descendents.[35]

This emphasizes the love of ritual characteristic of Dahomey (the society and the religion), the insistence on proper (and therefore expensive) commemorative pageantry, the context of honor and respect which is supposed to be implied by the economic outlay, and the connection between the daily contact with the ancestors and their "visiting" on ritual occasions.[36] The logic behind the richness of the ceremonies for the ancestral dead is seen in the fact that the living sib members represent those who are dead. When they are chosen to represent or impersonate their distinguished ancestors, the dancers "must be costumed as richly as their distinguished forbears had been, and in all other respects act as the rank of the ancestors requires."[37] Besides the sacrifices, there are even expenses connected with the journey of the dead, since the visit is conceived anthroposocially. The sib head lays gifts before the drums for the ancestors, in order to help them on the trip. Caury shells must be given so that they may buy anything they need. Drink is given (alcohol is very common in Dahomean ritual) for their refreshment. Both tobacco and cloths are given, since the ancestors must pay for their voyage across the mountains between the worlds of the dead and the living. Furthermore, not only are the great ceremonies richly decked to begin with; they become progressively more given to conspicuous consumption as the ritual continues. The rites are liturgical in character, with a highly trained personnel which "sells" religious services to its clients. The dancing is done by trained individuals, and the ceremonies are in charge of specialists who are careful that each step be properly performed.[38] Indeed, as commented on before in discussing the power of the sib head, there is considerable hesitancy in performing the supposedly and ideally annual ceremonies in honor of the ancestral dead in Dahomey. Part of the hesitancy, of course, is due to a fear of a too intimate contact with the dead. But it is also due to the expense, exemplified by the general rule that offerings be as worthy as possible. Slaves were the most suitable sacrifice in the days of the monarchy, as being the most expensive and royal gift.[39]

Aside from the "annual" customs for the royal dead, and the ritual attendant on the death of a king, perhaps the greatest economic burden on the distributive system of the collectivity is occasioned by the establishing of the ancestral dead, even though this occurs rather seldom. Some conception of the extent of the diversion of income to religious affairs can be obtained by following through some activities of the *dokpwegan* in his capacity as ritual organizer. The fact that it is the dokpwegan who attends to this establishment is interesting in itself, since the dokpwegan generally devotes his organizational energies to such productional activities as hoeing a field, building a house or making a wall. The institution of a *dokpwe* is a form of insurance, and for that reason has much economic interest. In Dahomean philosophy, everyone is liable for work in this cooperative labor, and through it any individual who needs help for a large enterprise, such as working for his father-in-law, or clearing land, may obtain help. Since everyone participates, no one loses his labor in the long run, while any emergency is met by this labor reserve. Its efficiency is possibly increased by the group activity, which is related to feasts, songs, chatter, rhythm, competition, and so forth.[40]

Even though the dokpwe is a secular and economic institution, it relates to religious patterns at three important points. One is the obvious case of installation of a dokpwegan, where the gods as well as men are called on for support in the career of this important official. Being head of the men of the village and "commanding their unquestioning obedience in all nonpolitical phases of life," he has a hereditary post, and calls particularly on the deities of the royal family: "the royal totem, . . . the spirits of the ancient kings, . . . the spirits of the royal tɔxɔsu" (those of royal family who are abnormally born) as well as the king himself. In the ceremony of installation, he points out that he must have help from all these sources, and a chorus of voices assures him that such help will be given. His relationship to these royal deities is part of the widespread pattern in Dahomean life of relating all powerful personages to the kingship. Here, this is done by relating the individual to the deities of the royal family.

The second main connection between the economic institution of the dokpwe and the religious pattern is found in funerary ritual. For the dokpwegan directs the burial ceremonies for everyone in his village.[42] He is one of the several persons notified when anyone dies. The work of the dokpwe begins with the funerary drumming, which does on day and night. On the night selected by the sib head for the partial burial, it is the dokpwegan who rolls the body of the dead man in native cloth, preparatory to the singing and dancing near the body. This dancing is difficult and strenuous, the young men vying with one another. From the time of the death until the definitive burial, a period of eleven days, the dokpwe continues to discharge its drumming duties. The dokpwegan himself continues to direct the various phases of the final ritual, including the erection of the temporary houses before the main entrance to the compound. The religious and the economic functions dovetail interestingly here, since it is usually he who collects the various gifts and offerings, some of which are to facilitate the journey of the dead, while others are to be used to prepare the body or to be spent on the ceremony.[43] Of course, some of the enormous quantities of cloths and other offerings are given to the dokpwegan and his dokpwe. It is the dokpwegan who sees to it that the dead man will have sufficient possessions in the world of the dead, by enclosing the gifts in the grave. He also destroys the man's shrine to Lɛgba, after the diviner has .ent the man's Fa *and kpɔli* (*sɛkpoli*, the fourth soul, possessed only by men to whom their full destiny has been revealed) on their way. The economic importance of this ritual obliteration of goods is obvious.

The third point at which the economic functionary called dokpwegan, with his dokpwe, relates closely to the pattern of religious observances is with reference to the consecration of the family dead. Here again this leader directs the process, and is in charge of the great quantities of offerings which are supposed to gain prestige for the spirits in the other world as well as for the family in this.

The entire complex of social pattern and rite which surrounds the deification of the sib dead is of interest as throwing light both on the religio-economic interrelationships as well as on the way in which the Dahomean thinks of the ancestral spirits. At death, the Dahomean does not immediately become a sacred ancestor. The funeral ceremonies for all dead adults must be completed within three years after death, so that the sib will not lose their souls.[44] Such dead ancestors should, ideally, be deified in a cycle of ceremonies taking place every ten years. The adult dead, who must cross three rivers and climb a mountain in order to reach the valley of their forbears, cannot become part of the august company there until they have been deified. This company includes the sib founders (tɔhwiyo) and their "associates," the personification of the

powerful unknown dead (Dambada Hwedo), and the deified sib dead
(*tovodun*).

It is dangerous not to deify the dead. Besides the fact that they may
feel neglected, to delay the deification opens the possibility of forgetting
one of them when the ceremonies do take place. This possibility is
fraught with grave danger. The danger derives from the anthroposocial
character of the deities. On the other hand, the danger is lessened because of the same characteristic. For the Dahomean assumes that he can
procrastinate, while evading the consequences of his inaction by placat-
ing the deities in other ways. He may consult a diviner in order to discover how best to ward off illness and danger, and to retain the friend-
liness of the spirits. The head of a collectivity continues to procrastinate,
since such ceremonies bring the initiators and directors of the rites in
very close contact with the spirits. This contact implies the possibility of
being taken by the dead. Although the Dahomean values highly the goal
of being worshipped by his descendants, the spiritual existence is not
rated so highly as life itself.[45] This evaluation is not changed substantially
by the fact that such a chief, or head of a group of collectivities, is likely
to be old and therefore near death. He will nevertheless attempt to postpone the fulfillment of his obligations to his ancestors, until misfortunes
seem to press too closely upon the sib members and the ancestral dead
to be remembered in the ritual may number from several hundred to a
thousand.

The extent of the economic burden of such a prolonged ritual may
be synoptically viewed by noting briefly the various tasks, contributions,
and expenses to be borne as the ceremonies progress:[46]

1. A cleared space in the bush.

2. A caury and a mat for every dead soul.

3. Several shelters of mats for women marrying into the sib, for the
male and female aborted and stillborn, and for the other dead who come
as spectators.

4. A lantern and small pot for every caury, which is sheltered within
its own mat.

5. Two full-sized shelters of bamboo, one of normal proportions and
one very long, for the living descendents.

6. Food for all who are to sleep in these shelters, this being furnished
by the men married to women of the deifying sib.

7. A chick only a few days old and a pot for each of the individual
dead.

8. Quantities of corn flour and palm oil to be placed in the pot when
the dead are to be called.

9. Cloths to swathe the pot when the chick is placed in it as a substitute soul for the one called.

10. Forty-one more chicks for those not individually named.

11. Cauries, palm oil, palm oil mixed with corn flour, and other gifts to welcome the dead.

12. Seven white cloths, seven white chickens, and seven francs fifty centimes for the chief of those who drum for the dead.

13. A ram for each dead man and a she-goat for each woman, together with still another buck (this is furnished by the first friend of the first of the family to die).

14. Two chickens, a pigeon and a duck (together with the ram) to be sacrificed by each person for his father; two chickens (together with the female goat) for his mother.

15. A ram, a female goat, and eleven chickens, sent by an important chief for the men who have died in his territory, the women, as well as for those unknown to him.

16. Money, white cloths, beads, drink, tobacco, bamboo fiber tinder, and pipes, to be thrown in seven circles drawn by the dokpwegan, each circle belonging to individuals or groups designated by him.

17. Two yards of cotton, a chick, and "much liquor" for each soul deified, together with forty-one cauries, seven castrated goats, seven she-goats, seven chickens, and seven cocks.

18. Ceremonial drums, which are buried in the final phase of the ritual.

19. Four large cloths, a male goat, and forty-one times seven francs fifty centimes, to be given to the dokpwegan.

20. Three small replicas of the altars (*asen*), to be kept for the next ritual series.

21. Sacrifices and offerings of beans, chickens, rum, and goats for the new temple erected in the compound of the founder of the collectivity.[47]

22. Two open pots (*agbanusu*) for each soul, and many pots peculiar to the children born malformed, and to the powerful unknown dead (the number is never stated; many calabashes, a mat for each soul, sixteen goats, two hundred and forty-one chickens, two lengths of white cloth (each forty-one yards long); all this is given to the chief priest.

23. Chickens, goats, "other animals," and figures of metals, to be used to celebrate the consecration (the chief priest takes everything used in the ritual except the pots).

24. Drums for the ancestral cult, at whatever price the maker asks, together with other gifts for the drummaker.

25. A number of pots, sacrifices, etc., equivalent to those used in the entire ceremony, to be used in parallel ceremonies to establish a house for Dambada Hwedo (there powerful unknown dead).

Even allowing for some Dahomean exaggeration, such a ritual is clearly very expensive. To say that such a burden positively is "functional for the survival of the society" gives a considerable latitude to the term. We may note the relationship between the economic and religious aspects of such rituals without insisting on their ultimate "value."

It is to be further noted that this is merely the economic burden of *establishment;* the cost of *maintaining* this temple represents still another religious demand upon the production of the group. Through the dokpwe not all of the offerings are lost, since they reenter the distributive channels. Nevertheless, a considerable portion is simply destroyed. The other side of this economic relationship is the obvious one that this religious goal of establishing one's ancestral dead causes a decrease in immediate consumption. That is, the quantities of objects are so enormous that years of saving are necessary as preparation. An additionally related aspect, one repeatedly found in Dahomey as elsewhere, is the extent to which conspicuous consumption is honorific. The gods, being like men in many traits of their character, enjoy witnessing elaborate and expensive ceremonials, and feel themselves neglected if men do not make offerings worthy of the deities. Thus the belief in certain religious goals requires concrete actions, setting into motion a complex group of economic processes, such as saving, consumption, distribution, and production, all conditioned and directed by, as well as conditioning and directing, religious activity. The situation in Dahomey may now be compared with that in a society at a much less developed technological level, the Manus.

# MANUS

The Manus represent an interestingly different case from the other societies discussed, at one significant economic point, for they are characterized by a strongly rational attitude which nevertheless contrasts with a rather low technological development. Apparently contractualistic elements figure even in the religious system. It has already been made evident that religious systems are likely to ask for favors from the gods, and the devotees are expected to return favors to the gods. At first glance, this appears to be simply a form of contract or agreement. However, it is equally evident that societies do not generally think of their own attitudes in such terms. The Tikopia, for example, consider themselves to be paying honor to the gods and to be receiving favors from them in order to be able to pay such honor. Further, their attitude is not to seek the minimum terms of such a "contract," but rather to be as lavish as possible in "payment."

Because of the importance of economic calculation in Manus life, the position of religion is interesting to analyze. The significance of this rational approach raises in the most crucial fashion the fundamental question being considered in this section of religio-economic interrelationships, whether economic matters are shaped and oriented by any religious patterns and goals. If the Manus actually do think of their Sir Ghosts only in terms of what the Sir Ghost can bring them in the form of food, prestige, power, health, and so on, then much of the previous analysis must be considered as less valid. For the attitude would thereby be a merely rational one which the individual takes toward powerful forces. The fear would be only that which we experience in avoiding a purely secular danger, such as nitroglycerine or storms. Any respect would be caused only by the power of Sir Ghost. The manipulative attitude would be merely that which is characteristic of handling any useful, though delicate, tool or force. This would remain the case even though such spirits were conceived in a completely "anthroposocial" fashion. For we are also able to assume such an attitude in dealing with other members of our society who are powerful. We may fear them, respect them, or manipulate them without at all "worshipping" them. This aspect of Manus religion, therefore, deserves a careful analysis.

*The Ward-Sir Ghost Relationship.* The strongly rationalistic element in the Manus economic system displays itself in a cool calculation of the profits to be made from various enterprises, and the exploitation of one's kin in various ways.[48] Since the religious system includes, as do other religions, requests for favors on the part of the worshipper, as well as giving favors to the spirits, one might expect a strong contractualistic bias in the Manus pattern of religious activity. To some extent this exists, as has already been noted in the brief summary of the system.

However, this relationship between the economic contract and the religious pattern does not turn out to be one of identity. Some of the contentions expounded in the introductory chapter are borne out here. It was maintained that rational calculation cannot alone constitute any basis for the continued existence of a society. Each society follows certain values, among which are religious ideas and practices, and these are not subject to logico-empirical proof or disproof. These partly furnish the motivation to action for the members of that society. However, if a religious system were found in which the individual merely manipulated

the sacred forces for personal advantage, in a cooly shrewd and impersonal manner, that general contention would have to be modified basically. Specifically, if the Manus actually do think of their Sir Ghosts
only in terms of what the Sir Ghost can bring them in the form of food,
health, wealth, and so forth, then this theory could not be accepted as it
has been presented.

In general terms, the answer is clear. The attitude of the Manus
toward the favors performed for Sir Ghost is that they express his solicitude for Sir Ghost.[49] Also, he does not think of his relationship to Sir
Ghost as merely a contractual one, worth only what it might bring on an
"open market." The relationship must rather be considered a covenant.[50]
It is not a relationship which is thought of merely in secular terms. It is
a solemn pact, moral in nature, between man on the one hand and a
divine being on the other. The force and sanction which motivate and
make this agreement effective are not a mere calculation of the empirical result of breach of contract (death on the part of the Manus,
destruction of Sir Ghost by the son of the Manus), but shame, guilt,
scorn, as well as sorrow.[51] The points at which this relationship clearly
deviates from a merely secular contract may be stated in more detail.

As against the usual conception of a contract, there is no choice of
partner by either part in the Manus–Sir Ghost relationship. Sir Ghost
may not choose another ward than his own, but must remain with his
ward.[52] The ward, on the other hand, does not exercise his theoretical
right to destroy the skull of Sir Ghost.[53] Actually, both grandfather and
father skulls usually wait on the deaths of brother skulls (i.e., other
males, more recently dead). That is, if Sir Ghost is not satisfactory, ward
does not immediately "choose another business partner" in any real
sense.[54] Furthermore, the attitude of the Manus that his devotion to Sir
Ghost is solicitude, a fact previously noted, is not the cooly impersonal
one of the rational calculation to be observed in a contractual relationship.[55]

Perhaps the most significant deviation from a merely contractualistic
definition of this relationship may be seen, however, *in its public and
moral nature*. Its functions are different from those of the Manus contract, which is individualistic and nonmoral.[56] For what seems at first to
be a mere trade of good fishing and health for some respect and a food
offering to a skull or spirit is, on closer examination, a public and moral
connection and an important factor in maintaining public morality.

This fact is most clearly seen by noting the situation which occurs
when there is a sexual offense, the greatest offense in Manus.[57] To begin
with, the affair cannot remain private because of the greater knowledge

of Sir Ghost, who knows most secret sin, even though he may not be omniscient.[58] So far as the individual is concerned, any such act is immediately known to any Sir Ghost of the family, as well as to that of his partner in sin. The act becomes, then, public knowledge in the spirit world, and is felt to be immoral.

Retribution itself extends the public character of the situation. If the relationship between an individual and Sir Ghost were merely an impersonal, contractual one, it would be expected that Sir Ghost might threaten the individual with punishment if he sinned. Further, that if sinning occurred, Sir Ghost would punish the individual unless he were persuaded by gifts not to do so. All this could occur privately and without shame. Actually, however, the entire village is brought into the situation. For retribution may not fall on the sinning individual himself. It is possible, of course, that either the girl or boy will be punished by sickness. Nevertheless, it is also possible that someone in the families of either boy or girl may be stricken, or someone in the family owning the house where the sin occurred.[59] Indeed, since there are so many other possible persons, there is perhaps a greater chance that someone besides the guilty pair may be hit.

This fact alone would prevent the Sir Ghost-ward relationship from being a private one. For what one individual does may cause retribution by his Sir Ghost to fall on someone else within his kinship group. Everyone, then, is potentially interested in what happens between a man and his Sir Ghost, and may be morally outraged by what a man does.

However, this does not exhaust the public and moral nature of this relationship. For when such an illness strikes anyone, the entire village is concerned, not merely the one made ill by Sir Ghost. "The moment such an illness occurs the community is all suspicion."[60] If there is any evidence at all—and with a whole village interested in everyone else's sin there is likely to be—the oracles will make the charge of sin against the couple. This, again, is not a secret charge. It is as public as the confession becomes.[61] The reaction to the confession is one of horror as well as an interest in making the tale known. Indeed, the public disapproval and shame which the couple must bear undoubtedly delay confession.[62]

Once confession is made, kinsmen hurry to make the expiatory payments which alone can return the stricken one to health and prevent further attacks. Here, again, knowledge of the sin remains mercilessly in view. If both boy and girl are unmarried, payment is made to the Sir Ghost of the family into which the girl is planning to marry.[63] The boy's kins also make payment to the Sir Ghost or Sir Ghosts of the family into which he is to marry. Possibly the Sir Ghosts of the house where the sin occurred may be included, if it does not belong to either side. Obviously, the payments are concretely made to the families themselves, and it may be noted in passing that their size make them significant as a type of economic distribution. In the case mentioned above, Kalo gens, to which Alupwai belonged, paid two canoes to the Sir Ghosts of Pwanau's kin, as well as two calico wraps, two fish spears, and a wooden chest with lock and key.[64] This was a poor gens, and it thus becomes evident that the interrelationships between economic and religious patterns cannot be described merely by saying that the religious system, or the relationship between ward and Sir Ghost, is merely an economic or contractualistic one based on an illusion. Rational calculation is not the sole explanatory factor in analyzing this relationship. It has been necessary to make this point at some length, since the importance of individualistic calculation and profit seeking in Manus society must be properly evaluated. It might otherwise be easy to fall into the error of thinking that ward continues his relationship with Sir Ghost only for the profit he makes from Sir Ghost's care, thus relegating religious ideas and practices to a simple economic pattern. Such a simple, but inaccurate, conception would discount the Manus religious system as a significant element in Manus social action and would cast serious doubt on an important sociological proposition, that a society does not exist solely upon a basis of individualistic, rational calculation. Patterns of non-rational action and belief must also exist, and these will be constituted in part by the religious system.[65]

However, to deny that the relationship between ward and Sir Ghost is that of a mere contract, and to explain this in various directions, is only part of an analysis at the economic level. It is useful to note still other points of economic motivation, and other places where Sir Ghost determines the allocation of the desirable but limited resources.

Sir Ghost requires of his ward that production and commerce be assiduously pursued. In Manus society, inefficiency, laziness, procrastination, or shiftlessness are never condoned.[66] Sir Ghost, although partly responsible for the prosperity of his ward, will insist on his ward being diligent at his tasks. Furthermore, this attitude is emphasized by other rules of economic action which are supported by Sir Ghost. Ward is impelled to meet his economic obligations on time, at the risk of incurring the severe displeasure of Sir Ghost.[67] Ward, furthermore, may not be wasteful or extravagant of his wealth. The Manus do not save or work in order to live comfortably, or retire at an early age. The wealth must be used for the recognition of crises such as marriage, death, spiritual activities, sin in the family, divorce, first menstruation, etc. In general, the wealth is used for high points in family affairs, the family conceived as including both the living and the dead. Sir Ghost will not approve of any purely individualistic or hedonistic use of the wealth, and it is sinful not to ask the opinion of Sir Ghost about any projected use of wealth.[68]

Payment of debts on time is conceived strictly, and it is expected that punishment for laxity will also be strict. The important economic exchanges are contracted many days ahead of the specific date on which the exchange falls due. "If one man is a day late in contributing his sago, for instance, and his baby is ill on the night of the day when it should have been contributed, this slight delay is diagnosed as the cause. His Sir Ghost is inflicting punishment for economic slackness."[69]

Since wealth is always a limited resource, any individual is constantly faced with the problem of allocation. The Manus is no exception. However, he must make certain that his Sir Ghost approves of his allocation. One member of his house may be due to go through the earpiercing ceremonial at the same time that a betrothal is to occur. Both require ceremonial feasts, and Sir Ghost may punish the house if he decides that one of the two members is getting too much of the limited wealth for his or her ceremonial. Sir Ghost may, of course, be consulted beforehand, but illness later may be probed by still another oracle, who may report that the earlier report on the opinion of Sir Ghost was not correct.[70] Similarly, the individual may succumb to a weakness for pig, and consume an animal which Sir Ghost thinks should have been used for the public validation of some event, that is, used to make a fine public showing in the public property exchanges.

It will be noted that Sir Ghost in thus shaping and directing activity which would be considered of an economic character even in our own society: producing, husbanding of resources, distributing them according to the most desirable plan in view of the limited amount available, not allowing temporary pleasures to use up resources needed for important events, and so forth.

This punishment for economic slackness is interestingly seen in connection with the adoption of a dead brother's child. The living brother must furnish the wealth required for the betrothal of the child, just as the father would have done had he lived. On the other hand, the mother's brother may himself advance the wealth if there is any delay, so that the children thus belong to his side of the family irrevocably. Sir Ghost may see this about to happen and strike someone in the house of father's brother. This is an act to spur the brother to act properly.[71]

Even bad luck in the important economic activity of fishing may be caused by Sir Ghost if the individual has not been meeting his economic obligations. This is a stern demand, and may be made even though the individual can claim justly that he is not able to meet the payments unless Sir Ghost will send the fish needed for exchange.[72] On the other hand, Sir Ghost will be appealed to when the time of spawning occurs, though not for daily fishing. Sir Ghost is expected to give the necessary guidance to the best fishing places, and an appeal may be made to his vanity or avarice, an interesting reflection of the Manus himself.

As a consequence, it must be accepted that the ward-Sir Ghost connection furnishes a constant impulse to be active in economic affairs. Punishment will otherwise occur, both directly as a result of Sir Ghost's displeasure at laziness, and indirectly as a result of the consequent failure to meet obligations. Fortune sums up this result by pointing out that:

Hard work is exacted up the limit. The Manus take very few siestas, except after all-night fishing. They are always up and doing in a torrid climate; they always "have work." And an observer cannot help but think that they die young, as they do, because of the speed and constancy of the work they do; which, in turn, is kept up by the heavy blame that falls upon a man who has rested for a very brief while, as a man accused of causing illness in his house.[73]

Acting upon Sir Ghost's desires projected from the other plane may go so far as to make gifts or payments on this plane for something happening on the other, such as a ghostly marriage. This, because somewhat arbitrary, may be resorted to when sin is difficult to find on this plane. However, a more concrete and expected economic activity, building a house, is also one which waits upon Sir Ghost's pleasure. Building a house is an involved and sacred crux of activity and relationships. The man does not plan to build until Sir Ghost has given the orders, complaining about the old one. The size of house is traditional for a given family. Building materials for the house are not actually bought by the man himself, but by others who receive large payments from the individual and who in turn acquire the materials from the land dwellers, as well as actually construct the house.[74]

It is to be noted that the Manus do not have the periodic ceremonies to be found in many other societies. This fact underlines the economic function of Sir Ghost as a director, guide, or motivator in daily affairs, since the season will not itself bring about a period for great religious and economic exchanges.[75] Such exchanges or gift payments are usually those, therefore, which arise out of the progress of the individual through the society and which are of social significance to both the society and Sir Ghosts. The validation of these by feasts, exchanges, and gifts in public ceremonial is expected by both the society and Sir Ghost, while the latter furnishes a strong motivation to carry out these ceremonials in the proper style and at the proper time. The ear-piercing ceremony, first menstruation and pre-marriage segregation of the girl coupled with the war blessing of the boy, marriage itself, pregnancy, child-birth, celebration of a long and prolific marriage (the *metcha*), and mourning, all call for the backing of some capitalist, who sees to it that payments of debts occur in time (through proper timing and planning) for each ceremony and who may advance the dogs' teeth or other necessary wealth for the occasion. There is thus a continuing chain of payment and debt, by which individuals, usually of fairly close kin, help to organize and pay for ceremonials demanded by the society and Sir Ghost, and in turn receive the same type of help.[76]

Thus it is evident that in this society of intense interest in economic affairs the religious pattern nevertheless helps to motivate and shape such action. Far from being merely a cold-blooded compact between the personal deity and the individual, privately made or broken, the relationship between Sir Ghost actually is in the nature of a covenant, moral in nature and publicly sanctioned and supported. Sir Ghost in turn is not merely the helper of the Manus, but insists on the other hand that the individual accept and live up to the demands of various economic obligations, by husbanding his resources, by allocating his wealth to the proper channels instead of using it selfishly or shortsightedly, and by producing energetically so as to make his payments when they are required. Sir Ghost even initiates demands of a productive nature by his desire for recognition on this plane. He further helps to motivate and keep to the mark any who would fail to recognize the important ceremonial events in the life of the individual and the family. The picture of economic affairs in Tikopia, where the matters of production, savings, trade, exchange, distribution, etc. do not play so active a part in daily consciousness, may be set against the Manus situation of active business, to see whether some of these patterns of motivation and allocation again play a part.

# 6. RELIGIOUS AND ECONOMIC ACTION (Continued)

## TIKOPIA

W<small>ITH REFERENCE</small> to the Tikopia, who are not far advanced technologically and who do not have a complex economic system, Firth notes:

There is a scarcity of the means available for satisfying wants, these wants are arranged on a broad scale of preferences, and on the whole choice is exercised in a rational manner in deciding how the means to hand shall be disposed of. The employment of the factors of production is governed by some recognition of the advantages of the division of labour and specialization in employments according to differential skill, and economies of scale are also secured in an elementary way in agriculture, fishing, and other cooperative work. Productive equipment and other goods are accumulated specifically to engage in further production, so that one may speak of the employment of capital, though it does not fulfill all the functions of this factor in a modern industrial system. Moreover, there is an implicit concept of a margin in the use of the various factors of production, as in the transference of labour from one area of land to another according to variation in its productive capacity, or from one type of fishing to another according to the conditions operating at the time, or in the tendency for the size of the working group to vary directly with type of employment . . . There is some realization of the operation of the law of diminishing returns . . . There is a system of property rights . . . Notions of value can be said to exist with the forces of supply and demand as a regulating influence . . . though . . . not expressed through a . . . system of exchange of commodities, or a price system . . .[1]

Though an economic analysis does not have to explain the choice of ends, the general analysis of an economic pattern must note their existence, so as to make clear what the group is attempting to achieve. As this relates to the Tikopia, it becomes clear that the ends which are sought are, for the most part, social in the broadest sense—i.e., there is social emulation more than economic emulation. Firth characterizes the Tikopia economy by saying that it is "non-competitive," or that labor is "a social service, not merely an economic service." He expresses it further in the form of three propositions: (1) the economic relations are personalized; (2) the profit-motive is prevented from free operation by "other psychological (in the terms of this study: sociological) factors concerning the social role of the accumulation and use of wealth"; and (3) economic transactions are governed by a broad code of reciprocity, but this is part "of a wider code which obtains for all types of social relationship(s) which . . . receive much more overt and institutionalized expression than in our type of society."[2] Furthermore, Firth found it necessary to examine ends, without attempting at all to explain or justify their origin, for he had to indicate why certain economic decisions were made, such as a failure to use productive equipment at a particular time (mourning). The explanatory factor of "maximization of satisfactions" as used by the economist had to be broken down into *different types of satisfactions*, since there are different types of satisfaction possible. The explanation becomes meaningless "as an aid to the changes in demand, or differential application of the factors of production" if it applies to all economic conduct.[3]

As in most societies, food is a primary goal of production in Tikopia, and therefore a prime factor in the economic processes. This follows from the commonsense and pragmatically obvious notion that in order to live one must eat. However, beyond this, not only is the Tikopia economy related to food: the social system itself is so oriented. The reason is not far to seek, taking into account several situations which have been previously described. It is not the nutritional value of the food which plays such a dominant role. It is rather that food is necessary for hospitality, in a culture given to dancing and visiting. It is a means for repaying obligations of various kinds, for showing respect to a chief, or acknowledging his suzerainty. It binds kinship units. It is, furthermore, a means of making religious offerings.[4]

It is at this point, therefore, that the system of ultimate values and beliefs called religion makes a pronounced impact. For just as, in another connection, religious elements impinge on the economic system through the political,[5] so here the emphasis is on the non-nutritional aspects of food exchange, production, and distribution, as well as the conditions surrounding all these. That is, ritual obligations and rules, impulses and beliefs, set certain ends, and aid in fixing means and conditions to these ends.[6]

Perhaps the most obvious relationship is expressed in the division of important food plants among the four principal chiefs, each one under the care of the peculiar deity of that chief, who is in turn responsible for rites (and therefore food production and offerings) in honor of that deity. Thus, the Ariki Kafika has control over the sacred yam, "the Ariki Tafua over the coconut, and the Ariki Taumak over the taro, and the Ariki Fangarere over the breadfruit. Each chief has his own set of rites to secure the prosperity of his food."[7] The rites of the last three are performed separately, but those for the sacred yam are the focus of much of the religious ritual of Tikopia, forming part of the seasonal cycle, the Work of the Gods.

Its importance is not simple and direct, however; it is only a small part of the total yam crop which must be fitted to the cycle. All but one type (not a distinct variety) may be planted and harvested at will.[8] It is of economic importance partly because it is a durable food, which can be kept over many months even in a tropical climate. However, its explicit and analytic importance does not lie in this, but in its relationship to the deity of the Ariki Kafika, to his position as chief and therefore as chief director of economic enterprises on the island. Furthermore, these integrated rituals are important for the food which must be produced for them and for the communal (and therefore intensified) endeavor which is set off and directed by such goals. Consequently, the significance of the yam extends beyond the Ariki Kafika and his direct relationship to the yam. This may be investigated in both these directions, and with a broader reference than to the Kafika chief himself. For substantially the same pattern holds true for other rites as well.

This is clearly shown in the case of the canoe rituals, which also call for increase and prosperity, such as in a formula used by Ariki Taumako:

I eat your excrement Tafaiata! (his title for the Atua i Kafika, when in his
    canoe court)
Turn to your timber is anointed there (the rite of oiling the canoe)
Anoint with power
Anoint for welfare
To ascend a flying fish on to your canoe.[9]

It is clear that this ritual is being used to obtain fish, asking the help of the deity in the production of fish for food. But it must be noted, also, that the reference is to "your canoe." The deity will simply not obtain suitable offerings if he does not furnish food in quantity and quality. The interest becomes more than merely selfish on the part of the Tikopia native, and his interest in fishing with renewed endeavor, in order to fulfill his obligation to the deity, is indicated. Thereby, also, an impulse is given to apply energy and time to repairing the equipment used in fishing. Firth suggests four main aims of this ritual activity: (1) the deities are brought again into contact with the canoes made by tools furnished (ultimately) by the deities; (2) the deities are stimulated to help to provide for their own worship; (3) the relations between the deities and the kinship groups are strengthened; and (4) the material fishing equipment is ritually charged again with *manu*.[10]

As to function, he remarks, "And in so doing, the ritual secures that these items of equipment, particularly the canoes, are in fact overhauled and made technically more effective. Moreover, the ritual provides a socially unifying occasion . . . the total result is an integration in technical, ritual, and social terms."[11] The description of this work, constituted by the productive and ritual parallels, indicates clearly how the presence of others in the group at a religious ceremony influences the individual to respond with alacrity and skill.[12] This is even more definitely the case than is at first apparent, when it is remembered that the gods are thought to demand promptitude and speed in their rituals. When the oven must be begun extremely early in the morning, in the ritual at Somosomo, the Pleiades are used to judge the time, and some individuals are deputed to wake others.[13] Speed and energy (the two concepts are close in Tikopia thought, as they are in Dahomey) must be characteristic of the worker for the gods. This is suggested even more strongly in the case of the first fruits ceremony for fishing, related to the repairing of the canoe mentioned above, and having as constituent parts certain formulae such as that given immediately above. The situation is thought of in symbolic terms. The gods of the (sacred) adze insist on receiving recognition for their aid to men (the tools ultimately came from the gods, and are used for repairing the canoes). But if men are slack in performing the ceremony, or do not obtain fish for the ceremony, these gods will become angry. The adze then will strike among men instead of among fish.

Hence there is always some haste to get the ceremony over, and if bad weather prevents the fleet from going out or if the catch is poor, uneasiness is felt in all the villages. It is during this time that the mats lie open in the canoe court and everyone is relieved when they are folded up; it is a sign that the due rites have been completed.[14]

The people of Kafika perform the ceremony three times at least, and if the catch is not good enough to include a large fish, the most desirable being a shark, the ceremony is again performed in Uta, the most sacred area in Tikopia. Thus the ritual sanction furnishes a strong push to perform the rites with dispatch. But the ceremonies depend upon the allocation of time and energy as well as equipment and rituals, to fishing. The deities will not be satisfied, and therefore fishing will be poor, unless proper offerings are made. These can be made only if the necessary repairs are made, work is expended on fishing, and many members of the clan cooperate and compete to achieve these goals. Besides the purely secular pride and admiration attached to an efficient and fast worker, the gods themselves approve. And the competitive context of the ceremony induces a greater expenditure of labor.

Even when competition is not a dominant motif, the ritual conditions may create a situation where a greater amount of work is demanded. In the plaiting of mats at Somosomo[15] by the women, for the "recarpeting," a more efficient situation is possibly created. At least, the energies of the women are not distracted from production. This is not a *purpose* of these ritual restrictions, but a latent or implicit function of them. The purpose is, of course, to emphasize the ritual sacredness of the action, which is imbued with religious feeling.

Because of respect for the sacred area of Uta, which lies close to the glade of Somosomo, the women must turn their backs to the seacoast and their faces toward Uta. Even though they worked in groups, and the Tikopia are given to light chatter and gossip, they were not supposed to speak at all, except for technical discussions about the actual plaiting.[16] Besides this tabu of silence, the elders warned the women not to stop or slow the work down, no matter what happened. At the time, a light shower had begun, but the task was too sacred to be stopped. Furthermore, no one was to approach the workers. The function of these ritual restrictions becomes clear, then, since the work would be speeded up greatly.

Some suggestion has already been made that the act which initiates the period of excitement, hard work, routine, and tapu (Work of the Gods) focuses on the chief as central religious head, and constitutes both an economic and a religious act. After the firestick has been thrown, the main question asked is an economic one, even though the context is sacred: how many days will be allowed to cut and plait the coconut mats?[17] The answer is a formal one,[18] but with this answer the ritual-economic period begins with hard work on the mat-making. Likewise, he initiates the collecting of food for the making of the sacred roi,[19] used at the kava ceremony preceding the lifting down of the adzes for the ritual canoe (and fishing) ceremonies. The ritual resacralization and actual repair of these canoes, discussed above, is also under the aegis of the chief. And, in a similar fashion, the change to intense fishing as an economic activity is instituted by the ritual necessity of fish, particularly

a shark, for the fishing welfare invocations of the chief, which were mentioned above. As ritual head, then, the chief initiates a diversion of economic activities in channels serving religious requirements, particularly
the demands of the deities. Partly, also, he diverts energies to the re-
placement of perishable objects or productive capital (canoes), this being
placed in a religious context. As a consequence, the significance of the
chief is very great. Both the economic and the political headship of the
Tikopia chief stem from his relation to the religious realm, in the thought
of the Tikopia. As representative of the deity of his clan, or, in the case
of the Ariki Kafika, of the whole tribe, he owns the land. But more important than this "ownership," which is nominal for most ordinary purposes, is his function as organizer and director of economic enterprise.
In this, there are several phases at which the element of the sacred is
introduced, since much of such enterprise is related to the wishes and
plans of the gods, not merely of men, and the aid of the gods is obtained
through the chief.[20]

The most obvious economic function served by the chief in his ritual
capacity is to divert energies toward preparations for sacred ceremonies,
for which great quantities of food, bark cloth, and coconut mats are
needed.[21] The Throwing of the Firestick begins a period of keeping the
fishing equipment as well as the gardens in working shape. Actually,
much of the diversion of energy is "wasted," in that energies are spent
on both productive equipment and purely sacred objects (e.g., mats).
Nevertheless, there is an imperious immediacy to the religious demands,
preventing procrastination, and the integration of the community's forces
as initiated by the chief is an important result.[22] An important political
function may also be served, in that the several chiefs are thus again
joined ritually, while the supreme place of the Ariki Kafika is emphasized.

Attention will be later directed to the politico-religious interrelationship at the points where the chief prohibits the use of one or another
commodity or area, and no detailed discussion need be given here. However, it should be emphasized that this is a pattern of saving, induced by
religious demands. Certain foods are consumed in smaller amounts, or
not at all, while others become dominant in the diet. The function and
purpose are the same, to save foods for the religious or secular ceremonials, particularly the former. Thus, Firth summarizes in tabular
fashion these shifts in patterns of economic consumption, and it is noticeable that all but one of the shifts are caused by the tapu of the chief in
particular.[23] This one is the individualistic restriction, to his own use, of
the cultivations of a given person. Others may be noted: (1) the Throw-

ing of the Firestick stops the felling of sago palms for nearly two months; (2) funeral prohibitions on: a. richer foods, b. plucking coconuts, c. reef or canoe fishing, cause a change in consumption habits by which some few reserves are accumulated, poorer foods are eaten, and production shifts from sea to land; and (3) restrictions on taking coconuts, which cause a diversion partly to other foods, and allow the accumulation of coconuts which can be used for creaming the ceremonial foods used as gifts or offerings. These are backed by religious sanctions, thus delineating sharply the close interrelationships holding between what would seem to be realms diametrically opposed.

This close direction of production and economic decisions with the chief in his capacity as religious head, and with sacred goals, can be seen most clearly in the manufacture of turmeric. This spice is related most closely to the Atua i Kafika, and thus to the Ariki Kafika, though turmeric is also manufactured by the other chiefs. The religious element is seen in that the food importance of termeric is comparatively little, and the coloring matter is used only in making a mark of ritual significance. It is considered attractive to the gods, and is used as a dye to color the bark cloths made as "toppings" or "coverings" for important food gifts to the Ariki Kafika.

As in the case of many other phases of the religious cycle, this is initiated by the Ariki Kafika, when he plants turmeric.[24] Firth witnessed the turmeric extraction of the Ariki Tafua, who is considered a turmeric expert. That he should be an expert is significant, since in this type of production great emphasis is laid on technical skill, as distinct from sacred power.[25] However, it remains true that the grinding and washing of the plant roots must be done every year by the chiefs, as a religious obligation,[26] while a commoner who produces at all will do so much less often. Even in the case of this technical procedure based on skill, it is thought by the Tikopia that the expert cannot rely on such skill alone. He must also use ritual formulae. For it is by his deity that such an expert obtains success in the separation of the pigment. Each will have a different deity, though it is understood that the ever-present Atua i Kafika is thought to preside over the process or season as a whole. It is also understood that the "chief, in accordance with his rank and esoteric functions, is always leader of the first unit in his own *nuanga*" (turmeric extraction),[27] the same order of precedence being maintained in the units throughout the procedure. The first batch of pigment is considered valuable, and is the chief's.

Here, again, capital equipment is renewed as a ritual necessity, while it is also a necessity for efficiency. The aqueducts are repaired or overhauled, being sections of split areca palm. The cutting of the first palm for this use is preceded by a short appeal to the particular deity of that *nuanga* unit, and later a libation and a food offering are made to the Kafika deity, informing him of the presence of a sufficiency of water. The deity is thus ceremonially notified that the secular aim has been achieved.

The ritual implications of the turmeric extraction are more clearly seen once the first grating of the roots begins, for it is from that time that a number of restrictions and prohibitions begin. The situation is well incorporated by the phrase, "living in the *nuanga*," as opposed to "those at the back."[28] Here, again, the imposition of the regulations is thought by the Tikopia to be of a merely religious nature, but the result is greater efficiency, for one of the important tabus is against sexual intercourse. To assure the efficacy of the prohibition, women and men separate both at night and for rest during the day. Affairs of sex might hurt the health of the people, or ruin the turmeric (it will be soft). Connected with this explicit bar against sexual intercourse is a series of prohibitions against certain postural positions: men must sleep on the back, while women must sleep on the face, and one may not squat with the knees hunched up, while it is permitted to "sit with crossed legs, or recline with the legs straight out in front."[29] These are considered less suggestive, sexually.

Similarly, there are food prohibitions, most of which attempt to induce the turmeric to become hard, by a symbolic process. Semi-liquid foods, or mush foods, or even sugar, must not be eaten. A less clear regulation insists on those "within the *nuanga*" eating only "hot foods." Those who eat the one must not come into contact with those outside, who eat "cold foods," otherwise the turmeric will not be satisfactory.[30] The remnants of the *nuanga* ovens, which would ordinarily become the cold food of the next day, are not thrown away, though this might be expected as a possibly symbolic rite. Instead, they are passed out from the *nuanga* into other households "outside." These rules are, it may be observed, significantly close to a magical pattern, though Firth does not remark on it. For a breach of these tabus is not punished by a deity presiding over or playing a part in the *nuanga*. The breach is rather the beginning of a (seemingly) cause-effect chain. Further, these are not tied to ritual formulae or any relationship to the deities, but are rather sanctions running "fairly evenly throughout the whole process."[31] Even children must obey the rules about food, which would not be expected if the sanction were less personalized. The impersonal pattern must be followed. This is particularly striking, since Tikopia children are usually allowed many breaches of tabus, being only gently (though repetitiously) admonished.

After the grating of the roots and the building of the filter stand for the funnel-like filtercloth of palm fiber, the extraction proper begins. Even though the expert is skillful, this is such an important point in the manufacture of the pigment that one could expect some ritual. At the time when the first batch of grated turmeric roots are being thrown into the filtercloth, the chief is given a cue by the one emptying the bowl, and then begins a formula called Fishing for Success.[32] It contains the usual metaphors of abasement, with several symbolic references to the turmeric, by the mention of redness in several connections. It is supposed to induce the greatest amount of turmeric from the materials being worked. The appeal is partly to the vanity of the deity being involved, who is Tuna, the Eel-God (who controls the fresh water used in filtering). This is related to other ceremonies in Tikopia, where there is a direct relationship to economic production, in that in each case the deity is told to help because the work is being done for him.

In spite of the insistence on genuine technical ability, the sacred (and partly magical) character of the whole process, noted before, continues to obtrude itself in this economic affair. That is, the expenditure of skill and energy on the process is not considered sufficient: the favor of the gods must also be obtained. For the final proportion between the edible, though less valuable, extract and the vermilion pigment is "believed to be not simply a physical relation, but one governed by spirit action."[33] This spiritual assistance is believed, in the Tikopia pattern of thought, to manifest itself in three main ways: (1) aiding the precipitation of the pigment; (2) transforming the edible portion into the vermilion precipitate; and (3) stealing pigment from others while guarding the home supply. This latter is done by the spirits, not by men, and the thieving is not to be done on the island, but elsewhere.

Somewhat the same phrasing is used in other formulae brought in later, in that a pattern of inducing the turmeric to be plentiful and well solidified is repeated. At every stage in the production of the pigment some ritual elements enter, some having a demonstrable function in increasing, or shifting the emphasis of, production, others (like the spiritual assistance petitioned for above) having none. In terms of the Tikopia ideology, each is necessary, and the Tikopia is not always conscious of the effect of the ritual, in economic or technical terms. Thus the enclosure to hold the bowls of turmeric while settling is tabu, once the bowls are filled, serving to leave the mass undisturbed during the precipitation.[34] Also, the sacred character of the pigment ensures a greater care in the handling of it, so that the actual production is greater.[35] This care is even more marked in the case of the first cylinder of turmeric from the oven of the Ariki Kafika. That is, the ritual motivation induces great care in production itself. This follows from the critical position of the chief. He is the initiator of the whole phase of turmeric manufacture, and leads the various units in beginning each step in the procedure. As the person most closely connected to the supreme deity of the island, who in turn is the deity of all most interested in the production of turmeric, it is felt that his pigment is crucial: ". . . if his pigment turns out well it is believed that this is a good augury for all the rest. . . . The Ariki Kafika himself, imbued with his responsibility, said that he recited formulae not for his turmeric alone, but that the nuanga of the whole land might be successful."[36]

Thus it is that the world of the supernatural and sacred, whatever its "illusory" qualities, actually interacts with this economic realm in definite, concrete ways, by shifting the ends to be achieved, and by furnishing a more imperiously immediate motivation for certain economic goals. The ways in which these ends may be achieved are conditioned by ritual sanctions which in some cases impair efficiency, in others increase it. In still others there is no perceptible way in which either could occur, the ritual sanction either having little effect, or consisting in a ritual formula which merely occupies an interval of waiting during a technological process. The demands of the sacred, then, divert scarce resources of time, energy, and capital equipment to certain activities at certain periods, changing eating and working patterns at the time, usually causing an increase either in the accumulation of wealth for later expenditures or, by repairs, in the heavy capital equipment of canoes, canoe sheds, turmeric equipment, adzes, etc.

It would not be expected that ritual elements would play such a directive role in economic production, without at the same time performing some distributive and exchange functions. That is, we should expect to find that the determination of the direction of distribution and its quantity would follow, at least in part, from ritual status, sacred obligations, and religious demands. It would also be expected that the focal point for such distribution or exchange as takes place must be the chiefs, in both a secular and a ritual capacity.

That is, he receives gifts as political head, and as representative of the clan deity.

Even the chief of the Kafika clan works in Tikopia. No one is a true member of the "leisure class," though it is true that the Ariki Kafika is allowed to work less, in terms of actual production, than other individuals. He is not, for example, allowed to shoulder burdens. Without a court or army to consume the gifts he receives, it becomes obvious that he must be a constant giver as well as recipient. This is even clearer in view of another fact, that his own possessions would more than cover his requirements and those of his family.

Stated briefly, he is the recipient from his people of periodic gifts of food and special types of raw material which, sporadic in the case of any individual contributor, nevertheless form *in toto* a steady stream of additions to his wealth. But . . . a great deal of what he receives he redistributes, and with his family's help he must reciprocate the initial gifts, though not necessarily to an equal extent.[37]

These gifts come from the chief's clan, but also come from people living nearby though from other clans, as well as those who are in other clans though closely related to the chief. The food gifts usually are constituted by a large basket of creamed pudding, or of fish, with "a mass of baked taro or yam tubers, breadfruit, or bananas."[38] They are also reciprocated soon afterwards. The reciprocating gifts usually come, of course, from contributions made by still others, thus forming a steady stream of income and outgo.[39] Besides the "first gifts," large fish are supposed to be brought to the chief. Further, "the border of the path is the orchard of the chief," that is, the food growing near the edge of the path may be taken by the chief, unless the owner takes it first. There are also food gifts indicating specific kinship ties, particularly the relationship to a common ancestor. These may be made when the chief is ill, or even in mourning.[40] Moreover, there are gifts which chiefs make to other chiefs when they attend ceremonies together. This is only one phase of his traditional role as a fountain of generosity, emphasized even more in other connection: "Toward poor commoners . . . a chief is expected to be generous without necessarily getting anything in return."[41]

Besides these sources of income, which are essentially secular, even though in many cases partly ceremonial, there are a great number of strictly religious rituals which include gifts to the chief, in particular to the Ariki Kafika. Such gifts include the *monotanga* of a sacred canoe, the *fonakava* from the recarpeting of a temple,[42] both given by commoners; *monotanga* of the very sacred canoes to the Ariki Kafika (given to him only), "the path of our ancestors (from Taumako to Kafika only), food from rebuilding a temple, and, possibly, the exchange of gifts at certain ceremonies, all the latter being gifts from other chiefs.[43] This does not include certain of the chiefly feasts, at which the chief composes songs to his deities, or at which the gods are brought in to witness the accession of the chief. This last, *te moringa,* is discussed in Chapter VIII. All of these call for return gifts of some sort.

It is not necessary to describe all these in detail, since the pattern is much the same. The quantity of food is large, an effort being made to express a general abundance. It is of the best quality, and is usually accompanied by something which is "extra," or "topped" by some contribution such as bark cloth. It is often redistributed at that point, or at least soon afterwards. The offering or gift is made when a particular ceremony is going to be performed, and is made at the place of performance, usually at a temple. The gift is made in view of the religious relation between the chief and the clan deities. Such a pattern is represented by the *fonakava*, mentioned immediately above.

Thus, the *fonakava* acknowledges the overlordship of the chief over the temple of the kinship groups in his clan.[44] As part of the Work of the Gods, the kava houses are reconsecrated. These are used by elders or chiefs on various occasions during the year. Even though the suzerainty of the chief over these several temples is only formal, the gift is considered very important. In the eyes of the Tikopia, this contribution made twice yearly is expressive of a fundamental connection between the gods of the chief and the deities of the kinship groups in the clan, and thus between the chief and the same groups. The ritual of reconsecration differs from case to case, since the characteristics of the different deities vary. Such an expression of relationship is involved in the ceremonies at Nukuora, when at one phase of the sacred ritual only the two chiefs of Fangarere and Kafika are present, with two helpers.[45] The Ariki Kafika makes the kava, while the temple itself belongs to the Ariki Fangarere by virtue of an ancestor buried there, who was saved by the Ariki Kafika at the time of the slaughter of the people of Ravenga.[46] Many libations to various gods were made at Nukuora, as well as thirteen offerings of roi, one for each god and ancestor, each on the proper mat. The morning previous to the setting out of the sacred roi, similarly large food gifts had been brought to Nukuora, though these were not of the sacred roi and were instead contributions to the Ariki Kafika as fonakava. This was again an acknowledgment of the relationship between Fangarere and Kafika, and a link forged because of the aid of the Kafika chief long before. This particular tie was made even more evident by the preparation of the roi, mentioned above, in the Kafika oven, and by a "coconut kava" on a grass plot between Kafika temple and the oven, but near Nukuora. In all this procedure, the economic function is not recognized by the Tikopia as being central at all. The most important goal is the reconsecration and recarpeting of the temples. The recarpeting is also economic, of course, since it is thus that the sacred property continues in good repair (unlike Polynesian temples elsewhere since the coming of white men). The distribution of food is also economic in character. But neither is thought of in such terms, the motivation for the economic processes being ritual and social in nature. The deities would be insulted, and the power of sacred objects would be destroyed, if they were not periodically refurbished, repaired, or renewed. This is consonant with both the attitude of the gods that men should be energetic and efficient in the ritual labor, and with the notion that some ritual objects lose their power when not "fresh." This is true of the several *tapu* knottings of palm leaf, as well as the circlets used by the chief when performing a ceremony.

It must be remembered that exchange for a concrete object of a secular nature is, though not pervaded by sacred elements, nevertheless noncompetitive and traditionalistic, somewhat like the food "exchange" which has been described. Here, using the concept of "equivalence,"[47] it is noticeable that certain objects are typically traded for one another, and that there is a graded series of "equivalents," even though the objects are not on the other hand expressible in terms of a universal medium of exchange. Furthermore, though this realm of exchange in a purely secular context is not so heavily motivated by sacred patterns, some few carryovers may be noted. Among these is the very set of concepts used to describe objects which are valuable. The term, *mafa*, is used to describe the "degree of ritual sanctity attaching to names of the gods, formulas and ceremonial institutions."[48] It does not mean precisely that in this connection, of course, but rather emphasizes an importance in the economic pattern. Even here, however, it happens that this economic importance is often related to the importance in the ritual scheme. Some objects, as we have seen, are important in production and in sacred ceremonies, such as turmeric bowls and equipment, the sacred canoes, the sacred adzes, etc. Furthermore, the same objects which figure largely in this secular exchange, such as sinnet, fish hooks, bowls, bark cloth, etc., are also those which are very important in the ceremonial exchanges at a funeral.[49]

Of all the objects which do play a role in this exchange, the most valuable, in terms of equivalents, are turmeric cylinders, canoes, and bonito hooks. The first two, as is known, are connected closely to sacred rituals and to a high social status. Turmeric and canoes are typically the property of the chief, whose relationship to them is not in terms of property and ownership but in terms of his function as religious officiant and representative. It must be confessed that the exact status of the bonito hook is not clear in either secular or ritual terms. It is true that the bonito, as a large fish, is wanted as an offering at the time of the repairing and reconsecrating of the canoes. However, as has been noted, the chief expression of desire is for a shark, while the shark hook is put by

Firth in a secondary position of equivalents, less than the bonito hook.[50] Part of its high value lies, of course, in "its ritual use for funerals, for atonement, etc."[51] but this sacred value would seem to be derivative, not primary. One possible explanation is that Firth is simply not clear as to the relationship of the shark hook and the bonito hook. Thus he does not make clear where the shark hook is related to the several "spheres" of values, except to say that ". . . the sinnet for the shark-hook is next to the bonito-hook, while next to it is the mat."[52] It may be that the two are the same thing, since when a bonito hook is given, the sinnet accompanying it is not "bonito sinnet," but "shark sinnet" or a "shark line." Further, as "weighty" goods the sinnet cord figures, but "that for catching sharks only." However, since Firth also remarks that the bonito hook "is primarily, after all, an instrument for catching bonito," the question must be left unanswered for the present.[53]

The exchange of most of these articles is fixed. One type of object calls for another object, or the same type, within its own sphere of equivalence. Food, of course, does not figure as an object of ordinary secular exchange, since most of such food exchanges are ceremonial in character, and not the result of someone coming to desire an object not now possessed. Furthermore, food is not durable. But, more important, *food is simply not an equivalent* of such objects as bonito hooks, shark cord, turmeric cylinders or canoes. In the case of these objects, "when the transfer of them from one individual to another takes place the situation is usually charged with emotional significance. Turmeric cylinders are broken over the body of a dead chief, bonito-hooks are hung round his neck, or in the lobes of his ears, a canoe is handed over to his mother's kin, as part of the payment for his burial."[54] These are, clearly, closest in their relationship to the sacred, while the next removed is the series of objects which Firth calls the bark cloth-sinnet group, which are sometimes used for ritual presentation. However, for the most part they are used for specialist skill in canoe or house building, for timber, bowls, damage to valuable tools, etc. The pandanus mat is "its highest expression."[55] Food is, of course, the ordinary payment for arm rings, the loan of a canoe, ordinary labor, paddling, and so forth. Its function in a genuinely religious context has already been discussed. In each case the equivalents are not derived from what we would call a market—Firth himself created the only situation comparable to a market, during his stay—or profit situation, but from traditionalized patterns which designate certain objects as occurring in the same sphere of values. These spheres nevertheless increase in value by degrees, as they approach objects which are peculiarly the property of the chiefs[56] and are sacred in many contexts. The economics of ordinary market competition cannot strictly fit this set of circumstances, even though there is emulation in the matter of work and efficiency, and in the effort to "live up to one's status," as well as elsewhere.[57]

Competition is limited, then, and Firth notes three main types of limitations to the "individual greed and acquisitiveness" characteristic of sharp competition. These are:

... firstly, there is the force of tradition, the binding obligations of kinship, respect for rank, and magico-religious taboo. Secondly, there is the lack of the means for individual economic assertion, the low level of material culture and the limited range of possible satisfactions. And, finally, there is the difficulty of evasion, the fact that in a small island community public opinion is hard to deceive, easily mobilized and effective by reason of the close and intimate nature of the personal bonds uniting the members of the community.[58]

Two of these types, it is seen, are personalized in nature, ranging from the effect of public opinion to the sanctions of the gods. The other merely expresses a lack of opportunity. These patterns are somewhat more difficult to analyze in the case of the Zuñi, in spite of its slightly more highly developed technology and its long contact with Western culture.

# ZUÑI

Although the technological development of the Zuñi lies somewhere between that of the Dahomey and the Tikopia, and considerably above that of the Manus, their orientation toward economic affairs is not strong. The center of tribal attention lies in the area of ceremonials, as we have already seen. Nevertheless, there are many points of interaction between those two levels of analysis and activity.

Actually, those who are considered poor in Zuñi constitute that half of the society who are without ceremonial property or connection.[59] Just as ceremonial poverty is apparently equated with economic poverty, so is wealth closely related with ceremonial activities and ceremonial possessions. This has a practical basis, of course, since religious activities in every society require a considerable expenditure of time, energy and goods. There is even a legendary basis for this relationship. Certain of the Zuñi masks are kept permanently in particular Zuñi houses. The explanation is given that "these Kachinas chose those houses to live in when they, the Kachinas, first visited Zuñi, knowing that in those houses, large and comfortable, they would be well entertained."[60] For example, when the permanent mask Ohewa Shalako (badger) chose this clan, it was on the basis of rich houses, "where men killed deer, and where the Shalako would get boiled venison and would not starve."[61]

Any family which "entertains" the Koyemshi during the winter dances must bear rather heavy expenses. A house must be built for this sheltering of these gods. In addition to the house-building, there must be a feast on the night of the arrival of the gods. Further, for six days after the ceremonial these "gods" will remain in retreat in the house, the family furnishing their food for that period. As a consequence, when the time comes for choosing the next year's family, there may be some hesitation in accepting such heavy expenses. The extra drain on food stores is particularly large, considering the low productive capacity of their dry or semi-arid farming and herding in this region. "Often the crook for entertaining the Koyemci is not taken, and their father is obliged to entertain them in his house. In that case the labor of house-building does not begin until the fall."[62]

This coincidence of wealth and ritual is seen in the element of economic display during ceremonies. At many of these, the Zuñi, like other peoples, make their rituals an opportunity for showing many of their personal treasures. Turquoise necklaces, the very best gowns and belts, coral beads, and so on, are worn at these times and the display is heightened somewhat by the fact that during these ceremonials every member of the fraternity bathes daily. Stevenson says: "Great pride is felt over the display of such wealth at these ceremonials."[63] Even small children may be loaded down with necklaces during the religious observances.

Further, the ritual periods are associated with considerable generosity. Many phases of the ceremonies call for food distribution as well as the distribution of other items. Also, the main festivals, particularly in Shalako, are associated with feasting in general. This period of religious observances is of great interest to all the Indians of the countryside as well as to the Zuñi. The larders are kept filled and there is feasting in all the houses except those where for a few days there may be ritual abstinence. The poorer classes of Zuñi will sometimes almost impoverish themselves by giving all they possess to their welcome or unwelcome guests.[64] Here, again, no claim is being made that such practices are necessary for the continuance of the society. We are merely noting the impact of religion on economic action.

Of course the actual participants in the ceremonies receive food and other offerings, at various phases. For example, after the breaking of baskets and pottery by the "gods," which takes place subsequent to the creation of the sand paintings, the Koyemshi go to the roof of Heiwa Kiva, and are told by a stuffed rabbit (which has previously been killed in a ritual rabbit hunt) that "your little grandfather is hungry; he wishes something to eat; bring him some food."[65] After this the Koyemshi go to the homes of the children who are to be initiated. In order, the first boy gives a bowl of cooked yellow beans, the next boy gives a bowl of cooked blue beans, then red, then multicolored, then black. The children give dried peas, stewed meat, etc. The food is carried back by the Koyemshi to the Heiwa Kiva, where it is distributed to the managers of the particular kivas.

As a matter of fact, it is considered desirable to have the office of Koyemshi, because of the heavy payments at the end of the religious service. Although they must work during the year at various houses which contribute services or goods, and must take part in all kachina dances as well as amuse the audience, and even distribute gifts to the people, they have the benefit of the exchange. When they are through with their dancing, and have been washed by the women, the latter give the Koyemshi a loaf of bread and a roll of wafer bread. After that they go to the plaza, where they receive many presents. Instead of the men bringing deer meat and the women bringing bread, many other gifts are made. "Now they bring whatever they have and presents from the store—meal and flour, meat, whole sheep, bolts of cloth, blankets, and new clothing."[66] These things are partially carried on the Koyemshi's back, and the rest is carried in a wagon to his place in the plaza.

At the close of the twelve days of ceremonies of the Apitlashiwanni (Bow priesthood), thirty-two women in two files of sixteen each carry a bowl or basket of food on their heads to the plazas. They are dressed up in their best finery, with silver beads and bangles, and white buckskin moccasins with black soles. This food is distributed to the participants. The corn and wheat consumed by the Bow Priesthood during this period are furnished by the father of the man who has taken a scalp, or, in modern times, one who is defined as being eligible for the priesthood. Similarly, at the close of these ceremonies, other gifts are distributed by the warriors as well as by their relatives and friends. "Some of these gifts are rather costly."[67] The gifts are divided among the dancers by the men who receive them. At the initiation of members into the fraternities, the women who belong to the fraternity father's family or the family of the candidate exchange gifts of flour, cornmeal, and so on. The women of the fraternity as well as the family of the male members supply their people with food cooked during these ceremonial days.

Some of the most elaborate of ritual food and gift distributions take place during the dance of the Kianakawa, following the dances for thanksgiving. Since these occur in the fall after the harvests, there is more food available. The contributions for the "first body of Ashiwanni" begin to arrive at the kiva during the dances. The offerings are carried in blankets and the men bring theirs in through the hatchway. The women hand theirs into the kiva. Usually, an aged man of the kiva receives these gifts.

There are deer and antelope, some that have not been flayed but simply drawn, with corn and other small offerings placed inside; others are flayed but the skins brought separately from the flesh; about three hundred watermelons, many of them covered with a netting of yucca containing a number of feathers, and a large quantity of corn on the cob. . . . A large number of birds are brought, the plumes of which are used by the Ashiwanni for their Telikinawe that are deposited at the solstice.[68]

However, deer and antelope have now practically disappeared. Similar offerings are made after the Chakwena, at the retirement of the Koyemshi.

Another ritually required economic activity is ritual destruction, usually of ritual objects such as prayer plumes (Telikinawe). Actually the prayer plumes are not destroyed; they are merely deposited. However, they are never touched again and in any case they are deposited in the ground, in the river, in springs, arroyos, fields, and even in the plaster of mud walls of homes. They are deposited by the hundreds, perhaps even thousands, since at several periods practically every male deposits one or several plumes of a given ceremony. This depositing of plumes takes place at all ceremonies, although at some ceremonies they are deposited only by a small number of priests.

Food is also deposited, and it is considered an offering, just as are the plumes. At the Kokokshi dances which follow the winter solstice ceremonies, the people are informed by the "gods" from Heiwa Kiva that the gods will come at night. At the same time, two men from the same kiva go through the village, receiving corn and all varieties of cultivated seeds in their blankets. This collection is mixed and put into five separate sacks. The following morning these sacks are deposited, each in a different place, such as in a corn field, the bed of a river, an arroyo, and so on. At this time practically every adult Zuñi "deposits food of every variety that has been made in the home into the river to Nanakwe (grandfathers) and Hotakwe (grandmothers)."[69] Similarly after the Solimobiya have made four visits to the village, each time with dances and distribution of seeds, practically every adult Zuñi "takes a bowl of food to the road leading to Kothluwalawa, praying as he goes, that the gods will bless the Ashiwi with rain to fructify the earth. . . . the food is emptied into the river as offerings to all the gods."[70]

Since the actual ceremonies require at times the participation of a large number of the people, it is not surprising that there should be economic cooperation for ritual ends. When the Shalako house is to be built for the winter ceremonies, it is clear that this alone would be a large economic drain on the family, aside from the actual gifts of food required. This drain is somewhat mitigated by help received from a group of men who have been detailed to work by the chief manager of the kiva from which the impersonators of the gods will come. They will work in the fields for the family that is to build or remodel a house for the Shalako festival. They also eat at the house for which they perform this service. However, the actual working force allows the family to stand this economic drain somewhat better.

Also, help in the actual building of the Shalako house is received. This is considered an obligation. Stevenson recounts that a man was returning from his peach orchard, his burro laden with peaches, at a time when the building was going on. He was stopped by the "gods" and "held up for trial for working in his orchard instead of assisting in building." He was allowed to proceed without further punishment after he was made to supply the party generously with peaches.[71]

A further mitigation of the economic drain on the family building this house takes place. When the time for the Shalako entertainment arrives, the woman of the house chosen goes about inviting all those who are on friendly terms with her household to come to the house. These people include blood relations, clanspeople and friends. The persons who are invited contribute services or supplies to the house during the year and the Advent.

On the fourth day of the winter solstice ceremonies, the new-year firemaker goes through the village for wood. The village cooperates with him in furnishing cedar for the ceremonies. He "collects a faggot of cedar from each house, the person giving the wood offering a prayer that the crops may be bountiful in the coming year. As the wood is collected it is tied together and when the firemaker has a load he takes it to the Keiwa Kiwitsine."[72] He continues this until every house has contributed its share. On a smaller scale, the Koyemshi go for wood about eight days before Shalako. Nine of them go out each day with a burro, coming back with the animal loaded. The wood is deposited before the new house that is to be dedicated, and is stacked by the women and the members of the clan. At several points in the ceremonial year, food is collected from the whole village, the participants in the ceremonies going about from house to house for this purpose. The ceremonial rabbit hunt, which may occur oftener than once in four years in times of great drought, is a cooperative hunt which incidentally brings in a large amount of meat for the tribe. This actually works for great efficiency, since in a large group of hunters, practically no rabbits escape.[73]

Of course, it is not possible to maintain the thesis that religious actions must lead to greater efficiency in all or even most cases. Since economic activity is secular, and sometimes indifferent to both goals and relationships of a religious order, it is likely that religious demands will sometimes curtail economic action as well as production. Ritual destruction is, of course, one example. In addition, in Zuñi at the winter solstice ceremonials, interest shifts to noneconomic operations. Indeed, after the prayer plumes have been planted on the fifth day, there will be "no trading of any description for four days, and to begin trading before ten days have expired is indicative of plebeianism."[74] Bunzel relates the Zuñi rationalization of this restriction on trading by saying:

The feeling about trade at these seasons seems to be that since these are periods of magical power, during which forthcoming events are preordained, if property passed out of one's hands during this time, all one's wealth would soon melt away. Therefore, during these periods, necessities are purchased at the store on credit, but no sales are made.[75]

Of course, some activities which are later curtailed may actually be intensified before the period of abstention arrives. This would have to be true, for example, in the case of food collection or wood gathering. With reference to the production of food for the winter solstice feasts, there must be a large amount of bread. This light bread is made into fanciful shapes by the women who bake it in their ovens, the fourth night being particularly one of greater activity. This is the last opportunity to use these ovens until the ceremonials end ten days later. The bread which is consumed during the ceremonials must, then, be prepared and stored for use at this time. This releases the women from two time-consuming activities, grinding and baking, so that they may attend or participate in the ceremonies. It also emphasizes the non-secular character of the ritual period.

A restriction of somewhat the same nature occurs with reference to the obtaining of salt from the Lake of Salt. Although the lake itself is almost inexhaustible, there being large deposits of salt already formed and constantly forming, the Zuñi are not allowed to take the salt during the year except at a specifically ritual period. Actually the quality of the salt is high and it is in much demand for trading purposes after a slight amount of cleansing.[76] The journey to the salt deposit is a sacred one attended by ceremonies which include the planting of many prayer plumes. This takes place "after the planting." Cushing suggests that this period was chosen because the journey was a dangerous one when the Zuñi lived in the old cliffs. Since the planting had been finished, the warriors would be free to accompany the party, so that no one would be killed by enemy raiders. At the present time the Zuñi live only two days' journey by foot from the lake, and there are regular commemorative and other pilgrimages to the place, though it is only at this one period in the year that salt is taken. On hunts or other excursions the Zuñi may even go as far as the neighborhood of the lake.

The sacred character of Kothuwalawa is indicated in another connection. Although game may be assumed to be as abundant near it as in any of the surrounding countryside, game is never taken from this area. Since the gods came from Kothuwalawa, assuming various forms on arrival, the hunter might actually be showing disrespect to a god in disguise. Thus religious sanctions actually restrict a possible source of game food.

Considering the intense religious interest in rain and its effect on the corn crop, it would be expected that the Zuñi are more attentive to their agricultural pursuits than they would be if corn were simply a type of food and nothing else. This would not be an explicit function, since the Zuñi themselves do not think in such terms. Rather, to the extent that social activity is focused upon one productive pattern, it would be expected that this activity would be carried out with less lapse of interest. This does not mean that the religious interest in corn would impel the Zuñi to accept new techniques of plowing, planting, or harvesting. Indeed, from what we know of the general effect of ritual interest, we would expect that technological innovations would be opposed precisely because of this sacred character.[77]

A further significant note on this religious orientation to productivity is the lack of attention paid in Zuñi ritual to sheepherding, horses, cows, or even wheat. Sheep play a large part in the external economy of modern Zuñi, but in the community's historical perspective they do not really matter so much as corn. This, on the other hand, is of ancient lineage, not from white contact. The time perspective of the community is long, and reaches back several hundred years. It is not surprising, then, that the rituals which are preserved with impressive integrity from one generation to another should reflect an earlier age when these modern food products were not significant.

A more direct motivation to work hard in the fields or at sheepherding is to be found in the desire of a man to have a mask, especially when he does not have any other sacerdotal relationships or objects to protect him. In former times, the good hunter could obtain a mask through his ability to provide feasts and skins for payment. He cannot be poor and acquire a mask. And he may be even driven to selling his beads for sheep to make a feast.[78] A native account of this situation, and the religious motivation for the economic activity, is significant:

. . . So if a man wants to have a mask made he will work very hard in the spring. He will plant a great deal and he will work very hard all summer so as to have good crops. Then after the crops are gathered in he will say to his wife, "Now I want my mask made." He will say this to his wife and his people. "That is why I have worked so hard." No one will say to him, "Do not do it; we are poor people and cannot afford it." No one will tell him that. They will be glad because they want something valuable in the house to pray for.[79]

Now that buckskin and buffalo hides are not obtainable as they once were, tanned leather from the store must be bought. After the headmen of the kiva have fitted it, and finished the sewing and ritual for making the mask sacred, the man must furnish a feast for the members of kiva. All the man's female relatives grind corn for this feast. All his people prepare for the occasion. He brings wheat and corn, and slaughters eight or ten sheep as well. On the other hand, the mask itself is valuable, including even the paint used for coloring it.

Initiation into a medicine society is also an economic drain on the individual's family, so much so that when a Zuñi is ill a decision must be made as to whether it is urgent enough to justify calling one of the societies instead of a particular shaman or doctor. Asking for the entire power of the society is "a last resort, since the expense of initiation is very great."[80] When the individual doctor is called, the individual has thereafter a ritual connection with him, being called the doctor's "child." The individual must go to the doctor's house at New Year, where his head is washed at the altar. At the time of treatment, the relatives of the ill person decide on a gift for the doctor.

When the medicine society as a whole is called, however, considerably more economic obligations are incurred. The patient must actually be initiated into the society, an increase in power which allows him to be completely free of the disease afterwards instead of being troubled or worried in spirit and therefore physically ill. This initiation is so expensive that several years may pass before the individual is able to bear the burden. When this time comes, the family informs the society father, and a date is set for the full moon of the month for initiations into this society. The ceremonies actually begin four days before this date, when after sunset there are prayers as well as the planting of prayer sticks. Then there is a four-day retreat, during which time the novice must do no work, and especially must lift no heavy weights. He must also eat and sleep very little. By the last day of the ceremonies, the ceremonial costume of the novice will have been bought or made. His relatives prepare an elaborate feast, and finally there are large gifts of food between the women of the initiate's family and those of his ceremonial father.[81]

It is thus seen that even in this society of little intensity of interest in economic affairs the patterns of religious activities have a concrete, as well as indirect and less tangible, effect on production and distribution, as well as exchange. The demands of the religious rituals and sanctions help to motivate as well as shape such economic activities. It will now be seen that this is true even for the Murngin, at a very low level of technological development.

# MURNGIN

Comment has already been made on the paucity of data presented by Warner on the economic system of Murngin, caused in the main by his conception of an economic system as a market or money economy only. This means concretely that many observations were ignored or not published on the grounds that they were irrelevant. This, of course, is familiar in the field of anthropology, for a common complaint of the critic is that the field investigator did not record a type of information in which the critic himself happened to be most interested. Nevertheless, even within these limitations, a number of relevant facts can be presented and analyzed.

The season of the most important Murngin ritual is at the same time the season of the most important economic activity, the gathering of food. This is the dry season, when the lakes have receded and food is plentiful.[82] Since the Murngin have been active in trade without the idea of profit, and are not manufacturers or agriculturists, the most important exchanges are not made with the goal of profit. They are rather gifts or exchanges of food or ritual objects, which are made for ceremonial purposes and in a religious context.[83]

*Land Ownership*. Land, however, does not figure in exchanges. It is rather protected from encroachment, whether or not permitted by the owners. This is not the kind of magical protection found in Tikopia or

Manus, to prevent theft. Instead, the land itself is identified with the owning clan and as such would be both useless and dangerous to any other group.[84] "Just as the totem, the creator, and the members are a permanent and inextricable part of the culture, so is the clan's ownership of the land."[85] This close relationship between the religious definition and the physical fact of ownership is even more clearly seen in the fact that it is especially the land about the water holes, not the intervening plains, which is definitely limited in its boundaries.[86] Such exact limits are also drawn near any body of water. These limits continue to exist, furthermore, even when a clan has been destroyed by another, because of the sacred character of local totems and of the wells in which the spirits of clan members dwell before birth and after death. This does not preclude the use of the land by other groups, however.[87]

*Food and Ritual Activities.* Since land is thought of as more or less like ceremonials, totems, or ritual knowledge, i.e., something which is essentially inalienable in ordinary trade, it can never be given or sold in exchange. More important in a society leaning heavily on kinship definitions for its general structure: the connections between groups cannot be emphasized, strengthened, or symbolized by a gift or exchange of such property. The Murngin do not accumulate large objects or objects in great quantity which might function similarly, since they value freedom of movement and avoid making or acquiring objects of a size or quantity which might hinder geographical mobility.[88] They do not even store food, and as a consequence the important gifts or exchanges of food must take place *during* the ritual dry season of plenty.

As the dry season begins, the unstable economic group which Warner calls the horde begins to accumulate.[89] The members will be related to only a few individuals. All will be closely intermarried clans, and any antagonisms are either held in abeyance or wiped out by a peace-making ceremony.[90] They will gather to enjoy the products of a particular local area, where cycad palm nuts are ripe, and oysters or other foods are easily available. Religious patterns immediately begin to play a role in this activity. This gathering of food could not go forward smoothly if the usual elements of strife were to continue, since physical avoidance is not possible. Ritual sanctions prevent such clashes from the beginning. And, as the more productive food locations become the setting for great rituals, the prohibition is even more definitive.[91] Thus the production which allows such rituals by providing enough food for large groups is in turn made possible by a ritual prevention of fighting.

This ritual period dictates a slight shift in the economy, since the men spend most of their time at their religious functions and hunt only casually.[92] Their contribution of meat becomes less certain, and most of the food is furnished by the women, who catch small animals, hunt shellfish, and gather all vegetable foods. The animals ordinarily killed by the men are, on the other hand, less necessary at this time, because of the greater quantity of other foods.

The gathering of people for food and for participation in religious ceremonies also allows a close relationship between the two activities by virtue of the presentation of food at certain points in the rituals. Following the sexual division of labor mentioned above, these gifts are made by the women to the men. These gifts express kinship solidarity, and indicate that women are not without importance in the economics of ritual life.[93]

One such situation occurs in the second part of the Dua Narra ceremony, when the totems are shown to the young men, and its further importance is seen at the conclusion of the ceremony, after the higher totems have been shown to the older men.[94] These totems are shown to the young men by lines of dancing older men, whose alternating movement represents the coming in and going out of the tide. However, before this dance begins, the women give palm food to the men. This is used by the leader to feed the men, but they are not allowed to eat it immediately. This prohibition is related to the ceremonial separation between men and women. Since the men are engaged in ritual activities, they may not stop to eat with the women. Further, women are not allowed inside the men's ceremonial ground. This means, then, that when the women have performed this economic function preceding the ceremony, the two groups separate, the men returning to the camp grounds.

Nevertheless, the food begins to take on more ritual importance. After the young men have been shown the totems, the older men go into the bush to look at the higher totems, or *rangas*.[95] There, when the string has been taken from the totemic emblems, it is presented to members of the opposite moiety or between *mari* (ego's mother's mother's brother) and *kutara* (sister's daughter's son) as a symbol of solidarity. Thereupon, the palm bread (or, possibly, yams) is sung over by the leader. He uses the totem names of the different *rangas*. In this manner the palm bread, which is cooked in ashes, becomes sacred itself. These "power names" suffuse the palm food with ritual power, so that the totemic spirit is actually in the bread. It is clear that only initiates and men of close relationship could partake of such food. Although food may be given to visiting friends, this particular food is not. If a leader does, "his own clanspeople would wait until there was an opportunity and kill him, because they do not want to have that name go to another tribe."[96] The food given by the women is made sacred by the leader, then, and becomes a symbol of close relationship in a ritual communion. "The Murngin always eat in this way after all ceremonies."[97]

A somewhat similar situation occurs in the Yiritja Narra ceremony, when the men dance into the women's camp.[98] The leader picks out a group to paint themselves in a manner symbolic of particular totems, such as a whale, bandicoot, water, and so on. While the men are painting, a group of younger men already painted as bandicoots, and others painted as banitjas (barrimundi fish) or Yiritja honeybee (because barrimundi came from an area having a honeybee totem), come into the camp. After the men have arrived at a point midway between the men's totem grounds and the camp, the leader stops and calls out,

"Bir-ka bir-ka bur-lum-bul (foam)

"Bir-ka bir-ka ko-wa-wa (yellow paint)

"Bir-ka bir-ka mar-ku-la (red and yellow paint)."[99] Then, calling out "Kar-ra-ark Ye!," they all dance into the camp looking for food. They go from hut to hut, and the women must rise to give them palm food or yam bread. They may give fish or honey. "If the men received nothing from the women they would become very angry and pick up their spears and threaten them. The women give because, say the informants, they see this Banitja painted on the men."[100]

This service performed by the women is not, however, enjoyed by these younger men who collect the food. It must rather be taken back to the older men who are on a higher sacred level. If the younger men were to eat the food, they would themselves become old men. Afterwards, the food is taken back to the totemic camp. Its final consumption is delayed until the lower totems have been shown to the younger men in a dance by the older men. The initiates are instructed in the meaning of the dances and totems at this time, by two men who stand beside them. When the younger men have seen the totems, the old men retire as in in the ceremony described immediately prior to this, to look on the higher totems. Then the totemic bread is eaten and the younger men are exhorted to live by the tribal rules. Food taboos against animal food are also placed on these initiates until they are painted in a totemic ceremony.[101] There is thus a ritually required change in consumption.

A result of such high ceremonies is also the lessened economic importance of the men and the dependence of the ceremonies on the food contribution of the women, with reference to both the daily necessities and the ceremonial food eaten at high totemic occasions. Thus there is a ritually created change in production patterns. A corollary result is that those with the higher religious positions consume more in relation to their production than usual, i.e., as ceremonial participants a greater proportion of the economic resources are allocated to them compared to their actual production. Thus the men work less at this time, and are more sacred. Furthermore, the best foods are appropriated by the most sacred people, who are the old men. At the top of the religious hierarchy, they also are privileged economically.

*Ritual Production and Gifts Other Than Food.* As has already been observed, the Murngin are not a trading or manufacturing people. Their technology is relatively simple, although it is often ingenious in its use of natural products with only little adaptation.[102] Nevertheless, some of the production is of great importance, the distribution of the objects taking place in ceremonial according to traditional pattern.

From one point of view such ritual giving is a method of distribution without monetary consideration. On the other hand, such gifts are important because they emphasize in a sacred context the closeness of certain totemic partners or kin. In fact, Warner maintains that Murngin economic behavior is dependent for its extension on two factors, the horde (i.e., the accumulation of many people at the time of plenty), and kinship reciprocals: "All the relatives of a Murngin ordinarily exchange gifts with him, but certain kinship personalities do this much more than others."[103] Not all of such gifts are elements in ritual, however. The mother's brother-sister's son (*gawel-waku*) relationship leans considerably toward a gift exchange of a trading character:

The mother's brother-sister's son relationship has been seized upon as the mechanism for enlarging the economic life of a Murngin man. "Far off" *wakus* and *gawels* are sought by a man, distant not only socially but geographically; the greater distance a man has between him and a trading *waku* or *gawel*, the greater pride he exhibits when displaying articles sent or brought to him by his relative, and the greater satisfaction he feels when sending or returning gifts.[104]

On the other hand, the mother's mother's brother-sister's daughter's son (*mari-kutara*) relationship leans more definitely toward ceremonial exchange:

The *mari-kutara* relationship is much the same, except that there is a tendency to indulge in ritual gifts more than in those from the ordinary material culture. The feathered string which has been the decorative covering of the totemic poles is sent by *mari* or *kutara* to the other. This exchange of ritual goods plays a prominent part in the economic life of the people, since if a *mari* receives a gift from *kutara* he must, in a not too great period of time, return a present of like ritual value.[105]

These are not merely symbolic gifts, but require considerable work and time. In particular, the feathered string mentioned above may be hundreds of feet long, usually being made by the women. As a ritual string for one of the larger totem poles, it will be copiously covered with feathers, so that it is necessary to kill many birds in the process. For some totemic emblems, only the breast feathers from the red-breasted parrot may be used. Feathers from the blue-eyed corella and the sulphur-crested cockatoo are also used for some totem strings. Hunting and daily searching for birds' nests are required. These ritual needs, then, cause an allocation of energy toward a production of sacred objects.

Furthermore, the gift exchanges with distant partners enter the economic picture, since many other materials or objects will be needed in the ritual, both for ceremonial exchange and sacred use. "This means that red ocher and other body paints, spear heads from the interior, carved wooden spears from the coastal belt, and other objects of economic value must be had to trade."[106]

The demands of the religious activities, therefore, affect more than food gathering and distribution at the economic level. (1) Such activities require the ceremonial distribution of other objects during the ritual, some of these objects having considerable ritual value and embodying a great amount of work. Further, (2) for both such ritual exchange and other parts of the ceremonial a great amount of production must take place. Totem emblems must be made. Ritual headdresses made of cockatoo feathers joined by beeswax and ironwood resin have to be fashioned. Bull-roarers, for producing the voice of the great snake, are to be made or refurbished. Also, (3) trade with distant partners must take place, in order to obtain some materials or objects used in the ceremonies.

As in the case of food gifts, the ritual gifts are often made by the women, indicating again the economic importance of the women in the Murngin ceremonies (in which the men consider them of little ritual significance). The women have perhaps their most obvious role in the Gunabibi ceremony of the Wawilak constellation.[107] The bull-roarer, or Mandelprindi, is used at many points. It is considered the voice of the great father, Muit the great python, calling for the initiates, since the uninitiates and the women are not shown the instrument. The man who whirls his flattened piece of wood at the end of eight or ten feet of hair rope in order to produce the bass viol reverberation stays out in the bush away from camp. After whirling it from left to right, he whirls it in the other direction. At each pause, the camp leader calls out in a shrill voice, "Ah! Yai! ah! Yai! ah! Yai!" and in quick tempo. Then the women chorus, "Le le le le le le le."[108] They represent the two Wawilak sisters calling out to the great snake.[109] After a number of representations of snake and of sea birds have been danced and sung, once each for male, female, and eggs, a number of other sacred areas, objects, and animals are also sung. Later, the women mass into a circle between the camp and the ceremonial grounds, under the leadership of an old man. Sitting under their mats, they are exhorted by two old women who beat the ground with sticks, telling them of the dire results of disobeying certain food taboos: again, a channeling of consumption.

Then a line of men, two of whom represent Yiritja water snakes, dance before and around these women and the uninitiated boys. The two snakes call out and the women answer with the call used in chorus with the bull-roarer. Then the women make presents to the men, which are turned over to the representatives of the snake.[110] These are ritual gifts, which are required of the women, under penalty of sickness or death.

The activities just sketched are mainly preparatory, and the same dance and gift ceremony is repeated later, after visiting clans have arrived. Further, these gifts from the women are related to high religious rank as in the case of food gifts, since they finally fall into the possession of the Dua leaders of the Gunabibi ceremony after hanging on a railing around the taboo well (i.e., after having been offered to Muit).

During the same ceremony, as in others, gifts are made between males as well, the ordinary presents being spears, tobacco and red ocher (used for purification) as well as the more sacred objects. The end of Gunabibi introduces, however, a different kind of gift, from the men to the women as well as from men to men. Distant tribal brothers exchange their wives for ceremonial sexual intercourse.[111] The preliminary arrangements are made through a man's younger brother, initiated by the local man, who sends presents to the distant relative. The recipient also sends ceremonial gifts.

Before the men return to the ritual grounds after the evening meal, they sit in a half circle, the women dancing in front of those who have become part of such arrangements. Their partners then rise and present gifts of value, including food. Later, but privately, each will give the woman additional secular gifts. Both presents are part of the relationship, it being usually assumed that the man and the woman are also having private intercourse before the licensed period at the end of Gunabibi.

*Religio-economic Influences.* Thus it is seen that in the limited economic activities of the Murngin the ritual patterns have considerable importance: (1) By ritually preventing open fighting during the horde gatherings, greater production is possible. (2) Through the identity of totem and land with a particular clan, encroachment on the property of another clan becomes impossible. (3) The normal division of labor between the vegetable foods obtained by the women and the large animal foods of the men is shifted, in that the women now produce almost all of the food. (4) The sacred leaders obtain more of the production, by virtue of their ritual position. (5) A number of sacred objects are produced for the ritual, as well as food. (6) Considerable trade must go on, in order to obtain materials from other regions for sacred objects. (7) Sacred objects and food are given or exchanged as an actual part of the ritual itself.

Of course, this ignores what is to the Murngin the most important of all relationships between the tribal economy and the religious forces: the dependence of nature on the ritual activities of man. Nature to the Murngin alternates between plenty and poverty, just as his social structure is sexually split between the unclean female and the clean male. The rituals reassert the superiority of the male and the purification of the whole tribe, while at the same time insuring, in the eyes of the Murngin, that there will be sufficient food. The economy could not function, if the rituals did not take place, for continual flood would result. As Warner sums it up,

... in these rituals the manipulation of the sacred totem insures the proper function of the seasons, a sufficient production of food, and a continuation of the natural surroundings proper for man. Thus that which is beyond man's technology or beyond his real powers of control becomes capable of manipulation because its symbols can be controlled and manipulated by the extraordinary powers of man's rituals . . . the identification . . . of the male and female principles with the seasonal cycles gives the adult men's group the necessary power to enforce its sanctions; the providing world of nature will not function if the rules of society are flouted and man's uncleanliness contaminates nature.[112]

This, then, represents to the Murngin the "actual" basis of the tribal economy, and not the more prosaic relationships between the ritual and economic aspects of action described above.

# SUMMARY

In spite of the greatly divergent societies being studied, and the varying interest in economic affairs, as well as the important differences in level of technological development, a number of fairly consistent patterns have begun to emerge from the data. These are in conformity with the theory of society and of religion which were discussed earlier.

One obvious point, which need not be expanded now, is that the "primitive" is not merely engaged in such a rude struggle for existence that he has no interest, time, or wealth for religious ceremonials. It has been seen that even at the low technological level of the Murngin a great amount of time, energy, and even "wealth" (the type afforded by the culture) is given to religious activities. Another is that in spite of the lack of industrial development found in Western culture there is a body of productive knowledge about the various fields of economic activity such as fishing, canoe building, making of string or packages, iron or brass work or corn raising and irrigation. A third general point is that economic affairs are usually closely bound up with one's family or more extended kin, i.e., gifts, payments, and exchanges are generally made to those who are relatives of one line or another. This is true even of Zuñi, the most "community oriented" of these cultures.

Closer to the actual problems of economics, it should be first noted that in each society a considerable amount of time, energy, and wealth was allocated to religious activities. There are ceremonial and ritual feasts; objects are used in the actual rituals; there is ritual destruction of objects, property, food, etc., or they are used up in some manner; and at various periods many people are spending a considerable portion of their time in actually observing the religious patterns. It has been further seen that the wealth or goods of the society are channeled by the religious demands in various ways, so that particular individuals receive more than others. Where there are separate officiants, these will receive payments of various kinds from the society, even when the officiant must nevertheless produce in his own right. The novice and his family figure in payments and exchanges, and indeed the various life crises generally call for some sort of public validation in which the gods are interested.

It also becomes evident that either explicitly or implicitly the religious demands motivate toward production. In order to please the gods one must save or acquire enough food or wealth for the payments, gifts, or offerings needed. One may not shirk these duties, because of the risk of the gods' displeasure. Savings will have to be made in order to meet these requirements of a religious nature. Furthermore, the greater importance of some products in the society, such as turmeric, corn, bullroarers, and so forth, may mean that more care is taken in their production, besides the greater motivation to expend energy in that direction.

On the other hand, it is equally clear that ritual restrictions also prevent production at the highest level of efficiency. Ritual demands for mourning may take some members of the society from their work for days or weeks. Some periods of the year may be given over to ritual instead of economic activities. Particular individuals who are important in the religious system may also be relieved from economic demands for a time, or at least given lesser duties. The requirement that particular economic activities be carried out in a ritual and thus formalized manner may prevent the introduction of the most efficient techniques possible. To be set against this one may mention the fact that in activities calling for group production, the very cooperation expected by ritual conformity may actually increase efficiency at the time.

In any event, it is clear that even in societies with or without a high technological or economic development, there is a definite economic system, in which the religious system helps to motivate, guide, distribute, and validate the productive and distributive energies of the individuals in it, not always in the most efficient way.

# 7. RELIGIOUS AND POLITICAL ACTION

W<small>E CAN ANALYZE</small> some economic choices by considering the activities of a single individual, isolated on an island in a classical Robinson Crusoe fashion. At such a level of analysis, political problems are not visible. However, when two or more men interact, social conflict emerges as a possibility. Their ends may be compatible, but they may need the same, limited means to those ends. Or their goals may be the same objects, which are themselves limited. Or, a further possibility, the goals themselves may be in contradiction.

Whatever these possibilities, the problem of "order" inevitably arises. Conceivably, an individual may attempt to use others by means of force, manipulation, or domination. He may rationally select the most efficient human means to his ends. Indeed, we may know of individuals who seem to do just that. Yet this can not be the foundation for a society. If such attitudes are generalized throughout the group, as Hobbes so brilliantly demonstrated, chaos would result.

The ultimate structure which prevents this chaos is that of common-value integration, as was outlined in the first three chapters. Nevertheless, the phenomena of power, conflict, and political order are aspects of social action requiring their own level of analysis. This is also true of economic phenomena as well, and in both cases we can assume the basic integration while holding to one focus as far as is possible.

An obvious debate then threatens: Do preliterate groups have "government and law"?[1] This is partly a matter of definition. There is, indeed, a temptation to claim that it is *only* a matter of definition. In some final, Pickwickian sense this is perhaps true. Such a sense is hardly adequate for science. We must, rather, attempt to relate our own focus to that of others, not only in order to communicate, but also because there seems to be some homogeneity in the phenomena.

The suggestion was made that conflict between individuals must be prevented or controlled. Differently phrased, *power and authority must be regulated institutionally.* As power dominates a geographical area, we usually call it *political authority.* In technologically developed societies, with a formal definition of political authority, we frequently call it *government.* The *state* then becomes a groupal structure centering around and claiming a monopoly over the legitimate use of coercion. Such an organization may develop a set of practices called a *system of law,* perhaps even a *court system.* We expect to find this latter phenomenon in formalistic, rationalistic, secular, and urban societies far more frequently than in their polar opposites.[2]

Let us make a few distinctions beyond these. A society will exhibit the phenomenon of political authority, or *power.* This may imply the existence of *law,* which again requires some description. Now, a law, or legal system, is surely not to be equated with the total complex of social custom or *mores.*[3] Nor is it useful to restrict it to court phenomena alone.[4]

Perhaps scientific convenience can guide us in the choice of definition, concept, or category.

Let us approach the matter from the concept of power, or authority. We then see that "the legal" is not a characteristic inherent in any particular group of *acts,* such as murder, quarrels, adultery, etc. It is rather a quality observable in a situation involving a broad, impersonal, societal norm which is threatened on the one hand, but which on the other is also protected by public coercion or its threat.

Several points are implied here. One is that a legal rule, as Malinowski correctly points out, is not usually called into play. The norm has been inculcated in the growing individual, and has become part of his value system. Moreover, the norm is "baited with inducements."[5] We refrain from murder because, for the most part, we have been reared to feel no such conscious inclinations, and we also derive some advantages from being law-abiding.[6]

Let us note further implications. *We expect conflict with the norms,* for the socialization process does not make the individual a complete conformist. Moreover, when such a conflict arises, the sole recourse is not a reliance upon the individual conscience: resort is made to force, as well. Following this out further, the matter is not a matter for the injured party to settle alone, *as an individual.* In addition, the application of the public coercion is in support of the societal norm. This implies the existence of *systematic pressure,* and the possibility of sociological *prediction.*

This prediction will deter some individuals from committing legally deplored acts, knowing the consequences. Beyond this, the public backing of the force makes the coercion *legitimate*: the creation of *authority*.[7]

We do not, then, speak of *all mores,* or customs, even though all have some social sanction behind them.[8] We must rather confine ourselves to the "formal and legitimate assignment and maintenance of legal authority, and the rules governing this patterned social activity."[9]

*The existence of a social system presupposes, then, a power system.* The converse is likewise true. Genetically, its chief aspects are achievement or ascription; functionally, they comprise the maintenance and exercise of power. Deposition, of course, is merely achievement or ascription in the eyes of the new officeholder.

Furthermore, the power-holder is not so dominant in this situation as he seems. However their philosophies conflict, leaders pay service, lip or other, to group values. Characteristically, they claim to be preserving the group from destruction, physical or moral.[10] In an efficiently ordered power structure, the ruler may assume his followers believe that he embodies their group values. In point of strategy and fact, he will do well to steer clear of both charge and refutation, and the clever ruler may manage to do so by making that embodiment apparent.

The point is further documented by the inability of even despots to break far from the pattern of values which the group generally follows.[11] The charismatic leader has a greater chance to do this, but even he must then remain a "constant deviant"—deviating in ways previously accepted by the group—in order to maintain his flock intact.[12] By the very act of group-value integration, the power holder is himself limited in his scope of action, precluding for the most part the coexistence of complete individual arbitrariness and a social system. The leader is dominant not because of his uniqueness, but rather because he is much like the rest of his followers, who find in him some symbol of, as well as a means to, their values and ends.

It would follow from these remarks, then, that any political system as a continuously operating unity is *legitimate.* In so far as the power system is not based on force alone—and none has functioned long on that basis—it derives its strength from being legitimized by the values which it upholds. Consequently, a *de facto* system as a going concern must become legitimate. Part of its struggle to become dominant, and most of its efforts to maintain itself, are to be catalogued under appeals to legitimacy—its *right* to possession. The traditional system has no such open struggle, disguising it in various ways.

It becomes evident that all societies have one or more central foci of political power. It is, then, significant to ask about the *explicitness* of the connections between legitimate power and other social phenomena. There is always a power structure, but it may be far more implicit than explicit.[13] And the extent to which other structures are explicit will vary. Such a formalized structure delineates *specific procedures* for attaining power. Further, power limits become more *stabilized,* in that the symbols for verbal and open resistance, or conformity, are closer to hand. *Social distance* is made more definite, reducing the importance of personality (charismatic) factors in the exercise of politics. Further, the structure comes to be partly autonomous, since it may not embody the ultimate authority at all.[14] This may vary independently of another factor within the structure, that of *inheritance,* or *ascription,* of political power. This is important, since it is related to defined classes or castes within the group; to social mobility (and therefore with religious prophets); to the necessity of removing a dynasty (Dahomey) or entire status instead of a particular person in order to change the political structure; as well as to the different types of socialization involved in the preparation of a child for his inherited or achieved position.

Moving from this point, the most significant orienting proposition is one iterated previously, that religious action takes place in this world, even though many of its ideas are directed to another. This means that most religious action has concrete effects in this world. One sins, for the most part, in this world. One is also, for the most part, punished here. Repentance and expiation, as well as exhortation and supplication, occur in this world, and the proposition holds for political action.

This means, then, that there will be some limits to the variation of worldly goals as they relate to the sacred direction of interest. In concrete terms, the goals of political action must integrate somewhat with those of religious action. There are always some mainly political ends which are partly gained by religious means.[15] There may be religious ends achieved by political means. Problems of authority and control may arise, since a clear-cut division may not exist. Since power is potentially capable of extension and generalization, the political official may at times be threatened by the power of religious officials or personalities. Legitimacy may be achieved through religious means. This legitimation may even be made formal as, e.g., when a ruler is formally accepted by the religious leader or sacred beings. Further, a proposition which seems likely, though difficult of proof, some emotional release through religion may function to divert attention from the repressions of political rule.

## DAHOMEY

It would be in Dahomey, the culture of great secular and sacred specialization, that we would expect the religious pattern to be most difficult to find at work in the political sphere.[16] The same difficulty, to a greater degree, appears in the attempt to analyze religion in our secularized Western society.

Before proceeding to less obvious interrelationships, the more evident might well be noted. The religious pattern in Dahomey, as among the Murngin, includes many magical patterns as well. The yehwe, or *vodun,* include the *azizan* who gave *gbo* fetishes, thus forming part of the magico-religious interweaving. There are a large number of such *gbo,* variant in concrete physical structure, but more especially in function. One curious type of *gbo* figures in a crucial fashion here. The *ordeal itself is a gbo.*[17] It is, like other magic, owned by a practitioner, and it distinguishes the guilty from the innocent. There were many such ordeals in Dahomey, most of them entirely comparable to those in our own past: if administered properly no one would ever be innocent. Some of these were placing a red-hot machete on the tongue of the accused (to see whether it blistered); taking an *adjikwin* seed from a pot of boiling oil (to see whether the oil burned the hand); placing a pepper under the eyelids (to determine whether the eyes would become inflamed); requiring the accused to kneel on broken palm-nut shells (to find out whether the skin were abrased); etc. Others were more primarily supernatural from the Western point of view: two magically treated seeds *(ago)* tied to a cord and lightly buried, the cord then being thrown about the neck of the accused to find out whether he could lift it; a similar test with pots; crossing the wrists, to determine whether the accused could separate them at command; washing the face in cold water, on the theory that if guilty his eyes would inflame.

As would follow from the preceding analysis, there is little if any difference between these in terms of social definition. In each case, it is the supernatural power which creates the efficacy, and it then becomes irrelevant whether, in terms of Western cause and effect, one group inevitably causes guilt to be adjudged, while the other results in innocence.[18] The magical, supernatural power is being used in the interests of justice.[19] Such ordeals were performed under the supervision of the village chief, who was and is the central figure in Dahomean political life.[20]

As is usual in a hierarchal political structure, the right of appeal existed. Thereupon the king would annul the ordeal, both as supreme political head and as possessor of superior magic: the religio-political parallel. His own ordeal then put the whole village to a poison test, begun by administering it to a representative of a quarter, then a compound, then the individuals, the actual poison being given to a cock (recovery meant innocence). The accused himself did not undergo the ordeal personally.

If the original culprit were again determined to be guilty, his punishment was even more severe, while if innocent he was free again.[21]

Similarly, two other types of trial may be noted, again using supernatural forces, this time definitely not magical. When the accused happens to be a member of a cult-group, he may be required to take an oath of his innocence, the retribution being death for false swearing. For he is to swear that if he be guilty he should die on the day his god "comes to his head."[22] Refusal, as in the case of ordeals everywhere, is a clear sign of guilt. A comparable type is the oath by which the individual takes earth in his hand, after saying, "If I am guilty, let the King of Dahomey take my head. Here is the earth of Dahomey." He then calls on the spirits of his sib dead, and eats the earth. If guilty, he will die in seven or sixteen (both sacred numbers) days. Calling on the sib dead is not to be taken lightly, since they are so close. The pattern is again followed, for men only, in an oath by Gu (god of iron), made when the man scoops up sand on a knife and swallows it. Rather than swear by the earth, the warrior will confess. This intrusion of the political into the religious, and vice versa, is entirely understandable in terms of our own culture, for not all the evidence is known to the whole group, and there is enough individualistic patterning and secularization for a very solemn and grave ordeal to be necessary.

The village chief, though apparently considered more as judge and conciliator than arbitrary ruler, was very powerful. On the other hand, he had to bear in mind one important source of *sacred limitations on political power*.[23] For "if the inhabitants of a village were members of one sib, then the representative of the sib-head in that village . . . exercised a considerable restraining influence on any untoward exercise of power to which the village chief might be tempted."[24] This is understandable not only from his position as head of an important group of people, but even more comprehensible from his semi-sacred character. The sib-head, who was and is the oldest male member, constitutes a link between the dead and the living. This is carried to its logical conclusion, in that his usually early death after assumption of office (explicable to us as a function of his age) is explained as a result of his contact with the dead. His religious duties include "establishing" the dead as deities, and if he forgets any, the forgotten soul will cause his death. Thus he was in a religious office, and likely to die. However, by virtue of that very contact which would kill him, he was in a powerful position from which to limit or deal with the more secular official, the chief.

Considering the intimate relationship held to exist between the gods and daily life in Dahomey, as elsewhere, it is not surprising that the vil-

lage chief would often have duties which extended into that realm. Not
thinking of disease as a primarily medical problem, the society required
him to act officially when epidemics occurred. At that time, he had to
call his diviner, to find out which gods had caused the situation, as well
as which gifts would influence them to take back the misfortune. He
thereupon acted as an official sacrifice collector for the gods in question,
assessing the villagers the amount of animals needed, ". . . and would
then set the date when the animals with the magic palm-fronds, or the
foodstuffs required, were to be brought to the chief-priest of the deity
in that village."[25] ". . . The chief is seen as the one who crystallizes
action in order to propitiate a supernatural power who, discontented
with some occurrence in the village, had endangered the lives of its
people."[26]

In Dahomey, property in land is not held to be inalienable in any
ordinary sense as is the pattern among the Murngin. Consequently,
titles may have to be validated. This situation may be one where the
political relates to one small element in the sacred complex. The sib-head
or head or collectivity may hold in trust a field or palm grove for a group
of heirs. If a division is to occur, the chief presides over the division, first
seating himself on his stool as a ritual act establishing legality. The
measure is in terms of bamboo lengths. However, this measure is not
merely noted in a secular fashion. There is an official to watch the proceedings, one element of which he watches particularly. At the boundaries of the bamboo measures either a sacred tree, *angya*, or "an equally
sacred bush called *desilisige*" is used as a mark. This bush or tree then
becomes the validating mark of the title, there for future generations to
use as an unquestioned boundary.

As in any autocratic political system, the political administration insists on having control over and knowledge of all occurrences and all
activities of the kingdom. Various devices were used to insure an adequate census, the collection of the honey and pepper crops,[27] and the
count of livestock, to mention only a few examples. This was partly
fiscal, but also it was merely part of a highly complex administrative
system, in which every individual was kept under definite control. In
most of these cases, the essence of the system was a double count by
different persons, one of which was not easily known to the individual
concerned. Two interesting examples may be mentioned, where the
sacred becomes an adjunct and useful tool to the administrator.

In order to tax the kill of the hunters, there were chiefs of the hunt
in each village, every one of whom was known to hunting chiefs at the
court (one for fishing and one for wild animals). It was through the

village *degan* (hunting chief) that the count was to be made. The actual count was made near Abomey, at the shrine to a spirit of the hunt (Gbwetin). The king came as a warrior, fresh from his annual campaign, sword in hand and (probably symbolically) the head of a conquered king in hand.[28] He met the assembled degan, and ordered them to come back to Djegbe (near Abomey) with the hunters who were officially under their supervision. At that time, these hunters were lined up with the degan for the count. However, the counting process was not made obvious, as it rarely was in Dahomey. Instead, hunters' knives were given each hunter and degan as they filed by. This was followed by a dance and festival, in which the hunters and the king danced, pantomiming the warrior. This seems to have been in honor of Gu, the god of iron, since he (as well as the king) was praised. He is symbolically associated in the Dahomean mind with war and weapons. The dance ended with a drink from a common cup by everyone, the water being drunk from a human cranium.[29] Then the hunting knives were heaped, and reconsecrated by sacrificial blood from bullocks, goats, and chickens donated by the king.[30] The hunters were not present at night, after having celebrated with food and drink from the king, when the chief-priest of Gu reported to the king. This sacred dignitary then collected the knives, taking them to the forest sacred to Gu, *guzume*, located at Ahwagan. There the assistants of the priest counted them, the result being the number of hunters in the kingdom.

It was not only at this point that the same deity figured, however, in the administration of the count. As would be expected, some degan knew why the knives were given out and returned in the ceremonial. To prevent them from concealing the accurate number, the number of knives was known, though it may have seemed an indiscriminate heap to the participants. Therefore, the number of knives taken to the sacred forest had to equal the number originally taken to the festival. When the numbers did not tally exactly, the degan were again called. This time, they were told that the deity of the hunt was aware of the discrepancy. Whatever cynicism they may have had about the source of the information, deity or mortal, there was no doubting the efficacy of the technique for forcing the individual to confess: the verdict of the supernatural, the ordeal. Thus at both points, the administrator utilized the sacred tools as means to achieve entirely secular ends.

This same technique was used for determining the production figures of those smithies which did not make hoes.[31] These figures were obtained, again, through religious dignitaries, the priests of Gu, the deity most closely concerned with iron. The procedure was for the king to set a date for Gu to be given food—"to eat"—at each of Gu's shrines. This food would be cocks, which were placed at the shrines, at the disposal of the chief-priests. This announcement was coupled with the statement that the deity, Gu, would punish any priests who failed to participate in this "feeding" by not taking their share of the birds. "The Dahomeans being devout, the priests invariably obeyed, and since every forge must have its shrine to Gu, the deity especially sacred to forgers, all the shrines were represented."[32] As each official came to the center of fiscal control (where those from outlying areas would have to go), he was to inform the secular official of the number of smiths working at the forge he represented. The procedure then simply consisted in counting the number of fowls taken.

On the other hand, the king could not overlook the power potential of such a highly organized system of religious worship. One aspect of this has already been mentioned, the conflict between Sagbata and the king, antagonism being expressed by the royal family against this cult. It was felt that its very title was presumptuous, besides the fact that several kings died of smallpox. Since the political regime was highly autocratic, proper control would be needed over other elements in this organization.[33] All cult houses, established for the worship of the "public deities" already outlined, were kept under the king's control. The procedure was to require a particular rattle for the chief-priest of any cult house to be established. This rattle could be obtained only through the monarchy. That is, a secular barrier is offered to a free expansion of sacred organizations.[34] Herskovits maintains that "no notation was made within the palace at the time these rattles were distributed, nor any account taken of those to whom they were given," however surprising this may seem. Nevertheless, at the time of the annual customs,[35] all priests of the ancestral cult had to come to a special ceremony on a certain day. They were to come with the rattles in question. The rattle had to be brought or sent, whether the priest happened to be ill or not. The other cults were not ignored in this process, for still other dates were set for them, when the principal ceremony took place. At that time, all the rattles were displayed. Their presence was consciously ritual and sacred, since this was (and is) the time for reconsecrating the rattles. It is necessary to have a rattle if one is to summon the deities. The control kept over the rattles was constituted by a record kept by the planter of the rattle calabashes. Each year he sent forty-one[36] calabashes of this type, and at the same time set aside a pebble for each one. When, at the end of the year, some were returned, it was known how many new rattles had been put in circulation, and, consequently, how many rattles in use there were in all the kingdom. One official counted those at the cult house, thus furnishing a close check on the actual number. A rattle might be replaced without authorization if broken, but two such rattles in the same cult house would weaken—"spoil"—the power of the deity.[37]

Though there seems to be no economic advantage to be derived from this information, a full knowledge of all details of the kingdom was held to be (as it certainly is) necessary for complete political control of the kingdom. Further, the king would then know what preparations to make for occasions of great significance, when the priests were to make sacrifices. More important, however, was the fact that through the cult the king reached more concretely and intimately into the lives of the people. For the chief-priest of each pantheon kept a tally of all the initiates entering a cult, a pebble being dropped, without looking at it or the receptacle, into a pouch, and one being taken away when a cult member died. The King could therefore find out from the chief-priest how many members there were in the cult. In this manner, rapid dissemination of knowledge about an edict could be achieved, while the power of the priests over the cultists could also be put to work. Herskovits expresses this situation concisely:

. . . since about half of all the inhabitants of the kingdom were numbered in the membership of the cult-groups, and the other half of the Dahomean people were related to cult-members and since, also, the religious convictions of these cult members and their relatives required implicit obedience to commands of the priests, control over the cult-houses by the king gave him a simple means of rapidly making known an edict to the people, and of assuring compliance with it.[38]

It is not from such uses of sacred techniques that the king's great political power stemmed, in the main.[39] The kingship was intimately associated with the rulers of the ancestral dead, the kingly dead. His person was actually sacred.[40] Abasement on the part of those who came before him was taken for granted. The royal family itself shared this characteristic.[41] This was accentuated by the enormous amount of ceremony which attended all his movements and those of his court, and by the extremely detailed fashion through which he kept abreast of all occurrences in the kingdom.

These apotheosized ancestors symbolically played a part in the king's very accession. The "grand customs," mentioned previously, which were the funeral ceremonies at the death of a monarch, had to be performed by the new incumbent before he would receive full title to his throne.[42] The actual ceremony of enstoolment is not, to my knowledge, extant in

the literature. The ceremony took place in Allada, ". . . where all
Dahomean kings had to go to be confirmed in their sovereignty,"[43] but of
its wider significance, or relationship to the ghostly deities, I find no
record.[44] The conclusion is inescapable that at such a time the incumbent
was given to their care, and he was exhorted to follow them, while the
subjects were told to obey.

Whatever the imposing qualities of such a kingly inauguration, the
kings took much of their awe-inspiring status from their constant identification with their deified ancestors. This was true not only of their ordinary associations, but it was significantly true even of the stories and history of the kings as well. That is, their historical past was kept partially
secret, and endowed with sacred implications. LeHerissé claims,

L'histoire revet, en effet, pour le Dahoméen un saint caractère; elle n'est pas
seulement le monument des gloires et des revêrs d'une tribu fondatrîce d'un
royaume, elle touche encore au merveilleux, parce qu'elle conserve la mémoire
d'origines mystérieuses et qu'elle enregistre les acts des ancêtres, heros
divinisés, protecteurs des "Danhomenou," "gens et chose du Danhome."

Les rois paraissent même avoir vu dans cette conception de l'histoire un
moyen d'augmenter leur prestige. Ils s'étaient reservés certain secrets sur leur
famille et leurs dieux. Ils ne les transmettaient qu'à l'heritier du royaume et
les anciens eux-mêmes les ignoraient, dit-on. Ainsi ils acqueraient la force du
mystérieux, la veneration de l'ignorant pour le savant, du simple pour le
genie.[45]

Though Herskovits does not attempt to probe precisely this set of relationships on a deep level of analysis, he summarizes several points of
interest in this regard:

Just as the King of Dahomey constituted a category apart in the social whole
that comprised the population of the kingdom, so the worship of the spirits
of the dead kings was a thing apart from the worship of any other category of
ancestors. It has been seen how the general class of tovodun encompasses the
nɛsuxwe, the souls of the princely dead. Over all these, in the world of the
dead as in the world of the living, the souls of the dead rulers of Dahomey
hold their exalted position. Their spiritual importance was reflected in the
implicit acknowledgment of their active collaboration with their living de-
scendant in the ruling of the kingdom. Thus their cult daily required a sacrifice as a matter of routine thank-offering for the King's awakening in health
to the new day. When their advice was desired concerning any matter of
policy, or when a remedy was sought for some unfavorable condition in the
kingdom, or when a campaign was to be launched against an enemy, or
when a crisis of any kind impended, sacrifices proportionate to the issue at
stake were made at the tombs that marked their graves, and they were called
upon to manifest their wisdom and will.[46]

This situation functions to give a great deal of emotional continuity to the reigning family. For in this manner the incumbent is not a single individual. The group came before the incumbent, and will make a place for him when he dies. He will receive advice and aid in crises from these deities. Just as they had power on earth, they now have it as supernaturals. They rule in each case, thus becoming "part of the structure of the universe," to the ordinary Dahomean, not to be questioned. The Dahomean came into a world where the king ruled. After death, he expected to go to a supernatural world where the king or his ancestors still ruled.

This was accentuated by the peculiar role which the prince or king played and plays in the rites for the royal ancestors. For the cult of the ancestral royal dead gives to the prince almost the status of an initiate in a cult. Like such cult members, he "may not be struck on the head, or across the cheek."[47] This would be akin to blasphemy. The rights of the initiate are his without the hardships of being initiated. He thus plays an important role in the royal ancestral ceremonies without actually being a cult member. For this cult ". . . approximates the worship of the gods in its following and ceremonialism. A prince can and does dance for the princely dead, but he is not thought to be serving the spirit of a dead prince, but rather to be representing this designated ancestor at the annual customs. In Dahomean theory, this means that annually, for the duration of the ceremony, the soul of the dead prince will enter his body, and he will not be himself but the dead man brought back from the land of the dead."[48]

It was in such ceremonies that the position of the king, from whom all power came, received its highest expression. In the ceremony witnessed by Herskovits, which must not be considered a greatly attenuated version of the former annual ceremonies,[49] the position was even made geographically clear, since in the large court where the dancing took place an area was laid off (the division was noted by early observers) by forming a rectangular space, delineated by bare palm branches. It was within this space that Behanzin's son, Daha, and his wives were to remain during the ceremony. Priests, members of the royal family, the chief-priest of the ancestral cult, elders, collateral relatives, etc. remained on the other side, approaching the "bamboo" boundary to prostrate themselves and kiss the earth before Daha.[50] Communication from the chief-priest to the "king" occurred by means of an elder wife of Daha, who would face the chief-priest at the boundary line, then carry the message to the chief.[51] To maintain this symbolically, "on one occasion an especially old man took up one of the palm ribs and, holding it before him, came close to Daha and talked directly to him."[52] As usual, animals were sacrificed,[53] the animals being tied very tightly so that their struggles could not impede the flow and catching of the blood. This blood was poured over the *asen*, or altars. A symbolic ritual was then enacted, by which a curtain placed in front of the altars was lowered both during the pouring of the blood and the bringing of food. It has been noted before that the monarch did not allow others (except as a mark of favor, and except for the case mentioned, of the hunters) to see him eat or drink. The lowering of the curtain, while the officiant called out "Zan!" or "Zanku!" (Night!), symbolized this ceremony of the king's meals, when he would be alone, set off from the others. Interestingly, the meat of one goat killed is not eaten, for it is a sacrifice made with a chant asking that the ancestors prevent princes and nobles now ruling from ever being sent away as slaves to foreign countries.[54] Several orchestras, of drums, gongs, and smaller drums, of flutists and singers, chanters with wands, and singers with gongs, played in succession, followed by the women in the palm barrier, who sang in solos and choruses. This was accompanied by body movements, the rhythms quickening. The intent of the songs was to praise the chief and his ancestors, and to call him to dance for the ancestral spirits. This pattern is, of course, highly traditional, the king never being a fine dancer, but rather a symbolic figure. In the ceremony witnessed by Herskovits, Daha finally came forward to dance.[55]

The audience became more excited, and the singing louder, as he danced, one of his wives behind him, twirling his umbrella. He was called back after his first dancing, and again circled the space while dancing. After this, the space reserved for his entourage was narrowed, so that the male performers might have more room for dancing. Other groups outside were later summoned in succession to pay "tribute with singing and dancing to the spirit of the dead King . . . The ritual itself was complete when the sacrifices had been made and the blood poured on the altars."[56] However, each group offered formulae of obeisance (and dance) during the afternoon. Though not actually part of the "annual customs," being commemorative of Behanzin's burial, it neatly expresses the general position of the king in the Dahomean society, while also helping to strengthen the kingly power. It also suggests the effectiveness of the "Great Customs" and the annual customs in supporting and re-emphasizing the far-reaching power and exalted rank of the kingly incumbent, from whom the power of his subordinates flowed. However, it is clear that this is *not mere support:* The political activities also hold the religious somewhat in check.

Thus at many points of basic significance, the political superstructure had a strong foundation in the supernatural sanctions, both minor magic and the greater ceremonies. Several others may be briefly mentioned. One of these concerns the position of the chief-priest, whose position as ruler over the "servants" of a given deity was extremely powerful. It has already been related how some control was maintained over him by the king. More than this was obtained, however, though it occurred only once in the lifetime of such a priest. His position was hereditary, and thus was not easily attacked. Nevertheless, he could not take over his office unless the king confirmed his accession. This was merely an elementary precaution, and thus enabled the king to wield more power through the religious organization. This type of control, the existence of which emphasizes the potential importance of the religious in crises, and the actual day-to-day significance of it as a possible political power, was further extended by the use of secular officials appointed by the king.[57] These officials were in at least nominal control over the priests and followers.[58] Furthermore, "religious offences committed by priests were judged by a court of priests presided over by the head-priest of *Zumadunu,* king of the royal tɔxɔsu,[59] in the presence of these officers, but offences against the state were judged exclusively by these officers, who were empowered to punish the culprits with beating, imprisonment, slavery or death."[60]

Furthermore, though the priest was to hold his position until death, and could not be shown publicly as a degraded criminal, the king could remove him for inciting to rebellion.[61] Recognizing further the power of the religious in this world, the political system forbade the existence of secret societies in Dahomey.[62] These might have constituted an even greater threat.

Though the extension of the supernatural into court procedure has already been shown in several connections, an interesting inter-relationship arises in the case of Fa, the system of Destiny, by which the will of the gods was to be known to human beings. The practitioners are thought of with great respect by most Dahomeans. It is true that those who have wielded power, the highest class members, are somewhat more sceptical, and condescending. Here, again, however, a supernatural system is used by those in power, understanding the locus of the sacred in this world, and its uses for personal or political ends. Indeed, Herskovits points out,

. . . in native "history" the *bokɔnɔn* (diviners), with their cult of Fa, are held to have been introduced into Dahomey as a means of attaining a more efficient control over society by the rulers, and to overcome the influence of those other divinatory systems which were less well organized and thus less easily controllable.[63]

Even today, all chiefs have a diviner for each of their destinies, and in former times the royal *bokɔnɔn* had great power. There were uses for such a diviner, aside from mere knowledge: Yet while the chiefs and princes and in earlier days the kings consistently consulted their diviners, the fact nevertheless remains that these same diviners in situations where it was politic to offer advice of a certain kind did not fail to pronounce as the will of Destiny what those in power desired to hear, or in mundane matters to read the lots in accordance with the best interests of their patrons.[64]

One more point, again with respect to fiscal policy, may be noted at which the regime was bolstered by the religious officiant. An adequate tax policy required information about the number of livestock, particularly cattle, goats, and sheep. The count of pigs was taken in another manner, but sometimes checked by this. On a great market day a crier made known to the people that a god living in a certain river had announced the coming of an epidemic and a poor harvest. The only way in which this misfortune could be averted would be for every man and woman to bring one caury shell for each head of livestock. These would be put in separate heaps, and the king, who was also part of the kingdom, would then add a great amount of palm oil, all this to be offered to the spirit. Since the predicted epidemic would probably not occur, the king thus received much emotional support for his leadership and economic contribution. Before these shells were taken to the priest of the river god, they were counted, a pebble being set aside for each shell, and placed in separate sacks with appropriate symbols sewn on them.[65]

In a society with such a high degree of formalized legal organization as Dahomey, the identity between secular legal officials and the religious officiants could not be expected to be close. Nevertheless, it has been seen that the hierarchy is bolstered at many important points by the religious system. This is true not only for the highest official, but also for such matters as the administration of justice and the taxation of the people. The potential power of various religious groups was consciously curbed. This recognized the necessity for keeping the political system secure, as well as the possible spread of temporal authority belonging to the priests. The constant support of the political authority by the gods is emphasized still, so that even under foreign domination the system has not changed basically. We may now take the case of the Manus society, with very little formalized authority, either political or priestly, in order to see how the emergent level of political structure appears, as well as the ways in which this may be related to the religious, both negatively and positively.

# 8. RELIGIOUS AND POLITICAL ACTION (Continued)

Once we move from the detailed formalistic organization of the technologically more advanced societies, particularly those of Western Africa, we thereby move to less secularized groups as a general rule, where the task of seeing the pervasiveness of religious orientation is less difficult. At the same time, the delineation of what is to be considered the economic, or the political, becomes correspondingly more difficult. In the following chapter, as in the previous chapter, some attention is given to this problem. In order not to fall into complex and abstract discussions, however, more attention will be rather paid to the concretely descriptive level, where there can be much more unanimity of agreement as to fact, than to the analytic significance of those facts.

What has been already noted, as theoretical formulation and concrete fact, is that the locus of political power interlocks with that of the sacred power. This reflects the analytic and concrete generalization that the two areas of potential competition for man's energy and time, secular and sacred power, will usually be somewhat integrated. Since the two are not aiming at precisely the same goals, and there is often a different personnel, traditional limits will be set. Direct opposition, if continued, would split the society. In many day-to-day situations, and at most ritual or ceremonial occasions, the secular leader is by inference, implication, and context allied with the sacred. This puts a stamp of approval implicitly, if not explicitly, on his acts.

*Manus.* Any attempt to analyze Manus political relationships in *political* terms is rendered difficult, as is later seen in the case of the Zuñi, by the lack of explicit and formalized lines of authority. There is no simple answer to the question, Who rules Manus? Ultimately and at a distance, the Australian Government rules Manus, just as the French rule Dahomey, and the United States rules the Zuñi. However, in spite of the impact of Western civilization on the culture, village life has not been

153

appreciably altered, even by the appointment of a native villager as "administrator."[1] White government, established in 1912, has begun to collect taxes, prohibit war, head-hunting, kidnapping the women of other tribes for prostitution, and keeping a public prostitute in the men's house. Outside authority makes patrols for medical inspection and tax collection, and at these times civil cases are heard in court.[2] The earlier native society had war leaders and men of rank, but these do not necessarily equate with this outside white authority, or even daily governmental action.[3] Mead claims that "as a result village life is anarchic, held together only by the stream of economic exchanges which bind all the families loosely together."[4] Actually, the evidence indicates clearly that this is a very inadequate generalization. A number of controls operate to prevent war, to prevent sin, to hinder or punish crime, to preserve order and honesty among the Manus, to see that debts are paid and serious matters are settled in court. In short, there is a considerable amount of implicit organization at the political level.

It must be admitted, however, that few if any great communal undertakings are organized in Manus by a specific political authority or leader. At present there is no "chief" who rules over the villages. War has been abolished, so that this important field of community action has been removed. The formal inter-village feasts given by the head man of a village, requiring the services of the whole village, are given infrequently. These were always rare events, and savings for years in advance were necessary.[5] The various villages are bound together by economic networks, but these are largely of individual origin. The religious system, as has been noted previously, does not have great seasonal cycles of ceremonies which would require the participation of all the villagers at once.

It is thus evident that the occasion and need for political action on a large scale are not frequent. However, order is a problem which must be settled in any society, small or large. The imposition of white authority upon Manus life has had an important effect in this particular sphere of action, more than in other spheres.[6] The Manus are trading people, and the abolition of war has freed them of a definite burden, while at the same time making the position of war leader, or some sort of village chieftain, less necessary. Yet, because the Manus are trading people, they are involved in countless disputes about debts, property, payments, and so on, and indeed seem to enjoy public arguments. As a consequence, the introduction of the court has been welcomed by the Manus as an opportunity for introducing more orderliness into such affairs, and for arbitration as well as formal speech-making.[7] This would commonly be a function of a political leader at the community or inter-community level, and it is now taken over by white administration. The fact that the Manus are already oriented toward trade means, further, that the pattern of saving, or of large economic undertakings, which in other societies would require the mobilizing authority of a central political leader, is in Manus under the direction of businessmen. It is true that these men are generally men of authority in their own right, but they function in this regard as businessmen, not as men of authority. That is, they may be men of no high rank, but their reliability as businessmen will insure the success of their large projects.

Thus it has occurred that the orderliness made possible by white administration of public peace and justice has been seized upon by the Manus, leaving their own political patterns with considerably less scope for action. In terms of this analysis, the system of authority has been made more diffuse. It has become difficult to call any particular person "chief" in the usual sense. What is necessary is to note various patterns of action of a political nature, taking account in each case of the locus of authority, and seeing where the religious pattern enters that of the political. It will be found, as a matter of fact, that even where the formal courts have entered, the Manus religion still plays an important role.

Earlier comments on the nature of Sir Ghost make evident how important it could be to the administration of law and justice. Sir Ghost has a public role in Manus society, and upholds the abstract idea of impersonal justice. Sir Ghost is always willing to punish his ward when the latter strays from the narrow path of honesty and virtue. Right and justice are not to be mitigated in individual cases because of the personal importance or weakness of a given man. Indeed, it seems likely that the Manus are more unbending in their attitude than the white administration. For example, Korotan had been a leader in economic affairs, head man, and a former war leader, but had become blind, so that he could no longer fulfill his obligations. He consumed his capital, and was being dunned by one of his creditors.[8] In spite of his connections, his former prestige, and his personal magic, he received no sympathy. His creditors were restrained from suing him in the white courts only by the knowledge that the white man would be much more lenient than the Manus code. It is expected that Sir Ghost will demand production and payment of debts even when Sir Ghost does not help ward to obtain the wherewithal to make payment, and even when Sir Ghost has allowed ward to become helpless, as in the case of Korotan. In any event, the Manus code of justice, backed as it is by the severity of the various Sir Ghosts, is stricter than even our own idea of justice. As Fortune sums it up,

. . . Sir Ghost . . . represents the law. The spirit of submission to a higher power expressed religiously represents also the spirit of submission to the just claims of persons who are on the outer circles of the society, considering a society as a series of widening circles of kin, clan, local group, and outside local groups.[9]

This means, then, that even when a case is brought up in a white court, or enforced by a native constable, the Sir Ghosts of the village support the decision and the act.[10] In fact, the detailed pictures of such conflicts as payment of debts or sexual transgressions would indicate that these native officials are not so much being supported by Sir Ghost as *rather supporting Sir Ghost* as the latter's judgment is given by the medium.[11]

An interesting case of what might be termed "legislation" in some sense occurred with the prohibition of prostitute capture. Formerly foreign women, or even a woman of another village, were sometimes kidnapped and used as prostitutes, thus affording an outlet for the men who might otherwise be tempted by the women of their own village. When this was made illegal, along with war, by the coming of the white administration, it also became sin to the Sir Ghosts of Manus.[12] The last such crime committed caused the culprit to be jailed by the white administration. However, he was killed by ghostly action while in prison. This was a new element in the Manus code, now definitely incorporated into it.

The most important crime in Manus society is sin. This is not so paradoxical as it appears. Their notion of sin has been characterized as akin to the historical Puritan conception.[13] It is associated with any sort of sexual transgression, of even the most minor sort, such as the accidental exposure of part of the body when a woman's grass skirt slips a bit. The Manus is constantly concerned with the idea of sin, just as he is with the fear of debts. What transforms this idea of sin into crime is not the nature of the transgression, which in itself might seem a matter of conscience, but the role of Sir Ghost. Although Sir Ghost is particularly concerned with his ward's activities, and will protect him against illness or danger, Sir Ghost will as quickly expose his own ward when the latter violates the code of the society. This is true whether sexual matters are involved, or the payment of debts, or honesty in business transactions. The exposure is not merely contained in the illness which Sir Ghost sends as punishment. This, again, might be construed as individual punishment, such as the gnawing of conscience. Sir Ghost *must also make public* the reasons for striking his ward. That is, there is an act which violates the code of the society, and it is punished in a particular and expected manner, made known to the entire society, and followed by payments made in public for the offense. Not only does the society know of the incident; it also supports it by active participation, hounding the accused, giving advice to the central persons involved, taking account of developments, and so on. In short, even though the area of action considered sinful in Manus is considered sinful in our own society also, it is not simple "sin," but rather comes under the category of crime. Our own society, which has recognized an explicit distinction between sin and crime, also considers serious sexual transgressions as crimes. The Manus do not have an explicit and formalized code, and do not make this formal distinction. Sin is crime, and is so treated.

This may be seen in a concrete case by briefly noting the crime of incest committed by Noan.[14] Noan, "worthless and somewhat feeble-minded," had in a moment of weakness bragged that he had had intercourse with several women, while sleeping in the house of Kemwai and Isole. Tcholai, to whom he bragged, treated this disclosure as the confession of crime. The kinship and house ramifications of the incidents were dangerous to all concerned, and he himself would be punished if he kept the matter a secret. Immediately he beat the slit gong in a tatoo for sexual transgression and war, rousing the entire village. He is not merely passing gossip along, it must be noted. He is announcing formally a serious transgression. The people of the village then act to take care of the situation.

Noan's bragging is not considered a sufficiently valid confession, until it has been made certain from the side of the others concerned, and, of course, confirmed on the ghostly plane.[15] That is, the public element is still lacking at this stage of proof. Since immediately afterwards neither Noan nor his fellow culprit would confess, the pressure of the public and ghostly information had to be used to extort admission. The functional role of this publicity and public pressure, as well as the importance of it in the definition of crime, is obvious. The public is being mobilized and organized to combat a transgression, and the pattern of the ghost cult furnishes the accepted and standard channels through which this public force may be expressed. In this particular case, the speeches were not formal and stereotyped in phraseology as in other cases, because of the seriousness of the charges. That the case was not merely one of general community indignation, upset by a transgression for which no pattern of action is recognized, is shown by the fact that an important marriage ceremonial, with canoe races and great exchanges of goods, took place at this period. This done, the case was resumed.[16]

When the son of the titular brother of one of the culprits was struck down, even more pressure was put on the latter to confess, which she did.

Immediately this fact was also made public, and later a public divination was held, which explained the punishment.[17] When a few members of the family attempted to hold a secret seance after everyone had retired, there was indignation among those who discovered this fact. This further underlines the statement that we are not merely dealing with a family or individual case of sin in the simple sense, but a public matter of transgression, which had to be dealt with by the group in a definite matter.

In a society so conscious of property rights, one may expect that trespass will be punished in some fashion. Here, again, Sir Ghost preserves the limits of such rights, even though he is also willing to forgive once expiation has been made.[18] Expiation in one case permitted the field anthropologists to have a permanent residence, since a man struck by a ghost for trespass (not his own Sir Ghost) was advised to build a house in his own territory, so that trespass would not be possible.[19] It must be remembered that such cases of trespass are also made public in the usual manner, through the medium.

With respect to theft, magic plays a somewhat more important role. There is not much individual land property belonging to the Manus, and very few Manus know any magic for protecting property. What is known has been bought from the land-dwellers. The forms of magic do not cause a large variety of diseases or deformities, and when they are placed on the property there are signs to indicate that the property is so protected.[20] However, most of these signs are not known by the Manus, and even the illnesses caused by the curses are not fixed in Manus thinking, so that in actuality they are frequently thought to strike down the culprit in any manner. Nevertheless, the respect for property is so well developed that this magical practice is integrated into the Sir Ghost conception. That is, divination proceeds in the usual manner to discover the cause of illness, the culprit is made to confess publicly, and expiation is made in the usual manner, as is true of any other crime. Even the land-dwelling spirits may be called into such a situation, although usually the Manus regard them somewhat humorously.[21] That is, there is no consistent belief in the automatic and individual working of the curse against theft. Instead, once the curse has had some effect, the general pattern of crime is played out, disclosing and punishing the culprit.

In addition to these supports, the religion now includes in one of its invocations an empowering to trade, instead of war, and it recognizes a type of soul-stuff which will strike those who wantonly break the peace after a peace-making ceremony.[22] Nevertheless, the functional role of the Manus religious system is most clearly seen in litigation, where the ghostly powers insist on probity, fair dealing, and the payment of debts.

In short, they support the court idea of justice in this as well as in the various sex crimes, where detection, confession, expiation, and payments follow a public pattern. The prohibitions against the crime of stealing are less frequently called into action, because of the Manus respect for property, but Sir Ghost punishes for this crime when it does occur. The mobilization of the entire community for the purpose of war has been stopped by the white administration, so that the ghostly powers are not supporters of this type of political action. Instead, they rather support the present prohibition against war. The Manus conception of justice, order, and conformity to law is thus expressed through the mediums of the various ghosts, so that opinion and action in this sphere are made official, public, and sanctioned.

However, this is a society in which trade, property, litigiousness, and a heavy consciousness of sin play important roles. The Polynesian society of Tikopia lays much less stress upon these cultural leanings, and thereby offers an interesting opportunity for contrasting the manner of interrelationship between these two types of activity, the religious and the political.

# TIKOPIA

In the case of the Dahomey, the politico-religious connection is an implicit and explicit alliance, though sometimes unknown to many commoners. In Tikopia, it becomes almost an identification. "Once elected as chief, a man is able to control the behavior of the members of his kinship group upon some of their most vital and personal issues, such as securing adequate food, freedom of recreation, and in the last resort even their right to live."[23] That the coordinating value of the chief is a reality to the people is shown by the anxiety which they show when a chief goes off on a voyage. ". . . At the present time the chief is the bridge between the kinship structure, the political organization, the ritual, and the economic system; he is the prime human integrating factor in the society."[24] The "identification" or "contiguity with the sacred" is most clearly expressed in the fact that the supreme deity of the island, Te Atua i Kafika, is peculiarly the deity of the Ariki Kafika, the supreme chief of the island, while lesser chiefs are more definitely the "mouthpieces" of lesser gods. However, much of the possible politico-religious friction between the chiefs is mitigated or averted by the little discussed division of privilege and honor in various ceremonies and contexts, one chief being supreme in one ceremony and not in another. For the supreme deity is part of the group of gods of each chief, though under a different name. Thus the basic fact of supremacy is kept intact, the Ariki Kafika maintains his headship, but much psychic or emotional satisfaction accrues to the other chiefs in both sacred and secular affairs. And since the larger part of daily life revolves about one's clan, the individual chiefs retain a considerable autonomy. A compact expression of many of these facts is the Fono of Rarokoka, formerly given by the Ariki Tafua, who has become a Christian.[25] Like other *fono* in Polynesia, matters of public moment, political, moral, ethical, or technological, were brought in for treatment. In Tikopia it differed in that it was not primarily secular at all, but intensely religious. It was, following one of the most basic characterizations of religious matters, stereotyped as to phraseology, place, personnel, and time. It was not, then, extemporaneous and bound to affairs of the moment. It was moral and political in tone, but ". . . it had strong religious associations, and the chief who spoke was deemed to be the mouthpiece of the gods. In other words the sanction of the *fono* in Rarokoka was not simply social and political, exercised through the authority of the presiding chiefs, but was intensely religious as well, receiving its validity from its superhuman origin."[26]

The Ariki Kafika initiates this ceremony, by "speeding the messengers of the chiefs" (informing the elders that it would be held in the morning) and by telling the Ariki Tafua to deliver the address. But the central place is held by the chief of Tafua. Its chief burden is an exhortation to social order, the basis of it being partly economic, partly ethico-moral and political. Indeed, its ethico-moral and economic advice especially relates to a central focus of the political: crime, in this case theft.

The areca nut and coconut are to be left alone, so goes the first section, so that the individual shall be prepared for ceremonial occasions. The mature coconut is indispensable as a main ingredient in the ceremonially required creamed puddings as gifts to go with a gift of food. If he does not restrain his appetite, there will be no mature coconuts for creaming, and he will be forced to steal. The disgrace would otherwise be too much to bear. The same general orientation is contained in the exhortation to watch to see what the chiefs are doing, in order to follow suit. This emphasizes the chiefs' leadership, but at the same time pointing out that if the commoner does not follow the chief in setting food aside for a public function, he will himself be without such food when the time comes. He will then have to steal, to avoid having no reciprocal contribution to make.

Similarly, the exhortation to avoid complete evacuation, which in the Tikopian attitude would not leave any food in the stomach. This causes a man to become hungry quickly, and he is thus more likely to steal food.

Even more striking is the suggestion in the version of the Ariki Tafua, which insists that a man shall have only one daughter and one son. The Tikopia are keenly aware of the food limitations of the island, and consciously attempt to limit the number of children.[27] The ideal social unit in Tikopia is one in which the odd jobs are done by the boy, while the minor household tasks and filling the water bottles are left for the daughter to do. But, beyond this, "there is an increase in food consumption without a corresponding increase in the value of the labour power."[28] The father can increase the supply of some foods in a short time, but not others, such as coconut, breadfruit, banana, etc. The alternative is, again, stealing, a crime. By the very emphasis on the proper pattern, leaving the alternative as something not to be contemplated, a greater push to avoid this crime is given.

Without bringing in all the various points discussed in the Fono, mention should be made of the prohibition on shrieking and cursing loudly. This is probably to be classed as a misdemeanor, and is related to rank, in that it is the commoner who would thus break the peace, and the man of chiefly family who would demand retribution. Tikopia law, like law generally, is class-conscious. Such shrieking is most common when food has been stolen, and the suggestion is made to "compress together his lips." "What is the use of shrieking? Does he wish to pay a fine to the next man of rank who comes along?"[29] Nevertheless, it must be noted, the Tikopia do shriek, though not if they know a man of a chiefly family is about, and not at all near a chief's house.

On a more serious level is the injunction to keep the peace in spite of evil, murderous thoughts. With respect to this section of the exhortation to public order, Firth says,

Private feuds are not uncommon in Tikopia, generated as a rule by either of the two universal causes of strife—land and women. Such men are said to ramarama, or firifiri toward each other, harbour in secret murderous thoughts which turn over and over in their minds. Usually such men seek to avoid each other, taking separate paths to their work. If they should meet a wordy argument is the result, ending often in blows. By the fono they are enjoined to dispute in speech only and that this being concluded they should turn their backs and each pursue his own way.[30]

Thus public order, with respect to both class privilege and the peace of the island, is enjoined in a highly emotionalized ritual, behind which lies all the power of the main deities of the island. The *ariki* who makes the Fono is for the time being the mouthpiece of *Te Atua i Tafua,* and the assembled audience is to remain with bowed heads and in silence.

The emotional sanction behind the Fono is more clearly seen when it is understood that a breach of even the rule against raising one's head during the ceremony amounted to a "crime": an act calling for a publicly approved chastisement by the secular authorities, following previously established and known patterns. The penalty was, theoretically, death. The method of imposition of sentence was suicide, the common method of expressing humility, defeat, and expiation in much of Polynesia. Actually, as in all societies, there are "institutional evasions of institutional rules," and the common method of paying for such a crime was to strip one's gardens and orchards of "great quantities of taro, breadfruit, bananas, and coconuts" and thus prepare large baskets of food.[31] These were presented to the *ariki* in abject humility and wailing, while the culprit pressed his nose to the chief's foot, and followed this by a dirge.[32]

Hardly a more revealing situation could be described to help in attaining an understanding of the position of this sacro-secular officiant. At every point in sacred rituals the chief figures as one, usually the main, officiant. His alliance with the gods is both felt and known in sacred or secular situations, the halo of the one carrying over to the other.

When the chief proclaims, the land must obey. However, such proclamations are almost always economic in nature; that is, most legislation is for a definite period, for definite situations, and is economic in basis, though political in administration. As the Fono would suggest, it is the chief who initiates and leads the important economic enterprises, particularly those having to do with the most sacred rituals requiring great quantities of food. ". . . The chief has been shown to be the most important single human factor in the economic life of the Tikopia. Not only does he play a part as producer, but . . . he gives direction to the productive work of the community . . . he imposes far-reaching restrictions on production and consumption."[33] Since he is not capitalist or entrepreneur, he has no economic holds over the tribe as such. Though he owns all the land (theoretically), it is not from this, but from his position of authority, that he commands them to strive for certain economic objectives, such as having sufficient mature coconut for creaming the ritual puddings. It is through his sacred character that a breach of an economic rule becomes a violation of law, for he makes public and approved such a regulation, while backing it with his potential influence with the gods.

One type of case involved may . be noted concretely, involving the Ariki Taumako, Pa Faitoka, and a taro area which the chief wanted to plant later in the season.[34] He planned to have it cleared, but did not wish to have it touched soon. Nevertheless, a brother-in-law of the chief,

Pa Faitoka began clearing the area without having announced his intention, together with another man. The chief discovered this when he went to bathe behind his house, hearing the sound of scrub brush being felled. His anger was immediate, being shown by five terrific yells of "Iefu"! which startled the whole village. Meeting his sister, after having found out who was to blame, he cursed her also, causing her to go off weeping. He then sent two men to the violators of the ground, to tell them that they must go off to the woods. That is, they were in effect banished from the village and area. The two sent as messengers were to go shouting, "a sign to all at large of his urgent displeasure, and a threat of disturbing consequences to the offenders."[35] The offenders were cursed and told to leave for Faea, or the woods.

Off they went, Pa Faitoka wailing as he proceeded . . . The same afternoon a party went over with the cognisance, though not at the express wish of the chief, to persuade him to return. This is called the "seeking." They were unsuccessful . . . but on the next day but one he came back, and after abasing himself before the chief and making the customary gift of food was received back into favour again.[36]

The people in general backed the Ariki Taumako completely in this matter, pointing out that the lands belonged to the Ariki. In ordinary terms, of course, this is not true, but at power crises the rulership is absolute. In this case, particularly, public opinion was behind the Ariki, since the general practices of the group had been violated. In the last resort, the power of the Tikopia chief is absolute. "If he tells a man to go to the woods, or to the sea, he must obey. There is no other refuge for him. As the natives put it, 'If the Ariki has become angry with him, where shall he go'?"[37]

The peculiar relationship of chief and deity means that there is no easy recourse to the supernatural, or to a group of deities, to prevent oppression or persecution. There are no separate "churches" with vowed cultists, or high priests with considerable power. Consequently, the people do not have any solution but the general pressure of public opinion, to which the chiefs are generally responsive. It is this which makes less actual the theoretical total power over the land by the chiefs. Normally a given orchard is worked only by the members of one house, and harvested by them. When, as will sometimes happen, a chief begins to take over an orchard, the owners leave it to him. However, they may later go through the customary ceremony of abasement, mentioned above, and request it. The chief will usually not refuse, since the people will favor the commoner who makes the request. The limitation on such extreme personal power is not another political power, or even a religious one, but a secular and social one.

The insistence on the public peace is embodied in the Fono and is part of the chief's ordinary political duties. Since the Tikopia chief does not have a court and retinue, and must do the larger part of his own productive work, there is no formal court or legal procedure. However, his technical ownership of the land, coupled with his real religious power, gives him the legal excuse and executing force to settle disputes. This is particularly true of quarrels between members of the same clan. He can literally compel them to obey. He may say, "Abandon your fighting that you are carrying on there. Plant food properly for the two of you in my ground."[38] He is technically correct in such a connection. Furthermore, if they continue to quarrel, the chief will inform them,

"Go the pair of you to your own place wherever it may be; go away from my ground." In fact, they have no ground then to resort to; their alternative is the ocean, so they capitulate. It may be noted that the chief usually intervenes only when there seems no prospect of an immediate settlement.[39]

"Legislation" may also be made in order to protect someone's real or fancied rights. Thus Taupe, a junior son of Moritiaki, who was in turn Ariki Tafua, wished to have his son inherit chiefly prerogatives, though his son could not succeed to the chieftainship, since his mother was from Anuta. His half-brothers were angry at this, and abandoned their father, though their own status was secure. Consequently, Taupe left to live alone, fishing and cooking in solitude. Finally, his father softened, and summoned Taupe. He gave him a

kit of sacred adze blades of clam shell of the small type known as pipi. He then accompanied him to Maungafaea and there buried the blades in various parts of the orchards. Here they served as barriers to secure the land to him in perpetuity and to ward off any possible encroachment by his brothers or their descendants . . . The pronouncement was also made that this house should send its gifts of food only occasionally to the Tafua chief instead of regularly, as is the duty of commoners.[40]

By this act a supernatural sanction would forever keep him secure in his land, even though he would remain a commoner. The sacred objects made the land "bitter," and would make those people ill who took any food from the orchards. Even the present Ariki Tafua, who sometimes encroaches on lands of clan members, has not encroached on these. That this was not a mere secular transfer of ownership is seen in the fact that impersonal property in land is not known in Tikopia, that the supernatural would not have to be invoked if there were such a conception, and that the land, in that sense, was never the "property" of Moritiaki. He was, in effect, passing a law for a specific situation, and using the sacred to administer it.

It is this type of sanction which figures most prominently in economic proclamations. One was described above, but the latter was of a more personal nature than the usual type, which is more general and pointed more definitely to a coming ritual.

For imposition of a *tapu* is political and economic in aim, while the sanction behind it is the sacred, wielded by a chief in many important cases. With reference to the term, *tapu*, it is true of Tikopia as it is of Polynesia in general, that the term refers to both the sacred and the forbidden. The meaning varies somewhat in particular contexts, though it must be obvious that the meanings are closely akin.

There are, of course, various types of prohibitions, necessary in a society without the corner policeman, which invoke the sacred and thus protect one's property. Individuals may want to prevent relatives or friends from taking too freely of areca nut or coconut, and use a sago frond lashing to notify others of this fact. This may be true of certain paths as well.

However, the Tikopia do not classify such a prohibition as a tapu, for there must be a definite material token and ritual performance to create such a sanction. The simplest kind are more powerful than the prohibition mentioned above. This simplest type is used by commoners, who obtain it from a medium or a member of a chiefly house. The power of the tapu stems from the control which these people have over supernatural beings. An immature coconut frond is used for the binding. There is a more powerful type, which uses the bottom leaves of the immature coconut frond. Ordinary people do not use this type of "binding."

The third type is used only by a chief, made from a mature coconut frond. This is used, as a rule, for the Canarium almond and a Tikopia fruit. The mature frond is thus the right of the chief, who wears it also as his ritual necklet. It is "associated with the chief's most powerful god and it is thought that breach of it will result in sickness or death." Thus, as in our society, the violation of the property rights has the law arrayed against it as well as ordinary opinion; for more serious and graver goals requiring a totality of effort external sanctions are likely to be applied. The ultimate sanction in each case is death, either directly caused by sacred beings or indirectly by a forced suicide.

Firth lists several categories of tapu. One of the most important is that imposed by the Throwing of the Firestick, by which the ritual season begins (the Work of the Gods). This prohibits the felling of sago palms in Uta, where the most sacred dancing area is located, for nearly two months. Here the set of prohibitions is much broader than the mere protection of property, or the saving of economic goods in preparation for later rituals. Consequently, no "binding" of a tree is made. The only knotting that takes place is that of a palm frond around the Ariki Kafika's neck. This necklet is most sacred, being the chief symbol of headship. At the "Throwing," then, these necklets are not thrown away, but carefully hung above the chief's seating place.[41] The whole ceremony of the Firestick imposes also a tapu on the whole land:

The performance of this symbolic act, brief as it is, has now rendered the land *tapu* and formally instituted the period of the sacred ceremonies. From this moment the way of life of the people changes and receives a fresh orientation. They must now act circumspectly: no one is expected to shout or make other loud noise in the whole island, no parties may sit out on the beach and talk, as is their wont, and dancing, the favourite evening amusement, is suspended. At night people are supposed to sit within their houses, and the Ariki Kafika may even periodically patrol the paths to see that this prohibition is observed.

On the whole, these restrictions are fairly closely observed.[42]

Most of these tapu have as their function, whatever the different purposes, the saving or storing of food, and in legal-administrative terms are comparable to rationing regulations: food for less important and individual goals is diverted to social, groupal goals. In both cases there may be cases of violations, and in both cases the penalties which are potentially to be invoked may be very severe. Nevertheless, the concomitant tapus on noise, excitement, and gayety are not analogous to anything in our own secular society, though perhaps they are to periods of sacred festivals or mourning in the Hebraic tradition. Breaches are dealt with directly, as when a deity causes illness or sickness; or indirectly, as when the chief administers punishment backed by sacred forces. The regulation is made public, and conformity is expected: the formula, libation, and invocation create a firm basis for such an expectation.[43]

Within such a political structure it would be indeed surprising, if the deities were asked merely to maintain a chief in his power, and did not also set a stamp of approval on his election.[44] Actually, very soon after the election of the chief, or it may be a couple of days after the end of the funeral rites of the old chief, there will be the first of several very important feasts in the lifetime of the new chief. Each of these has its particular name and may follow a definite order of precedence.

The first of these, which is the most important for the subject in hand, is *te moringa,* "the conveying," which "signifies the symbolic carriage of the new chief to his appropriate status."[45] He is "conveyed" to the sacred focus of the island, Marae, mentioned before in connection with the ceremonial dancing. At this feast the new chief first enters into ceremonial (but not sacred), economic and sacred relations with other powers, the first two with other chiefs, while the last two are with the gods of his clan. The type of feast, the men who are there, and the ritual incidents which occur, all bring in the sacred forces to witness the happenings there at the ritual ground of Marae. Like all other very sacred (or secular but ceremonial) meetings in Tikopia, this calls for great quantities of food from the clan orchards and those of the chief.[46] The chiefs assemble in the new chief's house, where the gods are invoked by a kava ceremony, libations being poured to the gods. The other chiefs participate also, cups of kava being carried to each. Following the libations a formal but non-sacred recital of thanks is given by representatives of each chief to the other chiefs. This contains certain conventional expressions of abasement and metaphors of flattery and approval. The reciters, experts in this task, are given food as acknowledgement. The end of the recital signals a beginning of eating for the particular chief praised.[47] Later, after the uncovering of the oven and the setting out of baskets of food, another ceremony takes place which introduces the gods, though still implicitly, as related to the new incumbent.

A procession of women enters, each bearing on her arm a pile of bark-cloths with a little package of turmeric on top. They come up behind the chief one by one to the tail end of his seating mat—the less sacred end—and he takes the gift from each and places it at the head of his mat. The women are representatives of the various ramages (paito), the *fuanga* of the dead chiefs . . . Each woman smears her turmeric on the belly and arms of the new chief [itself a sacred act, for turmeric is a chiefly substance and a sacred one, used only on solemn occasions] . . . The cloths are termed *a noforanga,* seats, and are regarded as being placed for the spirits of the dead chiefs to sit upon.[48]

Afterwards, baskets of food are carried to the temples of each chief, where again kava is made by the chief. Still later, the sacred portion of the food (at the sacred end of the chief's house) is carried to the bottom of Marae, and a "kava house" is built by ritual workers. A presentation of bark-cloth is made to each chief by the host chief (the new incumbent). "These are offerings not to the chiefs, but to their respective deities."[49] Thus, all through this first ceremony, which "establishes" the chief in his new office after election, the gods are brought in implicitly and explicitly to indicate the close relationship between them and the chief. Thus he is reinforced in his new position. The whole ceremony also functions to cement relations with the other chiefs, who must co-operate with him in the main projects and great ceremonies of the island.

Though for the most part the ordinary force of public opinion and personal exhortation and scolding are ample to control variations in sex practices, mention ought to be made of one case-type where secular and religious authority coincides. Since the case is perhaps somewhat controversial, it may be looked at from several points of view. This type of case, incest, is referred to by Firth when he briefly mentions political power: ". . . the forms of executive authority are vaguely defined, and come into operation only to cope with major breaches of the law, such as incest or direct insult to the chief."[50] Actually, it is almost impossible to detect brother-sister incest, since they may be sleeping close together, side by side.[51] They cannot, of course marry, ". . . and for a girl to become pregnant by her brother would be a scandalous proceeding. It is said that the pair would be made to put off to sea (fakaforau), with small chance of survival, as a punishment."[52] In consequence, they may practice *coitus interruptus*. From this, the conclusion is inescapable that here, as in many other cases, the power of the chief, which does extend to forcing any one to commit suicide by going out to sea,[53] is called out by such a scandal. However, there is more to the situation. Actually, there is a gradation of disapproval of marriages between close blood relations, ranging from ordinary public disapproval to "forcible restraint," of which, presumably, the authority of the chief would be the most obvious and ultimate expression.[54] Consequently, much of the Tikopia disapproval is merely verbal, with respect to even the marriage of half-brother and half-sister, a situation which Firth finds rather puzzling at first sight.[55] The solution lies in a supernatural sanction held to be operative in such cases. He points out,

The idea is firmly held that unions of close kin bear with them their own doom, their *mara*. This concept is the opposite of that of *manu* . . . *Mara* may be rendered therefore as failure, or as ill-luck, misfortune. The idea essentially concerns barrenness . . . The peculiar barrenness of an incestuous union consists not in the absence of children, but in their illness or death, or some other mishap, as the periodic lunacy believed to result from the incest of mother and son mentioned above. The idea that the offspring of a marriage between near kin are weakly and likely to die young is stoutly held by these natives and examples are adduced to prove it . . .

This generalization . . . is a belief in the operation of supernatural forces . . . the resentment of the parents of the guilty pair, who . . . after death vent their accumulated spleen on the offspring.[56]

This vengeance can be satisfied, sometimes, by less than all the offspring. The Tikopia believe this evil retribution works constantly, and will document it by empirical evidence, the evil coming only after the parents have died. It is held that in the realm of the spirits the parents are shamed by other spirits, thus creating the motivation.[57] A similar situation, dreaming of incest, arouses anger and fear at possible loss of vitality and strength.[58] Thus the two sanctions overlap in this prohibition of one type of scandalous behavior. The secular or political authority is here the chosen agency to act when a genuine case of (true) brother-sister incest occurs, and the penalty is ultimate, death. The force behind that authority is sacred. However, this case is not historically known in Tikopia,[59] so that the case is merely a technical point at law. Marriage within a less proscribed degree with close blood relatives is not prevented or penalized by the political authority, and instead is the recipient of evil from the spirits of parents. Presumably the extreme cases would also cause supernatural retribution. In such cases, however, the ordinary processes of action by a supernatural personality would not offer the immediacy and the public, official directness of death by order of the *ariki*. On the other hand, the chief does not usually introduce his authority in cases where the gradual processes of public opinion, or the supernatural entities, will ultimately erase what is not an extremely serious scandal. The alliance between the two is thus made explicit in their division of labor.

The active role which the Tikopia chiefs play in both secular and sacred affairs create an identity of interest as well as an adjustment of the demands between the two activities. In the Zuñi society, politically secular affairs are minimized and turned over to a definite group, aside from the matters which have come to fall under the jurisdiction of white society. As a consequence, in spite of the dependence of the political officers upon the religious authorities, analysis is not simple.

# ZUÑI

Stevenson, writing of the period at the turn of the century, dealt very little with political life among the Zuñi, but summed up the relationship between the political and the religious by assimilating the former to the latter: "The government of Zuñi is hierarchical, four fundamental religious groups . . . being concerned."[60] A generation later, Bunzel reported that: "The real political authority of the tribe is vested in the council of priests," thus reaffirming the earlier statement.[61] However, the problem of analysis is not so simple as would appear from these observations. Here, as in Manus, war is no longer a function of the political authorities, and the introduction of white courts as an alterna-

tive avenue of justice has narrowed somewhat the area of activity of the
political authorities. Unlike Manus, however, this society does not have
its interest focussed on trade, property, or argument, thus narrowing further its use for any important development of administrative or legal
structure. Crimes of personal violence are infrequent, theft is rare, and
sexual transgressions are not usually considered important by the authorities. Roughly expressed, the Zuñi live quiet, self-contained lives in
which the broader political activities are much less important than their
ceremonial life. In consequence, any discussion of interrelationships between political and religious elements must refer to the smaller details of
political action.

However, the most obvious point of contact is a broad one, having
many implications. There are secular officers in the pueblo, headed by
the Governor and Lieutenant-Governor, and including eight tenientes or
deputies.[62] They have under their jurisdiction most of the matters which
we could call "political," such as

. . . adjudication of civil suits, such as boundaries, water rights, inheritance,
restitution for loss or injury to livestock, management of cooperative enterprises of a nonreligious character, such as road building, cleaning of irrigation
ditches, execution of Government ordnances regarding registration, etc., and
all manner of negotiation with outside powers.[63]

It is clear that with the greatly increasing relationships with the whites,
these officers have more duties and influence. Nevertheless, the office of
Governor still lacks prestige among the Zuñi. The orientation toward
ceremonial matters as being of prime importance, and the desire to avoid
the strife which necessarily comes with outside contact and negotiations,
make this an undesirable office.

Because of this formal separation of secular, political affairs from
the religious, important chiefs such as Rain Chiefs will not be found on
the Governor's staff.[64] Yet, these secular officers have no power in themselves, and are rather dependent upon the priests. These holders of
religious power select the Governor and his staff, and may also remove
him at any time. Stevenson reports a case of deposition in 1891.[65] After
a complaint made by an associate Rain Priest to the Rain Priest of the
North, a meeting was held by the priests to discuss the matter. The accusation was that the Governor had stolen horses from the people, and
traded them to the Mexicans for sheep. The later deposition meeting was
as dignified and formal as any impeachment proceeding might be. The
Governor made his speech of defense, which was answered by the elder
brother Bow Priest. The verdict was announced by the judges, who were

the "first body of Rain priests," whereupon all left the plaza without further discussion.[66]

This does not mean, of course, that the Ashiwanni or council of chiefs of the rain societies are occupied constantly with the affairs of the Governor. The affairs which they are most intimately concerned with are the selection of impersonators of the gods, the interpolation of particular ceremonies (such as initiation) into the usual calendar of ceremonial activities, what should be done in the case of earthquakes or drought, or tribal policy as it touches mainly ceremonial matters.[67]

At the installation of the Governor, the Ashiwanni are present and the Bow Priests are to summon the outgoing officers.[68] Prayers are said, and the incoming Governor expresses by a kinship term ("my father") his recognition of the authority of the Sun Priest. The Indians present underlined the prayers by words meaning "that is so," emphasizing the public character of the installation. The cane of office is empowered by the ritual of breathing on or from it, giving it life.

Bunzel claims that "the only crime that is recognized is witchcraft."[69] Although this is a supernatural act, it is actually treated as a secular crime, at least to the extent that it is believed to cause injury, and is answered by public action. When the relatives of someone killed by sorcery bring this charge, the Bow Priests, who are the group empowered to enforce order, examine the accused. In former times the accused was hung from a beam by his wrists being placed behind his back, until he confessed. By revealing the source and nature of his power, he also lost it. He might then be released or executed. At the present time, torture is no longer permitted by the whites.[70] However, an individual may be nagged into confessing.

No one is brought to such a trial unless someone is near death. However, when death has occurred, the reality of the charge is accepted. Violence against such a person is taken as a matter of course. Thus in Stevenson's time a woman was killed by the father of a child, because he thought the woman had bewitched the child.[71] The man was not punished, the court accepting the charge of witchcraft as valid. At the present time, "Actual executions are probably quite rare, and a person may live under suspicion of being a witch for a long time without anything happening."[72] Nevertheless, there is no denying the right of a War Captain to kill a witch. Public execution would probably not occur, due to the power of the whites, but convicted witches would be killed secretly unless they managed to escape to other villages—a groupal act nevertheless.[73] After the official interrogation and torture by the Bow Priests, the public confession was required of the convicted person, and the execution was sanctioned by the pueblo, the Bow Priests carrying the verdict out, following the pattern of crime, conviction, and punishment of the criminal situation expected in a society.[74]

The Zuñi are taught to be pleasant and generous, without the drive and tempestuousness of the Plains people. The severe characteristics of hewing close to an abstract principle in the face of opposition, or of intense personal loyalties in spite of social disapproval, are not esteemed.[75] It is interesting, consequently, to note the disapproval of such a seemingly minor element of action as quarreling, which is actually incorporated into the religious system. That is, the public peace is protected by specific religious prohibitions. Mention has been made already of the great number of prayer stick offerings, one of the most fundamental elements in Zuñi ritual. When such plumes are offered as part of ritual, the individual must refrain from quarreling for four days afterwards.[76] Since the religious officiant represents the highest Zuñi ideal, the system prohibits any such person, including those holding temporary offices, from quarreling or disputing with members of the community or with outsiders. "The priest should be gentle, humble, and kind."[77] In short, those in power must never contribute to public disorder.

The problem of public order arises at times when there are Navahos in the town, and in particular at the distribution of gifts from the housetops. When the people are scrambling for these gifts during the dances of thanksgiving, there is generally no fighting or unamiability. The outsiders do not usually attempt to scramble, but if they do so fairly the Zuñi do not object. However, if they do trip or act in some other manner to gain an advantage, they will be "hustled off the plaza by the police, who are ever on the alert to preserve order there when a number of 'Navahos are in the town.' "[78]

A combination of magical technique and the priestly function is found in the case of theft. Not of frequent occurrence, it does not constitute a cause for formal legal action within the community. When it does occur, the family of the guilty person must pay the family of the one who has been wronged.[79] To discover the thief, a Rain Priest is summoned to a private session. Here he administers datura (jimson weed) to the man who lost the property. After this, the priest keeps a vigil through the night, listening to the man. The latter is expected to call out the name of the thief.[80] In the morning, the priest holds a usual Zuñi purification ceremony: he returns to the house, after having told the man the name mentioned, with his wife and other female members of his family. These make yucca suds for washing the man's head. After the washing, the priest gives corn, cloth, or other presents, and the women return to their house, from which they bring food for the man's family. It is assumed that the culprit will return the property, but the War Chiefs do not enter the case to force the issue beyond the point of detection reached by the Rain Priest.

The intense, personal, romantic love approved in our own society is not the ideal of Zuñi, where a much more casual attitude toward sex is taken. "Adultery is not a crime. Along with stinginess and ill temper it is a frequent source of domestic infelicity and divorce, but is never regarded as a violation of rights. Sexual jealously is no justification for violence."[81] Nevertheless, although sexual transgression is not a crime as it is in Manus, there are situations in which it is classed as a nonsecular crime. Such situations may occur when someone who is chosen to impersonate one of the gods violates the code. Two cases of this sort may be mentioned. In one of them, the elder sister of the Sun Priest had been "approached with undue familiarity" at night, when the man was her guest. This was a public matter, since the man had been chosen to impersonate a god at Shalako. Her own importance probably intensified the indignation. He was tried by the Ashiwanni, found guilty, and was expelled from his office.[82] The offense, under other conditions, would be grounds for no more than gossip. Here, it becomes, the occasion for formal, definite public condemnation. A later offense of this nature occurred, which added the charge of incest to adultery, since the man accused was a kiva brother of the woman. The Bow Priest responsible for expulsion was not ordered to do so, however, since the time for the ceremony was too near, and a substitute could not be found quickly.[83] The woman concerned was not the wife of an important man, furthermore. Instead, a sharp public rebuke is given by the Bow Priest at the next monthly planting of prayer sticks.

Revealing cult secrets to outsiders or the uninitiated is a grave offense, called by Bunzel "a crime against the gods."[84] The importance of such a transgression must be evident from the Pueblo emphasis on ritual. The character of secrecy in the society makes such revelation almost akin to treason. Just as in the case of witchcraft power, the potency of ritual is lost or weakened when it is revealed.[85] Individuals who let others learn their sacerdotal secrets lose the protection which such information gives.[86] This is one reason why Christian missionaries appear ridiculous to the Zuñi. It is clear to the society that this outside religion has little to offer, since it is handed out as though of no value at all.[87] As a consequence, revelation of kachina cult secrets is simply giving away the protection possessed by the tribe. Without such sacred powers as protection, the society would be helpless against drought or any other calamity.

Death by beheading is the punishment for such a crime, and is supposed to be carried out by those who impersonate the gods.[88] This severity reflects the general societal attitude.[89] However, in point of fact no one living has any memory of such an execution. Considering the interest of the pueblo in past events, it is evident that no concrete instance of such punishment is effectual today or in the recent past as a deterrent against this crime. The actual substitute is flogging, by the masked impersonators.[90]

The Zuñi pattern of turning over most secular political affairs to a group of officers, dependent on the highest religious leaders for its power and authority, functions to free these leaders from contact with the strife and turmoil which this society considers inconsistent with the calm necessary to approach the sacred. The gradual encroaching by the white society on many aspects of the pueblo life during the past several hundred years merely emphasizes the importance of this "separation." In the case of the Murngin discussed below, outside contact has been sporadic and slight, so that even warfare or blood feuds have not been wiped out by the white administration, thus leaving an important field for political action open to the political leader. On the other hand, outsiders as powerful as the whites might have created new fields for such action. As in Zuñi society, the Murngin center of interest lies in a complex series of sacred observances, so that there has been little formalization of political action. In fact, there is much less in Murngin, and far fewer patterns of action which may be accepted as "legal" or "political."

## MURNGIN

In dealing with Murngin patterns of this kind, one is likely to attempt to speak of "tribal law" where there is no tribe.[91] "The tribes of northeastern Arnhem Land . . . are very weak social units, and when measured by the ordinary definitions of what constitutes a tribe fail almost completely. The tribe is not the war-making group . . . Even clans well toward the center of a tribe's territory will . . . range themselves with another group . . ."[92] It is perhaps rather to be called a large cultural group.[93] Nevertheless, the cultural similarities are great enough, and there is enough of some kind of emotional unity, that definite patterns of action toward other clans in the same "tribe" are maintained by the leaders of a given clan. The totemic relationships are not to be ignored as factors in unity. The clan and moiety are the two most important local groupings, and it is the clan which is the most important political or legal entity. These are the largest "units of social solidarity" and violence does not occur within them, or between a man's clan and his wife's and mother's clan.[94] Since "it is through his clan that a man establishes his totemic relations and identifies himself with the sacred world," it is not surprising that it is this same clan which would preserve order, and punish the rebellious or illicit. One might also expect both sacred and secular penalties and threats as instruments toward such ends. For the larger framework of Murngin society is religious, however secular many details. Such controls are the more necessary, since the Murngin society is, by our standards, bloody and violent. The violence is both day-to-day and mystical. The violence must be held in check within the clan, since it would be destroyed. Within the society there are checks of custom, also, which tend to mitigate much of the potential death-dealing.

The locus of secular power is identical with that of the sacred power: the old men. To speak of a gerontocracy is not sufficient, since the strata of the society are organized in terms of age grades, and it is therefore not the higher leaders alone who are fixed or placed in a rank. Since sexual bifurcation is part of the system of age grading, there is created, for both men and women, a fixed pattern of secular powers at any given time, the fixity made even more definite by the existence of the extremely complex kinskip system, according to which everyone in the clan is related to everyone else in a specific manner.

The problem is somewhat complicated in the case of the Murngin by Warner's liberal use of the term "tribal law." Apparently influenced by Durkheim, he often uses it where other anthropologists would use the older term, "custom," or "institution," or "norm of conduct," or "rule." Thus, for example:

Mutual fidelity is demanded by husband and wife. She is supposed to stay away from all other men, and according to tribal law he is not allowed to cohabit with any women except his wives . . . Frequently women have had intercourse with other dué before starting to live openly with their own husbands. This causes much indignation and usually results in a beating for the girl and a heated quarrel between the husband and the lover . . . the lover and the tribe recognize that he is in the wrong . . .[95]

The same situation is repeated in the curious tale of the man who found that his galle had had sexual relations with another, and left her to die in a deep hole inside a high rock.[96] The story is told to influence women to be faithful, and believed to be true by the women. A woman may attack with obscenity and a tongue lashing when her husband has been unfaithful. Nevertheless, the identification of this pattern with a legal situation is dubious. Mere conflict does not produce a legal situation, and neither does a mere contravention of the norms, though these are necessary. This remains true, even when the husband feels it a positive duty to beat his wife.[97]

It is true, granted, that the situation begins to approach a legal one when the community demands certain penalties for certain acts, choosing, perhaps, the injured party to perform the punishment, and it is very close when the community itself takes action. It becomes specifically political or legal when the constituted authorities—and there is no society without them—resolve the problem, even if the whole community takes part. Thus, the situation begins to approach a politico-legal one in the case of gross infidelity. "If a wife continues to be unfaithful she might be killed by her dué and members of her own family. Usually the dué would depend upon a magician to accomplish this."[98] In the other direction, several cases of infidelity, as in the quotation given at length above, call for threats and growling, with the lover accepting the scolding as proper.

From this pattern to the case of killing the unfaithful one by magic for a continued, public affair is one step toward the politico-legal structure. Certainly the step into such a structure *is* made in the case of a *makarata* ceremony. Taking up a concrete case of this type, boys are not supposed to have contacts with girls before marriage, though they usually succeed in having such experiences. Both mother's brother and the parents will watch the actions of the youngsters. "A young man said to me, 'We do not sleep with girls before we are married because we are afraid of the old people. Sometimes a girl who belongs to another man says yes and we do. If it is found out the proper husband raises a row, and maybe her father. Sometimes a boy gets killed this way and sometimes they only cut him until the blood comes' (in a makarata)"[99] "The makarata is a ceremonial peace-making fight," as Warner characterizes it. On the other hand, it is also a public, official, legally controlled method of punishment for a more serious offence. As in the case of punishment elsewhere, the same method is actually used for other purposes, such as merely making peace, or preventing further bloodshed. In the case under consideration, the individual goes through the ceremony as a member of a group, which sees to it that he is not punished too severely, again emphasizing its nonpersonal character. It is the injured party or group which sends the invitation to a makarata.[100] This is a highly ceremonial affair, in which the injured group paint themselves with white clay and dance in to the dueling ground, "singing a song which is descriptive of the water of their totemic well."[101] The other side is also covered with white clay. Each side stands just outside spear-throwing distance, with a jungle fighting cover behind them, in case the ceremony turns into a genuine fight. The injured group will then dance a non-sacred totemic performance toward the others, then retire, walking. The others perform, also, after which the fighting starts.

In the case of killers, the first throwing does not attempt to punish them, but there is rather a method of allowing the injured group to work out some emotion by throwing at the men who are supposed to have "pushed" the killers.[102] This is a standard method, which is presumably not followed in the case of an individual violator of the sexual rule under consideration. No spears with stone heads are thrown at the pushers, who have two relatives accompanying them in their zig-zag run in the middle of the field. These deter the injured group from being too serious about hurling the spears, since these are also kin to the other side. They also aid in knocking down the spears which are thrown. All the members of the injured group hurl spears, and some, more outraged, throw many or even continue approaching and hurling until they have driven the runners into the jungle. No retaliation is permitted, even to the cursing which they must also bear.

It is the secular leaders, the old men, who decide that they have had enough. The decision is made by the old men of the offended group, thus emphasizing their role as public leaders. It is then that the real culprit must take his punishment. For this time the spear head remains on the shaft, a potentially death-dealing weapon. First as a whole, then as individuals, the offended group will throw their spears, until their indignation subsides. The cathartic function is obvious.

At this point, also, the control of the old men, who are in another connection the religiously privileged, is seen:

While all this is taking place, the old men of both sides walk back and forth from one group to the other, telling the throwers to be careful and not kill or hurt anyone. The offending clan's old men ask the younger men to be quiet and not to become angry, and when they hear insults thrown at them not to reply or throw spears since they are in the wrong. When the old men of the injured clan feel that they have sated their anger as a group they call out to the young men to stop, and each man then throws singly at the killers.[103]

In the general heat of emotion, of course, the old men may fail in their attempt.

After this phase is over, one of the offended group, in this case presumably the husband, jabs a spear through the thighs of the offender, after the latter has danced with his group up to them. If this is not done, or if only a slight wound is made, it is to be expected that more violence will occur at a later time, and that vengeance has not been sated. After the jabbing, the two groups dance together as a sign of solidarity and ritual peace.[104]

As mentioned, this general pattern holds also for killers, and this procedure becomes an efficient tool in the hands of the old men of the clan, for preventing too much bloodshed or for wiping out ill will between groups. Since among the Murngin there are long-standing feuds, which do result in ambushes and death, some political mechanism must exist in order to avoid a situation of total hostility. This has importance in another direction, since without such a mechanism the unstable economic group of the horde could never come together. This group, which accumulates during the dry season when food is plentiful, can exist only to the extent that the clans are friendly. The better areas may have several clan groups on them, though a given area may be owned by only one of them. The makarata is the method by which some antagonisms are suppressed.

At this time, then, the makarata helps preserve order. However, there will also be some suppression of ill will.[105] This is done by ritual sanctions, which take the place of a genuine tribal, political organization, at least to some extent.

The belief that the totem will be offended if clashes occur between opposing clansmen usually keeps the peace . . . Peoples with a background of feud and warfare who might not otherwise risk meeting one another can be fairly certain of peace in a horde gathered for a ritual. Since the local clans which start the ceremony have it well under way and the totemic emblems have been made and are in the camp by the time the first guests arrive, hesitant visitors can feel comparatively safe in coming to the ceremony.[106]

Also at this time the old men, who have an interest in keeping order for their sacred rituals, and as well as the power to help maintain it, will be with the hotheads as moderating elements. Thus is seen the structure of keeping the peace in a non-formalistic manner: (1) the use of the *makarata* as a technique for erasing tendencies toward the ultimate of political antagonisms, war; (2) the presence of numerous old men who have the power to maintain the public peace at a time of sacred rituals; and (3) the threat of supernatural sanctions, which are powerful enough to cause the death of the culprits.

It must be emphasized that these sacred sanctions are not necessarily used by the ceremonial leaders, the old men, at least in this connection.

As Warner saw, "Warfare is in direct opposition to ceremony."[107] Sacred rituals, in Australia or anywhere else, are unifying in tendency. They increase the devotion to and support of groupal ends, while intensifying conformity to group norms. Being expressions of the value-structure of the society, warfare *within* that society[108] is directly antithetical. It is not surprising that the ritual is stopped if armed conflict breaks out during its celebration. The violators are criminals. The leaders of the ceremonies will consider the action a direct insult to the totem. "It is believed that the totem itself would seek vengeance upon any leader who did not protect its interests at such a time."[109] The participants fear death from the fighters, and death from the totem. This totemic penalty is not, it must be repeated, directed by these leaders. The criminals will simply die, or those celebrating the totem will suffer illness. Or, perhaps the totemic and real ancestors will not allow a soul to enter the womb of the woman, and the culprit will have no children.[110] Or—this has been noted before —the totemic ancestors will not help the culprit in a time of need, or when he has died in a fight and his soul is supposed to be directed to the totemic water hole.

To a significant degree, then, in the absence of a formal political system the same ends are gained through control by the old men and the sacred sanctions. The control goes further, however, than has been mentioned. These culprits may also be punished by the ceremonial or clan leaders. Thus, sexual relations which are illicit will cause the same result, and in both cases the leader may exert his authority and suggest that the culprits be punished—even killed.[111] Thus Warner saw two women narrowly escape death at a Narra ceremony when caught in adultery.[112] At this time the ceremony was not stopped, even though fighting broke out. The presumption was that the punishment of the culprits would avoid any totemic penalties. The women escaped only by swimming at night to a nearby island. Similarly, when a man has seen a totem for the first time, he is not supposed to have sexual intercourse with his wife. "It is said that the ceremonial leader for the totem would be so angry that he would attempt to spear the culprit.[113]

The same effect may be attained when an individual within the clan is a continual trouble maker, or killer. When there is a killing, this is not an occasion for outsiders, or near relatives from other clans, or even retaliation by clan members. The situation is rather a public one, and the penalty is death by the group. Here again, presumably the decision is one made by the old men who have seen the higher totems.[114] Similarly, divulging secrets to the women or the uninitiated which are supposed to be in the possession only of the old men, or for looking at ritual things before initiation, may call for the death penalty, again a political solution for a ritual crime.[115]

Though it may be true that "age grading in Murngin societies is highly ritualistic and controls a man's religious life far more than it does his ordinary daily existence,"[116] in the sphere of authority this is less true, since age grading is crucial, as suggested before. Though much of the authority is a quite secular fear, the general principle of the "contiguity of the sacred" ought not to be forgotten. The external sanctions, such as being able to prevent a young Murngin man from moving upward, are important. However, the source of these sanctions is not "external." The old men are much more intimately associated with the clan ancestors and totems. The association is real, since passage through the age grades makes the individual actually more sacred, by his participation in the sacredness of the clan well through becoming part of the Python spirit in the Python's Djungguan rite. The "halo of the sacred" becomes a necessary fact, in that those who are supposed to have secular authority also have sacred authority, and that in the larger framework of the ritual constituting the Murngin philosophy the capstone and symbol is the totem, close to which there is no living human being except the old men. This identification, of course, prevents potential conflict between these types of behavior. This is further emphasized by the fact that the secular authority does not act at many points, simply because the sacred entities, whose rites are oriented toward the old men, themselves enforce public peace and conformity.

## SUMMARY

Thus we see the interlocking details between religious and political action. The support which the religious system gives the political is not merely explicit, but also implicit and symbolic. Further, this relationship is not one-sided. For the political system also supports even where it is not identified with the religious. Where the two are not identified in the same personnel, there are institutional patterns for avoiding conflict. This, of course, partly follows from the proposition, that the society is a cultural emergent which is not a mere aggregation or addition of several hypothetical "individuals." It thus has manifest and latent aims of its own, and these must possess some sort of compatibility if the group is to continue as a society. It then becomes incautious to speak of any sphere or level of social action as being more "basic," and attention must rather be given to the manner in which these relate to one another.[117] Then it is seen more clearly how the religious actional system is in the world about us, conditioned by it and conditioning it. The doctrines are not merely philosophy, but become motivationally concrete outside the strict limits of the dogmas, lending both power and significance to secular institutions as well as limiting these institutions in many ways.

# 9. FAMILY AND RELIGION

Patently the psychoanalytic theory of religion is not universally correct which contends the religious structure is simply a projection of the parent-child relationship.[1] Nevertheless, it is true that the relationship between man and the gods, spirits, or natural forces which he conceives to be sacred, is a social one. This fact is particularly obvious where the gods are conceived in symbolically familial terms such as those expounded by psychoanalysts, but it is true even in religious systems in which this is not the case.

Two facts are evidently correlated here. One is the social character of the religious forces, and the other is the fact of socialization within a family or kinship structure. The assumption of communication between social creatures, whether men or gods, the acceptance of some authority, indeed, the learning of all of social behavior, occur within such a structure. That this learning primarily involves social objects is to be expected, even when those objects are sacred. The question of priority need not concern us here.

The main social function of the family, whatever its structure in a given society, is a composite one embracing several aspects of *creating new members of the society*: the reproduction, maintenance, status ascription, and socialization of the child.[2] This also includes the old age and burial of a member of the society, the completion of the cycle. Like the society of which it is a part, the family achieves its results by enlisting the energies of its members, giving them security, affection, sexual gratification, etc.

These functions taken together require a structure which is not to be found in any other institution. It must be a *biological* grouping, since at least two of the participants are linked sexually; and some kind of biological relationship, real or assumed, exists between its members. However, this does not alone define the familial relationships or structure. In addition, the pattern must contain *economic* relationships, since the feeding and general care of the new members requires it, just as does the continued support of the adults. For the *ascription of status,* the members of the family must have a similar status, thus allowing considerable determination of such status by the mere fact of birth in a particular family. Furthermore, this pattern must be one of *long duration,* for the period of socialization in man is long, as is the period of dependence. Even though the adulthood and marriage of the children partly loosen the links between the participants in this structure, this period of common life, with its mutual habituation, gratifications, and conflicts, is nevertheless fundamental in the formation of the individual personality, as well as in the sentimental cohesion of all the familial members.

The chief points of relationship between this familial structure and religious activity are those of *status and sanctions.* The ramifications of status are of course many, involving such matters as birth, status ascription as well as the achievement of status, rites of passage and initiation, definition of various kinship positions, legitimacy, and certain aspects of marriage. Sanctions involve the socialization of the child, with reference to both secular and nonsecular matters, ritual and secular conformity and punishment, and so on. Or, in reciprocal terms: It is within the kin group that religious socialization occurs, and these learned sanctions in turn support much of the familial structure.

"An individual life, whatever the type of society, consists in passing successively from one age to another, and from one occupation to another."[3] As a general rule, the most significant of such acts of succession or passage are set off by ritual and ceremony. The most important are usually birth, adulthood, marriage, and death.[4] Such birth rituals seem to have as their chief function the announcement to the community of the existence of a child, and an acceptance of that announcement, as well as the familial acceptance of a delegated responsibility, the sustenance and socialization of the child. All societies seem to take note of birth in some manner.[5] The passage of the individual *after* birth reflects the fundamental system of stratification, of status and role. A morally accepted and sanctioned pattern of action is to apply to each position in any society.[6] The person who makes the passage is officially empowered by the ritual to fit the pattern of action, and the society *gives notice that it will expect that pattern.* It is a part of the common value system that just those statuses should exist, and that this person should occupy them or it. This becomes particularly relevant to the familial system, since any growth in the individual, i.e., change in a determinate direction, must mean a change in his familial relationships. In fact, these individual status changes reflect most immediately on the family, not the society. Any puberty or other passage ceremonies will explicitly change the status of the individual in the society at large, but the locus of primary experience and orientation for that individual will be his family or kin group. The social adjustments called for in the new status will mostly be made by the family, not the society, unless the individual is the only one of his class (e.g., a monarch). The society itself is little affected as a whole, since the process merely allows one generation to replace another. The structure, the systematized set of social relationships or elements, may for the most part stay the same. These remarks also hold in a broad way for the passage into puberty and adulthood, or marriage. Being social events, however, they receive some attention in the form of ritual. Since adulthood or puberty is so intrinsically related with sexual maturity and potential reproduction, the ritual is likely to reflect that fact by having reference in symbolic or explicit ways to the sexual organs and their use.[7]

It must be remembered that it is *not the mere licensing of a sexual union* which makes marriage important, since in many societies a rather wide sexual freedom is allowed outside of marriage.[8] Undoubtedly of more importance is the entrance of a new member into one familial or kin group, or the leaving of an old member. Yet even such changes are less important than the actual *creation of a complete family* which is implied by the union. This is suggested by the facts on illegitimacy and incest. It may now be taken as a truism that whatever the ideas of a given tribe about premarital sexual unions, even those lasting for a long time, no society allows indiscriminate *childbearing*.[9] Malinowski states the principle in terms of fatherhood, by pointing out that ". . . no child can be brought into the world without a man, and one man at that, assuming the role of sociological father, i.e., guardian and protector, the male link between the child and the rest of the community."[10] Malinowski might actually have gone further, by pointing out that a sociological mother is required as well as a sociological father. It is in these terms, then, that rituals relating to marriage have their significance, giving a stamp of approval to children and kinship beginnings. In a sense, that is, the society is validating and accepting future parents. Once accepted, the child must be socialized. This is a long process, of both an informal and a formal character. Skills must be acquired, and many value patterns must form the structure of his personality. Religious instruction is likely to be part of the child's daily life. He will be forbidden to touch sacred objects. He may be threatened by godly wrath if his actions are not proper. At major stages in his growth process, the transition may be marked by rituals, and at such rituals he will be given moral injunctions, emphasized by the sacred situation. He will learn the tabus of kinship, as well as those of religion, and come to accept their reciprocal supports unthinkingly. By the time he is an adult, they will be so much a part of his action pattern that passing them on to his children in turn will not need to be a rationally planned, "educative" process. His children will learn them from everything he does.

The exit of a human being from the tribe and his entrance into another state or world are the occasion of ritual, but it usually waits upon the definitive fact of death: complete lack of expected social response. This is a social definition of a physiological state. This type of social definition is common enough. However, it is understandable that death should have the social immediacy and finality of a "stubborn fact" far more than birth or puberty. Though in the case of birth there must be a recognition of something having entered this world, this need not be, and sometimes is not, considered human. The distinction is simple enough, since being human is a product of the socialization—"humanizing"—process, and before the child has formed a part of "humanity" it is possible to ignore its birth as having no social significance as yet. Although puberty rites presumably recognize a physiological fact, available evidence is clear that they do not necessarily occur contemporaneously with either reproductional or sexual maturity, coming much later or much earlier than either. But to the extent that the activities of the group are dependent on social interaction, death is inevitably and immediately noticed. The new-born child is first of all a *thing*, with few if any social expectations to meet at once. The man who has just died forces the group to recognize his new state, because there are such expectations, and he fails to meet them.

This does not mean, of course, that the dead individual immediately disappears from his family or society. Aside from the living memory of the dead, they often remain as part of the supernatural forces, even in societies which are not cases of "ancestor worship."[11] In fact, practically every primitive religious system imputes both power and interest to the dead. It is significant that in spite of the wide disparity between the societies treated in this investigation, all of them consider the dead to figure largely among the sacred forces. This suggests two important questions. One of them is, Why is there a sacred funeral ritual? The other is possibly related to it, whence this power of the dead in these religions?

Death is rarely impersonal. It is a brute fact, and is inevitably recognized, but for clear reasons it is not a physiological fact alone. This is true, whether one thinks of the cause of death, the realm to which the dead go, or familial and group bereavement. As many others have pointed out, whatever our scientific preconceptions, we do not tend to think of the death of a loved one in terms of purely physical causation. The question stemming from our feelings is *Why?* not *How?* That is, we seek an anthroposocial explanation, one couched in terms of will and motivation, not physical process alone. Primary group interaction, and this is even more intensely true for close familial interaction, depends on a tight interweaving of personalities, sentiments, attitudes, cooperation, and ideas. One's whole personality is involved in the relationship. When one member leaves, the gap cannot be filled by another in quite the same fashion. All the daily expectations of action, sentiment, and thought are frustrated, and the emotional props based on the lost one are gone.

Two inferences may be drawn from this. One is that to prevent familial or group disorganization from becoming too widespread, there must be some techniques for bridging the emotional gap. This is perhaps the most important implicit function of the mortuary ritual. The other is that even when the dead are not themselves sacred, they are nevertheless related to the supernatural world. This is abundantly shown in the symbolism of the ritual.

The society enjoins particular types of mourning and funeral ritual.[12] This means that at the moment of greatest preoccupation with one's own sorrow, the group forces those most concerned, the family, to take part in something which points beyond sorrow itself to other interests, social and sacred. The solidarity of the family has been temporarily broken by the removal of an integral part, and the collective mourning and ritual serve to realign the unity in an emotionally satisfactory and socially approved manner.[13] Communal activity is required at a time when the emotional shock might otherwise lead to complete lack of action. Mourning and ritual adjust the individual to the reality of death.[14] That is, there is a forced catharsis and a deviation of interest from sentiment to activity.

Certainly part of the reference of the dead to the sacred forces arises from the division of the universe into the day-to-day profane, impersonal phenomena on the one hand, and the sacred, moral and supernatural on the other, wherein the dead clearly do not fall into the first category. Naturally, they are not necessarily identified with the sacred completely, but such a division leaves them more closely related to that supernatural system of forces than to the impersonal, prosaic ones. Let us look at these connections.

First of all, there is one of *common moral interest*. Both the gods or spiritual forces and the dead have considerable common cause in maintaining the traditional morals, particularly those of the familial group. This is not so completely true of the living members, who may also be motivated in this direction to the extent that they are adequately socialized, but whose own physiological, intensely individual, or immediate

drives precipitate conflict with those *mores* from time to time. The dead
and the spiritual forces may have passions of their own, if they are conceived anthropomorphically, but it is the passions and the moral actions
*of the living* which they are interested in directing. Morality being, in
all cultures, something which one is somewhat more interested in forcing
on others than on oneself, there is again a break between the gods and
the dead on the one hand, and the living on the other. Besides this link
between the dead and the sacred, there is another in their common motivation *toward helping the group*. No society believes in spiritual powers
which are even for the most part inimical. Although these forces are
sometimes whimsical, mischievous, or even vengeful (for contravention
of the *mores*) in the main their explicit task consists in helping the
society with regard to food, fecundity, and health, as well as in more
purely spiritual affairs.

A further relationship between the dead, the living and the sacredness of the mortuary ritual may be seen in the fact that the individual
*comes from the dead*. This is true, of course, for any society, with or without an ancestral cult. More to home, the individual comes from the
ancestors of the immediate family, for they are his ancestors, usually
physiologically and always sociologically. Thus there is always a link
with the dead, even the unknown dead. This is true for the dead whom
one did know, for the links are based on both kinship and *Gemeinschaft*.
Moreover, *everyone returns ultimately to the dead*. This does not exhaust,
however, the possibilities of relations or occasions of respect, especially
when clan solidarity insists so much on the unity of the living and the
dead. *It is the dead who are great*. This is true from the rational point
of view that numerically there will always be a larger number of great
men in the past than at any given time in the present. But, more important, it is the judgment of the only members in the tribe who have
seen both the old and the new, who have a rational advantage in maintaining this point of view, and who usually are in a dominant enough
position to impose it on the rest: the old, generally the old men. Furthermore, the *dead are the personnel of the sacred myths, legends, and sacred
beliefs*. In any society, the past great are respected, by definition, and to
the extent that the society singles out members of past generations to
whom tribute is to be paid. When this body of legend and sacred myths
and beliefs is symbolized in a sacred well, as in the case of the Murngin,
the possible implications are many and clear. All that is great and glorious
in the past of the family or clan is collected there, and it then must follow that all of value in the present had to issue from that source. Whether
symbolized as a sacred well or not, any society will at least implicitly

recognize this circular process, in which all come from the ancestors and all become ancestors in turn. These general points may perhaps be clarified further by treating these societies in somewhat greater detail.

# DAHOMEY

The Dahomey attach great social importance to the marriage of its members, suggesting a fruitful approach to the study of family and religion. The fact that the Dahomey family includes both the living and the dead would imply that anyone entering or leaving the family by marriage must also obtain the approval of the ancestral spirits. Actually, a number of the steps in the marriage process are marked by questions asked of both Fate and the ancestors. Further, the sib head, who is the oldest living family member and the closest to the spirits, plays a significant role. Also, gifts are made to both the living and dead family members, showing respect to the gods. And, of course, this knowledge becomes part of the content of the socialization process.

These facts may be seen more clearly by noting briefly the more important steps which the prospective couple goes through in order to enter the main type of married state, the *akwenusi*.[15] The father of a daughter ready for marriage consults his Fate in order to determine which of a list of prospective sons-in-law is acceptable. Thus, even before the future son-in-law knows officially of a possible marriage, the supernatural world has been consulted. When the man is approached, he is not supposed to refuse, but he will consult his own diviner to ascertain the will of his Fate, or Destiny. If both men's Fates agree, the prospective husband brings gifts to the family of his proposed bride, accompanied by older women and men of his family. He also begins to donate various services and presents to the family of his betrothed, such as firewood, planting, and other field work.[16] He keeps account of the value given, since he will demand an equivalent in return if the marriage arrangements are not completed.

When the girl's family consider that the formal requirements have been adequately fulfilled, the man asks that the woman be sent to him. It is then that the sib head of the girl's family orders the ceremony. The man brings the sib head[17] a number of presents, cloths, caury shells, salt and a goat. The sib ancestral spirits are thus informed of the marriage. The following night two men and two women, selected by the man's sib head, carry a basket of presents from the man's home to his father-in-law. After the formality of looking for the bride is observed, the girl's betrothed comes to spread out the gifts, which are matched by the girl's belongings and gifts to the girl from her family. It is at this time that one of the important older women of the girl's sib, an *akɔvi*, calls upon the ancestors to bless the girl.

Although these points of connection between the supernatural world and the various steps in the formalities of getting married are important, other religious observances must be noted.[18] The most important are performed by the girl's father. Two days before the marriage ceremony itself, he offers food to the tɔhwiyo (sib founder), as also to the deified ancestors themselves. The pantheon gods which the girl worships also receive a food offering at the time.[19] The setting of the marriage date, though apparently determined by the sib head, was first discovered by consulting Fate. On this occasion, as usual, Lɛgba receives a portion.[20] When the girl goes to her husband, Lɛgba receives an offering especially for himself.

In addition, the woman herself may be a member of a cult group, in which case she must consult her own deity, as also her own Destiny. She thus discovers whether her shrine, in the house of her father, may be transported. To insure that the ancestors of both the man and the woman learn of the match, ". . . all the offerings to the spirit of the founder of the girl's sib must have remained for two days in the house of worship dedicated to that spirit, and these same offerings must also have been left for a time in the shrine of the ancestral spirits of the bridegroom's sib . . ."[21]

The first night at her husband's house the woman spends with women belonging to his house, after she has been given a dish of beans to eat.[22] She does not sleep with her husband until the second night, at which time the mothers of both are present. The following morning, after the marriage mat has been sent to her father, the woman is given her new name. This is the occasion for gifts to the man from his society, as well as dancing and feasting.[23]

Other marriages in which the father retains control over the children are different from this mainly in that there are different approaches to the union: the man may make the request of the woman's father; there may be a previous elopement, which is then "legitimized"; eligible girls of two families may be exchanged; and so on. These types do not, however, ignore the religious ceremonies, even though some of the services owed by the husband to his father-in-law and mother-in-law may not be performed. Since marriage in Dahomey involves heavy financial obligations, sib pressure, usually through the ancestors, is sometimes brought to bear to push the couple into a formally acceptable relationship. This relationship to the sib ancestors is important after the marriage, in enforcing social requirements in certain crucial situations. One case concerns the prized character of children in this culture. Although it would seem that barrenness or impotence would be ridiculed, actually neither a man nor a woman is taunted for such a reason. It is felt that the sib ancestors would avenge this indiscretion by making the ridiculing one either barren or impotent.[24] The other side of this situation is observed when a girl states that a given man is the father of her child or the cause of her first pregnancy. His ancestors will punish him by sterility if he denies this charge, even though he knows the accusation to be false.

Since the main forms of marriage are approved, or finally become approved, by the ancestors of both the parties, divorce finds them likewise interested. Just as a man must not refuse a woman offered to him divorce must be demanded by the woman, at least openly. His own sib ancestors, not those of his wife, will wreak vengeance upon him if he disobeys his injunction.[25] Consequently, he must make the marriage relationship impossible for the wife to endure. This may be done by obvious ways of persecution. However, the more serious methods involve lack of respect to the woman's relatives, and in particular to her ancestors. Perhaps the most serious is failure to take a proper role in the funeral ceremonies for his mother-in-law or father-in-law, or in the annual sib ceremonies for his wife's ancestors.[26] That is, he must maintain a proper attitude in public toward his wife and her sib, because he is watched by the ancestral spirits.[27]

Up to this point attention has been paid only to the couple marrying and the manner in which the supernatural world impinges on their relationship. However, it must be remembered that the marital relationship is socially significant also in that it produces new members of the society. This process is a slow one, embodying constantly changing patterns with respect to both the larger society and the family itself. The child, in a sense, "grows into" this larger society, finally establishing a family of his own. Even though Dahomey society does not set up sharp gradations throughout this series of changes, it cannot entirely ignore them any more than the religious system itself can do so. Consequently, as the individual gradually assumes different familial and social roles, his position in the religious sphere also changes.

This is most clearly seen in the Dahomean conception of old age, as opposed to youth, i.e., the two extremes of the individual and familial cycle. The kinship system of Dahomey pays great respect to age, a fact which is paralleled in the religious structure. The oldest male member of a sib is the sib head, and is also the one who mediates between the living and the ancestors, as has been noted before. The oldest ancestors are the most powerful among the Dahomean family deities. Similarly, the old women of the sib are extremely powerful.

This respect paid to the aged does not mean, however, that no attention is paid to the development of the child. Even before conception this interest is shown by the desire of the Dahomean to have children. As would be expected, failure to bear children is met by consulting supernatural powers and the use of charms.[28] Similarly, supernatural precautions are observed during the growth of the fetus, to avoid mishaps, as well as at birth.[29] Even before the child is born, the supernatural world is consulted, for the diviner is asked to ascertain which deities must be propitiated to ensure a safe birth.[30] If, when the child is born, it is deformed or is physically misshapen in some way, the supernatural world is again consulted to determine whether it is to be kept. Such a child is actually not born to the family in the social sense until the priests of the abnormally born have discovered from Fate what should be done with it.

The naming of a Dahomean child is of great significance, since knowledge of a man's name can be used to harm him, and since these names are related to different deities.[31] Actually, a *series* of names is acquired by the individual. He obtains a very secret name from his mother, as well as a name from the mother's deity (assuming that she has such a deity), and one from his father's deity (under the same assumption). This is aside from names which are derived from the particular circumstances of the individual's birth (born after twins, or of prolonged pregnancy, and others). If neither parent is a cult initiate, the child derives his name from the Fa of his father. Related to this is the determination of the name of the child's *djɔtɔ*, or guardian spirit,[32] a question which is asked of the supernatural world by the diviner when the child has attained the age of five months. Another name is added to this series when a young man has reached the age of eighteen or twenty years. A parallel name is given to a young girl when she marries, the name being given to her by her husband. When the individual later becomes an initiate into a cult an additional name is acquired.

The first social recognition given the infant after the first naming occurs at a "little ceremony" which seems to have the function of introducing the child as a member of the family. This occurs five days after birth. Raffia bands are placed about several parts of the body, and the child is carried as far as the threshold. A hen and cock are sacrificed, the blood and bones being placed in a hole in front of the door. There are festivities, such as singing and dancing, to mark the occasion. No such ceremony occurs when the child finally ventures from the house.

A minor ceremony intervenes at the age of three months, which does not appear to have religious significance. Five months after birth, as has been noted before, the ceremony of determining the child's *djɔtɔ* occurs.[33]

Although the child thus can learn the name of his "guardian spirit" at an early age, his Destiny or Fa is not unveiled to him until he is ten to twelve years of age.[34] And even this is only his partial Fa. Except for the rare cases when a woman becomes a compound head, a woman never obtains more than a partial Fa.[35] In order to obtain his partial Fate, the boy takes palm oil, beans, and seven chickens to the diviner, who has eighteen palm kernels for this purpose. The diviner gives food to the boy's Fate. After a period which is thought of as five days, the boy returns to the diviner. He handles the palm kernels as is done when querying Destiny, and the resulting pattern of marks tells the diviner which Fa the boy has. This characteristic pattern is taught to the boy, as well as food and place taboos. The kernels themselves are given to the boy, as well as a chicken for his own Lɛgba.[36] With the kernels and his Lɛgba pot outside his compound, the boy now has his partial Fate.

A few years later the Dahomean boy and girl undergo another recognition of their changing roles with respect to marriage, although apparently no religious ceremony is related to it. These are the ceremonies of circumcision and cicatrization.[37] Individuals who will not permit these operations are laughed at.[38] Nevertheless, the cuts on the girl are made shortly after menstruation, and the date is set by a diviner.[39] Offerings are made to Lɛgba and to the god of iron, to prevent any evil flowing from the operation. The entire series of such cuts may take place over a period of a year.

The case of circumcision has changed somewhat by the contact of Dahomey with European medical technique. Instead of circumcising between seventeen and nineteen years of age, many Dahomeans have their sons circumcised in the hospital shortly after birth. Further, when this is the case, no offering is made.[40] When circumcision is delayed until early or late adolescence, the occasion does exhibit some ceremony, although the purpose is still hygienic, it is claimed.[41] In any event, after circumcision and the subsequent intercourse with a post-climacteric widow, the youth may marry.[42]

However, even though a young man has been circumcised, this does not mean that he has attained his full Fa, or Fate. As a matter of fact, even though this ritual is a highly important sacred event it does not occur at any fixed point in a man's life. The ritual is instead performed after the man has had a run of bad luck, when he may be told by his diviner that his Fate is the root of the trouble. It is through this ceremony that he obtains the earthly counterpart of his fourth soul (sɛkpɔli).[43]

In obtaining his full Fate, as in obtaining his partial Fate, the man takes offerings to his diviner. These include sixteen chickens, six goats, a hoe, much strong liquor, and a sack of raffia.[44] The two go to a special place which the particular diviner uses for Fa ceremonies. When the night of rituals and offerings is over, the man has received his *sɛkpɔli*, in the form of a replica on earth. This is the sand bearing the marks of the palm kernels thrown to reveal the man's complete Fate. This is also sewn into white cotton cloth, and the man also obtains the other equipment of Fa, palm kernels, white clay or meal, and the carved horn-like objects used to call Fa. A man will always consult his Fate at any important juncture, and will sacrifice to it several times a year. This is an occasion for dancing and the distribution of gifts to the diviners.

Through Fa, as well as through the worship of the ancestors and the Great Gods, the Dahomean maintains contact with the sacred world during his lifetime as he shifts his kinship status from infant to adult. Nevertheless, as he approaches death, he changes his relationship to his family again by his increasing nearness to the gods. This has been seen in the intensified respect paid by the family to the aged, whether man or woman. In their closer contact with the family and sib ancestors is seen a reflection of the fact that the aged of the family will soon also become ancestors, finally to be deified. This final stage in the relationship of an individual to his family begins when he or she dies, and sacred ceremonies are performed by the family for the deceased family member.

Death in Dahomey is the occasion for perhaps the most elaborate of all Dahomean rituals. This is, of course, true of the death of royalty, but it is also true to a somewhat lesser extent for others. A number of important facts may be brought out at this point. One is that, aside from personal power, a man with a large family will receive a very elaborate funeral, for his many relatives by blood and marriage will all take part, bringing many gifts. On the other hand, a child, who can hardly be said to have begun participation in family life, ". . . has practically no funeral at all."[45] As the individual approaches the age of marriage, the funeral becomes more elaborate.

This relationship is also seen in the belief that one who is powerful and rich in life will also enjoy these privileges after death. One's family helps attain these privileges after death by furnishing a good funeral at death. A good funeral is more than a recognition of importance; it is also a means of continuing this importance into the next world.

The ceremonies also represent an affirmation of the familial and sib connections of the individual. It is necessary to prevent the loss of any soul, a loss which could be caused by evil magic during the individual's life or at death, or by failing to recognize him or her at or after death. This requirement holds for those who die away from Dahomey, or by suicide, or in circumstances considered abnormal by the Dahomean.[46] When the dead are "established," or finally deified, the unknown dead are included as well as the dead who did not die normally or in Dahomey. Further, in all cases of persons who die abnormally or away from Dahomey, a final funeral is given before three years have elapsed, even though at the time of death no elaborate ceremony is offered.[47] A normal funeral does not permit such a delay. All souls of the family and sib must be kept, in order for new members to be born, and the funeral insures permanent existence for the soul.

The "conspicuous consumption" of the funeral ceremonies, by which the lavish display of wealth and the giving of valuables emphasize the importance of the family position, brings out the relationship of the relatives by marriage. This was noted briefly in discussing the duties of the son-in-law toward the wife's relatives when death occurs. For messengers are sent to the sons-in-law, informing them of the death, whereupon they are expected to send their wives back to the family. The unity of the family is thus reasserted at death, against the ties of marriage itself. Further, the sons-in-law themselves must come, bringing many gifts, and prepared to furnish a band for certain phases of the ritual. This separation of husband and wife continues until the mourning period is over, after the definitive burial, a process which may take several months.

Thus the individual Dahomean remains under the care of his gods constantly as he begins his journey through the various familial relationships from birth until death and his final assumption of a place among the ancestors. The deities, either directly or through his Fate, inform him of their objections to his acts, and also tell him what he must do to avoid serious retribution. The various steps in his changes of status are marked by various rituals and many deviations from accepted behavior will be punished by these interested forces. The sacred ancestors and gods who took part in familial relationships either on this earth or in their supernatural abode continue to direct attention toward lives of their worshippers. These patterns may now be noted as they appear under different forms in a Melanesian society, the Manus.

# MANUS

The Manus Sir Ghost maintains his interest in his family and his family relationships, and in addition engages in such relationships on the ghostly plane. Marriages, births, family quarrels, and other phenomena of daily family living are to be found in his life.[48] His interest in the affairs of mortals on the earthly sphere causes him to take a hand in their direction at various points. His concern with sexual sin in its various manifestations, as well as in the economic exchanges which are a part of the ramifications of Manus kinship, indicates the necessarily detailed character of that direction. His desire to uphold the ways of propriety and virtue suggest the type of influence to be expected.

The relationship between Sir Ghost and the ward is a close parallel to that between father and son.[49] Sir Ghost is unrelenting in his punishment for sin, just as the father is. However, like the father, he is expected to gratify the wishes of the ward. The child, like the ward, is often ill-tempered toward the father who does not gratify whims, and the relationship of respect is momentarily lessened somewhat. Father and Sir Ghost are not omniscient, but do know more about important facts, especially derelictions, than the dependent. Father and Sir Ghost are supposed to insure the prosperity which will allow marriages, exchanges, a new house, and so on. Further, Sir Ghost inevitably fails in his obligations to his ward, just as the father does, for the high death rate insures that most Manus men die before reaching old age.[50]

Similarly, the subordinate position of the woman is reflected in the Sir Ghost system, since it is the dead male who takes over these functions, not the female. "It is a patrilineal cult widely removed from all matrilineal sentiment."[51] It is the adult male who stands in the ward-Sir Ghost relationship, not the female. She is rather expected to be living under the protection of her husband or elder male relative and his Sir Ghost. When a woman or a child dies in spite of the pleas of the family to Sir Ghost, asking that he help the ill person, usually no skull is thrown out or destroyed.[52] Sir Ghost may, however, be scolded for remissness.

The Manus kinship system does not bring theory and practice closely together, for there are many points at which the ideal pattern of relationship is not followed.[53] However, within the practicing kinship relationships there are many definitions in ceremonial terms. That is, the various kinship positions carry with them definite obligations of a ceremonial sort, aside from the obvious and broad ones falling to the lot of the family head as keeper of Sir Ghost. Some of these may be mentioned briefly to indicate the close connection between ceremonial functions and kinship in Manus: (1) The mother's brother names the child, pierces ears, catches the fish for his sister's daughter when she goes through the segregation for first menstruation, and keeps those weapons which have shed the blood of sister's child. (2) Father's mother, father's sisters, and father's sisters' daughters ceremonially invoke the double line of male and female ghosts at various ritual occasions such as release from first menstruation segregation; war blessing; premarriage segregation for girl; on a woman after the birth of a child; a widow at the end of mourning; or a ghost immediately after death. (3) Father's sister's son performs a similar invocation in order to release his male cross-cousin from mourning. (4) Child of male line of the mother of the dead has the ritual obligation of tearing down the house of the recently dead person (his father's sister's son). (5) The paternal grandfather ceremonially blesses his son's son, formerly as a preparation for war, but now rather for prosperity.[54] Other minor rites are performed by other kin. The invocation of the ancestral ghosts by children-of-sister in favor of children-of-brother is called magical in character by Fortune.[55] However, it is open and public in favor of a known group and for ends which are accepted by the kin group and the society, and occurs at explicitly recognized life crises. Their designation as "magical" is modified somewhat by Fortune later, by his stating that "The religious forms connected with life crises are thus semi-magical in their nature."[50] The ghosts are expected to respond more or less automatically, but the other elements of magical action are lacking, so that this ceremonial function is semireligious in character. Indeed, these are situations "where the ghosts are used aberrantly."[57] That is, there are evident signs of relationship with the religious cult of ghosts, according to Fortune, and apparently the religious forms ordinarily presented in a different spirit are handled aberrantly, i.e., somewhat like magic.

It has already been made evident how Sir Ghost acts to enforce conformity with ideal behavior within the family. The morality of everyone within the family is his concern, as well as that of anyone who visits the house in which his skull rests. In addition to activity which is specifically sin, other types of familial action, such as preparing for marriage or puberty exchanges, arranging for marriages, celebrations of a long and prosperous marriage, and so forth, are part of his concern. Even a child's sex play, Mead suggests, is curbed by the fear of spirit rage.[58] Sir Ghost is quick to punish transgressions both before and after puberty and marriage, emphasizing his power in the socialization process.

An interesting relationship occurs between Sir Ghost, conformity, and the practice of magic, when a widow remarries. That religious activity sometimes ramifies into magical practices has already been made evident. This happens in the case of widow remarriage because of inconsistencies in the Manus attitudes concerning such behavior. In ordinary sexual matters there is a single standard of morality for both men and women in Manus. Transgression is equally punished by Sir Ghost, no matter what the sex of the violator. When a husband dies, he is expected to punish severely any attempt on the part of his living wife to remarry, the punishment falling on the man as well as the woman. However, when a wife dies, her ghost is not nearly so powerful as the male ghost, and as a result widowers who remarry do so without much fear that the ghost of their dead wives will harm them. There is also an economic aspect to this situation, since women are expected to work for their dead husband's heirs or financiers. Also, the children will be left motherless, since they are expected to stay with the patrilineal gens.

Nevertheless, widows and widowers do marry. As an adult, and more independent than a young man entering marriage for the first time, the widower is better able to arrange a marriage. On the other hand, the practice of child betrothal makes it difficult for the widower to select a wife from the young girls, so that widower and widow are likely to come together in a new marriage. ". . . Widow remarriage is not effectually prevented by former husband's ghostly revenges or by public opinion."[59] The remarriage of widows is usual, differing in this respect from sexual transgression or economic failure. That is, the disapproval does not succeed in enforcing conformity.

The pressure to remarry, with the difference in standards for the two sexes, act together with still another element in this magico-religious situation, the lack of any basic moral intensity on the part of the society against remarriage. In spite of the upsetting nature of such marriages or elopements, "public opinion is . . . decidedly nonmoral about widow remarriage."[60] In short, the religious system is *not a strong support for conformity* here, precisely because the value structure of the society is not strongly opposed to this type of behavior. There is fear that ghostly wrath will hurt members of the family, and indignation at abandonment of the children, or of the economic obligations to heirs, but no clearly defined attitude that this action is sinful can be said to be prevalent. Nevertheless, the husband's ghost is indignant, just as the wife's ghost may be. As a consequence, two patterns of what seems to be magical action enter at this point. In order to prevent the husband's ghost from wreaking vengeance upon the couple, magic is used. Charmed ginger may be put between the teeth of the skull, effectively rendering the ghost impotent. It is to be noted that in this connection it is *ghost,* and not *Sir Ghost,* who is acting, since the situation is not clearly defined as a moral one. The magic may be performed secretly, or with the approval of ward. As against this situation, another possible magical pattern may be found, since ward may actually attempt to incite his own Sir Ghost to punish either the remarrying widow or friends who help her.[61] Sir Ghost acting in this capacity is not *Sir Ghost* any longer, or a sacred force to be respected, but is *ghost.* This is, as Fortune points out, the "borderline of magic."[62] That is, where the code to be followed is no longer clear, and there is room for conflicting interests to express themselves, Sir Ghost and malicious ghostly forces lose their religious character, and magical manipulation becomes possible.

In view of the intensely emotional attitude toward sexual offenses in Manus, the element of cross-cousin jesting and obscenity takes significance as a problem in familial conformity. In the ordinary relationship between Manus spouses there is little or no sex play or easy familiarity. Romantic elements and caresses are not considered necessary or desirable. However, for the Manus there is an emotional outlet for any deprivation this structural situation may cause. With one's cross-cousin of the opposite sex a jesting relationship holds, and suggestive badinage is in order. The man may accuse the woman of sexual transgressions, play roughly with her body, or even hold her breasts.[63] Nevertheless, conformity is demanded in this pattern as well, for not only must this activity be always public, but Sir Ghost takes an interest in it. If the play becomes too obscene, or ventures too far toward intimacy, it is expected that Sir Ghost will cause illness to be visited on the parties concerned.

An important support for conformity in the relationship between the family and the Sir Ghost pattern must not be overlooked. To a considerable extent the entire set of kin of a transgressor is responsible for the acts of the transgressor. The Sir Ghost wrath may not always be directed toward the violator himself, but toward any member of his close kin. This tends to force all members of the kin grouping to be actively interested in the conformity of others. A practical consequence of this is that even the closest of confidants, cross-cousins, succumb to the dread of Sir Ghostly anger, and betray the secrets which the familial structure permits only between these two.[64]

Since it is through the death of a kinsman that the ward-Sir Ghost relationship is created, the connection between various kin is emphasized at death. The man who is to be ward to the newly created Sir Ghost is part of a large group of mourners, and places many strings of native currency on the body, so that Sir Ghost may purchase a wife in the spirit world.[65] The manifest function of this, of course, is to direct Sir Ghost's interest toward the supernatural sphere, so that he will not long too much for the mortals left behind, and thus drag them after him. It is no longer necessary to kill or kidnap a man for ransom in order to end the mourning period, and now a large turtle will suffice.[66] Recovery of the skull and other bones is achieved by exposing the corpse on neighboring islets until they have been washed clean. The connection between mortal and supernatural kin is further severed by a magical exorcism at the final disposal of the body.[67] The chief mourners are the *pin papu*, i.e., the father's father's sisters and their female descendants. Once they were supposed to sleep with the corpse for twenty days, washing it each day. Now the period is three days.[68] They also bury the corpse, or place it on an islet. The father's mother, father's sisters and the daughters of the latter also play a part in these rites, including the ritual appeal to the double line of male and female ancestral ghost, for the Sir Ghost immediately after death, and for the widow at the end of her mourning period.[69] The important economic aspect of this death is the requirement that a funerary feast be furnished Sir Ghost by his ward, a requirement which is supported on the religious side by Sir Ghostly anger. This anger will be expressed in the usual fashion, by sending illness to the kin of Sir Ghost.[70]

Considering the almost filial-paternal relationship holding between ward and Sir Ghost, the close relationship between the family structure in Manus and the religious activity is to be expected. The ritual simplicity of the religious pattern means that the many different types of relationships to be found in Dahomey are not evident here, but the broad character of the rules enforces a pervasiveness of connection which is as complete as in any society. This is particularly true with respect to conformity with familial rules regarding sexual matters and the economic obligations of kinship, which were discussed in the earlier section on Manus economic action. The primary character which sexual transgression assumes for the Manus in both familial and religious spheres requires a considerable amount of interconnection between the two, a relationship which extends in some cases to action bordering on the magical when there is a lack of clarity as to the proper behavior. The obligations of kinship are also emphasized at the death of the mortal who becomes Sir Ghost, the supernatural force which will in turn protect the kin left behind. This apparent simplicity of religious structure is not to be found in Tikopia, so that the relationships between familial and religious activity are not nearly so explicit, and are at the same time somewhat more varied.

# 10. FAMILY AND RELIGION
## (Continued)

## TIKOPIA

THE GREAT INTEREST which Polynesian societies have in family descent, together with an insistence on inherited differences in ritual rank, would suggest how intimately the family structure and activities must relate to the religious in Tikopia. Since those who are by far the most important in the religious system are so defined by their place in the wider kin system, one would expect to find many interrelationships on the detailed level which would buttress this major connection.

The interest in kinship among the Tikopia is borne out by their conception of the individual family, made up of parents and children, as being part of an unbroken line of patrilineal descent. Each such family is one element in a larger group, the *paito*, or "house." The other families which make up this group are also parts of this unbroken line, which traces back to a common male ancestor, always through male ancestors. We have noted before how the sacred prerogatives and duties have been passed along this line of descent, the male headship also functioning as religious officiant. The patrilineal descent principle is strictly enforced, and when there is no obvious heir, such as the son of a chief, the house "explores the collaterals to the utmost to find an heir to a chief or elder, while all the time the immediate sister's son is never considered."[1] This consciousness of the long line of descent and inheritance is emphasized in the religious relationship by the fact that the original dwelling of the common ancestor is usually continued as a temple for the rituals to the gods and ancestors.

The "houses" of Tikopia are separated from one another on the basis of their different relationships to ritual obligations and rights handed down from their ancestors, just as they are connected with one another by the common character of this descent. The chiefly and commoner families are not primarily distinguished on the basis of their wealth, but

200

on the basis of ritual division. The commoner families in turn are divided
into those which have a ritual elder as head, and those which do not.
However, the man who serves as elder, whether he be a ritual elder or
not, will serve as the "channel of communication with the gods and
ancestors."[2] And in this case, the choice is made on the basis of seniority
of descent, not mere age. In the direction of the larger aggregations, the
various houses are bound to one of the four *kiananga*, or kin groupings,
and here also membership is patrilineal, with the headship falling to the
ritually senior chief. These four chiefs are, in turn, kinsfolk.

Although the position of chief or ritual elder is not the only possible
approach to understanding the Tikopia family, the position of chief, and
the religious and familial relationships involved in the latter position,
clarify those of the former. The relationship of the chief to the food
supply of the society has already been discussed, since the chief's status
as clan or society head defines his relationship to the gods and their gifts
of yam, coconut, taro, and breadfruit. This ritual position is indicated
further by the restrictions on ordinary people, who are not permitted to
take an officiating role in the ceremonies such as those at Somosomo.[3]
Analogously, it is the male head of the individual family who officiates at
lesser ceremonials within the home, such as a libation. Just as the chief
takes the center of ritual attention, and is on close terms with the sacred,
so it is the household head who sits on the "sacred" side of the house,
and is the focus of such matters as ritual exchange. The respect for those
in authority within the family is carried so far that the personal names
of both father and mother are not to be spoken by the children.[4] Here,
the prohibition is most emphasized in the case of the father's name, to
such an extent that an individual will declare that he simply does not
know the name. This avoidance is not merely verbal, however. Children
may not, for example, touch the head of their father, even though his
own brother or mother's brother may do so. The distinction between this
respect for the father and that for the chiefly father is indicated by the
fact that the commoner father may ask his son to delouse his hair, while
the chiefly *tapu* prohibits such a service at any time.[5] This type of respect
includes the father's personal articles as well, and is particularly strict in
the case of the chiefly father, though in these cases the tapus are relaxed
after the death of the father. The rules are not so strict, moreover, in the
case of the mother, and they tend to become reversed with respect to the
eldest son as he becomes older, thus emphasizing the ritual and familial
importance of male status.

The ritual and familial importance of the adult male is defined, naturally, in a negative fashion as well. The female correspondingly occu-

pies a somewhat lower position. This lower position is reflected in the religious observances at many points. For example, the sacred adzes ". . . are kept on a special shelf at the site of the temple and are handled by no one but the chief and then only on ceremonial occasions. The women and children may not even see them."[6] It is true, of course, that there is a particular female deity who is the patroness of the women, and at certain points in the ceremonies the women do play a part. However, even at these points their function is more usually that of preparing food, tending the ovens, plaiting the mats, and such work.[7] Attendance at the Kava is rare, except in the case of the women of Kafika. The central role in the dancing at Uta is taken by the men. When the circular post of Resiake temple is washed, no commoner or woman may touch it, since this is a sacred point in the temple.[8]

Mention has already been made of the sacred character of turmeric making. The status of women is interestingly sidelighted in this connection by the fact that the last batch of turmeric is considered the least valuable, just as the first batch is the most valuable. It is thus the last batch which is considered to be related to the women. The first batch is usually kept as property for years, while that "of the women" apparently forms part of the ordinary domestic supply. Even with reference to the actual production of the substance, women may not take part until the batch belonging to the chief of all the Tikopia has been filtered and baked.

This sex differentiation is begun at an early age. The role which the male plays in rituals is based on years of association with rituals as observer, while the female very often is not even an observer. Boys are admitted to religious ceremonies at the very earliest ages, even though it is understood that they will not understand them, and of course may even create a minor disturbance by their ignorance of what conformity is. On the other hand, a girl will in all likelihood be told to move away from such a ceremony, even though she is not punished severely.[9] However, in spite of the fact that this difference in sexual status is tied closely to the greater ritual importance of the male in Tikopia, it must be made clear that his authority is not all-powerful, nor is he sacred in any deep sense. Though great respect is paid to him, there is also a considerable amount of affection between him and his wife and their children. Relations within the family are rather informal. "Mutual deference is the norm aimed at."[10] Although the husband may scold the wife in certain situations, and does, the wife may also scold the husband, and may even offer physical violence to him at times. A case of this might be when she is very jealous because of his infidelity. Each spouse may give orders within the family, and it is expected that they will be obeyed. Neither is a drudge, since both work together in the fields, and both have household work of some kind. The man, for example, will weave the nets for the household, cut the trees for making bark-cloth, as well as make repairs on the house.

Similarly, although the children show great respect for their parents, it must not be believed that the children stand in deep awe of their parents. The many tapus associated with respect for parents do not prevent a great amount of affection between children and parents. Naturally, as is to be expected, this affection mitigates considerable the *tapu* character of the parent. As a consequence, in many situations, the child will disobey the parents or stubbornly insist on privileges which are not his, or (more rarely), even strike the parent. As a matter of fact, the society recognizes that there will be so much affection within the family that it makes specific efforts to wean the child from the immediate family into the larger group.[11] Adults will speak lovingly to the child, telling him not to cry for his parents but to call for them, the others, and to remember them instead. Similarly, the relationships between male siblings are marked more by non-religious elements than ritual ones. In a type of society preferring harmony and affection, and without the strict notions of sex common among the Manus, one would expect that siblings would be on rather free terms with one another. The elder children are often in charge of the rearing of the younger ones, giving them orders and instructing them with regard to etiquette as well as matters of *tapu* and techniques for various activities and play. Girls rather than boys tend to act as mentors of the young.[12]

Nevertheless, even in these close relationships, some elements of minor religious importance are to be seen. One obvious point is that the eldest son stands in a different relationship to his parents and to the rest of the children, by virtue of his inheritance of ritual position. He will become the focus of ritual activities in his own family and if he is the eldest son of an elder, or chief, he will of course grow into a great number of religious relationships which are not open to the other siblings. Since he is the future ritual head, members of the family or close relatives who possess ritual knowledge may spend considerable time with him, instructing him in his religious duties. Naturally, the most secret or sacred and less known information about ceremonies and ritual will be transmitted to him by his father. As the eldest son grows older, his relationships with the other siblings must change because of the increased respect which must be paid to him, and increased power which accrues to him. He may even take over the leadership of his house upon his father's death, assuming the family name borne by the occupier of the ancestral house.[13] In this case the younger members of the family would remain until they had married.

The sisters of the father have somewhat the same functions as other classificatory mothers. That is to say, they substitute for the mother in teaching, protecting, feeding, etc. Thus their functions are parallel to those assumed by classificatory fathers in Tikopia. The relations, however, are different in the direction of *tapu* and ritual, whatever the informal relationships may be which involve love, warmth, affection, etc. One may curse most of one's blood kin in Tikopia. This is not true for the father's sister. One may not strike her, curse her, or utter indecent words in her presence. This would be a wrong, one punishable by the family ancestors.[14] Like the father, she personifies authority over family property and may possess religious knowledge. If a man of rank believes that he will die while his son is still young, he may pass on his ritual knowledge to his sister. She must not pass this knowledge on to her own son but must see that her brother's eldest child receives this information at a proper time. It is to be expected, of course, that this situation would occur only in families of rank.

Emphasis in Tikopia ritual is on the relatives through the male line. This does not mean, however, that the family of one's mother has little importance. Assistance may be obtained from this line for ritual and practical demands when the individual grows into maturity. Many formal gifts are made between the two lines. Further, it is the mother's relatives who bury the individual and it is her ancestors who take charge of one's soul. They see that it arrives at its appropriate heaven after having been purified. In addition, if an individual is a man of rank, the gods of one's mother's family may be ritually appealed to in times of need, for aid while living. The mother's brother also plays an important ritual role as the child becomes an adult. The rite of superincision before reaching manhood places the mother's brother in a central position. It is he who supports the youngster both physically and morally during the operation, and he also makes many formal gifts at this time to celebrate the change of status. Similarly, the first time that the individual takes part in the sacred dances at Marae, it is the mother's brother (or brothers) who must take care of the novice and guide him through the dance, shielding him from the crowd by standing in front of him. He holds up the youngster's arms in this process and prevents him from being ashamed because of his ignorance or shyness.[15]

The process of socialization also takes account of these ritual, religious associations between the family and the sacred observances. Note has already been taken of the fact that elder siblings attempt to inculcate proper conduct, decorum, and respect for sacred things and various *tapus* in the younger siblings. Other adults will also take part in the socialization process. As the child stands up and wanders about in, say, the dwelling house of the Ariki Kafika, someone will grab him and point out that the house is sacred, and that he must sit down. Similarly, the child must stand away from the sacred side of the house and is constantly reminded of the *tapu* character of personal possessions of his father as well as the sacred character of many articles in the household. Although violent physical punishment is not generally used, the child will be shaken or given a sharp blow to emphasize the verbal instruction. The good-natured tolerance of this is seen in the fact that the adult generally "behaves to a child as one free spirit to another, and gives an order to another adult in just as peremptory a fashion. Indifference to commands is common to children and persists in adult years."[16]

As has been noted before, a grandfather may spend considerable time in this socialization process, informing the child of events in the society's past, origins of things and the land, the doings of the gods, etc. Even though the more esoteric information is passed on by the father, when through some accident the father fails to pass along the information, very likely some of this gap will be filled by a father's brother or father's sister. Children may not turn their back on the ritual elders or men of rank, and instruction of this nature in a specific situation may be given by anyone present. Such people will, of course, generally be relatives. These instructions are repeated continually. The *tapu* character of temples, certain canoes, certain house posts or spears, as well as particular people, is impressed upon the child on many occasions. The respect for the parent is impressed upon the child at a very early age. In fact, there is a ritual formula which is recited over the child very shortly after birth, in which the duty of providing food for the parent in his or her old age is expressed. Likewise, the ritual mourning of the dead parent is a duty imposed upon the child. Since the formalized exchanges and gifts which are made at the time of a parent's death constitute a great drain on the economic resources of any family, children who live with their parents must acquire and maintain a large supply of bark-cloth and pandanus mats for the occasion of a parent's death. Even outsiders may express to the young people their disapproval of any such lack of filial piety.[17]

Although there are ritual elements in the initiation ceremony of superincision, it must be kept in mind that this is not overtly religious in character.[18] The initiates are not instructed in the myth lying back of the ceremony. It is permitted to use a razor blade in the actual cutting process.

The wailing and weeping on the day of the operation are apparently formal, and the songs are not sacred in character, one of them even having two words of English in it. Calling the Tikopia initiation ritual "atypical," Firth adds, "There is no secrecy about its methods, no seclusion of the initiates, few or no food taboos to observe, and those which exist refer to comparatively unimportant substances, no expressed tests of manhood and indeed a positive attempt at mitigation of physical pain, no instruction of a moral order."[19] Yet entirely aside from the implied or symbolically ritual significance in the name of the ceremony as relating to death or injury ceremonies, in the food *tapus* with their connection with ritual obedience, with the historical and magical significance of the origin of the ceremony from the Tafua clan god, the ceremony has importance as an educative force. Firth maintains that the initiation situation is functionally the same in Tikopia as in Australia or Africa, where instruction in sacred and moral knowledge is explicit, or in Melanesia, where it is less obvious.[20] That is, the boy is shaped to his position, sacred or secular, in the community. His place in the kinship structure is emphasized by the role which his relatives play in the elaborate gift exchanges and in the actual performance of the operation. Although the religious position and action are not specifically underlined, the general social function of the ritual includes these implicitly as well. Firth sums up the symbolic and functional effect of this phase of the child's growth:

The suppression of the individual, the disregard of his normal freedom of choice and action is important. In ordinary life he can obey and disobey; at initiation he must submit. He is taken in hand by his elders, treated by them as an object, carried about, gripped in strong arms, and then forced to undergo an operation from which he shrinks. . . . It would be strange if at this time he did not become aware of the power of traditional procedure, made manifest in the personalities of his social environment. On the other hand . . . he is the focus of attention. He is smeared with turmeric, adorned, fed with choice foods, wailed over and caressed, and later treated as an honoured guest in many households . . . A new status is conferred upon him, and his maturity becomes patent to him . . . he is now admitted to participation in adult assemblies and is no longer specifically forbidden sex intercourse.[21]

Participation in the sacred dances at Marae is not allowed to the Tikopia male until he has gone through this initiation ceremony. If a boy of rank is concerned, his first participation as a novice is celebrated by the singing and dancing of the *tau*. This is a focus for both religious and familial relationships. The bonds of kinship are emphasized by the formalized gifts exchanges which are part of the celebration, and by the actual physical role of the relatives as they sustain, protect, and guide the novice through the dancing. The *tau* singing and dancing performed in Marae are themselves sacred. Besides marking another stage in his social development and acceptance, it places him in the center of religious observances where he must function in the future.[22]

The exhortations concerning the family which are to be found in the Fono of Rarokoka were not thought of primarily as socialization, although this was one function of the Fono.[23] This proclamation was heard with great reverence by the people, and was given as part of a sacred ceremony before the religious dances and songs in Marae. The principal gods of the island were thus speaking to the people through their representative, the chief of Tafua, and the assembled group bowed their heads in respect. Two interesting injunctions relating to the family occur in it. The first is simply the suggestion to married couples that quarreling not be allowed to get out of hand. The husband is specifically warned that if quarreling becomes so bitter that the husband drives his wife away, it may be difficult to get her to come back. This is simply a kind of empirical wisdom, but most moral or religious exhortation as relates to the world must be of this order, while yet backed by the religious sanction.

The second injunction has many interesting ramifications for the social scientist, which cannot be dealt with here. It is a plea to restrict the population by *coitus interruptus,* so that the food produced by the land will be sufficient for all. The high sacredness of the Fono would suggest that this has been a conscious problem for the Tikopia for generations. The people are told in effect that the ideal family consists in one boy and one girl, thus reproducing the generation. In this fashion all the possible kinship lines will be made in each generation, continuing the importance of the individual family.

The strong interest in kinship lines and the close connection between these lines and ritual authority in Tikopia insures a close relationship between familial and religious action. The status of the sexes, as well as that of various kinship positions, is partly defined in ritual terms. Religious instruction is given by relatives, and in turn religious sanctions are utilized by the society to aid conformity to familial patterns. Ritual mourning is part of the familial duties, and certain of these duties are partly inculcated through the religious activities. However, in Tikopia much of the orientation of daily life is toward kinship lines, and these relationships with religious patterns become almost obvious when kinship heads are the religious officiants. The situation is somewhat different in Zuñi, oriented as it is toward communal action, more than toward individual kinship interests.

# ZUÑI

The analysis of religious action as it has been given up to this point would suggest that in Zuñi society one would expect to encounter greater difficulty in tracing the inter-relationships between the family and the religious system than in the other societies studied. For in Zuñi the explicit family structure has much less social attention focussed on it than in other societies. The dominating focus of interest in the pueblo is the communal ritual and ceremonial life, and many individual or personal activities are not stressed by public attention. Bunzel suggests this community action type of interest by stating:

In fact, the only sphere in which he acts as an individual rather than as a member of a group is that of sex. A man's courtship and marriage are matters of individual choice. In the bid for attention they suffer from being entirely divorced from group activity. At Zuñi no action that is entirely personal and individual receives more than passing interest. Births, deaths, and initiations figure largely in local gossip—marriages do not.[24]

The point is made more obvious by remembering that among the Hopi, marriages are accompanied by important gift exchanges, and, as one would expect, marriages enjoy considerable social attention in that pueblo.

However, courtship and marriage are only a part of family activities, and in spite of the greater interest among the Zuñi in larger communal affairs such as the rituals than in the narrower and more personal affairs of kinship groups, some ritual attention is paid to such affairs. This may be seen in such matters as birth, initiation, and funerary rituals, the functions of kin groups, the status of the women, the learning of religious lore, as well as the socialization of children and other related items.

Although Zuñi society has been divided into clans, Kroeber has pointed out that there is little relationship between these and the important aspects of social life, including the religious. The narrower relationships of blood kin are more significant in daily action. In the religious connection, clan functions "give color, variety, and interest to the life of the tribe . . . But they are only an ornamental excrescence upon Zuñi life, whose warp is the family of actual blood relations and whose woof is the house."[25] The individual will consider himself to be part of his mother's clan, and allied to his father's clan, but as such the clans do not participate in the life of the pueblo to an important degree. There is no central clan meeting house, no recognized head, no meeting or organization, and the clan never acts as a body. Nor are they associated with the kivas. There is "little connection with the religious societies or fraternities either in name, function, or membership except in certain special and limited cases."[26] There is no worship of the clan totem. The general social lack of importance of the clan groupings is a reflection of their lack of great religious importance.

Propitiation of the sacred powers actually may begin before the birth of the child. During the winter solstice ceremonies, after the beginning of the fire taboo, the family uses fertility "magic" to promote the growth of crops and the fecundity of the women. The females of the household make clay objects like those on the priestly altars, and these are set out at night with other sacred objects, such as sacred ears of corn or medicine bundles, masks, or rain fetishes. The following dawn sacred prayers and songs are repeated by the family, asking for fertility.[27] When a woman is pregnant during this period, and especially if she has had difficulties with previous babies, she may visit Corn Mountain, to deposit prayer plumes and possibly a doll fetish. She is accompanied by a priest and her husband to this shrine, where she scrapes dust from the rock from one side or the other, depending upon whether she wants a boy or girl. This is swallowed.

If a woman has difficulty in delivering her child, the medicine priests may be called by her family.[28] On the birth of the child, it must be "cooked." Accompanied by prayers of the priest, a sand bed is made with hot stones and sand, and the child is placed in it. Aside from the prayers for long life and health for the child, the symbolic significance of the "cooking" must be taken into account. It ritually cuts off the child from the supernatural world from which he comes, and places him definitely in this world. Supernatural entities are referred to as "raw" or "uncooked" beings in Zuñi. After four days, the child is brought to the Sun Father at dawn, when it is ritually washed with yucca suds at a point marked by a line of corn meal from the house. Prayers are offered for the health, long life, happiness, and goodness of heart of the child.[29] The mother is also ritually washed, just as she was previously placed in a warmed sand bed like that for her child.

This new human element in the family may observe public ceremonial activities from the earliest days of his life. However, he does not go through initiation until he is about five years or older.[30] This is not the admission of a novice into a religious organization, since no secrets are revealed to the child. It is rather the formal acceptance by the gods of the child" . . . It partakes of the essence of Zuñi initiation, which is the formation of a bond between the individual and powerful supernatural forces."[31] Children do not have any ceremonial status before this, and would not join the sacred dead at Kothluwalawa if they should die. The initiation is the occasion for the dancing of several of the masked gods. The fathers of the children carry their children into the kiva, after the kachina chief and pekwin have made certain the fathers have not put too many blankets on the children. The whipping of the children is evidently exorcistic and purificatory. The use of the giant yucca blades as whips is frequent in Zuñi ritual. In this case, after each group of strokes by the participating masked gods, a blanket is removed. However, the boy's father is in front of the boy.[32] After the usual four nights of fasting from animal food, there are gift exchanges between the women of the fathers' clan, who have been grinding food for such exchanges, and the ceremonial father's relatives.

"Final" social initiation may occur late in modern Zuñi society, because some of the boys have been away to school, forcing them to delay until the age of eighteen or nineteen. The age was supposed to be from ten to twelve years old, when the child had attained sufficient judgment to keep the secrets of the kachina cult. Again the ceremonial father of the boy takes charge of the boy's participation, and again there is whipping by the masked gods, this time considerably harder and more painful. The boys are told stories of what happened to young people who revealed religious secrets, so as to frighten them into silence. They may have a mask, and to symbolize this attainment of ceremonial maturity they must in turn whip the kachinas, also. Again the women relatives have prepared food for the ceremonial fathers and priests, as well as other people of the house where the boys were whipped.[33]

Initiation into one of the rain or medicine societies is an even more important step for the growing member of the society, and will probably take place years after his initiation into kachina society, because of the expense involved.[34] Here, also, there is a ceremonial father, the one (in the case of medicine society initiation) who took the man as patient. The boy's assembled family receives notification that the ceremonies will begin, the "father" praying at this meeting. All members of the society make prayer sticks for the man to plant, and the boy's ceremonial father also prepares a personal fetish as well as regalia and costume. In turn, the novice is backed in this religious step by an elaborate feast furnished by his own relatives. After the four day retreat following the initiation, the women of the boy's family exchange gifts with those of the ceremonial father.[35]

When the individual is lost to his family by death, ceremonies are simple. Bunzel claims that the attitude toward the dead is one of fear.[36]

There is also a feeling of reverence, but "fear is the predominant feeling actuating the rites for the dead." Violations of the taboos of mourning are considered more dangerous than other violations, because of the feeling of the recently dead, who wish to draw the loved ones toward himself. The connection between the recently dead and the loved ones of his family must be "darkened" with black corn meal, and he is implored to cease troubling the living. Funerary rites are simple and are carried out almost immediately after death. The body has been bathed with yucca suds and rubbed with corn meal, preparatory to the simple dressing and wrapping up in the best clothes and blankets. The male members of the family have the responsibility of digging the grave.[37] Immediate members of the family must also bury the object belonging to the dead. The spirit of the dead person is expected to hover about the village for four days before starting on his trip to Kothluwalawa. A surviving spouse must be purified by yucca suds after the burial, and is protected during the four days by the parents or sisters of the deceased. These sleep at his or her side during the period.

The fact that house ownership and lineage are traced through the maternal line does not mean that this is a "matriarchal" society. Kroeber points out that the status of the sexes is not significantly different from that in "nonmatriarchal nations."[38] While the husband occupies the house, he is master of it. This subsidiary role of the female sex is also reflected in the religious system. There are "no women priests nor fraternity officers—only associates—; and while women are not excluded from religious activity, their participation is obviously subsidiary."[39] Initiation is almost entirely for boys or men. Household duties begin for the girl long before puberty, while the young man is comparatively free between initiation and marriage, often a fairly long period.[40] Men object to their wives going about in ceremonial activities, and also object to the periods of continence imposed by the retreats. At many points, of course, the women participate in some aspect of the ritual, such as distributing food gifts, or ritually washing a dancer.[41]

Socialization of the children is aided by the sacred beings, a fact of some importance in a society where physical force is rarely used on children.[42] The fear of the sacred powers possessed by the gods is used to frighten the children into conformity. The Atoshle are particularly used. "The Atoshle also carry giant yucca . . . and they are supplied with large stone knives with which they threaten to cut off the heads of naughty or disobedient children."[43] Parsons gives a vivid picture of the emotional reaction of the child to a visit of Atoshle.[44] These bogeys also guard peach orchards against child depredations. Atoshle may come in a dance, but may also come at other times. A mother will secretly ask Atoshle to come in order to frighten a naughty child into submission. She will then "protect" the child against the accusations.[45] There are also other elements in the religious system for inculcating virtue in the child. When Tchakwena dances after Shalako he may include advice to the young, advising them to respect their parents as well as to follow other lesser advice.[46] Benedict adds the note that the times she observed this dance the homilies were not included, but the disciplinary function remained, since reference was instead made to breaches of ceremony on the part of individuals.[47] Bow Priests may also administer public rebukes, as noted in the discussion of Zuñi political action.

A number of religious duties are taken care of within the family. A particular family generally has charge of certain masks, among the most sacred of Zuñi sacerdotal objects. These houses are not necessarily the ones from which the impersonators of the masks come. If a family line dies out, the masks must be removed, of course, but in any case will remain in the care of the same clan.[48] Sometimes, the mask will be "fed" by a child of the family: Some food will be thrown at it, together with a prayer. As noted previously, particular ritual functions are similarly performed by particular clan members. For example, fire-making at the winter solstice is the function of Badger clan.[49] Naturally, inheritance of such functions, like other clan functions, is through maternal descent. Although descent is maternal, the fact that one's religious affiliations are not determined for the most part by this lineage means that instruction in religious lore and ceremonial may as easily come from the father. This, in fact, happens in an informal manner, the child learning elementary prayers for the household and less public situations.[50] More esoteric lore is, of course, learned from the child's ceremonial father.[51]

# MURNGIN

The categories of kinship to be found in Murngin society are more complex than those of other societies under discussion in this study. Likewise, the myths of the religious system are extremely complex, even though the rituals themselves are comparatively simple. This interest in myths and in kinship would suggest that there are important relationships between the two. In addition to these, however, we may expect to find many connections of a somewhat more concrete nature, as in other societies.

Overshadowing and shaping any detailed connections is the nature of the totemic system itself, by which the kinship bond is extended to include both animate and inanimate objects of a sacred nature. Or, expressing it differently, the ritual or sacred bond is extended to include such objects, which are also in a kinship relationship to human beings.[52] In such a system, objects of importance to the tribe are symbols referring to particular kinship groups, and are also ritually symbolic. In short, the fundamental religious conception is one of kinship. In Murngin society this conception has its central apex in the idea of the sacred well, which is in turn symbolic of all the group's dead kin, to whom and from whom all members return or emerge.[53]

The myths which are the basis of Murngin ritual are highly sacred, and not to be classed as merely for entertainment purposes. Warner states this by suggesting that ". . . the story is not a myth to them but a dogma and has the same ceremonial significance to the Murngin as the Mass to a believing Catholic." In view of this fact, the connection between various elements in Murngin myths and the kinship structure takes on more significance.

One of the most fundamental of distinctions in Murngin myth, ceremonial, and family structure is that between the sexes. The female is the subordinate, the less powerful, the unclean, and the male element contrasts with it in these respects. This is a motif threading its way through all the most important Murngin myths. In the myth of the Wawilak women, the sisters traveled toward the sea, naming plants and animals as they went. After they had stopped so that one of them could bear a child, all the plants and animals which they had gathered or killed ran into the clans' totemic well, a symbolic return which is also part of the Murngin conception of human beings. However, menstrual blood from the older women fell into the totemic well.[54] This was pollution, and the great python in the well finally emerged to swallow them. Before swallowing them, he caused heavy rains and a great flood. This is correlated in Murngin thought with the female element and with the undesirable, as the dry season is one of plenty, associated with the male element. The blood which figures at many points in Murngin ritual is symbolic of the mythical blood. The fact that the Wawilak sisters copulated incestuously with one of their own clans men before the journey, and on the journey the older sister profaned the pool, is considered to be the cause of the rainy season flooding the earth. The python swallows the earth as it did the women. In the rituals, the snake is consequently played by the men, while the uninitiated children play the part of the sisters. Since the flooding is also a fertilizing process, its further identification with the importance of men is made evident. The deeper relationship between the ritual and myth, and the age-grading and sex bifurcation may be summed up:

The men's age grade is a snake and purifying element, and the sociological women's group is the unclean group. The male snake-group in the act of swallowing the unclean group "swallows" the initiates into the ritually pure masculine age grade, and at the same time the whole ritual purifies the whole group or tribe.[55]

In the camp division at the time of rituals, the part of the ground where both women and uninitiated children may enter is called "the camp of those who do not belong," and is thought of contemptuously.

This mythical and ritual subordination is reflected in the greater authority of the older men, whose authority increases as they approach the higher totems and the sacred well. This becomes the source of specific sanctions as they apply to the family structure. The sacredness which increases in the man as he proceeds through the age-graded initiations is able to subordinate the profane or less sacred elements of the young and the female. " 'This man married wrong or that woman has had illegal sexual relations, and our whole group is . . . made sick.' "[56] The sanctions in turn have their effect upon the men, who must learn to conform as well. The conformity as it relates to warfare and ritual was discussed in the chapter on political activity.[57] The deeper sanctions of the totemic system present Murngin society with its ultimate unity.

The significance of the sexual element is further seen in the fact that as women lose their sexual functions they enter more fully into the ritual activities. The menstruating woman is seen as the obvious expression of the female, and is ritually most unclean. The woman approaching menopause, or past it, is much less an expression of this principle, and may take part in several rituals.

The myth may shade off into a folk story, which is in turn believed by the native and may also attempt to point a moral. Such a tale is one in which a man discovers that his betrothed was no longer a virgin, and the man leaves her to starve to death. The tale is expected to have some effect upon girls as well as married women.[58]

Aside from the social division on the basis of sex, the family and kinship relations depend on age-grading, a point which has been mentioned a number of times previously with reference to the Murngin. Each step in this process is important from the standpoint of both family and religion. Within the kinship group the individual takes on more authority and a larger sphere of action, and this is true ritualistically as well. The young boy is comparatively undifferentiated until he is six or eight years of age, when circumcision takes place. At that time he moves to the men's camp, where he remains until he establishes a family of his own. Later, he is allowed to see the low totems, which move him a step further in the society. Seeing the high totems, followed by death, completes the man's cycle. Residence in the men's camp is not merely a ritual definition, however, since even after seeing the low totems a man will remain there until he obtains a wife.[59] Normally, of course, the two coincide.

While in this ritualistically subordinate position, the young man receives instruction in proper behavior, toward both men and women. The sister taboo begins for the young man at this time. Removing him is expected also to prevent the young boy from learning too much about sex at an early age.[60] Kinship and the authority of age both determine who will instruct the young. The oldest male in the camp, naturally, gives instruction, but the near relatives also reprimand wrongdoers. The old men, as well as the boy's parents, attempt to prevent the boy from a wrong marriage or even to have contact with a girl. In addition to specific moral instruction, the boys learn of the tribal lore and tradition. If a given boy is son to a ceremonial leader, the latter may have given such instruction before circumcision as well, telling him of songs, dances, and ritual words.[61]

When a man's family has been completely established through the birth of a child, he participates still more fully in the social and ritual life. The higher totems in the Narra ceremonies are not usually seen until that time.[62] Dietary taboos are removed from the man when he becomes a father. This ritual reflection of a change in familial status is also to be found in the case of the woman, from whom definite dietary taboos are removed.[63] Since Murngin society recognizes a large number of kinship categories, the concrete creation of a family of procreation means that the father now has established a number of new and important relationships with his kin, through the child. If the child is the son of a ceremonial leader, a further set of relationships is begun at birth, since the boy inherits this leadership, assuming that he is old enough when his father dies.

Rules with respect to kinship or sexual activity are impressed upon the individual at various ritual points, emphasizing the close connection between the two. At the time of circumcision, and before the operation has been performed, the trumpet which represents the python is blown, and the initiates are asked to try to blow it. Then they are commanded to "'respect their fathers and mothers,' 'never to tell lies,' 'not to run after women who do not belong to them,' 'not to divulge any of the secrets of the men to the women, men who belong to a lower division of the association, or uninitiated boys.' "[64] This type of injunction is again given after the operation, when the boys are steamed. On a much deeper level of implicit function, the entire set of ceremonies dramatizing the Wawilak myth acts to hold back the individual from the profane or unclean actions which would prevent the dry season of plenty from occurring. It is for this reason, Warner suggests, that a young man who refuses to copulate with a woman at the time of wife exchange is considered to threaten both himself and his partner with illness.[65] That is, any lack of conformity is ritually dangerous.

This ceremonial wife exchange which takes place at the close of one group of rituals based on the Wawilak myth, called Gunabibi, has other aspects relating to kinship and religion. As might be expected in a society highly interested in kinship relationships, the Murngin discuss tribal relationships with one another at these major rituals which bring distant visitors to the ceremonial grounds. This tracing of kinship lines is, naturally, indulged in most by the older men. Through this intellectual activity, an individual may learn that another is a tribal brother from a distant clan. The two will then exchange wives for ceremonial copulation. The fact that the tribal brother lives far away means that the ceremonial relationship will not ripen into an intrigue threatening the established family. On the other hand, the kinship relationship itself suggests that there is a kind of equivalence which prevents the sexual connection from being mere promiscuity. This bar is also felt on the ritual side, since the definition of the situation is also a religious one, separating it from ordinary intrigue. The copulation is preceded by dancing and ceremonial gift exchanges, and is succeeded by the husband's putting his own sweat on the legs and arms of his wife's partner for the night, to prevent any supernatural ill effects from the act.[66] Even the sexual position assumed is different from the usual Murngin custom. Further, if either partner objects, he or she is told that both will be made ill by the python. Thus a distant kinship relationship is symbolically made close in a ritual situation, reinforcing the unity of the tribe. There is a consciously accepted (manifest) function for this element of the ceremonial, in the minds of the Murngin, the purification of the individuals: " 'This makes everybody clean. It makes everyone's body good until next dry season.' "[67] It is thus related to the idea of fertility, and the cycle of growth.

The increasingly sacred character of the individual as he approaches the totemic well of death suggests that it is in funerary rituals that one would expect to find a high degree of development, and a close connection between kinship and ritual. Thus the death of a son requires the actual father and his brothers to take the leading role in mourning ceremonies, and the death of a father demands that all those defined as son in the clan take the lead. The father must open the grave after burial and, with the father's sister's son, clean the bones.[68]

However, many other kinship relationships enter this final ritual pattern of the individual's life. The ceremonials begin before the actual physiological death takes place, and a man's relatives will wail over him while he is still dying. The songs at this time recognize implicitly the close connection between the dying and living, and their purpose is to cause the man's soul to refrain from hurting the remaining kin. As he dies, the songs of his own clan and moiety must be sung, underlining the patrilineal nature of his inheritance and status as well as of the ancestors to whom the songs are also being sung.[69] This phase of the death is not an organized one. The man's female relatives are expected to show the most grief, and cut themselves as an indication of this sorrow.

A few hours later, the clan of the dead man or woman paints the clan design on his or her body, just as was done in the case of the man when he was circumcised, and when he saw his totemic emblem. This again emphasizes the kinship relationship between the living and the dead, for it announces to the ancestors where the soul should go. The evil spirits cannot then lead the individual's soul astray. The dead soul must also be forced to leave, and this is done by a "communion" of palm-nut bread, which a near relative has the women make. Since the dead man is not participating, he is expected to leave. Relatives are also brushed by smoking green leaves, from a fire built by the father or other close relatives, the function here being again that of forcing the dead man from his living kin. Following these expressions of relationship, a long series of ritual songs is used to complete the funeral ceremonies.[70] A cycle of songs is also used when the body is exhumed in order to cleanse the bones for final interment in a hollow log receptacle. In these final ceremonies, too, the close relatives of the dead are the chief participants, some of whom take individual bones as mementos.[71] These ceremonies include many dances, before the bones are finally separated from the kin group.

## SUMMARY

In this section on the relationship between the elements of kinship and familial action on the one hand, and religious action on the other, it has become clear that the expected connection between these most important areas of social activity is actually very close. The basic distinction in a society between the sexes, recognized in a status conferred by birth, is also a part of the religious pattern, wherein the female normally has a much more restricted participation in the more sacred activities. This is more particularly true on the conscious level, since it is clear that women play important auxiliary roles, such as furnishing food for participants, dancing or serving in lesser rituals, or making objects such as mats for certain ceremonials.

The nature of the unsocialized members of the society, i.e., the children, is usually recognized by a series of ceremonies which carry the individual from the earliest stage of nonparticipation in either society or religion to the last stages when his social role has been widely developed in such activities. Further, the attitudes and actions of the children with respect to authority in the family are also taken into account, the religious admonitions often pointing out the duties of the children. Other kinship positions may also be considered by the religious system, and this is particularly true of mortuary rituals, where particular members of the kin group must participate on a relative's death.

The various steps by which an individual comes to play a wider role in his family and society have another aspect to them, the process of socialization. In part, this is recognized explicitly by the members of the society, who may at various points in certain religious ceremonies formally instruct the young in duties of a familial and nonfamilial nature. However, the very process of changing the status of the individual is an element in socialization, since the attitudes and requirements of others with respect to the individual have now changed. A different pattern of action is in order in the new situation, causing the individual to change his activities and patterns of attitude to correspond. Furthermore, there are religious sanctions which help to enforce the new demands, as well as to sustain the old.

It has also become evident that marriage is not so much a focus of social attention as the established family itself, i.e., the kinship group with the new generation now born. That is, the consummation of marriage is the *family*, not the legal joining of male and female. As a consequence, the children themselves figure more significantly in the rituals involving the family than the actual sexual joining. The birth of children confers a new status on man or wife more than the actual marriage, since the parents figure in religious arrangements for the children.

Besides these obvious levels of interconnection between family and religion, it is evident that other and deeper levels can be discovered. Here, the structure and statuses of the family are often to be seen in the structure of the religion, in such elements as the central deity, the authority of the deity and male headship, the pattern of subordination, the interest in kin, the protection of kin, the organization of the religious activities with reference to kin groups or lines, and so on. Thus the familial or kinship structure not only is supported by, and supports, the religious, but both utilize elements from the other, symbolically as well as at an explicit level.

# 11. CONCLUSION

Even the kindly must grant that the foregoing detailed iteration of specific facts has at times seemed less than enthralling. This is a conflict forever waged, between the broad, perhaps at times deep, exploration of grand ideas, a task which is usually exciting; and the closely bound, hemming attention to the facts which are the only acceptable demonstration of those ideas. We become impatient, and must move on. It is, however, most necessary to control this impatience when examining religion as its impulses move men. The temptation to speculate about such high issues is strong in all of us, and a scientific scepticism, indeed, a formal agnosticism or emotional atheism, does not lessen the temptation.

There are two directions of speculation which seem most attractive to any thinker concerned with the great moral problems of our times. One of these, broadly stated, is to wonder anew as to the ultimate truth of any religious idea. We are a generation lost, lost in the only fashion which is really troubling, that is, by our own self-judgment lost. We do not have the bitter, hard, even defiant, lostness of the Twenties. That has succeeded to what may seem far more poignant and damaging, a grim, dogged, consciousness that the aloneness and lack of guidance will likely persist into the future. Yet we continue to seek guidance.

The sociologist cannot, unfortunately, do better than record this feeling, just as the literary artist may use it as material for creation. It is not true to say that the sociologist thereby furnishes no compass. Yet the compass only tells us our direction: It says nothing of our ultimate arrival, or, far more needful, of what destinations may even exist. It does not tell us in which direction we should go, or indeed whether we ought to move at all.

Believing all this to be true of the limits of social science, one would become a false scientist by attempting the role of glib prophet. There is a place for the prophet. Perhaps there is a need for him. But his strength

219

and his vision must have richer sources than science alone. For these reasons, the present study has eschewed prophecy.

Hewing to this line, by limiting the study to those sociological aspects of religion which are empirically demonstrable, a number of important, related questions were of necessity left untouched. Which religion is "better," whether religion is in general "good," and whether there is an ultimate religious "reality" to which these religious ideas refer, all these are problems with which no science is competent to deal. These are questions of value, or they refer to essentially nonempirical phenomena, matters outside the range of the senses. We can analyze the effects of such religious beliefs, and the connections of such beliefs with still other doctrines and actions. Still, we must accept the limitations of scientific investigation. If we can develop a body of demonstrated fact and theory, perhaps we will have a base which may allow some of those judgments which require both evaluating standard and an adequate understanding of the empirical world. Certainly, our values remain irrelevant to any problem until we know the facts. It is the function of science to furnish those facts.

Similarly, the problem of the "origins of the gods" is outside the realm of ascertainable fact. This is a different type of problem than the preceding ones, since this is at least an empirical question.

It is no strain on faith to believe there was a beginning to religion, that there was a time when our ape-like cousins-far-removed began to believe. This occurrence, or occurrences, was a definite point in history —definite, unknown, and unknowable. The data are not available, and they will not appear. The discovery of artifacts, useful as they are for many purposes, will not open the meaning of religious life at that period. Here we are almost lost until we move forward to the stage when man began to record his actions. Even "good guesses" about Neolithic man do not tell us of the first beginnings of religion, which surely occurred long before that period. It is difficult to demonstrate hypotheses concerning modern primitive men, about whom we have fairly good field reports. It is wasteful to attempt this concerning primeval man, unless we are merely interested in the pleasures of speculation.

The second main direction for speculation has at least the merit of good precedent. It is the temptation to believe that the conclusions drawn in this book from primitive religions are also valid for modern religions and Western society. It is clear that many of them do possess such a wider validity. However, it must be made clear that their wider correctness has not been demonstrated, and that they must stand or fall to the extent that they actually do fit the data from still other primitive societies.

Further, we know that our analyses of modern religion are hampered by a "surplus" of facts, as are those concerning Western man generally. This is a state of affairs which is rapidly coming to be true of primitive societies as well. For within the past generation we have become painfully conscious of more conflicting details. Edward Sapir records, in a late essay, his shock at J. O. Dorsey's casual offer of an Omaha example, late in the 19th Century, of the degree of individual variation within *every* society, primitive or not. Perhaps we can draw facile conclusions from primitive societies precisely because we have only skimmed the surface of social action in them. We may, indeed, in the present study, have sketched the *basic* lines of action, but of necessity left out immense areas of disagreement in individual cases. We now know that there are devout men and doubters within these societies, fervent traditionalists and reformers, philosophers and pedants, and a statement about a "required ritual" must contain a qualified suspicion that some participants may not agree that it is required, after all.

Yet we can work only from previous analyses and reports, and laboriously continue to build a set of ideas which are at least clear enough to be attacked or demonstrated by later data. We cannot leap at once to a set of judgments which would encompass all such phenomena wherever found, in Western society or in an isolated area in the Polynesian triangle. It is to be hoped that other scholars will continue their work in formulating and testing hypotheses for Western society as well, and still others can develop the integrating ideas for both of these groups, as well as for other developed civilizations.

That this study begins with primitive religious action does not mean that it is thought to be simpler. Rather, it is a convenient beginning, and seems to be an interesting one. That it may be infinitely complex is amply demonstrated by the study itself. For all these reasons, it has seemed justifiable to avoid the second temptation, that of guessing that the many conclusions of this study must be also valid for Western society.

It is also clear that no conclusion emerges that religion is "the" mainspring of all human action. It is, rather, often so intertwined with other pushes and motivations that one cannot isolate it as an independent factor at present. True enough, it shapes much of economic behavior, but the latter is often shaper in turn, and one would be nonplussed at the task of completely unravelling the threads.

At a different level, let us see what conclusions of a general order seem to emerge from this survey.

First of all, we see what the devout understand better than the doubters, that religion is action, not merely a set of philosophic speculations about another world. Religion is not something which is only *believed*: It is *lived*, and its impact is no less upon the doubter who sceptically follows religious form, than upon the believer who gives himself unhesitatingly to a jointure with the infinite. Religious belief demands action at every turn, action in this world, toward this world. That such action has other facets and sequelae goes without saying. Since nearly all tribal members move within the same sphere, the actional demands of religious belief have an impact on the activities of all, whether or not they themselves participate in a given ritual, become a novice or initiate, or make offerings.

A great number of such interrelationships between religious action and other spheres have been traced in detail, in the course of the present analysis. Yet no claim is made that this captures the emotional reality of religion. It may safely be claimed that the emotion itself must exist within action, and be rewarded or supported by such relationships. In turn, however, the emotion is intrinsic to religion. Without it, there would be no impulse to carry on the activities which have been traced here. Still deeper, moreover, the sociologist is not the artist, and does not seek to evoke the images and worshipful yielding which are of the essence of religion as it is lived by the faithful, in this or any other society.

Yet the teasing out of many of these relationships is of great value for an analysis of social action. We are accustomed to speak of the "fact of social integration" without seeing how the various spheres and levels of social action actually do relate to one another. Sometimes the relationship occurs simply because of overlap of personnel. In other cases, the religious may be a necessary arm for the political. In still others, both are seeking the same goals. The integration has to be specified, if we are to assert it.

Several points emerge from such a detailed study. First of all, we see how weak a tool is the idea that men are seeking only their advantage. When we define the hedonistic psychology in this fashion, its weakness is self-evident, but in a cynical age we are likely to utilize it in many connections, because it is simple. We see, rather, that even in political and economic action a rationalistic self-seeking does not reign. Men must also believe their behavior to be just, or right, or moral. To point out that many structural relationships of religion function to uphold the *status quo,* or to yield material rewards of religious officiants, does not invalidate this proposition. Nor can this be interpreted merely as "unconscious" motivation. The officiants are aware of the rewards, and one need not claim that they have no interest in them. Rather, these are not sufficient, and one may test this—as one may do in our own society—by offering comparable material rewards for alternative modes of behavior which do not possess such legitimacy, or religious meaning. In short, if one were to express the matter with modern cynicism, the devout are "taken in" by their own preachments.

A further point is to be noted, this time with respect to the matter of integration. In outlining the general theory of religion which is being partly exemplified, partly tested, in this manuscript, religion was seen as a level of integration, offering common, societal values which help to direct the society as a whole. Religion *expresses* the unity of society, but it also helps to *create* that unity. It is for this reason that the anthropologist or sociologist may state that "the major function of religion is the integration of social action," with varying phraseology according to his particular school. Yet we have seen that this does not express with sufficient accuracy the manifold relationships of religion with other types of activity. Such relationships are not necessarily positively functional, for they may inhibit other areas of action. For example, the preoccupation with religious ritual may hinder a rational solution of a technical problem, or may cause considerable economic waste. The religious allegiances may occasion a division of loyalty, as between family and religion, or political subordination and the religious. Even if one narrows the term "functional" to mean "the continued existence of the society," such a positive function is not always visible. It may be true that almost any system of interlocking habits is mainly "integrative," else they would not interlock. Yet at many points it is possible to see either latent or manifest disfunctions, of many types.

Moreover, we see that the "function" of religion—in the meaning used in this study, i.e., the *effect of the relationship*—are not to be seen as either "good" or "bad," or even inhibitory or stimulating. The effect may be rather to shape social relationships in a particular way, or to start an activity at one time rather than another, or to use one artistic design as against another. It is an error of reduction to classify all these functions as merely positive or negative. In a basic sense, we must widen and deepen our classification of functions.

A further conclusion was not adequately tested, although it was mentioned in Chapter III. Does religion offer solace for personal misfortune? Is it a source of emotional security, as it often is in our own society? For the societies under consideration, it would be difficult to give such an answer, except for a few, isolated remarks. On the other hand, it is clear that at a higher level of generalization this conclusion is possible: The general world-view offered by the system of religious belief does suggest that the cosmos has meaning; that man has an understandable place in it; and that the gods do not coolly ignore the fate of the tribe. On this cosmic level, it is erroneous to speak of personal solace, but that tribal tragedy can be rationalized from this basis must be clear.

This investigation has also attempted to utilize the emerging insight that magic and religion are not always separate, antagonistic modes of behavior. Rather, they form a continuum composed of a number of characteristics. Any given magical or religious system will fall somewhere between the two ideal-typical poles, but they will inevitably overlap somewhat. Many elements in a magical system will fall close to the religious pole, and a number of religious elements are very similar to magic. When we see this clearly, we are no longer surprised to find magical practices being used by priests, or being systematically used to uphold a given economic or political practice. Further, we are able to see that even within developed religions of modern European or Asiatic societies there are magical elements. These, then, are not to be seen as intrusive or alien elements. They are integral to the whole supernatural complex.

A further insight, also emerging from previous analysts of religion, was developed still further in this study, the social character of the gods. This element has an obvious function in rationalizing the position of man in an often hostile universe. However, on any level of action the logic of this social character has its effects. We do not find it strange, therefore, to find a man threatening the gods—and if our religious experience is wide, we know that this behavior is to be found in our own society as well. We see this reaction as directly related to the social relationship existing between man and the supernatural entities. That they should express resentment at being ignored is a natural enough idea, once we see that their personalities are likely to be structured similarly to those of tribal members. This does not exclude a feeling of awe or worship, but those emotions are in a setting of social interaction between gods and men. They are not merely a reaction to a philosophic contemplation of the infinite.

That the main body of this study has been occupied with detailed facts should not obscure our primary goal, that of developing further a sociological theory of primitive religion. It is for this reason that the salient hypotheses have been explicitly stated. They are thus in a form which makes them vulnerable to attack. But the very process of attack on explicit hypotheses is fruitful: science grows by the negation of the old. It is difficult to refute the vague, but it is equally difficult to build upon it.

This primacy of interest in the facts and hypotheses has meant that the basic problems of research design have for the most part been placed in footnotes and appendices. Thus the critique of alternative theories of primitive religion constitutes Appendix II, and an outline of a typology of primitive religion forms Appendix I. The criteria by which the societies were selected has been, for reasons of space, made into the final footnote for Chapter III.

Thus, the major hypotheses as well as the framework in which they are examined, have been presented, in an effort to facilitate critical review. It is the contention of this study that the selection of a group of societies of very different structures and religious beliefs (Chapter IV and Appendix I), by criteria which have nothing to do with whether they might "fit the theory," offers at least a good foundation for the wider validity of a sociological theory. That these societies might fit the theory by accident remains a possibility, although, in view of the disparate character of the societies, not a strong one. A still wider investigation will settle these matters, and it is to be hoped that such a wider investigation will follow. That the present theory must be modified, as it has modified those presented in Appendix II, can be taken for granted. This is simply the normal process of scientific cumulation and growth.

In addition to the main problems which have been broached here, others may become the focus of future research. One question of increasing concern is that of cultural change. Most modern primitives are succumbing to the onslaught of Western civilization. This is partly a matter of gunpowder, though not entirely. Soon there will be no "untouched" societies, if there are any now. The problems of acculturation, which have always been of interest to the anthropologist, become crucial. Furthermore, as we recognize that there are common characteristics to social interaction, all such processes are necessary grist for the social analyst's mill.

We may learn, then, which religious systems are most susceptible to change. It may be that we shall learn to what extent a religious system is conservative, and at what points. If magic is really a sort of primitive science, it will be destroyed first. This hypothesis is now being tested before our eyes. Perhaps we shall not be able to specify which religious components change first, without further specification of their relationship to the total pattern of social action. This should furnish interesting hypotheses for social change in our own society.

As we accumulate a better understanding of the relationships between the structural and functional aspects of social action, we should be able to state more clearly not only what structures do exist, but just how they limit the range of possible functions, or alternatively, just which structures are necessary for given functions. We may have to work out not only a typology of structures, but criteria for comparing structures. At present, we must use general descriptive phrases. We have no general set of indexes, or characteristics, or patterns for comparison, to be used in analyzing structures or functions. These are necessary as general tools, and more especially for primitive religion.

On the basis of such an accumulation of structural-functional theories, we should be able to state whether given cultural elements, such as religion, are necessary for the continued existence of any society, and to what degree, or in what form. Such a level of generalization, of course, presupposes an organized body of demonstrated theories which are valid for both primitive societies as well as urban civilizations.

Perhaps, also—for even the most austere scientist hopes that his work will be useful, in embarrassed secrecy hopes it will move men—such data will ultimately help to teach the prophet who will some day offer us the guidance we now need.

# APPENDIX I. VARIATION OF RELIGIOUS SYSTEMS IN TYPOLOGICAL TERMS

THE METHOD of selecting the societies seemed to avoid the danger of choosing several religious systems merely on the basis of whether they would fit certain preconceived notions about religion. However, such a claim is buttressed if we check the result. This can be done by determining whether the religions are actually very different from one another. If it can be shown that the religious systems under consideration are different from one another *with respect to variables important for religion,* we have better grounds for our claim that a theory which fits those systems should have a still wider validity.

This is essentially a structural analysis. Now, without developing a complete taxonomy, we can at least indicate the *basis* for such a taxonomy. This foundation for a typology should include the elements or variables of most importance in a primitive religious system. These seem to be the following: (1) personnel; (2) societal matrix; (3) sacred entities; (4) ritual; and (5) belief. However, no effort will be made to create a special nomenclature for all the types which are logically possible, and even for the present religions only simple, roughly descriptive phrases will be used.

Instead, the effort will be to show that these religious systems vary from one another in their most important relationships. When, therefore, it is demonstrated that the theory in question adequately analyzes these particular religions, we have some basis for considering the theory adequate not merely for religions "all of one type, the type chosen only to fit the theory," but for systems so different from one another that this theoretical adequacy cannot be a statistical accident. Instead, it becomes likely that the "fitness" of the theory rather indicates a wider scientific validity for that theory.

*Variation in Religious Personnel.* "Personnel" as used here refers to both religious leaders as well as followers. Its main modes of variation are two, A. the extent of formal religious training, and B. the extent of identification of the secular with the sacred leaders and followers. As to the first, it is obvious that not all religious systems provide for specifically religious training for those who are participants or observers. Thus, among the Manus, there is no effort to send any individual through a particular course of education or training in the techniques of getting in touch with the spirits.[1] This is related, of course, to the general lack of such formal training in other affairs within the same society.[2] *Those who call on the practitioners* among the Manus likewise are without any specialized, formal training. On the other hand, among the Dahomey there is almost a "monastery" system, according to which individuals are chosen to become followers or priests in a particular cult or church.[3] These individuals go through a long period of training in esoteric lore, while isolated almost entirely from the rest of the society.[4] Here, then, is a high development of formal education in religious techniques for both practitioner and layman.

These two societies represent extreme opposite points among the societies investigated in this study, with respect to this particular mode of variation, the formalization of training. For the Manus give formal training to *neither* the religious practitioner nor layman. The Dahomeans give some training to *both* priest and devotee.[5] Beginning, therefore, from the group with least formalized training, the Manus, one can arrange a rough graduation of such training: (1) Manus; (2) Tikopia; (3) Murngin; (4) Zuñi; and (5) Dahomey. The Tikopia give such formal training only to the religious practitioners, who are also the repository of much other tribal lore.[6] This is, as the student will recognize, a common Polynesian pattern. Neither women nor ordinary children go through any such training.[7] Only the sons of chiefs or elders, who may in time themselves lead or participate in important ceremonies, are taught the spells, prayers, exhortations, communications, names of gods, etc., which are necessary for the continuation of the religious system. Thus this training is limited to a very small part of the tribe, though others in the tribe know much of this lore from ordinary observation.

Such training is much more widespread among the Murngin than among the Tikopia, for all boys are given such training in a series of rites of passage leading to the final phase of seeing the high totems.[8] Sacred lore is taught to them at these periods, the information being increasingly secret and sacred each time.[9] The women, on the other hand, who have little explicit function in Murngin ceremonialism,[10] are not given any such training, and it is, indeed, from the women (as well as the "uniniti-ated" youths) that the information must be kept secret.

Dahomey and Zuñi are close with respect to this particular mode of variation. Both men and women are given ritual instruction. Not every-one belongs to a "training" group. In both cases, it is the men who receive the most intense and important training, since the burden of religious leadership falls on them, for the most part. In both cases, there are formally structured religious organizations—usually called "societies" in Zuñi and "cults" or "churches" in Dahomey—which, for the given society, have a generally similar pattern. In both cases, ritual instruction is necessitated by the complexity and richness of ceremonial. Neverthe-less, Dahomey may be considered to have a greater intensity of formal training, and perhaps a greater extensity (the groups to which such train-ing extends). That is, in terms of the classes, types, or proportions of people who are to receive such training the two may be rather close.[11] But Dahomey gives those who receive this instruction a longer, much more intense, period of study.[12] Consequently, the ranking suggested above seems to be fairly accurate.

This mode of variation in terms of formalized personnel training is independent of the second mode, that *of the extent of identification of the sacred with the secular personnel structure,* both expert and layman. This second mode answers the question, To what extent are the secular leaders also the religious leaders, or the religious followers identified with the secular followers? That this is independent of the first is seen from that fact that in Dahomey there is considerable formalization of training, but a separation of the secular and sacred leaders,[13] while in Tikopia there is training for a small group of persons who will be *both* secular and sacred leaders.[14] This latter proposition is also true for the Murngin.[15] And in Zuñi the identification is likely to be indirect and incomplete;[16] on the other hand, in Manus there *may* be such an identi-fication,[17] though it is not a necessary one. Thus in terms of decreasing identification of the sacred with the secular personnel structure, these societies may be ranked in this manner: (1) Murngin and Tikopia, where the identification is complete; (2) Zuñi, where such an identifi-cation is very likely, though still not necessarily complete; (3) Manus, where the identification seems to be fortuitous and possible, though not necessary or predictable; (4) Dahomey, where the separation is complete.

*Variation in Type of Societal Matrix.* Since religious action always takes place in a societal context, even when the moment of ritual finds only one person present, some variation in religious systems will be ex-pressible in terms of the type of society of which that religion is a part.

This goes on the obvious and explicit assumption, that one cannot easily analyze the religious system without some reference to the fact that the members of the society do other things besides pay respect to the gods, and that these other activities are important for an understanding of the religious system.

Though it is clear that many types of variables could be used to characterize a given society, a composite one is most consistently applied here, that often used by the sociologist, the degree of *cultural* approach to or deviation from the "ideal type" of the "Western" civilization, or even "urban" society. This is rough, but concrete qualifications and more precise descriptions can be added at any necessary points. It must be emphasized that neither this variable nor any other used implies any ranking of inferiority or superiority among societies, or any belief that there is a unilinear evolutionary growth to societies. This particular variable will usually be roughly correlated with that of technological levels, though in this study the general field of technology is not a major focus.

In order to characterize this variable somewhat more precisely, it may be pointed out that it is a composite of at least five other elements: (1) rationality, (2) self-interest, (3) universalism, (4) functional specificity, and (5) impersonality of daily social interaction.[18] (1) *Rationality* refers to the emphasis on efficiency in the choice of means to a given end. Action varies from this extreme toward that of traditionalism, which refers to action without reference to the possibility of improving efficiency. (2) *Self-interest* refers to the pursuit of one's personal gain, as against the abstract principle of assiduous devotion to certain groupal ends without regard to personal gains (honest or dishonest). In terms of occupational stereotypes, the contrast might be between the salesman as the self-interested, with the physician or priest as the disinterested, person. (3) *Universalism* refers to the pattern of social interaction being determined not by the particular intimate, friendly, or even hostile previous personal relationships of the individuals involved, but rather on the basis of prior, accepted patterns holding for *any* individual or for that particular class. For example, ethical universalism is a very common value in Western Protestant countries. That is, to take an example, one is supposed to be honest with strangers, friends, or enemies. As is well-known, "rural" social relationships are often characterized as particularistic, varying from the universalism of "urban" bureaucracy. In our society, both medicine and business are supposed to tend toward universalism, in that the same treatment is to be given to patient or customer without regard to any *particular* ties between these latter two and the physician or business man. They contrast, however, with respect to disinterestedness, since the primary object of the latter is assumed to be personal gain. (4) *Functional specificity* refers to the pattern of rights and obligations being narrowly and explicitly defined both in minimum and maximum terms. The contract is the type example. Friendship and family relationships contrast with this pattern, since rights and obligations are explicitly defined in minimum or negative terms but institutionally or culturally defined in maximum terms: every obligation is to be fulfilled which does not conflict with a higher obligation. Though business and medicine are variant with regard to disinterestedness, they are both functionally specific: the social relationship exists only for a definite purpose. As is well known, social relationships within urban societies are frequently thought of as tending toward the functionally specific. (5) *Impersonality* refers to social patterns which do not enjoin strong emotional attitudes, such as the administration of justice or economic transactions, varying toward war or marriage, which do. This category or element may be considered partly residual, in that it includes any type of emotion not related to the four previous elements.

In terms of these elements which constitute the composite variable mentioned as the "societal matrix," that is, the variation from traditionalistic, disinterested, particularistic, functionally diffuse, and emotionalistic societies to rationalistic, self-interested, universalistic, functionally specific, and impersonalistic ones, the attempt may be made to rank the societies treated. The rank suggested here is: (1) Murngin; (2) Zuñi; (3) Tikopia; (4) Manus; and (5) Dahomey. It is understood that this ranking is only approximate, but the reasons for it may be noted.

That the extremes are represented by Murngin and Dahomey seems obvious, for Dahomey society approaches almost a "developed" civilization. Dahomey has for centuries carried on trade with other tribes for economic gain.[19] It has a complex judicial and administrative organization.[20] Many relationships are determined on a purely economic or legal basis.[21] There is a great development of rationality in its technology.[22] It is "urban." The Murngin possess much less technical skill and specialization. It is an isolated tribe, with no regular trading with the outside world.[23] There are few, if any, relationships which could be called contractual.[24] Most relationships are highly particularistic, depending for their definition on the kinship system.[25] There is little, if any, "rational self-interest in the pursuit of gain." Much of the daily social interaction seems emotional.

The ranking of the other three between these two points is, of course, much more difficult. Still, it can be done with some objectivity. The Zuñi are ranked between the Murngin and the Tikopia, since the emphasis in

Zuñi life on high group solidarity,[26] distrust of self-interest[27] or changes in traditional methods of even production,[28] the insistence on treating outsiders as intruders whom one is permitted to trick as well as on the width of institutional obligations (as opposed to a narrow or specific definition),[29] all indicate a type of society far from the "urbanism" of Dahomey. It lies further in this direction, nevertheless, than Murngin, partly because Zuñi life has been affected somewhat by both Anglo-Saxon and Spanish cultures for many generations, and partly because of its inherent development. There is, thus, a trade system which allows at least some pursuit of self-interest as well as functional specificity. Furthermore, this specificity is seen in other realms of activity, such as specialized production of a technological nature: tourist goods, pottery, and irrigation. Furthermore, some development of universalism has been necessitated within the society itself by the development of a village system, since living in settled groups means that many patterns of action arise which may be applied to any other Zuñi, whether friend or stranger. That is, the number of people constantly in one small area means that these relationships cannot be defined entirely particularistically through kinship, but must be part of an impersonalistic, universalistic pattern of meeting and greeting, buying or trading, etc. On the other hand, though the Tikopia have not been in constant contact with other societies, and have no real market system,[30] there is no complete group repudiation of self-interest.[31] The individual is swallowed up much less in the Tikopia group. The subordination is rather more definitely (i.e., much more functionally specific) to officials.[32] Particularistic patterns are confined to a greater extent to the immediate family or to very close kinship relationships.[33] Wider tribal patterns have arisen which allow smooth social interaction with strangers, particularly since members of one clan may live in an area dominated by another. Considerable technical skill is shown,[34] though granted that it is rather firmly traditionalized. Some break in the traditional is indicated in Tikopia by the inclusion of formerly secular objects or tools within sacred rituals, often as technical "improvements." For example, the iron or steel adze, even in ritual situations, has taken the place of the clam shell as a cutting instrument.[35] Similar processes have occurred in Zuñi.[36]

At first glance, it would seem that Manus society, seemingly "backward," should be ranked farther from Dahomey than the Tikopia or Zuñi. However, it must be remembered that Manus society lays great emphasis on the self-interested, impersonal action, and the contractual obligation.[37] Kinship is important, but most social interaction is not of this particularistic kind. It is of a much more widespread, generalized type, which allows the Manus tribesmen to meet both Manus and strangers without having to decide what relationship they hold to him in particular.[38] Manus society, though technologically on a low plane of development, is a "radical, ascetic, capitalist" society.[39] Ethical universalism, i.e., honesty in one's obligations toward everyone, is highly emphasized. A technique of increasing efficiency or of making money is accepted more easily than in Tikopia. The shift from the tribal settlement of disputes to white men's courts, for example, was easily made.[40] The possibility of conversion to Christianity is discussed calmly.[41] Therefore, with all its lack of population, or highly developed administrative machinery, or mechanical skill, the Manus society approaches much more closely to the cultural pattern of a "developed" civilization, or even "urban society," than the Murngin, Tikopia, or Zuñi, with respect particularly to the elements important in the definition of their religious systems.

*Variation in Sacred Entities.* As is known to students of primitive religion, the variation in "gods and spirits" and sacred things is almost infinite. Even the most casual perusal of Frazer's work[42] would substantiate this proposition. Of course, many so-called "spirits," such as stones, trees, rivers, etc., constituting much of the variation, are to be actually analyzed into a simple external symbol and some indwelling force or "personality." Nevertheless, part of the definition of religion must include a description of the sacred entities, personalities, or "spirits" which are the focus of most of the religious action and are defined by that society as sacred. This variation is not easily expressible in terms of a single or composite characteristic to be described in any given case as existing more, or less, than in another society. Thus, among the Murngin, the focus of the ritual attention is the Great Serpent, whose spirit is thought to be immanent in many other phenomena. The "god" is, like many clan totems, a type of animal. Both the Tikopia and the Manus pay respect to "ancestors," though the Tikopia lay greater emphasis on a culture-hero, as well as on secondary totems. The Zuñi pay their respect to the Sun, the Uwanami (rain-makers), Kachinas, the Beast Gods, and (to a lesser degree) the War Gods, and find sacred forces in many natural phenomena. The Dahomey worship Mawu and other pantheons of gods, including several types of ancestors.[43] The variation here is great, and may be characterized roughly by pointing out that such entities are usually classifiable as varying from a *highly abstract, distant entity not clearly defined, through broad, natural forces* (such as the sun, rain, fire, etc.), *various degrees of anthropomorphism in gods and spirits, to animals, plants and other natural objects* (usually increasingly totemic). Such a variation merely expresses an increasingly definite, concrete, and prosaic character. In the case of any particular religion, however, the definition of the variation should also be given a concrete description. With respect to the direction of variation mentioned, the religious systems may be related in this fashion: (1) Dahomey; (2) Zuñi; (3) Tikopia; (4) Manus; and (5) Murngin.

The difficulty of applying such a mode of variation is the fact that each religious system will have many different kinds of sacred entities within it. Thus the Dahomean Lɛgba is as earthy an anthropomorphic deity to be found anywhere,[44] and within the heart of the Dahomean set of beliefs is a system of ancestor worship.[45] Similarly, although the central Tikopian deity is a culture-hero, there are many totemic elements.[46] This would perhaps hold true for any primitive religious system. One need not attempt to show that all these variations merely cover an original or basic monotheism.[47] It is descriptively useful, however, to recognize the type of entity on which the religious system lays most emphasis. Thus the Sky Pantheon, Mawu, certainly has more of an abstract, distant character than the Tikopia culture-hero, the Manus ancestor-worship, Zuñi rain-spirits and the Sun, or the Murngin Great Serpent.[48]

Similarly, in spite of the sacred character of corn, springs, Kilowisi the horned serpent, and especially the sacred ancestors (awonawilona) in Zuñi,[49] the system emphasizes certain "vague impersonal forces," among which ". . . are certain clearly defined individuals and classes of beings who definitely influence human affairs . . . such as the sun, the earth, the corn, prey animals, and the gods of war . . . Clouds and rain are the attributes of all the supernaturals . . ."[50]

Likewise, the Tikopian emphasis is clearly on the culture-hero, Atua i Kafika, even though behind him (yet not equal in power) are certain "great deities" who have never lived as men.[51] The "anthropomorphism" of the Manus "deity" or spirit is much less open to question, since it is almost always a man's own father.[52] The case of the Murngin is parallel, since its totemic character is well known, approaching other Australian systems.

*Variation in Ritual.* The necessity of including the structural element of ritual in any classification of religious systems must be apparent, since this is the most obvious behavioral aspect of religious practices. It is true that one might conceivably use a concretely descriptive type of classification of ritual practices, with several sub-categories of classification, such as relationship to seasons, whether there is adoration, threats, or gratitude paid to the gods, or the asking of good will, or perhaps the extent of symbolism, the gestures, objects manipulated, etc. However, most of these can be considered dependent on other variables. Thus the question of the task which the ritual is supposed to perform—magical increase, adoration and respect, obtaining advice or good will, making threats or expressing gratitude—is more correctly subsumed under the *variable of belief*, since these are really part of the meaning of ritual, as discussed in Chapter III. The relationship to the seasons is partly a function of belief, since the meaning of the ritual determines whether the ritual has some connection with the seasonal (usually, productional) calendar. This relationship to the seasons is also partly connected to the type of sacred entities, since their interest in the seasons (sidereal, agricultural, fishing, rain and drought, etc.) partly defines their characters.

The extent of symbolism is, on the other hand, a function of a perhaps more important characteristic, the *degree of elaboration of the ritual*. That this is important is seen from the fact that it is in a society with a high degree of such ritual elaboration that a greater interest in religious action itself will be found. Since symbolic elements are found in every ritual, the elaboration of the ritual itself means that symbolism is also more highly developed. This elaboration further determines the extent to which the productivity of the society is devoted to religious purposes, as well as the extent of pervasiveness of religious attitudes and ideas in other than seemingly religious spheres of action, such as family life, agriculture, war, etc.

This characteristic, furthermore, is actually an independent variable with respect to the second variable, *the type of societal matrix*. It is not even dependent on the level of technological skill, or the development of a surplus for market (and thus for religious contributions). For the ranking of the five societies used, in terms of the *increasing degree of elaboration* would be roughly this: (1) Manus; (2) Tikopia; (3) Zuñi and Dahomey; and (4) Murngin. The reasons for this suggested ranking deserve some mention.

That the Manus have the least degree of ritual elaboration can be accepted without further discussion, since the ritual practices there are very simple. There are no grouped cult activities, and no elaborate seasonal ceremonies.[53] It might be also accepted though, with slightly more comment, that the Murngin have the most complex ritual ceremonies of all five. For a considerable portion of the life of the Murngin tribes revolves at certain periods around complex ceremonies.

As Warner's description shows, there is also a vast series of interrelated "cycles" of ceremonies among the Murngin.[54] Furthermore, there are innumerable narrowly totemic (clan) ceremonies, figuring in mortuary[55] as well as other ceremonial situations. These groups are considered to have a more elaborate ritual development than the Tikopia, not merely because of the extremely interwoven complexities of the Murngin ritual, but also because at important periods most of the population, both day and night, centers its activities about the rituals. Further, much of the apparent elaboration of Zuñi, Dahomean, and Tikopia ritual is to be interpreted differently. Zuñi ritual, for all its color, is not elaborate in content, but in organization.[56] That is, the basic elements of the ritual are simple, such as the phraseology of prayer, the manipulation of sacred objects, offerings, abstinence, etc., but are: A. recombined in various ways, and B. performed by different groups at different ceremonies, or even at different phases in the same ceremony.[57] It is perhaps this aspect of Zuñi ritual which Parsons suggests, when she writes:

> Pueblo ritual is kaleidoscopic. There are many ritual patterns or rites, and, almost as accommodating as tale incidents, they combine in many ways. Thus ritual is both fixed and mobile. Mobilized into a comparatively constant combination, a group of rites may form a ceremony, sometimes without a dramatic idea.[58]

On the other hand, although the greater population and the wealth of Dahomey allowed and still allow large offerings and ceremonies with many devotees, much of the apparent elaboration is merely duplication. For there are "churches" in Dahomey.[59] That is, the ritual of a single cult-group alone does not have the complexity of Murngin ritual. Further, much of the "elaboration" is the mechanical repetition of the same rhythm or movement.[60] This is also the case in the Tikopia ritual, whose basic *kava* ceremony is repeated in many places. Further, in the case of the Tikopia, no ritual occupies the attention of the whole society as happens in Murngin, even though a large cycle is the focus of conversation at times. Such a case happened in Dahomey only for the "great customs" of the royal ancestor cult, and at the death of a king. The latter, of course, no longer occur, since Dahomey is ruled by France, and the former are much reduced.[61]

The relative ranking of Zuñi, Dahomey, and Tikopia is facilitated by the simplicity of the basic Tikopia ceremony, the *kava*. The elaboration of sacred objects has not developed to the degree apparent in Zuñi or Dahomey. Also, there is less activity which is purely ritual. Much of the ritual program consists in a few ceremonials, which initiate, continue, or close a period of technological activity, such as mat-weaving, turmeric making, or the laying of thatch. Zuñi or Dahomean rituals, on the other hand, often exist as traditionalized, integrated, complex wholes, elaborate enough in themselves to require a long period of entirely ceremonial action.

*Variation in Religious Beliefs.* It will be recognized here, as in the case of variation in sacred entities or rituals, that the possibilities of variation seem almost infinite. Nevertheless, some general sub-categories can be discovered. Here there is no possibility of defining religious beliefs as merely variations of one characteristic, simple or composite, in one direction. Instead, the definition must be concrete, in terms of the particular religious system involved. The differences between various systems of religious beliefs can, however, be roughly classified, since a number of common themes are to be found rather widely distributed over the earth. Within such categories, of course, the concrete content will always have to be defined for the particular society.

These categories may be briefly noted. (1) There are beliefs about human souls. These beliefs, or set of integrated ideas, describe where souls come from, before they come to this earth. There is also a statement of where they go after the human being dies. This does not mean at all that there is a widespread belief in the immortality of human souls, only that there is general agreement that human beings do not immediately cease to exist when they die. Exactly what kind of place they go to or from will vary tremendously, as is known. (2) A second classificatory sub-category is the pattern of explaining the ritual or ceremony of activities. That is, the rituals in themselves do not constitute a self-enclosed system. Rather, the gestures, words, objects, movements, etc., derive their significance from the meaning invested in them by the system of belief. This does not mean, of course, that every element in a ceremony actually has an explicit known meaning. Many elements in a given ritual or ceremony will not have been thought of by the society; they will simply accept it as having existed always. Many such elements, however, may have some meaning given them, when the field anthropologist questions the natives about the meaning of that ritual. (3) Religious beliefs extend also to another group of ideas, that of punishment by the spiritual forces for sins, breaches of tabu, or any noncompliance with some religious injunction. Precisely what it is which is to be the occasion of punishment, or the type of punishment, or the ways of avoiding the consequences, must be determined concretely in the case of each religion. The definition, again, must be in terms of the meanings given by the society, and not in terms of, say, Christian morality and sin. Since religious gestures, movements, objects, etc., vary greatly, the possible breaches of their sanctity are also great in number, so that concrete description of this sub-category of belief will be required as part of any classification of religious systems.

(4) One will ordinarily have to include still another area of belief

in the classification of religious systems, the origin of gods and men, as well as the later "historical" interrelationships of gods with gods, and with men. It is possible that in many cases part of this origin belief will come to be enacted in ritual, endowing the latter with its meaning. These beliefs also help to define the characteristics of the sacred entities which are the center of attention of the religion, by describing their experiences in an early period. They are, then, often closely related to other types of belief. Furthermore, it ought to be noted that "beliefs" of this kind shade off in sacredness toward those stories of origins which are merely told for entertainment and which have little, if any religious function. The distinction between story, legend, myth, and sacred history is often a subtle one, and is to be defined by the attitudes of the participants in the culture themselves.[62]

*Typological Characterizations.* Since the foregoing discussion has attempted to relate these societies to one another through variables important for the classification of primitive religious systems, we may take the further step of deriving from that discussion some brief descriptive terms to emphasize the differing character of these religions. These terms are linguistically not precise, unless it is understood that their meaning is only to be found in the preceding discussion, not in any other connotations they may have as words. The following characterizations seem appropriate:

MURNGIN
Totemistic, basic-rural, sacro-secular, formal ritualistic;

ZUÑI
Naturalistic, basic-village, semi-sacro-secular, formal ritualistic;

TIKOPIA
Culture-hero ancestral, basic-village, sacro-secular, semi-formal, semi-ritualistic;

MANUS
Paternal ancestral, basic-urban, secular, informal, nonritualistic;

DAHOMEY
Creator-god pantheonistic, basic-urban, secular, monastic ritualistic.

The meaning of the first phrase in each characterization is fairly obvious, since in each case the reference is to the type of sacred entity or entities which are the focus of the religious practices, such as "culture-hero," "father's ghost," etc. The terms "basic-rural," "basic-village," and "basic-urban," do not, of course, mean that these societies are to be considered in ordinary terms as "cities," "towns," or "open country." Rather, the reference is to the meaning given in the discussion of the *societal matrix.* No inferences beyond those elements comprising that composite variable ought to be read into these three terms. They represent merely *approximate ways of stating the variation* already suggested by "societal matrix." "Sacro-secular" refers to the situation in which the sacred and lay personnel structures are identified with each other, as in Tikopia and Murngin. "Secular" refers to the separation of the two, as in Dahomey. The term "formal" does not refer to formality in the ordinary sense, but merely to the fact of *formalized training* for lay or practitioner in the religious system. The term "monastic" suggests an extreme degree of this training. The concept "ritualistic" refers to the existence of a considerable *elaboration* of *ritual* in the religion. This is true of all these five groups, except the Manus, even though it has been seen that there are important gradations between them.

It seems clear, then, that the religious systems under study vary widely in the variables or elements important for primitive religions, and that we can therefore analyze them with some assurance that a theory which fits these groups may have a wider validity than for these groups alone.

# APPENDIX II. A CRITIQUE OF PRIMITIVE RELIGION

As AN ORIENTING REMARKING, it ought to be repeated that much of the enormous literature on religion is irrelevant to the main problems of this study. Our object is not to discover whence religion came historically, or what its ultimate origins were. We can in some cases trace movements of religions in historical times, though in the case of nonliterates we may find the distinction between fact and folklore somewhat hazy. As to its ultimate origins, our data are irrevocably gone. We shall never be able to make more than reasonable deductions, without any possibility of finally testing them.[1] The possession of a Paleolithic artifact tells us almost nothing about its religious meaning. In the present study we have attempted to use sources which can be corroborated. This seems to be a more fruitful starting point.

A further difficulty must be noted in passing, this time an *apologia*. This section is a critique of major groups of theories which have been used to analyze primitive religion. At present, there is no adequate compendium of these theories, although they are discussed in a number of works.[2] The writer has of necessity relied upon his own scholarship. However, this scholarship is essentially American, and lacks the traditionally encyclopedic character of Continental scholarship. This is not false modesty. The reader may simply infer from this statement that the following critique is written with some humility before the overwhelming body of research which would have to be digested, in order to make this critique entirely satisfactory.

This analysis has, furthermore, led to several points of view which it would require a general debate to defend. First, a closer rereading of the classical works of Tylor, Schmidt, Marett, Lang, Frazer, and others has led the writer through two radical shifts in opinion. There was a preliminary period when all of them seemed naive in their conceptions and unsound in their choice of data. After that, and at present, there ensued a feeling that the differences between a modern analyst and any of them are not at all fundamental; that they were often very close to a sound understanding of religion, even when the interest of the times focussed their attention on problems different from ours.

Second, a number of re-evaluations seemed in order, although they are not significant except to a historian of ideas. Andrew Lang, for example, becomes a much sounder and more discriminating analyst than even Tylor, who was one of the best. In the precision of his logic and the deep interpretation of data, Lang deserves more attention than is usually given to him, at least in American circles. Frazer, on the other hand, becomes a masterly, energetic compiler. Further, the eclectic Lowie, coming much later, has written an able analysis of religion and of society which compares with the best analyses from the more colorful Malinowski. And, finally, the work done by the classicists—Gilbert Murray, Jane Ellen Harrison, and Francis Cornford—seems far more sophisticated in its implicit understanding of religion and society than anything that has been written since that time. And, it must be remembered, "that time" was the period in which Durkheim was making his own investigations into religion.

Since this critique does not aim at a historical treatment, the major ideas must be the focus of attention, not the men. On the other hand, no attempt will be made to analyze these ideas on the most abstract level.[3] A possible classification of these theories, in a somewhat schematic fashion, is presented here:

1. Animist-Manist
2. Naturistic
3. Psychoanalytic
4. Theological
5. Cultural-Historical
6. Sociological

We must remember that for many of these writers, in each of these groups, the problem of evolution was primary. We need not investigate here the historical situation which made that problem of primary concern in the last quarter of the nineteenth century. However, even when the evolutionary problem was a central concern, the implicit ideas about religion shaped these discussions, so that many common points of interest can be found.

When we ignore the problem of origins, and concentrate on the treatment of religion, the differences between Tylor's animism, Spencer's manism, and Müller's naturism are reduced to slight proportions. Let us look at Tylor's classic statement, preceding by several years that of Spencer:

In the first place, what is it that makes the difference between a living body and a dead one; what causes waking, sleep, trance, disease, death? In the second place, what are those human shapes which appear in dreams and visions? . . . the ancient savage philosophers probably made their first step by the obvious inference that every man has two things belonging to him, namely, a life and a phantom.[4]

The personal spirit which is thus created becomes the "apparitional-soul," a ghost-soul. It is the source of life and thought, and possesses the individual. It can leave the body, during as well as after life, and can enter animals as well as things. Tylor continues, "They are doctrines answering in the most forcible way to the plain evidence of men's senses, as interpreted by a fairly consistent and rational primitive philosophy."[5] Again, "The early animistic theory of vitality, regarding the functions of life as caused by the soul, offers to the savage mind an explanation of several bodily and mental conditions, as being effects of a departure of the soul or some of its constituent spirits."[6] Both visions and dreams give similar evidence to the primitive mind in its attempts to explain the soul, for the savage or barbarian "has never learned to make that rigid distinction between subjective and objective, between imagination and reality, to enforce which is one of the main results of scientific education."[7] These, then, are the source of the idea that souls are "ethereal images of bodies."[8] In short, this most primitive form of religion is a product of the mind working on data furnished by the senses, by obvious and direct experience. Spencer agrees in the main with this proposition. It is equally clear that from such "simple" beginnings, inanimate or natural objects may come to be possessed by a soul, so that polytheism and nature worship can develop. Furthermore, one spirit may achieve dominance, to become a great god, ruling over the others as well as over men. Although Tylor did not assume that only the "higher races" could evolve the notion of monotheism, the final step has generally been taken by civilized groups.

What concerns us here is not the accuracy of the evolutionary sequence, but the conception of religion which is implicit in this treatment. This conception is to be found equally implicit in Comte's work a generation earlier.[9] This conception looks upon religion as essentially an intellectual effort, an early type of philosophy which orders both physical and social facts. Its view is that the only significant orientation toward the world that man can have is that which is to be derived from science. In this narrow sense, Tylor's work can be called "positivistic."[10] The religious doctrines and practices are treated as theological systems created by human reason.[11] The systematics of animism are viewed as the attempt to understand the common events of human experience— death, breath, the movements and activities of natural phenomena as well as animals. This is essentially a cognitive process, and the primitive believer is a logician, rationally analyzing the universe. The same conception is to be seen in the case of magic:

Magic has not its origin in fraud. . . . what we find is an elaborate and systematic pseudo-science. It is, in fact, a sincere but fallacious system of philosophy . . .[12]

Tylor's approach, then, is essentially rationalistic and cognitive. It is, furthermore, individualistic. Following a long tradition of nineteenth century thought, he attempted to analyze religion as the activity of individuals, rather than of the society.[13] It is from the experiences of individuals that religion arises. The fallacious reasoning of individuals leads to "higher" forms of religion, a process in which other individuals in the society also share. The relationship between individual and society has been discussed at several points in this study, and needs no great elaboration here. However, a few comments may be added with respect to animism-naturism, in particular.

There is, first of all, no quarrel with the idea that the originator of any idea might have been an individual. This would be true for innovation, generally, we may suppose, since any act must be done by an individual. This admission does not, however, change the essentially social character of religious activities, and we may look at the failures which arise from the individualistic conception.

If we attempt to look at religion as an individual activity, or as one originated by an individual, we cannot explain the integration of the social structure. To the extent that the wants or desires (in hedonistic economics), or individual experiences (in animistic and naturistic theories of primitive religion) are individual, they are properly random. A society will always be somewhat heterogeneous with respect to the sex, age, status, occupation, personality of its members, and they cannot have had precisely the same experiences. There would, then, be extremely variant experiences and reactions, and the structure becomes indeed a puzzle.

We fail to understand, furthermore, the obligatory character of religious activities, as to symbolism, ritual, language, or belief. So long as the experiences and the philosophical interpretations of them are random, there is no particular force or process by which other members come to accept them.

Moreover, any such interpretations would have only a fortuitous relationship to the group values, if they were merely rationalistic explanations of the universe.

The rationalistic approach, then, fails to take into account the emotional, obligatory character of these beliefs and practices. The individualistic approach fails in its attempts to explain the integrative character of religion, as well as the integrated character of the social structure. This means, concretely, failing to see the close connection between religious activities and the moral aspects of behavior.[14] In addition, this means that Tylor does not see religion as *analytically necessary*. There is merely evidence that religion is a universal social phenomenon, an entirely different matter. In Tylor's statement,

Though the theoretical niche is ready (for a tribe without religion) and convenient, the actual statue to fill it is not forthcoming. The case is in some degree similar to that of the tribes asserted to exist without language or without the use of fire; nothing in the nature of things seems to forbid the possibility of such existence, but as a matter of fact the tribes are not found.[15]

It is a tribute to Tylor, however, that we must still discuss his theories. At a time when few men examined anthropological materials critically, he was able to produce a treatise which is readable even now. Although he accepted the evolutionary framework of his day, and spoke of "lower" and "higher" races, he insisted that the laws of the mind were essentially the same for all of mankind. Furthermore, although we have here pointed out the weakness of the purely cognitive approach to religious phenomena, it must be remembered that this is one necessary element in any understanding of religion. In addition, by the happy chance of his focus, animism, he was well aware of the "anthropopsychic" character of sacred entities.

The naturism of Friedrich Max Müller does not require an extended treatment, since its essential conceptions are similar to those of animism-manism.[16] Instead of using Spencer's ghosts, or Tylor's visions and dreams, he decided that religion rested mainly upon spontaneous feelings of awe, wonder, and terror which natural phenomena inspired in early human beings. The enormously powerful forces of nature and the diversity of its manifestations so impressed early man that he responded with those feelings and thought which we designate as religious. This idea, which is common even yet, was only a beginning, a foundation.[17] The awe is an emotion, but it has little intellectual structure. There are as yet no spirits, and these arise in part through a *process of linguistic confusion: between the metaphorical use of a term and its more strictly denotative usage.*[18] Thus, the sun might be called something, or an entity, which hurls golden bolts through space, allowing a subsequent personification.

A whole world of such spirits might thus be created, and the cult would arise from the necessity of propitiating these powerful entities. At times taking an extreme position, Müller became interested in the extent to which language and myth in turn shape human thought, almost becoming thought itself. Indeed, the myth becomes "a disease of thought,"[19] and his main focus of interest.

We need not discuss the labyrinth of linguistic questions which are relevant to naturism.[20] Müller's conception of religion is very close to that of animism, except for the specific discussion of evolutionary problems. These were, of course, his main focus throughout his linguistic researches. We can be surprised at this new use of the Robinson Crusoe situation—man, at the dawn of history: naked like Adam, but a grown person; fully socialized, but without any experience; the result of several hundreds of millions of years of evolution, but seeing the sun for the first time. For many of the things which seem so awe-inspiring to us have, as Durkheim phrased it, "a regularity which approaches monotony."[21] Man's long animal history precludes his "discovery" of many of these phenomena.

Furthermore, an enormous number of the sacred entities to be found among human societies are not at all awe-inspiring, so far as we can use this type of reasoning: an impressive list of totemic animals, to use only one section of such beings.

These are, nevertheless, but quibbles. What is significant is that this approach, in spite of its accepting the emotional element in religion, is another attempt to analyze religion as a pre-scientific explanation of the world. Man is seen as developing a kind of natural history, even though the precipitating experience is emotional. The ideas that he develops at this dawn of mankind are, naturally, erroneous, but they are his first intellectual activities on such a scale.

On this level, then, naturism and animism-manism have the same failure. Consequently, neither can explain the continuance of religion. Tylor was faced with the problem of explaining the survival of animistic notions into modern life, and indicates that under the impact of science it is fading. Similarly, if religious systems are a result of a first emotional contact with natural phenomena, they should disappear when we have understood their origin. However, it is precisely the integrative and integrated character of religious action which causes this lasting strength, and viewing religion as a purely *cognitive* activity, or as a merely *individual* product, inevitably leaves these matters unexplained and indeed inexplicable.

In both cases, moreover, there is the attempt to find order among the *objects* worshipped: Tylor and Spencer by positing an in-dwelling spirit from ghosts, visions and dreams, Müller by finding gods or spirits in natural phenomena. This is, naturally, the result of a rationalistic approach, which expects to find such an order, since it is assumed the religious ideas are early attempts at rational explanation. Such an approach is akin to the numerous attempts to find cross-cultural order in the religious symbols themselves.[22]

*A transition from animism.* More eclectic than his predecessors, and more sophisticated in his understanding of society, Andrew Lang represents a transition figure of importance for several groups, among them the cultural-historical and the theological. He began his work as a Tylorian animist.[23] Later, however, he took a more critical view, both as to the religious *beliefs* of the primitive as well as to the integration of religion with the rest of social action. His own starting point was rationalistic, an attempt to understand these ideas as cognitive, within an evolutionary framework. Although he did not entirely throw over this basic assumption, by 1901 he was able to write, "The study of the origins of religion is impeded by the impossibility of obtaining historical evidence on the subject."[24] And in his printed version of the Gifford Lectures he was able to present telling criticisms of some of Tylor's ideas.[25]

He had also begun to develop a more functionalist view of religion, combined with the growing idea that morality and religion were more closely interrelated than a purely individualistic or rationalistic approach would indicate.[26] The possibility that high-gods were rather common had begun to play a part in his thinking, a matter of great importance for the later notions of W. Schmidt. He is able to see that magic and religion do not constitute a dichotomy, and also accepts the notion that science will not necessarily destroy religion.[27]

His approach, however, remains evolutionary in character, and his focus of interest is usually that of religious beliefs. His main emphasis remains cognitive.[28]

Sir James George Frazer first published *The Golden Bough* in 1890, and expanded his original work into a twelve-volume opus by the period 1911-1915, but he is not a transition figure in the same sense as Andrew

Lang.[29] As Malinowski has implicitly affirmed in his extended essay giving honor to Frazer, the contribution of the latter was not that of forwarding the theory of religion.[30] A humanist and a scholar, he was able to re-create from field reports something of the drama of primitive life. He became the source and inspiration of much work, but remained with a previous generation in his basic conceptions. He makes the magician into a clever, cool manipulator of other individuals at one time, while thinking of him as also a kind of early scientist.[31] He resurrects the distinction between magic and religion in outmoded terms, ignoring Lang's criticisms. He is essentially an individualistic rationalist. It is quite true, of course, that much more is to be found in Frazer. His very attempt to re-create the life of the primitive frequently forced him to present entirely different data: the magician becomes at times a priest, the sacred entities are anthropopsychic, the integration of moral and religious action is presented in certain cases, etc. However, in the main, his work became a compendium of far-ranging anthropological data with evolution as a central problem, within a framework of individualistic rationalism.

Two main emphases do represent contributions, however, although in both cases he does not make them central ideas, and both of them were being worked out by other writers at the same period.[32] He pointed out that, in contrast to the work of previous analysts, religion must be thought of as *action,* not as a doctrine alone; and he tied up religious activities with great life crises, especially birth and death.[33]

*Psychoanalysis and Primitive Religion.* Although most of us are somewhat sceptical of the psychoanalytical explanations of primeval thinking, it is worth remembering that all of the thinkers mentioned up to this point had no hesitation about making such explanations. The ratiocination of primeval man is sketched in every one of these earlier works, and with hardly more data than Freud, who had his patients as well as Frazer, Wundt, and Reinach as sources.

Although the basis of orthodox psychoanalysis has been, and still is, predominantly biological and hereditary, its most fruitful contributions have been those dealing with social relationships and the socialization process. Its position is further interesting, in that social scientists generally reject the theoretical schema of psychoanalysis, while in banter and personal conversation utilizing Freudian ideas extensively. Moreover, the modern developments in psychoanalysis have been in the direction of assimilating sociological ideas.

With reference to religion, however, psychoanalysis has been relatively unfruitful. Its ideas have not been sharpened over a period of several decades, and "research" has consisted in the main of applying rigidly a set of deductive principles to field reports. Since psychoanalysis has begun from what was previously termed a "positivistic" approach, it has treated religion as an illusion, as a major pathology, which general human enlightenment would inevitably erase. The cult aspects of psychoanalysis, of course, leave the field open to a return accusation.[34]

Even if one does not accept Kroeber's re-evaluation of Freud's *Totem and Taboo* as a fantasy, *The Future of an Illusion* is clearly the sounder work. However, the basic ideas of both are almost identical, as is true of the more specialized treatment, *Moses and Monotheism*.[35] Here, dealing mainly with Western society, Freud points out what he considers the two main aspects of culture. These are: A. the knowledge and power man possesses for mastering nature (technology), and B. the regulations of relationships between human beings (value systems). Man cannot live in isolation, but culture has to be defended against the individual, since it is burdensome to him. If it were not protected, he could kill whom he pleased, take any woman he chose, and satisfy any of his hidden desires. Yet such a situation would be chaotic. There are other beings whose desires must be satisfied in turn. It is only through culture that a communal existence is possible.[36]

Man is thus hemmed in by his culture, other men, and nature. He must, then, have a defense for his "innate narcissism," particularly as this situation relates to nature.[37]

Culture, then, humanizes nature. This is of great importance, since it is these impersonal forces which are most heartrending in their coldness. If we endow nature with a will, we can understand it, for we are then dealing with familiar things. We can propitiate, threaten, and plead. As has been noted previously in this study, an important function of religion is that of making certain aspects of the universe *meaningful* to us, in a sense different from the merely scientific.[38]

This step, on the other hand, has a primeval and an early infantile aspect. It is phylogenetic as well as ontogenetic: the early relationship of helplessness and fear before the parents. The two situations, in this conception, are the same. The forces of nature are made into gods with the characteristics of the father, just as in our helplessness before the father we endow him with less terrible qualities. Even when natural science develops, the gods continue their threefold task:

. . . they must exorcise the terrors of nature, they must reconcile one to the cruelty of fate, particularly as shown in death, and they must make amends for the sufferings and privations that the communal life of culture has imposed on men.[39]

The gods, however, recede into the background, except for occasional miracles.

But this last development is hazardous for the gods, since the suspicion remains that in the fateful working out of things the gods themselves are creatures of an inscrutable fate.[40] The third task, then, becomes the main work of the gods, and morality their chief domain. They must:

. . . adjust the defects and evils of culture . . . attend to the sufferings that men inflict on each other in their communal life, and . . . see that the laws of culture, which men obey so ill, are carried out.[41]

Now a further step, by which this justice, goodness, and wisdom, are imputed to one divine being, the condensation of the gods of antiquity. As one could predict, for Freud this is revealed as the father figure, and as a consequence the intimacy and intensity of the child-father relationship could now be recovered. The parent-child relationship is, we see, projected into the external world. It is this illusion, this pathology, which lies behind all religion.[42]

This type of "historical" reconstruction is also followed in *Totem and Taboo,* which need not concern us here. With more specific reference to the development of the incest tabu, the same theme is worked out: the origin of moral and religious ideas from the archetypal, phylogenetically internalized Oedipal complex.

The strength of this illusion lies in the "oldest, strongest and most insistent wishes of mankind," those relating to infantile helplessness, the need of protection, the allaying of anxiety, fulfilling of justice, the promise of a future life, the origin of things.[43] Freud suggests, nevertheless, that it is time we try other means to happiness, since religion has been tried and found wanting.

As is easily seen, in spite of an acceptance of false biological conceptions, this approach does recognize the interrelationships between various aspects of the value structure. In spite of this view of religion as a false "theory," he sees its emotional importance. Freud was not able to manipulate data from other cultures without applying a mechanical set of principles, however, and as a result was not able to develop and sharpen his ideas on religion as he was able to do with specifically clinical conceptions.

*Theology and Primitive Religion.* Ordinarily in a scientific work the conclusions of theologians are ignored. They are somewhat more relevant in the case of primitive religion, and especially so since some of the impulse toward the cultural-historical position came from theological circles. This position represented a way out of certain problems posed by the animistic theories. Without attempting a really adequate analysis, it is clear that the animistic theories were extremely relativistic. They were thereby opposed to the authoritarian absoluteness of church—any church —doctrines. By looking at a wide range of morality, the bases of Christian morality were questioned. Furthermore, those religious groups which laid great emphasis on revelation were faced with primitive groups which presumably could not have had such a revelation. In addition, the primitives had to go through a long period of education before even accepting such doctrines intellectually. Finally, the evolutionary framework left the developed Christian religion as merely one more step in the growth of religious practices, leading just possibly to the twilight of the gods as the end point.

The materialism of primitive animism, not to mention its dark and bloody concerns, also suggested unclean roots for developed religion.

Actually, as Schmidt amply documents, the significance of animism for the Christian religion was at first overlooked.[44] By the turn of the century, however, a number of theologians began to busy themselves with these problems.[45] Unfortunately, however, they did not see the importance of animism, and, as Schmidt notes, made many errors in their attacks on animism, as well as in their own attempts at analysis.[46] Gradually, as missionaries began to collect ethnographic data systematically, some of these errors were erased.

For our purposes, it is most significant that this group finally seized on the opportunity to accept a primitive, natural monotheism closely related to morality as the ultimate basis and forerunner of all religion. This idea, in a similar form, was accepted by scholars of the cultural-historical school, in particular those grouping about the journal, *Anthropos*. The works of Lang in particular were of great importance for this development, for he had repeatedly pointed to the widespread occurrence of the high-god, removed from the world while lesser spirits came into more direct contact with men. Furthermore, according to Lang, the origin of the high-god is not necessarily spiritual, for he was a powerful, though non-natural man, created by men to answer their questions about the world. Lang had also exploded many of the facile evolutionary propositions dealing with religion. That those writing from a theological position were led to examine animism critically, and then to gather further data, is worthy of note, even when their aim was not that of science alone.

Writing from a theological point of view, they were at least aware of the close relationship between "morality" and religion, after an earlier phase of identifying morality with Christian morality. A major weakness is their emphasis on doctrine, but they were able to accept the emotional element in religion, as well as the fact that religious doctrines offer a number of answers as to the meaning of the world and its events. They did not see the crucial importance of religious action, as the focus of both doctrine and social structure, and their significance is now seen in the impetus they furnished toward actual field reports of primitive societies.

*Socialist-Communist Position.* Only a brief glance will be given the socialist-communist attempts at theorizing about primitive religion, and that mainly for some completeness of discussion. This group exemplifies clearly a conclusion to be drawn from Parsons' *Structure of Social Action,* that it is only those theorists who constantly return to empirical data who are able to forge ahead in the development of adequate theory.[47] The theological group, for all its interest in buttressing Christianity, became far better versed in the facts of ethnology, and many of them actually did excellent field research. Junod, Koppers, Schmidt, Schebesta, and Gusinde are among the better known names, but the group is large in number and impressive in its field researches. It is an ironical twist that the "materialistic" socialist followers have never bothered to absorb the data of other researchers, or go into the field themselves.[48] This is the case not only for religion, but also for the study of the family as well.[49]

In both cases, the "theory" is developed deductively from Marxian notions, with citations of many isolated bits of data to "demonstrate" it. Actually, there is no complete and systematic theoretical system. There are, however, a few early works which attempt some comment on primitive religion. And, as is usual when the object of analysis is not Western capitalism, the analysis can be classed as "vulgar Marxism": the religious ideas are held to follow directly from the economic structure, i.e., the forces and relationships of production or ownership. Religion is no more than a reflection, in the minds of men, of the external powers which rule them. These natural forces come to take on the form of the supernatural. Other Marxian writers also followed Müller to some degree.[50]

Since, in this conception, "the religious world is but the reflex of the real world," Christianity—especially in its bourgeois form—with its notion of "abstract man," admirably fits the demands of the economic system which treats man as a commodity.[51] When, however, there was a low development of labor's productivity, there was as a consequence a very narrow range of social relationships between man and man, and between man and nature. This is reflected in the "ancient worship of

Nature, and in the other elements of popular religions."[52] It will be only when the relationships between men are reasonable and intelligible that this religious reflex will vanish.

As in the case of socialist speculations about the family, the evolutionary framework is imposed on the data under the common assumption that certain societies, such as Polynesia and Australia, could be identified with those existing in the Paleolithic period.[53] There is, nevertheless, little attempt to indicate just how and when some particular complex of production relationships actually created, or influenced, or determined, the religious system. H. Eilderman goes so far in his speculations as to postulate, in a fashion reminiscent of an earlier generation, an original society of force, in which the strong took what they wanted, in an environment of want.[54]

The rationalism which characterizes Marxism, causing Lenin to refer to "the religious opium which stupefies the people,"[55] must treat religion as epiphenomenal and an instrument for the manipulation of the exploited. Thus, Plekhanov:[56]

Both the innovators and the conservatives invoke the aid of the gods, placing various institutions under their protection or even claiming that they are an expression of divine will. It goes without saying that the Eumenides, whom the ancient Greeks regarded as the upholders of the mother right, did as little in its defense as Minerva did for the triumph of the father. Men simply wasted their time and effort in calling upon the aid of the gods and fetishes; but the ignorance did not prevent the Greek conservatives . . . from realizing that . . . the old customary law was a better guarantee of their interests.

Or, Engels, upholding Morgan's "economic determinism" against Bachoften (though basically accepting the "stages" postulated by both):

Dass eine solche Auffassung, wo die Religion als der entscheidende Hebel der Weltgeschichte gilt, schlieszlich auf reinen Mystizismus hinauslaufen musz ist klar.[57]

Rather: "Nach der materialistischer Auffassung ist das in letzter Instanz bestimmende Moment in der Geschichte: die Produktion und Reproduktion des unmittelbaren Lebens."[58] That nostalgia which in Marxist thought viewed early man as living in a primitive communism, in which no one questioned the legitimacy of a child, property was held in common, and there was a "free voluntary respect enjoyed by the organs of the tribal (clan) society,"[59] saw the accumulation of property and the development of property rights as having destroyed that healthy life.[60] Religion becomes the goal of the exploiters, the owners; in the future, when these relationships are destroyed, religion will also be eliminated.

Unfortunately, the undoubtedly close integration between power, wealth, and religion was never fully analyzed. The basic rationalistic errors, the failure to see the necessity for ultimate value structures in a society, and the failure to use data beyond Morgan, prevented the development of an important insight.

*The Cultural-Historical School.* Schmidt occupies a central role in the development of the cultural-historical school of anthropology, a system of data organization first propounded by F. Graebner.[61] Schmidt accepted some of Lang's conclusions, and fitted them to Graebner's method. The cultural problem was attacked mainly in terms of the diffusion of cultural phenomena and artifacts. Here, again, the specific problem was not that investigated in this study. Its significance lies, as in the case of Lang and the theological group, in the attention drawn to otherwise unnoticed elements in primitive religions. We must remember once more, however, that the primary intellectual problem was doctrine rather than other elements in religion.

For Schmidt, the most primeval cultural form available is among the Bushmen, the Congo Pygmies, the Semang of the Malay Peninsula, the Andaman Islanders, the Tasmanians, i.e., those mainly on a low plane of technological development.[62] As most American anthropologists, as against European scholars, would point out: though these are "primitive," they are not "primeval," but may represent a long line of evolution and change of their own, whatever the usual conservatism among primitive societies. Schmidt attempts to prove that: A. these most archaic cultures all have a high-god religious pattern, and that therefore, B. this pattern must be the primal archetype, with animistic developments coming later. In fact, he would maintain that all groups had a revelation experience, in which this primal pattern was central. The distinction between "primeval" and "primitive," however, throws doubt on this formulation, since beliefs, like tools, also go through changes and processes, and there is little reason to believe that we have reached, say, a Paleolithic level when we study the Semang. Nevertheless, as Lowie shrewdly points out, there is a considerable conservatism in religious beliefs and practices, and some elements may be preserved for millennia.[63] It would then be methodologically acceptable to assume, as one would in dealing with technological remains, that if one found such tribes, all of them isolated for centuries, with the same high-god complex, this complex could be considered older.[64]

Schmidt attempts in several volumes to prove this. However, it still remains to be proved, except in Catholic circles, because of both inadequacy and contradictoriness of data. Actually, there seems to be a strong animistic or quasi-animistic set of spirits even in the cases cited, so far as adequate evidence can be collected. There is genuine prayer to other than a high-god, and the high-god him-(her)self will have human attributes and therefore foibles.[65] The concrete evidence would indicate that the animistic conceptions are at least as entitled as the high-god to be considered primal.

This group is significant in that by investigating these problems, it uncovered an enormous mass of data which, as in the case of Lang, had long been overlooked. They threw their weight against the survivals from evolutionistic animism, and proved the existence of certain high-gods even among technologically backward tribes. True enough, they overlooked some of the trickster elements and apparently failed to see that each culture validates the values within it, so that what seems to us the trickster creator chastising for whim alone, may be upholding a value of functional significance. Thus they tended to gloss over such evidence. However, Lowie suggests, the acceptance of a creative entity as an intellectual notion in the minds of such tribes shows up a fact of great importance for understanding the much-deprecated "primitive mind."[66]

In addition, and more important for our purposes, there is a good grasp of the intimate relationship between the moral system of the society and the religious ideas. The approach, sophisticated in its geographical and temporal perspective, was relativisitic enough that the Christian morality did not constitute the standard for judging whether the tribe had a moral system. Its emphasis on doctrine, and to some extent on those segments of ritual which seemed to be spread from one area to another, did not allow a focus on the interrelatedness of all the religious elements with other aspects of the society. This is especially true for Graebner's analysis of the "World and View" of the primitive.[67]

*Sociological Position.* To speak of a "sociological school" is unfortunate, since the major structure of social analysis is not basically different between cultural anthropology and sociology. Indeed, as has been pointed out earlier, without adequate documentation, one may say that the differences in approach between cultural anthropology, sociology, and social psychology are primarily occupational, not based upon important theoretical considerations. The term, "sociological school," then, is used here only because the best known of the group was Emile Durkheim, a sociologist.

The French side of this group is well known. Most of Durkheim's works have been translated. His colleagues on *L'Année Sociologique* at the turn of the century, Henri Hubert and Marcel Mauss, are also read in this country, and Lucien Levy-Bruhl is still widely quoted.[68] They have, indeed, not only become well known, but also well damned.[69]

Since the present study is in the tradition of the sociological school, especially that of Durkheim, the present section is directed mainly toward pointing out elements in the earlier formulations which are explicitly rejected. Nevertheless, at least a brief tribute ought to be paid to the English group, who were not sociologists, but classicists: Especially so, since the inspiration for both was William Robertson Smith. In addition, the English group, centering about Gilbert Murray and having as its two most distinguished scholars Jane Ellen Harrison and Francis M. Cornford, kept abreast of developments in France. Indeed, a careful reading of Harrison's work might indicate that she was more cautious in interpretation while as deeply interpretative, compared to Durkheim.[70] As some mitigation of this judgment, let us remember that the standards of criticism in the classics, as well as the quantity of verified data, were both superior to those in anthropology, at the turn of the century. This is a considerable mitigation if we believe, and this is my own faith, that there can be a science of society. Because they were primarily concerned with the elucidation of Greek classics, both philosophy and literature, they frequently attacked problems which are not central for the sociologist. Nevertheless, their approach is implicitly that of good sociology, while centering their analysis on such specifically historical and linguistic problems.

As to the rejected elements in the Smith-Durkheim formulations, a few comments will suffice. No longer can we accept easily the "stages" of evolution which were part of the intellectual structure of that time. Nor do we need to accept totemism as the most primitive of religions, or promiscuity as the most primitive or reproductive "institutions."[71]

Smith's idea of primitive mentality, implicit in Durkheim and explicit in Levy-Bruhl, according to which the tribesman simply cannot distinguish between many things which are clearly different to the "civilized" man, is an idea which modern analysis has also rejected in part.[72]

Both Smith and Durkheim held the notion that the typical primitive society represents a homogeneous milieu, in which the members are almost an undifferentiated kin group who feel as one, both with themselves and (during rituals) with the gods. The individual is almost completely absorbed.[73] As against this, the anthropologist has come to see that there is great individual variation within any society. Although many anthropologists have seen this, including Boas, it is perhaps Paul Radin who has most emphatically insisted upon the point.[74] In any event, the matter is the subject at present of many joint researches done by anthropologists and those trained in psychology or psychiatry.

Smith, of an earlier generation than Durkheim, falls into another type of confusion, one which has already been discussed in Chapter II. He considers as almost part of the definition of religion the idea that the system is, inherently, "good," "beneficent," favorable to the community.[75] As has already been noted, no matter what values one holds, the religious activities will be in some measure ambivalent. They do not even unequivocally and universally support the political structure.

As to the conception of magic held by Smith and Durkheim, both stated that the two were distinct. For Smith, there was a moral antithesis between magic and religion; Durkheim accepts this, and emphasizes as well a supposed professional antagonism.[76] As has already been discussed in Chapter III, the distinction between the two is best seen as a continuum, if we are to have a formulation which fits the facts.

Although Smith attempts to analyze many types of sacrifices (sacred or unclean animals, types of vegetable foods, etc.) and sacred places (cairns, caves, stones, trees, etc.) in terms which make it evident that these objects have some inherent characteristics which would make them sacred to the group, Durkheim himself rejects such a theory by pointing out the infinite variability in these items.[77] Yet a synthesis is seen between these two, one which has only been suggested in this study, that the symbols used, and therefore the items defined as sacred, will not vary at random, but will be limited in part by the items which are important within the society. This is an idea which is also implicit in Durkheim's discussions of totemism, cited above, as well as in the work of the English classicists.

A final element in the Durkheim formulation must be mentioned, the notion that in investigating religion one is discovering the "reality" which religion expresses.[78] This is part of a wider positivistic framework in which Durkheim's thought is couched, and is closely connected to the idea frequently held by positivists (as often by Durkheim), that it is possible to create an ethic or a religion on a "scientific" basis. It means, in essence, a denial of the basic separation of the logico-empirical or scientific, and the value-judgmental.

The basis for rejecting this notion of a religious "reality" demands some discussion, which must extend to the point of view from which Durkheim began his investigations. Most importantly, Durkheim was led to ask the question concerning the "reality" expressed by religion because of his rejection of two widespread explanations of religion, already discussed in this study. One is, that religious ideas are attempts to describe or analyze the external environment, the heavens, or the actual origins of physical things. The other is that the various religions or sacred objects, places, words, or situations derived their sacredness from some intrinsic characteristic which automatically inspired the feeling of awe in the perceiver.

Against the first of these explanations Durkheim made the objection already noted, that the spread of science would have rapidly wiped out religion as a social force if it had been merely an attempt by early man to explain the physical universe. Against the second, Durkheim pointed out that the mere variety of sacred objects would deny any such intrinsically religious character. The characteristic which is common is really the emotional reaction in the believer. Consequently, these sacred things are to be considered symbols. Durkheim does not, of course, accept the notion that religious ideas are "mere illusions." This set of ideas led Durkheim to state the proposition that these religious things— gods, robes and vestments, sacred words, etc.—were symbolic of "society." That is, one cannot speak of symbols unless there is a referent for those symbols.

It is here, however, that Durkheim falls into serious error. For he then thinks of these symbols as being essentially the type of symbols used in scientific statements, i.e., essentially linguistic pointers referring to a specific reality. But he then has returned to the *first* type of theory already rejected: "Religious ideas must, then, be distorted representations of an empirical reality which is capable of correct analysis by an empirical science, this time sociology."[79] Instead of conceiving religion as the central element in the normative complex, it merely becomes a metaphorical description of some elements in the concrete social group. Actually, when we insist on the importance of the subjective factor in the analysis of social action, it is seen that "*no* empirical reality in the scientific sense underlies religious ideas."[80] The referents in question are ultimate value-elements, nonscientific and nonlogical in nature. If there were really an empirical reality being expressed in religion, no need would exist for the particular kind of symbolism found in religions.[81] This reality could be "expressed" directly, as in any scientific description.

This does not deny, however, that it is through the socialization process that religious attitudes are developed. Further, it must be admitted that the attitudes toward religious precepts and sacred things are like those toward moral precepts and acts, and that both are social in nature. Or, expressing the relationship as transformed by Parsons, "*society* is a *religious* phenomenon."[82]

Durkheim fell into this positivistic error easily because of another such error, that of thinking of the actor as being "constrained" by the moral elements in society. Granted that this is not a consistent point of view, nevertheless its presence at any point means that the actor is sometimes thought of as only an individual, adjusting himself to both the social and physical environment. Consequently, it becomes easy to think of the religious objects as being symbolic of the concrete source of "constraint," the concrete society which "imposes" its moral and religious patterns on the members of the group.

In all the preceding discussions, the attempt has not been made to stress a criticism couched only in terms of the particular problems of this study, but rather to understand the problem in terms of the formulator. However, since the aim here is not history, a separation has been attempted between the purely historical materials and the implicit formulations which helped to shape the earlier analysis of origins. In most of these cases, a considerable amount of common residue is to be found, suggesting often a more precise theoretical formulation as a working hypothesis. Such a general formulation, it has been further intimated, must relate closely with a general theory of society, since most of the earlier works failed because of an individualistic and rationalistic bias. It must, further, emphasize broadly the meaningful, emotional, and actional elements. Moreover, no arbitrarily monistic theory of the *kind* of entity or thing worshipped can be accepted, to judge by the evidence. The reasons for this may be noted in the sociological analysis of Chapters II and III. Further, the encyclopedic system of adducing materials out of context or merely as "another case to be cited," ignoring important gaps in the sources, or citing corroborative materials from otherwise rejected sources, must be thrown aside for a while. Until our anthropological data actually cover satisfactorily the many tribes utilized in such a treatment, we must rather attempt the more modest, yet intensive analysis of fewer, but better understood, tribes.

# BIBLIOGRAPHY

Allen, Clifford, *Modern Discoveries in Medical Psychology*, 2nd ed., N. Y., Macmillan, 1949.

Allier, Raoul, *Magie et Religion*, Berger Levrault, Paris, 1936.

Ashley-Montagu, M. R., *Coming into Being Among the Australian Aborigines*, Routledge, London, 1937.

Ashley-Montagu, M. R., *Man's Most Dangerous Myth: The Fallacy of Race*, N. Y., Columbia University, 1945.

Ashley-Montagu, M. R., and Merton, Robert K., "Crime and the Anthropologist," *American Anthropologist* 42 (1940), pp. 384-408.

Aupiais, F., "Cérémonies fétichistes dites ahuandida á Bohicon (Dahomey) ches le chef féticheur Tongodo, le 1er mars 1930," *Anthropos*, vol. XXXI (1936), pp. 239-241.

Ayres, C. E., *Science the False Messiah*, Bobbs-Merrill, Indianapolis, 1927.

Bachofen, J. J., *Urreligion und Antike Symbole*, 3 vols., Leipzig, Philipp Reclam, 1926 (from various works written up to his death in 1887).

Barber, Bernard, "Acculturation and Messianic Movements," *American Sociological Review*, vol. VI (1941), pp. 663-669.

Bartet, A., "Les rois du Bas-Dahomey," *Societé de Geographie de Rochefort Bulletin*, vol. XXX (1908), pp. 179-216.

Basedow, Herbert, "Subincision and Kindred Rites of the Australian Aboriginal," *Journal of the Royal Anthropological Institute*, vol. LVII (1927), pp. 123-156.

Bateson, Gregory, *Naven*, Cambridge University, Cambridge, 1936.

Becker, Howard, "The Sorrow of Bereavement," *"Journal of Abnormal Psychology*, vol. XXVII (1932), pp. 391-410.

Bell, F. L. S., "The Place of Food in the Social Life of Central Polynesia," *Oceania*, vol. II (1931), pp. 117-135.

Benedict, Ruth Fulton, *The Concept of the Guardian Spirit in North America, American Anthropological Association Memoirs* (1923), no. 29.

Benedict, Ruth Fulton, *Zuñi Mythology, Columbia University Contributions to Anthropology*, vol. XXI, N. Y., 1935.

Bennett, John W., and Tumin, Melvin M., *Social Life*, N. Y., Knopf, 1948.

Bernard, L. L., *Instinct*, N. Y., Holt, 1944.

Bertho, Jacques, "La science du destin au Dahomey," *Africa*, vol. IX (1936), pp. 359-376.

Bertho, Jacques, "Les Houeda," *Les Missions Catholiques*, 1935, Nos. 3233, 3234.

Besson, Maurice, *Le Totemism*, les Editions Rieder, Paris, 1929.

Beth, Karl, "Die Religion im Urteil der Psychoanalyse," *Archiv für Religionspsychologie*, vol. II (1929), pp. 676-87.

Binet, Edouard, "Observations sur les Dahomens," *Société D'Anthropologie de Paris, Bulletin et Mémoires*, series 5, vol. I (1900), pp. 244-252.

Boas, Franz, "History and Science in Anthropology: A Reply," *Am. Anthrop.* 38 (1936), pp. 137-141.

Bose, G., "Nature of Intelligence and its Measurement," *Indiana Journal of Psychology* 19 (1944), pp. 58-65.

Bosman, William, *A New and Accurate Description of the Coast of Guinea, Divided into the Gold, the Slave, and the Ivory Coasts*, 2nd ed., London, 1721.

Breal, Michel, *Hercule et Cacus. Etude de Mythologie Comparée*, Paris, Durand, 1863.

Bros, A., *L'Ethnologie Religieuse*, Librairie Bloui et Gay, Paris, 1936.

Bros, A., *Le Religion des Peuples Non-Civilisés*, Paris, Lethielleux, 1907.

Brown, A. R., "The Definition of Totemism," *Anthropos*, vol. IX (1914), pp. 622-630.

Bücher, Karl, *Industrial Evolution*, trans. S. M. Wickett, N. Y., Holt, 1912.

Bunzel, Ruth L., "Introduction to Zuñi Ceremonialism," *Bureau of American Ethnology Annual Reports*, vol. XLVII, pp. 467-544, 1932.

Bunzel, Ruth L., "Zuñi Katcinas," *Bureau of American Ethnology Annual Reports*, vol. XLVII, pp. 827-1086, 1932.

Bunzel, Ruth L., "Zuñi Origin Myths," *Bureau of American Ethnology Annual Reports*, vol. XLVII, pp. 545-609, 1932.

Bunzel, Ruth L., "Zuñi Ritual Poetry," *Bureau of American Ethnology Annual Reports*, vol. XLVII, pp. 611-835, 1932.

Bunzel, Ruth L., *Zuñi Texts, American Ethnological Society Publications*, vol. XV, N. Y., 1933.

Burton, Richard F., *A Mission to Gelele, King of Dahomey*, vols. I and II, 2d ed., Tinsley Bros., London, 1864.

Cannon, W. B., *The Wisdom of the Body*, London, Routledge, 1932.

Cornford, Francis, *From Religion to Philosophy*, Holt, N. Y., 1913.

Cunow, H., *Ursprung der Religion und des Gottesglaubens*, Berlin, Dietz, 1913.

Cushing, Frank Hamilton, "Outlines of Zuñi Creation Myths," *Bureau of American Ethnology Reports*, vol. XIII (1891-1892).

Cushing, Frank Hamilton, "Zuñi Fetiches," *Bureau of American Ethnology Reports*, vol. II, pp. 9-50.

Cyrille, Guillaume, "Ethnographie dahoméene," *Outre-Mer*, vol. IV (1932), pp. 144-154.

Davis, Kingsley, "A Conceptual Analysis of Stratification," *American Sociological Review*, vol. VII (1942), pp. 309-322.

Davis, Kingsley, *Human Society*, N. Y., Macmillan, 1949.

Davis, Kingsley, "The Theory of Primitive Religion," unpub. mss., given before the Philadelphia Anthropological Society, 1939.

Dietzgen, W., *Sämtliche Schriften*, in 3 vols., vol. III, Dietzgen Wiesbaden, 1911.

Dunbar, H. F., *Emotions and Bodily Changes*, N. Y., Columbia University, 1946.

Durand, Moïse, "Le paysan dahoméen vu par un Dahoméen," *Le Monde Colonial Illustré*, no. LXIX (1939), pp. 129-132.

Durkheim, Émile, "De la Définition des Phénomènes Religieux," *L'Année Sociologique*, vol. II (1897-8), pp. 1-28.

Durkheim, Émile, *L'Education Morale*, Paris, Alcan, 1925 (materials from 1902).

Durkheim, Émile, *The Elementary Forms of the Religious Life*, trans. Joseph Ward Swain, Macmillan, N. Y., 1926.

Eildermann, H., *Urkommunismus und Urreligion*, Internationale Arbeiter-Bibliothek, Berlin, 1921.

Elkin, A. P., "Studies in Australian Totemism—The Nature of Australian Totemism," *Oceania*, vol. IV (1933-4), pp. 113-131.

Elkin, A. P., *Studies in Australian Totemism, The Oceania Monographs*, No. 2, Sydney, 1937.

English, O. Spurgeon, "Psychiatric Treatment in Psychosomatic Illnesses," *Med. Surg. J.*, 101 (1949), pp. 565-573.

Engels, F., *Der Ursprung der Familie, des Privateigentums u. des Staats*, 5th ed., Stuttgart, Dietz, 1892.

Evans-Pritchard, E. E., "The Morphology and Function of Magic," *American Anthropologist*, vol. XXXI (1929).

Evans-Pritchard, E. E., "The Zande Corporations of Witchdoctors," *Journal of the Royal Anthropological Institute*, vol. LXII (1932), pp. 291-336, and vol. LXIII (1933), pp. 63-100.

Evans-Pritchard, E. E., *Witchcraft, Oracles and Magic Among the Azande*, Clarendon Press, Oxford, 1937.

Evans-Pritchard, E. E., "Zande Theology," *Sudan Notes and Records*, vol. XXX (1936), pp. 5-46.

Firth, Raymond, *Primitive Economics of the New Zealand Maori*, Dutton, N. Y., 1929.

Firth, Raymond, *Primitive Polynesian Economy*, Routledge, London, 1939.

Firth, Raymond, *Report on Research in Tikopia, Oceania*, vol. I (1930-1), pp. 113-114.

Firth, Raymond, "The Economic Psychology of the Maori," *Journal of the Royal Anthropological Institute*, vol. LV (1925), pp. 340-62.

Firth, Raymond, *The Work of the Gods in Tikopia*, 2 vols., Lund, Humphries, London, 1940.

Firth, Raymond, "Totemism in Polynesia," *Oceania*, vol. I (1930-31), pp. 291-321.

Firth, Raymond, *We, the Tikopia,* American, N. Y., 1936.

Fortes, M., and Evans-Pritchard, E. E., *African Political Systems,* Oxford University, London, 1941.

Fortune, Reo F., "Manus Religion," *Oceania,* vol. II (1931), No. 1, pp. 74-108.

Fortune, Reo F., *Manus Religion, Memoirs of the American Philosophical Society,* vol. III, Philadelphia, 1935.

Fortune, Reo F., *Sorcerers of Dobu,* Routledge, London, 1932.

Frazer, Sir James G., "The Beginnings of Religion and Totemism Among the Australian Aborigines," *Fortnightly Review,* 1905, pp. 151-162, 452-467.

Frazer, Sir James G., *The Golden Bough,* 1 vol. ed., N. Y., Macmillan, 1935.

Frazer, Sir James G., *Totemism and Exogamy,* 4 vols., Macmillan, London, 1910.

Freud, Sigmund, "Mourning and Melancholia," in *Collected Papers,* vol. IV, International Psychoanalytic Press, Wien, 1924-5, pp. 152-170.

Freud, Sigmund, *Totem and Tabu,* trans. A. A. Brill, N. Y., Dodd Mead, n.d. (materials date from 1912-1913).

Freud, Sigmund, *Moses and Monotheism,* trans. Katherine Jones, N. Y., Knopf, 1939.

Freud, Sigmund, *The Future of an Illusion,* trans. W. D. Robson-Scott, Horace Liveright, Edinburgh, 1928.

Goldenweiser, A. A., *Early Civilization,* Knopf, N. Y., 1922.

Goldenweiser, A. A., "Religion and Society: A Critique of Durkheim's Theory of the Origin and Nature of Religion," *J. Philos., Psych. and Sci. Meth.,* vol. IV (1917), pp. 113-124.

Goode, William J., "Conceptual Schemata in the Field of Social Disorganization," *Social Forces,* 26 (1947), pp. 19-25.

Goode, William J., "Magic and Religion: A Continuum," *Ethnos,* 1949: Nos. 2-4.

Graebner, Fritz, *Das Weltbild der Primitiven,* München, Reinhardt, 1924.

Graebner, Fritz, *Methods der Ethnologie,* Heidelberg, Winter, 1911.

Graebner, Fritz, "Kulturkreise u. Kulturschichten in Ozeanien," *Z.f. Ethnologie,* 1905, pp. 28 ff.

Gutmann, Bruno, *Das Recht der Dschagga,* Beck, München, 1926.

Handy, Edward S., "Zuñi Tales," *Journal of American Folk-lore,* vol. XXXI (1918), pp. 451-471.

Harrasser, Albert, "Die Rechtsverletzung bei den australischen Eingeborenen," Beilagheft zur *Zeitschrift für Vergleichende Rechtseissenschaft,* vol. L (1938), Stuttgart.

Harrison, Jane, *Ancient Art and Ritual,* Holt, N. Y., 1913.

Härtter, G., "Das Gottesgericht bei den Ewe," *Zeitschrift für Ethnologie,* vol. LXIX (1937), pp. 63-72.

Hazoumé, Paul, "Le pacte de sang au Dahomey," *Travaux et Mémoires de l'Institut d'Ethnologie,* vol. XXV (1937), pp. viii-170.

Herskovits, M. J., *Dahomey*, 2 vols., Augustin, N. Y., 1938.

Herskovits, M. J., "A Note on 'Woman Marriage' in Dahomey," *Africa*, vol. X, No. 3 (1937), pp. 335-341.

Herskovits, M. J., and F. S., *An Outline of Dahomean Religious Belief*, *Memoirs of the American Anthropological Association*, No. 41 (1933).

Herskovits, M. J., "Population Statistics in the Kingdom of Dahomey," *Human Biology*, vol. IV, No. 2 (1932), pp. 252-261.

Herskovits, M. J., "Some Aspects of Dahomean Ethnology," *Africa*, vol. V (1932), pp. 266-296.

Herskovits, M. J., and F. S., "The Art of Dahomey: I, Brasscasting and Appliqué Cloths," *American Magazine of Art*, vol. XXVII (1934), pp. 66-67; "II, Wood-carving," vol. XXVII, pp. 124-131.

Hoebel, E. Adamson, *The Political Organization and Law-ways of the Comanche Indians*, *American Anthropological Association Memoirs*, No. 54, 1940.

Hogbin, H. Ian, "The Social Reaction to Crime: Law and Morals in the Schouten Islands, New Guinea," *Journal of the Royal Anthropological Institute*, vol. LXVIII, pp. 223-262.

Hogbin, H. Ian, *Law and Order in Polynesia*, N. Y., Harcourt, 1934.

Hubert, Henri, and Mauss, Marcel, "Esquisse d'une Théorie Générale de la magie," *L'Anneé Sociologique*, vol. VII (1902-3), pp. 1-146.

Hubert, Henri, and Mauss, Marcel, "Essai sur la nature et la fonction du sacrifice," *L'Anneé Sociologique*, vol. II (1897-8), pp. 29-138.

Hugen, Thomas H., "Freudism and Religion," *Philosopher*, vol. XII (1931), pp. 63-72.

Hunter, Monica, *Reaction to Conquest*, Oxford, Int. Inst. for African Languages and Cultures, 1936.

Kalten, Horace, "Functionalism" in *Encyclopedia of the Social Sciences*.

Jones, Ernest, "The Psychology of Religion," International Congress of Psychology, Groningen, 1930; abstract in *Psychoanalytic Review*, vol. XVII, p. 356.

Junod, Henri, *The Life of a South African Tribe*, 2nd ed., Macmillan, London, 1927.

Kinkel, J., "The Problem of the Psychological Foundation and of the Origin of Religion, *Imago*, vol. VIII (1927), No. 1; Rev. in *Psychoanalytic Review*, vol. XII (1925), pp. 473-4; and vol. XIII (1926), pp. 484-6.

Kiti, Gabriel, "Consécration à un fétiche (Dahomey)," *Anthropos*, vol. XXXII (1937), pp. 283-287.

Kiti, Gabriel, "Quelques rites expiatoires au Dahomey," *Anthropos*, vol. XXXII (1937), pp. 978-980.

Kiti, Gabriel, "Rites funéraires des Goun (Dahomey)," *Anthropos*, vol. XXXII (1937), pp. 283-287.

Klineberg, Otto, *Negro Intelligence and Selective Migration*, N. Y., Columbia University, 1935.

Kolnai, A., "Psychoanalytic Sociology," *Imago*, vol. VIII, No. 2.

König, Herbert, "Das Recht der Polarvölker," *Anthropos*, vol. XXII, pp. 689-746.

Koppers, W., "Die Ethnologische Wirtschaftsforschung," *Anthropos*, vol. X-XI, pp. 611-651, 971-1079.

Krauskopf, Alfred Artus, *Die Religionstheorie Sigmund Freuds*, C. Neuenhahn, C. m. b. j., 1933.

Kroeber, A. L., "History and Science in Anthropology," *Am. Anthrop.*, 37 (1935), pp. 539-569.

Kroeber, A. L., "Thoughts on Zuñi Religion," *Holmes Anniversary Volume*, Washington, 1916, pp. 269-277.

Kroeber, A. L., *Zuñi Kin and Clan*, Anthropological Papers of the American Museum of Natural History, vol. XVIII, Pt. II, N. Y., 1917.

Kuhn, Adalbert, *Herabkunft des Feuers und Goettertranks*, Berlin, Dummler, 1859.

La Barre, Weston, *The Peyote Cult*, Yale University Publications in Anthropology, New Haven, 1938.

Labouret, N., and Rivet, P., *Le Royaume D'Ardra et Son Evangelisation au XVIIe Siecle*, Travaux et Mémoires de l'Institut d'Ethnologie, vol. VII, 1929.

Lang, Andrew, *Custom and Myth*, Longmans, Green, London, 1887.

Lang, Andrew, *Myth, Ritual, and Religion*, 2 vols., Longmans, Green, London, 1867.

Lang, Andrew, *Social Origins*, Longmans, Green, London, 1903.

Lang, Andrew, *The Making of Religion*, Longmans, Green, London, 3d ed., 1909.

LeFaivre, Henri, "Les derniers rois du Dahomey," *Revue D'Historie des Colonies*, vol. XXV (1937), pp. 25-76.

Le Herissé, A., *L'Ancien Royaume du Dahomey*, E. Larose, Paris, 1911.

Lehman, F. Rudolf, "Die Religionen Australiens und der Südsee 1911-1930," *Archiv für Religionswissenschaft*, vol. XXIX (1931), pp. 139-186.

Leiris, Michel, "Fragments sur le Dahomey," *Minotaure*, No. 2 (1933), pp. 57-61.

Lenin, Nicolai, *Imperialism, the State and Revolution*, N. Y., Vanguard, 1929.

Le Roy, A., *Les Pygmées*, Tours A. Name, 1905.

Le Roy, A., *The Religion of the Primitives*, trans. Newton Thompson, N. Y., Macmillan, 1922.

Lesser, A., "Function in Social Anthropology," *Am. Anthrop.*, 37 (1935), pp. 386-393.

Levy-Bruhl, Lucien, *Primitive Mentality*, trans. L. A. Clare, Macmillan, N. Y., 1923.

Li, An-che, "Zuñi—Some Observations and Queries," *Am. Anthrop.*, 39 (1937), pp. 62-76.

Linton, Ralph, *The Study of Man*, Stud. Ed., Appleton-Century, N. Y., 1936.

Llewellyn, K. N., and Hoebel, E. S., *The Cheyenne Way*, University of Oklahoma, Norman (Oklahoma), 1941.

Lowie, Robert, *Primitive Religion*, Routledge, London, 1925.

Lowie, Robert, *The Crow Indians*, Farrar and Rinehart, N. Y., 1935.

Lowie, Robert H., *The History of Ethnological Theory*, N. Y., Farrar and Rinehart, 1937, Chapter XIII.

Lütgenau, Fr., *Natürliche und Soziale Religion*, Stuttgart, Dietz, 1894.

Mair, L. P., *Native Policies in Africa*, Routledge, London, 1936.

Malinowski, Bronislaw, *Coral Gardens and Their Magic*, 2 vols., American, N. Y., 1935.

Malinowski, Bronislaw, *Crime and Custom in Savage Society*, Harcourt, N. Y., 1926.

Malinowski, Bronislaw, "Magic, Science and Religion," in *Science, Religion and Reality*, ed. Joseph Needham, Macmillan, N. Y., 1925, pp. 19-85.

Malinowski, Bronislaw, "Parenthood—the Basis of Social Structure," in V. F. Calverton, and S. D. Schmalhausen, *The New Generation*, MaCauley, N. Y., 1930.

Malinowski, Bronislaw, *Sex and Repression*, Harcourt, Brace, N. Y., 1927.

Malinowski, Bronislaw, *The Sexual Life of Savages*, N. Y., Halycon, 1929.

Malinowski, Bronislaw, *The Family Life of the Australian Aborigines*, London, Hodder, 1913.

Marett, R. R., "Preanimistic Religion," *Folklore*, vol. XI (1900), pp. 162-182.

Marett, R. R., *The Threshold of Religion*, 2nd ed., London, 1914.

Maupoil, Bernard, "Le culte de Vaudou, M. J. Herskovits et l'ethnographie afro-americaine," *L'Afrique Francaise*, vol. IX (1937), pp. 358-360.

Mead, Margaret, "An Investigation of the Thought of Primitive Children, with Special Reference to Animism," *Journal of the Royal Anthropological Institute*, vol. LXII (1932), pp. 173-190.

Mead, Margaret, *Growing Up in New Guinea*, Blue Ribbon, N. Y., 1930.

Mead, Margaret, *Kinship in the Admiralty Islands, Anthropological Papers of the American Museum of Natural History*, vol. XXXIV, Pt. II, N. Y., 1934.

Mead, Margaret, "Melanesian Middlemen," *Natural History*, vol. XXX, pp. 115-130.

Mead, Margaret, *Social Organization of Manu'a, Bishop Museum Bulletin*, no. 76, Honolulu, 1930.

Merton, Robert K., *Social Theory and Social Structure*, Glencoe, Illinois, The Free Press, 1949.

Merton, Robert K., "Social Structure and Anomie," *American Sociological Review* 3 (1938), pp. 672-682.

Merton, Robert K., and Ashley-Montagu, M., "Crime and the Anthropologist," *American Anthropologist*, vol. 42 (1940), pp. 384-408.

Mooney, James, "The Ghost Dance Religion and Sioux Outbreak of 1890," *Bureau of American Ethnology Annual Reports*, vol. XIII, 1892.

Morgan, Lewis Henry, *Systems of Consanguinity and Affinity*, 1877.

Müller, F. Max, "Comparative Mythology," in *Oxford Essays*, vol. 2 (1856), pp. 1-87.

Müller, F. Max, *Anthropological Religion,* Longmans, Green, London, 1892.

Müller, F. Max, *Contributions to the Science of Mythology,* 2 vols, Longmans, Green, London, 1897, vol. I.

Müller, F. Max, *Lectures on the Origin and Growth of Religion,* Longmans, Green, London, 1878.

Müller-Braunschweig, C., "Normal Nucleus of the Religious Attitude of Mind," 11th International Psychoanalytic Congress, Oxford, 1929; Abst. in *Psychoanalytic Review,* vol. XVII, pp. 492-493.

Murray, Gilbert, *The Rise of the Greek Epic,* Oxford, Clarendon, 1907.

Murray, Gilbert, *Five Stages of Greek Religion,* Oxford, Clarendon, 1925.

Neff, W. S., "Social-economic Status and Intelligence: A Critical Survey," *Psych. Bull.* 35 (1938), pp. 727-757.

Nimuendaju, Curt, "Die Sagen von der Erschaffung und Vernichtung der Welt als Grundlagen der Religion der Apapoçuva—Guarani," z. f. *Ethnologie* 116 (1914): 284-403.

Olivier, Leroy, *Essai D' Introduction Critique a L'Etude de L'Economie Primitive,* Lib. Orientaliste Paul Geunthner, Paris, 1925.

Pareto, Vi Ynedo, *The Mind and Society,* trans. Andrew Bongiorno and Arthur Livingston, 4 vols., N. Y., Harcourt, 1935.

Parkinson, R., *Dreissig Jahre in dem Südsee,* Stuttgart, Strecken u- Schröder, 1907.

Parsons, E. C., "A Few Zuñi Death Beliefs and Practices," *American Anthropologist,* vol. XVIII (1916), pp. 245-256.

Parsons, E. C., "A Zuñi Detective," *Man,* vol. XVI (1916), pp. 168-170.

Parsons, E. C., "Ceremonial Friendship at Zuñi," *American Anthropologist,* vol. XIX (1917), pp. 1-2.

Parsons, E. C., *Hopi and Zuñi Ceremonialism, Memoirs of the American Anthropological Association,* no. 39, 1933.

Parsons, E. C., "Increase by Magic: A Zuñi Pattern," *American Anthropologist,* vol. XXI (1919), pp. 279-286.

Parsons, E. C., *Notes on Zuñi,* 2 pts., *Memoirs of the American Anthropological Association,* vol. IV, No. 4, 1917.

Parsons, E. C., *Pueblo Indian Religion,* 2 vols., Chicago University, Chicago, 1939.

Parsons, E. C., "Spanish Elements in the Kachina Cult of the Pueblos," *Proceedings of the Twenty-third International Congress of Americanists* (1928), pp. 582-603.

Parsons, E. C., "The Origin Myth of Zuñi," *Journal of American Folklore,* vol. XXXVI (1923), pp. 135-162.

Parsons, E. C., "The Religion of the Pueblo Indians," *Proceedings of the Twenty-first International Congress of Americanists* (1924), pp. 140-148.

Parsons, E. C., "Winter and Summer Dance Series in Zuñi in 1918," *University of California Publications in American Archeology and Ethnology,* vol. XVII, No. 3 (1922), pp. 171-216.

Parsons, E. C., "Zuñi Conception and Pregnancy Beliefs," *Proceedings of the Nineteenth International Congress of Americanists* (1917), pp. 379-383.

Parsons, Talcott, *Essays in Sociological Theory Pure and Applied,* Glencoe, Ill., The Free Press, 1949.

Parsons, Talcott, *The Structure of Social Action,* McGraw-Hill, N. Y., 1937, pp. 757 ff.

Porteus, S. D., *The Psychology of a Primitive People,* London, Longmans, 1931.

Pettazzoni, Raffaele, "Allwissende höchste Wesen bei primitivsten Völkern," trans. A. Pauletig, *Archiv für Religionswissenschaft,* vol. XXIX (1931), pp. 108-129; 209-243.

Plekhanov, George, *Essays in Historical Materialism,* N. Y., International, 1940.

Preuss, K. Th., "Religiöser Gehalt der Mythen," in *Sammlung Gemeinverstaendige Vortraege,* No. 162, Mohr, Tübingen, 1933.

Radcliffe-Brown, A. R., "Notes on Totemism in Eastern Australia," *Journal of the Royal Anthropological Institute,* vol. LIX (1929), pp. 399-415.

Radcliffe-Brown, A. R., "On the Conception of Function in Social Science," *American Anthropologist,* vol. XXXVII (1935), pp. 394-402.

Radcliffe-Brown, A. R., *The Andaman Islanders,* Cambridge University, Cambridge, 1933.

Radcliffe-Brown, A. R., "The Rainbow Serpent Myth of Australia," *Journal of the Royal Anthropological Institute,* vol. LVI (1926), pp. 19-25.

Radcliffe-Brown, A. R., "The Social Organization of Australian Tribes," *Oceania,* vol. I (1930), pp. 34-63; 206-246; 426-456.

Radcliffe-Brown, "The Sociological Theory of Totemism," *Proceedings of the Fourth Pacific Science Congress, Java,* 1929, vol. III; *Biological Papers,* Maks and Van Der Klits, Batavia-Bandoeng, 1930, pp. 295-309.

Radin, Paul, *Crashing Thunder, the Autobiography of an American Indian,* Appleton-Century, N. Y., 1926.

Radin, Paul, *Monotheism Among Primitive Peoples,* Allen and Unwin, London, 1924.

Radin, Paul, "Personal Reminiscences of a Winnebago Indian," *University of California Bureau of American Archeology and Ethnology,* vol. XXVI (1913), pp. 243-318.

Radin, Paul, *Primitive Man as Philosopher,* Appleton-Century, N. Y., 1927.

Radin, Paul, *Primitive Religion,* Viking, N. Y., 1937.

Radin, Paul, *The Winnebago Tribe, Bureau of American Ethnology Reports,* vol. XXXVII (1932).

Rank, Otto, *Seelenglaube und Psychologie,* Deuticke, Leipzig und Wien, 1930.

Rattray, R. S., *Ashanti Law and Constitution,* Clarendon, Oxford, 1929.

Rattray, R. S., *Religion and Art in Ashanti,* Clarendon, Oxford, 1927.

Reik, Theodor, *The Psychological Problem of Religion,* trans. 2d ed., ed. Douglas Bryan, N. Y., Farrar Straus, 1946.

Rivers, W. H. R., *The History of Melanesian Society,* vol. I, Cambridge University, Cambridge, 1914.

Rivers, W. H. R., *The Todas,* Macmillan, London, 1906.

Rivers, W. H. R., "Totemism in Polynesia and Melanesia," *Journal of the Royal Anthropological Institute,* vol. XXXIX (1909), pp. 156-180.

Roheim, Géza, "Dying Gods and Puberty Ceremonies," *J. Royal Anthr. Inst.,* vol. 59 (1929), pp. 181, 197.

Roheim, Géza, "Freud and Anthropology," *Man,* vol. XXXVI (1906), Nos. 98 and 141.

Schmidt, W., "Der Monotheismus der Primitiven," *Anthropos,* vol. XXV (1930), pp. 703-709.

Schmidt, W., *Der Ursprung der Gottesidee,* 6 vols., Aschendorff, Munster, i.W., 1926-1935.

Schmidt, W., "L'Origine de l'Idee de Dieu," trans. P. J. Pietsch, *Anthropos,* vol. III (1908), pp. 125-163; 336-368; 559-611; 811-836; 1081-1120; vol. IV, pp. 207-250; 505-524; 1075-1091; vol. V, pp. 231-246.

Schmidt, W., "The Position of Women with Regard to Property in Primitive Society," *American Anthropologist,* vol. XXXVII (1935), pp. 244-256.

Schmidt, W., and Koppers, W., *Völker und Kulturen,* Regensburg, 1924, vol. I.

Schröder, Theodore, "The Psychoanalytic Approach to Religious Experience," *Psychoanalytic Review,* vol. XVI (1929), pp. 361-376.

Schweisinger, *Heredity and Environment,* N. Y., Macmillan, 1933.

Schwartz, F. L. W., *Der Ursprung der Mythologie,* Berlin, Hertz, 1860.

Seagle, William, "Primitive Law and Professor Malinowski," *American Anthropologist,* vol. XXXIX (1937), pp. 275-290.

Skertchley, J. A., *Dahomey as It Is,* Chapman and Hall, London, 1874.

Smith, W. Robertson, *Kinship and Marriage in Early Arabia,* Cambridge University, Cambridge, 1885.

Smith, W. Robertson, *Lectures on the Religion of the Semites,* rev. ed., Black, Edinburgh, 1894.

Spencer, Herbert, *The Principles of Sociology,* 3 vols. in 5, N. Y., Appleton, 1880-96, vols. II, III.

Spieth, Jakob, *Die Religion der Eweer in Süd-Togo,* Göttingen, 1911.

Stevenson, M. C., *The Zuñi Indians, Bureau of American Ethnology Reports, Annual Reports,* vol. XXIII, 1901-2.

Thurnwald, Richard, *Economics in Primitive Communities,* Oxford University, London, 1932.

Torday, E., "The Child's Place in African Religions," *Revue Internationale de L'Enfant,* vol. XI (1931), pp. 331-353.

Tylor, E. B., "On a Method of Investigating the Development of Institutions; applied to Laws of Marriage and Descent," *Journal of the Royal Anthropological Institute,* vol. XVIII (1888), pp. 245-272.

Tylor, E. B., *Primitive Culture,* 2 vols., G. P. Putnam's Sons, 6th ed., N. Y., 1920.

von Bertalanffy, Ludwig, "The Theory of Open Systems in Physics, and Biology," *Science III* (1940), pp. 23-29.

Van Gennep, Arnold, *Les Rites de Passage, Librairie Critique* (Emile Mourry), Paris, 1909.

Viljoen, Stephan, *The Economics of Primitive Peoples*, King, London, 1936.

Vinogradoff, Sir Paul, *Outlines of Historical Jurisprudence*, 2 vols., Oxford University, London, 1920-2.

Waller, Willard, *The Family*, Cordon, N. Y., 1938.

Wallis, Wilson D., *Messiahs: Christian and Pagan*, Badger, Boston, 1918.

Wallis, Wilson E., *Religion in Primitive Society*, Crofts, N. Y., 1939.

Warner, W. Lloyd, "Murngin Warfare," *Oceania*, vol. I (1930), pp. 457-494.

Warner, W. Lloyd, *A Black Civilization*, Harper, N. Y., 1937.

Webb, Clement C. J., *Group Theories of Religion and the Individual*, N. Y., Macmillan, 1916.

Weber, Max, *Gesammelte Aufsaetze zur Religionssoziologie*, 3 vols., J. C. B. Mohr (Paul Siebeck), Tübingen, 1920-1.

Weber, Max, *The Protestant Ethic and the Spirit of Capitalism*, trans. Talcott Parsons, Allen and Unwin, London, 1930.

Weber, Max, *Wirtschaft und Gesellschaft*, J. B. C. Mohr (Paul Siebeck), Tübingen, 1922.

White, Leslie A., *The Science of Culture*, N. Y., Farrar, Straus, 1949.

Williams, Joseph J., *Africa's God II. Dahomey, Anthropological Series of the Boston College Graduate School*, Chestnut Hill (Massachusetts), vol. I, No. 2 (1936), pp. 85-182.

Winthuis, J., *Mythos u. Kult der Steinzeit*, Stuttgart, Strecker u. Schröder, 1935.

Witte, A. P., "Der Zwillingskult bei den Ewe-Negern in Westafrika," *Anthropos*, vol. XXIV (1929), pp. 943-51.

Woodworth, Robert S., *Heredity and Environment*, N. Y., Social Science Research Council, 1941.

Wucherer, Alfons, "Der Markt in Süd-Togo," *Zeitschrift fuer Ethnologie*, vol. LXVII (1935), pp. 32-43.

# NOTES

## CHAPTER 2

1. See Talcott Parsons, *The Structure of Social Action*, N. Y., McGraw-Hill, 1937, pp. 757 ff., for a more detailed statement of the sociological approach, and its relationship to other social sciences.

2. Parsons, *Ibid.*, gives the most elaborate and adequate analysis of this development in human thought.

3. For a good elementary statement of this process, see John W. Bennett and Melvin M. Tumin, *Social Life*, N. Y., Knopf, 1948, chapters 16, 17, 18.

4. A good analysis of integration and *anomie*, see Robert K. Merton, "Social Structure and Anomie," *American Sociological Review* 3 (1938), pp. 672-682. The problem was a central one throughout Durkheim's work.

5. For its temporary popularity, however, see L. L. Bernard, *Instinct*, N. Y., Holt, 1944.

6. A recent and implicitly radical analysis of race is that of M. Ashley-Montagu, *Man's Most Dangerous Myth: The Fallacy of Race*, N. Y., Columbia University, 1945; as also the interesting article, "Crime and the Anthropologist," with Robert K. Merton, *American Anthropologist* 42 (1940), pp. 384-408. The racist literature is well known and enormous.

7. See the classic study by Otto Klineberg, *Negro Intelligence and Selective Migration*, N. Y., Columbia University, 1935. For some intercultural comparisons, see G. Bose, "Nature of Intelligence and its Measurement," *Indiana Journal of Psychology* (19) (1944), pp. 58-65, as well as in S. D. Porteus, *The Psychology of a Primitive People*. London, Longmans, 1931. Socioeconomic correlations have also been a focus in some of these studies: W. S. Neff, "Social-economic Status and Intelligence: A Critical Survey," *Psych. Bull.* 35 (1938), pp. 727-757; Gladys C. Schwesinger, *Heredity and Environment*, N. Y., Macmillan, 1933; and Robert S. Woodworth, *Heredity and Environment*, N. Y., Social Science Research Council, 1941.

8. An extended treatment, aside from that implicit in Freudianism, is that of H. F. Dunbar, *Emotions and Bodily Changes*, N. Y., Columbia University, 1946. Also: Clifford Allen, *Modern Discoveries in Medical Psychology*, 2nd ed., N. Y., Macmillan, 1949, and O. Spurgeon English, "Psychiatric Treatment in Psychosomatic Illnesses," *Med. Surg. J.* 101 (1949), pp. 565-573.

8a. The reader will by now have understood that "sociological" is merely a short way of referring to sociological and/or anthropological and/or social-psychological. Most of the apparent distinctions between these "approaches" are occupational, and not of fundamental significance for this study.

9. The best recent analysis of functionalism is to be found in Chapter I of Robert K. Merton's *Social Theory and Social Structure*, Glencoe, Illinois, The Free Press, 1949. See also Robert H. Lowie, *The History of Ethnological Theory*,

N. Y., Farrar and Rinehart, 1937, Chapter XIII. See also the article by Horace Kalten, "Functionalism" in *Encyclopedia of the Social Sciences*. From the biological point of view, the classic is W. B. Cannon, *The Wisdom of the Body*, London, Rutledge, 1932. For a more recent, abstract development, see Ludwig von Bertalanffy, "The Theory of Open Systems in Physics and Biology" in *Science* 111 (1950), pp. 23-29, as well as others of his works. For several discussions of the anthropological point of view, see A. Lesser, "Function in Social Anthropology," pp. 386-393; A. R. Radcliffe-Brown, "On the Concept of Function in Social Science," pp. 394-402; and A. L. Kroeber, "History and Science in Anthropology," pp. 539-569, in *Am. Anthrop.* 37 (1935); also Franz Boas, "History and Science in Anthropology: A Reply," *Am. Anthrop.* 38 (1936), pp. 137-141.

10. This is from an earlier manuscript version of Kingsley Davis' *Human Society*, N. Y., Macmillan, 1949. It is a restatement of A. R. Radcliffe-Brown, "On the Conception of Function in Social Science," *Am. Anthrop.* 37 (1935), p. 395.

11. Cf. the series cited above in the *Am. Anthrop.*, vols. 37, 38.

12. This is also the position taken by Lowie, *Op. cit.*, p. 237, where he calls functionalism "a worthy program for ascertaining what intracultural bonds may exist."

12a. A similar situation exists in the field of social disorganization. See William J. Goode, "Conceptual Schemata in the Field of Social Disorganization," *Social Forces* 26 (1947), pp. 19-25.

13. Merton. *Social Theory and Social Structure*, Chapter I.

14. For a simpler statement of function, see the extended treatment in Bennett and Tumin, *Op. cit.*, pp. 73ff., 169ff., 187ff.

15. To cite examples at random: Combustion as a process of oxidation, offspring as exclusively originating from previously existing organisms, disease as caused by germs.

16. These exact observations are hypothetical. However, the facts are very close. See Reo F. Fortune, *Manus Religion* (*Memoirs of the American Philosophical Society*, vol. III), Philadelphia, 1935, pp. 40, 52, 118, 250, 252, 253.

17. See Bronislaw Malinowski, *The Sexual Life of Savages*, N. Y., Halcyon, 1929, as well as *Coral Gardens and Their Magic*, 2 vols., N. Y., American, 1935.

# CHAPTER 3

1. This is not a reference to "feral" children, but to the more fundamental element in such situations, social isolation. See Kingsley Davis, "Extreme Social Isolation of a Child," in *Am. J. Soc.*, 45 (1940) pp. 554-565, and "Final Note on a Case of Extreme Isolation," *Am. J. Soc.*, 52 (1947), pp. 432-437, for a good analysis of this situation. Also: Marie K. Mason "Learning to Speak After Six and One-half Years of Silence," *J. Speech Disorders*, 7 (1942), pp. 295-304; and J. A. L. Singh and Robert M. Zingg, *Wolf-Children and Feral Man*, N. Y., Harper, 1941.

2. Cf. Parsons, *op. cit.*, "The Unit of Action Systems," pp. 43 ff.

3. Cf. Herbert Goldhamer and Edward A. Shils, "Types of Power and Status," *Am. J. Soc.* 45, (1940), pp. 171-182.

4. Much of this statement comes from Kingsley Davis, unpublished paper

before The Philadelphia Anthropological Association, 1939, "A Theory of Primitive Religion."

5. The most fruitful analytic use of this distinction was made by William Robertson Smith and Émile Durkheim, although the distinction is implicit in most analysts of religion. See W. R. Smith, *Kinship and Marriage in Early Arabia*, Cambridge University, 1885; as also *Lectures on the Religion of the Semites*, Black, Edinburgh, 1889, etc. Note also the methodological discussions and concrete researches of Emile Durkheim, esp. *The Elementary Forms of the Religious Life*, trans. J. W. Swain, Macmillan, N. Y., 1915, as well as *L'Education Morale*, Alcan, Paris, 1925 (materials from 1902). See also the extended exposition of Durkheim's growth from an earlier positivistic position, in Parsons, *op. cit.* perhaps the most elaborate and intensive application of a sociological point of view to the religions of "developed" civilizations is Max Weber's *Gesammelte Aufsaetze Zur Religions-Soziologie*, 3 vols., J. C. B. Mohr (P. Siebeck), Tubingen, 1920-1.

6. As the critic may be quick to point out, neither Confucianism nor Buddhism, to mention only two examples, is theistic. On the level of developed civilizations, this is possible both as philosophy and religion. It is interesting, however, that in both cases, as in Hinduism generally, the mass of believers insistently break from this intellectualist tradition for the relative emotional security and personal response of anthroposocial entities.

7. Cf., for example, Raffaele Pettazzoni (trans. A. Pauletig), "Allwissende höchste Wesen bei primitivsten Völkern," in *Archiv F. Religionswissenschaft*, 29 (1939): 108-129; 209-243.

8. As merely one example, note later how the Dahomean myths reflect this, by pointing out the contribution of each god, or the ways in which the general welfare of man was served after a conflict between gods, etc., M. J. Herskovits, *Dahomey*, New York: Augustin, 1938, vol. II, pp. 130-4.

9. Raymond Firth, *The Work of the Gods in Tikopia*, 2 Vols., Lund, Humphries, London, 1940, vol. II, p. 310. The formula thus calls the attention of the god to the self-abasement of the reciter, and communicates to it the fact that this is being done for the god himself, but only *through* the welfare which will come to the land. Surely this is subtle flattery.

10. Radin, *Primitive Man as Philosopher*, New York: Appleton, 1927, p. 347. As a matter of fact, it is the Trickster, though fickle, who ultimately or unexpectedly brings good things which were refused by other gods.

11. This is expressed in an extreme fashion by the Murngin with respect to the weather, as they "assume a direct false causal relation between the good or bad behavior of society and the state of nature." (W. Lloyd Warner, *A Black Civilization*, N. Y., Harper, 1937, p. 409.

12. See Max Weber, *Wirtschaft und Gesellschaft*, J. C. B. Mohr (P. Siebeck), Tübingen, 1922, "Zauberer-Priester," pp. 241-3, and Bronislaw Malinowski, *Magic, Science and Religion*, Glencoe, Ill., The Free Press, 1948 (the essay is from 1925), Sect. V.

13. As Lowie has shrewdly pointed out for even the "individualistic" Plains Indians. See Robert H. Lowie, *The Crow Indians*, Farrar and Rinehart, N. Y., 1935, as well as Ch. I of his *Primitive Religion*, N. Y., Boni and Liveright, 1924, and his extended series of papers on the Crow, in the *Anthropological Papers of the American Museum of Natural History, 1912-1925*.

14. Firth, *op. cit.*, vol. II, pp. 307-8.

15. Herskovits, *op. cit.*, vol. II, pp. 117-8.

16. Firth, *op. cit.*, vol. I, pp. 43, 74, 108.

17. Parsons, *op. cit.*, p. 431.

18. This has been most ably analyzed by Max Weber. See the essay on his contribution, among others, in Talcott Parsons, "The Theoretical Development of the Sociology of Religion," in *Essays in Sociological Theory Pure and Applied,* Glencoe, Ill., The Free Press, 1949, pp. 52-66.

19. Unless Professor Nock is correct, as quoted by Talcott Parsons, in maintaining that "men do not in general 'believe' their religious ideas in quite the same sense that they believe the sun rises every morning." T. Parsons, *Structure of Social Action,* p. 425.

20. This symbolism has much of the character of the simple symbolism involved in language as a cue, but is clearly more complex.

21. Durkheim's *sacré,* Weber's *charismatisch,* Pareto's *non-logical:* they can be related to *mana, orenda, wakan, manitu,* etc., although these are sometimes thought of as specifically religious. See Émile Durkheim, *The Elementary Forms of the Religious Life;* Vilfredo Pareto, *The Mind and Society,* (trans. Andrew Bongiorno and Arthur Livingston, New York, 4 vols. Harcourt, 1935, esp. vol. I, Chs. 2 and 4), New York, 1935; Émile Durkheim, *De la Definition des Phénomènes Religieux* (L'Année Sociologique, vol. II, 1897-1898, pp. 1-28; Francis Cornford, *From Religion to Philosophy,* New York: Holt, 1913, etc.

23. E. B. Tylor, *Primitive Culture,* New York: 6th ed. Putnam's, 1920, vol. I, pp. 117-141.

24. Bronislaw Malinowski, *Crime and Custom,* New York: Harcourt, 1926, pp. 85-92, and H. Ian Hogbin, *Law and Order in Polynesia,* New York: Harcourt, 1934, pp. 216-222.

25. Max Weber, *Wirtschaft und Gesellschaft,* Tübingen, 1922, "Zauber-Priester" pp. 241-243; B. Malinowski, *Magic, Science, and Religion;* see also his *Coral Gardens and Their Magic,* New York: American, 1925, which depicts many magical situations closely approximating a "religious" pattern. This is to be seen, similarly, in E. E. Evans-Pritchard, *Witchcraft, Oracles and Magic among the Azande,* Oxford: Clarendon, 1937, the proliferations of magic into "closed associations" amounting to cults. Cf. his "The Zande Corporations of Witchdoctors" (*Journal of the Royal Anthropological Institute,* vol. LXII, 1932, pp. 291-336, and vol. LXIII, 1933, pp. 63-100). His earlier conception of magic is to be found in "The Morphology and Function of Magic" (*American Anthropologist,* vol. 31, 1929).

26. Robert H. Lowie, *Primitive Religion,* pp. 136-151.

27. *Ibid.,* p. 141.

28. Malinowski, *Magic, Science, and Religion,* sect. V. Also *Coral Gardens and their Magic,* vol. II, "The Magical Word," pp. 213-250. Note, in addition, that only the garden magician would dare to utter the well known spells (*Ibid.,* vol. I, p. 105), and only the magician would venture into the grove playing a part in Tilakaya magic, under penalty of a swelling of the sexual organs (*Ibid.,* p. 278).

29. Evans-Pritchard, *op. cit.,* p. 452.

30. Lowie, *Primitive Religion,* p. 142; cf. Henri Junod, *The Life of a South African Tribe,* London: Macmillan, 1912, vol. II, pp. 485 ff.

31. Seconded, however, for different reasons. Cf. Paul Radin, *Primitive*

*Religion,* New York: Viking, 1937, Ch. IV; Vide Lowie, *Primitive Religion,* pp. 144 ff.

32. Radin, *op. cit.,* p. 64: ". . . no great changes are required to change it into an invocation and prayer." Lowie, *Primitive Religion,* pp. 144-147: ". . . the magical has been found to partake of the psychological character of the religious." Lowie's main interest in the discussion is to refute Frazer's notion of the temporal (historical) priority of magic, a priority which Radin fully accepts.

33. Cf. R. R. Marett, *Psychology and Folklore,* London, 1920, pp. 168 ff.; A. A. Goldenweiser, *Early Civilization,* New York, 1922; M. J. Herskovits, *op. cit.,* vol. II, p. 262; M. J. and F. S. Herskovits, *An Outline of Dahomean Religious Belief* (*Mem. Am. Anthrop. Ass.,* no. 41, 1933, p. 68).

34. W. L. Warner, *op. cit.,* p. 229.

35. Raymond Firth, *We, the Tikopia,* New York: American, 1936, cf. pp. 485-487, 523. Also his *Primitive Polynesian Economy,* London: Routledge, 1939, pp. 269-270.

36. See Parsons, *op. cit.,* pp. 601 ff. A condensed statement of its characteristics is given in Wm. J. Goode, A Note on the Ideal Type (*American Sociological Review,* August, 1947, pp. 473-474). The concept is associated with Max Weber, who elaborated its self-conscious use theoretically in his essays in *Gesammelte Aufsätze zur Wissenschaftslehre,* Tübingen, 1922, and empirically in his monumental *Gesammelte Aufsätze zur Religionssoziologie,* Tübingen, 1920-1921. Howard Becker has discussed the term extensively, especially its less specialized form, the ideal type, in various essays (see, e.g., Howard Becker, Constructive Typology in the Social Science in Harry E. Barnes, Howard Becker, and Frances B. Becker, *Contemporary Social Theory,* New York, 1940, pp. 17-46, also his "Interpretive Sociology and Constructive Typology" (*Twentieth Century Sociology,* Philosophical Library, New York, 1946, pp. 70-95).

37. If one wishes to follow the current pattern of constructing indexes, one might weigh each characteristic, and construct an index number for a given system of supernaturalism.

38. "Individual" ends include both *common,* personal goals, held by *each* individual member of the group, as well as those held by only a few, or one.

39. However, in case of failure, there is no general application of pragmatism with reference to the whole body of magic, just as is true of science or religion. One assumes that: a. the technique was specifically wrong; b. it was carried out incorrectly; or c. there were counterinfluences, of the same character.

40. The relevant bibliographical references are given later in this exposition. It may suffice here to note that the Murngin are a people living in East Arnhem Land in Northeastern Australia, about 3000 (1926-1929) individuals constituting the society; the Dahomey live in West Africa, with a population of over 250,000 (1931); the Manus live off the shores of Great Admiralty Island, and are a Melanesian group with about 2000 (1928-1929) members; the Tikopia live on an isolated island in the Solomon Islands Protectorate in the Western Polynesian area, numbering 1281 (1929); and the Zuñi are a Pueblo society in the Southwestern United States, with a population of about 2080 (1937).

These societies were selected, without consideration as to whether they might fit a preconceived theory, on the basis of: 1. whether the society is still functioning; 2. extensity of data; 3. intensity of data; and 4. whether at least one major field investigation had been made by modern anthropological techniques.

The Yale Cross-Cultural Survey, now the Human Relations Area Files, has not as yet produced a monograph on primitive religion. However, the first major publication from this source, George P. Murdock's *Social Structure* (New York: Macmillan, 1949) indicates that enormous gaps exist even for kinship, a primary datum for anthropological reports. Such a statistical coverage, when it is done, should supersede the present analysis. Yet, for most tribes, the data needed do not exist.

# CHAPTER 4

1. Melville J. Herskovits' *Dahomey*, Augustin, N. Y., 1938, is undoubtedly the standard work on the subject. Other specific references by him and Frances S. Herskovits will be noted later. E. Foa, *Le Dahomey*, Paris, 1895, is not useful for present purposes, since the coastal people, especially Porto Novo, are the object of study. A. Le Herissé, A. *L'Ancien Royaume du Dahomey*, Larose, Paris, 1911, is much more significant, though he never was clear about certain points in the religious system which Herskovits finally clarified. I have not made direct use of Gabriel Kiti's several articles in *Anthropos* 32 (1937): 75-86; 283-7; 419-434; and 978-80, dealing with sections of ceremonial, mainly because they did not add anything significant to the analysis. The earlier travelers' reports, especially those of Bosman, Dalzel, Burton, Snelgrave, Skertchly, etc. (see the Bibliography for these works) have been consulted for complementary materials and background, but the present analysis is mainly couched in the present. J. J. Williams' *Africa's God; Dahomey*, Boston College Graduate School, Anthrop. Series, vol. I, No. 2, Boston 1936, is not used because of its Catholic bias.

2. Melville J. Herskovits and Frances S. Herskovits, *An Outline of Dahomean Religious Belief*, Men. An. Anth. Anth. Ass. No. 41, 1933, p. 9.

3. *Ibid.*, p. 11.

4. Early missionaries used Lisa as the translation of Jesus, Mawu for God: note H. Labouret and P. Rivet, *Le Royaume d'Ardra et Son Evangelisation, au XVII Siecle (Travaux et Mémoires de L'Institut D'Ethnologie* (1929), vol. VII.

5. It must be noted that such variation is to be expected in this society, which is not isolated, and which is secular. These variations have often figured in the literature on Dahomey. Cf. Herskovits and Herskovits, *Outline*, pp. 11. Further, *folk variations are likely to abound where much religious life is esoteric.*

6. "Symbol," since the Sky-God, like Thunder, and Earth or Aido Hwedo, to mention a few examples, are really a *group*, with these heads as symbols.

7. Herskovits and Herskovits, *Outline*, p. 12.

8. *Ibid.*, p. 16.

9. Herskovits, *Dahomey*, vol. II, p. 103.

10. Herskovits and Herskovits, *Outline*, p. 14; Herskovits, *Dahomey*, vol. II, p. 105.

11. His "character" is often thought of as a merely impersonal force.

12. Herskovits and Herskovits, *Outline*, p. 15.

13. At first reading, the Herskovits's seem to be at least verbally inconsistent on this point. In the *Outline*, p. 14, they write, "In time Mawu and Lisa bore children, the oldest being Sogbo . . . Next came Sagbata . . ." But on p. 16: ". . . Sagbata in the mythology of this Earth cult symbolizes the first-born son

of Mawu-Lisa . . ." However, Professor Herskovits writes me that the statement on p. 14 is the more current belief. Further, any such inconsistencies to be found in similar expositions must be explained by the inconsistencies between different versions, from different cult heads. For in these West African cultures there are many such variations in belief.

14. Herskovits and Herskovits, *Outline*, pp. 16-7.

15. *Ibid.*, p. 17.

16. As the Herskovits's have noted, the attitude of detestation by the Dahomean kings toward the cult is understandable when it is learned that four Dahomean kings are known historically to have died of the disease.

17. That is, the high god in these cases does move farther from the immediacies of the world, but keeps the balance of the most important powers, especially creation. This parallels the Dahomean social pattern, where the King was high and far removed but still maintained a reigning and powerful hand on things.

18. The Herskovits's are quite sure of this disputed point, Cf. *Outline*, p. 23, as well as *Dahomey*, vol. I, pp. 165 ff. However, it is actually a sort of "secondary" totemism.

19. Unless otherwise noted any final "n" of Dahomean words used here is nasalized.

20. In Whydah. However, this was once thought to be even more widespread, and the idea itself is intriguing to the Western mind.

21. Relating the summary to the later formulation is the attitude of the Dahomeans toward Dan. Dan is not loved, but is a thief, and does not forgive readily, whereas Lɛgba does (who is loved). It seems evident that Dan is impersonal, non-human, less motivationally understandable than Lɛgba, whose foibles and quirks are "human" to the Dahomean.

22. Herskovits, *Dahomey*, vol. II, pp. 201-2.

23. The "n" in sɛmɛkɔkanto is also nasalized.

24. Herskovits, *Dahomey*, vol. II, p. 234.

25. Pottery vessels are made by the Manus settlement near the island of Mbuke (see Mead, *Kinship*, p. 189). A few islets are owned, as well as rubble platforms used for important gift exchanges.

26. *Ibid.*, p. 190.

27. *Ibid.*

28. Reo F. Fortune, "Manus Religion," *Oceania*, vol. II, p. 77; *Manus Religion*, p. 12.

29. *Ibid.*, p. 1.

30. Fortune, *loc. cit.*, pp. 79, 84.

31. *Manus Religion*, p. 37.

32. Fortune, *loc. cit.*, p. 82.

33. Fortune, in a personal communication (October, 1943), informs me that one danger is the prevalence of malaria in a virulent form, which seems to attack the brain.

34. *Manus Religion*, p. 10.

35. *Ibid.*, p. 16.

36. This is not entirely a consistent practice, since Sir Ghost may be sent on an errand (ward's business), or may go about its own affairs. See Mead, *Kinship*, footnote p. 198.

37. *Manus Religion*, pp. 17, 21.

38. *Ibid.,* pp. 21-2.

39. *Ibid.,* p. 29.

40. *Ibid.,* p. 32.

41. *Ibid.,* p. 51; Mead, *Kinship,* p. 191.

42. *Manus Religion,* p. 40.

43. *Ibid.*

44. *Ibid.,* p. 41; "Manus Religion," p. 97.

45. I.e., there is no way to cure the person, since the only curative technique would be confession and expiation.

46. *Manus Religion,* p. 23.

47. *Ibid.*

48. *Ibid.,* pp. 10, 38, 51. As might be surmised, this type of conclusion is not liked, since Sir Ghost thereby becomes arbitrary, and further removed from his major role, enforcing the rules of mortal affairs.

49. *Ibid.,* p. 74.

50. Fortune suggests that perhaps the Manus have used magic for generations, but are constantly losing it, there being no genuine magical practitioners to create magic anew (see *Ibid.,* pp. 63-64).

51. See Fortune's tables, *Ibid.,* pp. 71-3.

52. Fortune suggests (*Ibid.,* p. 74, and "Manus Magic," p. 106) that this division of sickness allows the system to be predominantly moral, since it can thus emphasize mortal action, and not attend carefully to the social activities of the ghosts.

53. See Mead, *Growing,* pp. 31 ff., where she reports that her and Fortune's possessions were safe from Manus two- and three-year-olds, although vandalism and thievery would be expected in other societies. Also she notes (*Kinship,* p. 203), a child who would pick up a banana floating a few yards from a strange house (therefore upon the "property" belonging to the house) would be branded as "a thief."

54. "Manus Religion," p. 107; *Manus Religion,* p. 78; Mead, *Kinship,* p. 302.

55. *Manus Religion,* p. 78.

56. Raymond Firth, "Totemism in Polynesia," *Oceania I* (1930-1); pp. 291-321, 377-98.

57. *Ibid.,* p. 291.

58. This I would call a concrete generalization, though mainly because the analysis of the causes is not complete. I suspect that it would be universally true.

59. Raymond Firth, "Report on Research in Tikopia," *Oceania I* (1930-1); pp. 113-4.

60. There is a fourth group, individuals of a natural species considered inedible. Here, Firth claims, there seems to be an entirely different sense, and no element of the supernatural. However ("Totemism . . . ," p. 297), he also says: "Any object which is regarded as an *atua* may not be eaten, and anything which is fit for human consumption cannot be in itself an *atua*—though it may become associated temporarily with *atua*." Thus the relationship to the fourth group, though more tenuous, seems nevertheless real enough.

61. W. H. R. Rivers, *The History of Melanesian Society,* vol. I, Cambridge, 1914, pp. 298, 362. Rivers obtained most of his information from John Maresere, who was actually a native of Uves, though he had lived in Tikopia for twenty years. Rivers also used Rev. Durrad's materials.

62. Raymond Firth, *The Work of the Gods in Tikopia*, Lund, Humphries, London, 1940.

63. *Ibid.*, p. 1.

64. Firth, "Report," p. 114.

65. *Ibid.*, p. 114.

66. Firth, *Work*, vol. I, p. 91; cf. also "Totemism."

67. The present site of Zuñi has probably had a town on it for the last five or six centuries, according to both Spier's excavations and Kroeber's analysis. See Kroeber, *op cit.*, pp. 200 ff.

68. For a description of Zuñi agricultural techniques, see F. H. Cushing, "Zuñi Breadstuffs," in *Indian Notes and Monographs*, vol. VIII, Museum of the American Indian, N. Y., 1920.

69. Bunzel, "Introduction to Zuñi Ceremonialism," p. 475.

70. Kroeber, *op. cit.*, p. 183.

71. Bunzel, "Introduction to Zuñi Ceremonialism," p. 476.

72. Kroeber, *op. cit.*, p. 47. It ought to be added parenthetically that the importance of these primary associations within the family is not to be discounted even in a society where the kinship system does not emphasize the immediate family.

73. Kroeber, *op. cit.*, p. 48.

74. And, rarely, a female may be initiated. See Bunzel, "Introduction to Zuñi Ceremonialism," pp. 517-8. There were four in 1902 according to Stevenson: M. C. Stevenson, "The Zuñi Indians," Twenty-third *Annual Report of the Bureau of American Ethnology*, Washington, 1901-2, p. 65. As noted previously, this does not exhaust female cult activities.

75. The folded hand is held before the nose.

76. Bunzel, "Introduction to Zuñi Ceremonialism," p. 480.

77. *Ibid.*, p. 509.

78. However, other supernaturals are also so identified.

79. *Ibid.*, p. 511.

80. *Ibid.*, p. 511. A list of the rain priesthood for 1896 is given by Stevenson, *op. cit.*, pp. 165 ff.

81. Parsons, "Hopi and Zuñi Ceremonialism" (*Men. An. Anthrop. Ass.*, No. 39, 1938, p. 16) gives the number as fifteen, as she includes all those listed by Kroeber (*op. cit.*, pp. 170-1). Bunzel, "Introduction to Zuñi Ceremonialism," p. 513, omits *pekwin*, the bow priests, and apparently Big Shell people (Kroeber's No. 11), of which group Parsons says (Ibid.) they "are not Ashiwanni (rain societies), although they 'go in' with the Ashiwanni of the South on the fifth day of their retreat." In any event, the number of priesthoods is large, even though the number in each may be rather small.

82. It hardly needs to be pointed out how sacred are these fetishes, or *etowe*, in Zuni worship. It is through these most sacred objects that the power of the priests exists. They are brought from the depths of the earth at the emergence of the people, and are kept in sealed jars except when being used in a few secret rites.

83. Stevenson, *op. cit.*, p. 180, gives the order of these retreats.

84. Ruth L. Bunzel, "Zuñi Katchinas," 47th *Annual Report of the Bureau of American Enthnology*, 1929-30, Washington, 1932, pp. 843-4.

85. See *Ibid.*, pp. 922 ff., for many tales about different "masks."

86. *Ibid.*, p. 845.

87. *Ibid.*, pp. 975, 998.

88. *Ibid.*, p. 976.

89. The Shalako ceremonies. In the sticks, of course, rests supernatural power.

90. Bunzel, "Introduction to Zuñi Ceremonialism," p. 523.

91. The Koyemshi remain in retreat during the period of the masked dancing by each kiva, a period of five days and nights. Their participation is in addition to their summer clowning (see Elsie C. Parsons, *Notes on Zuñi, Memoirs of the American Anthropological Association,* vol. IV, No. 4, 1917, esp. pt. II, the section titled *"Newekwe* and *Koyemshi,"* pp. 229 ff.

92. It is twofold restriction: all who kill must belong, and no one who does not kill may belong. The priesthood supplies the spiritual protection for those who have killed and who would thus be open to the vengeance of the ghost. Bunzel (*Ibid.*, p. 526) says that in 1928 there were only three members.

93. Kroeber, *op. cit.,* pp. 156-7, found that thirty-four of forty-two members entered in this manner. "Trespass" is also possible, since those who blunder into a ritual meeting are supposed to be initiated. This Kroeber calls a mere "ritualistic device."

94. Bunzel, "Introduction to Zuñi Ceremonialism," p. 531: "The participants gradually work themselves into a state of mental excitement bordering on hysteria." This is in contrast to the general lack of Zuñi religious intensity (see p. 480).

95. W. L. Warner, *A Black Civilization,* Harper, N. Y., 1937. It is to be remembered that Warner is using this term only for convenience, since there is no such designation for the group of clans, not organized into a "Murngin tribe," which speak somewhat the same language. Also, v. Warner, "Malay Influence on the Aboriginal Cult of Northeast Arnhem Land." *Oceania* 2 (1931-2): 476-495; T. Theodor Webb, "Tribal Organization in East Arnhem Land," *Oceania* 3 (1932-3): 466 ff.; A. P. Elkin, "Marriage and Descent in East Arnhem Land," *Oceania* 3 (1932-3): 41206; Webb, "Aboriginal Medical Practice in East Arnhem Land," *Oceania* 4 (1933-4): 91-98; Webb. "The Making of a Marrngit," *Oceania* 6 (1935-6): 336-44, etc. The literature on this area is excellent, though not extensive, and furnishes a desirable check on the ethnology of the central tribes and other tribes now entirely changed by the coming of white men. With respect to these changes, cf. a A. P. Elkin *Australian Aborigines and How to Understand Them,* Angue and Robertson, Sidney and London, 1938.

96. W. L. Warner, *op. cit.,* p. 16.

97. *Ibid.*, p. 21.

98. *Ibid.*, p. 23-4. This seems adequately to fill the gap left by Spencer and Gillen, who insisted that the Arunta, Luritcha, and Ilparra tribes did not know "where babies come from." Warner's statements on these points seem sound. They raise the question again of the extent of Trobriand ignorance in the matter.

99. *Ibid.*, p. 126. Criteria for ordinary status: 1. responsibility in blood feuds, and 2. children; for ritual status: 1. sacred areas one may penetrate, and 2. parts of the graded ritual in which one may participate.

100. Warner, *Ibid.*, p. 131.

101. *Ibid.*

102. *Ibid.*, p. 244.

103. *Ibid.*, p. 244.

104. *Ibid.*

105. *Ibid.*

106. *Ibid.*, p. 387. This "deeper" level is almost certainly not conscious.

107. Warner, *op. cit.*, p. 399.

108. There are two, the totemic (and important) soul, and the less significant trickster (ghost, *mokoi*) soul.

# CHAPTER 5

1. Talcott, Parsons, *op. cit.*, pp. 757-775.

2. Implied in the frequent use, in traditional economics, of the "Robinson Crusoe analogy."

3. Parsons, *op. cit.*, p. 655.

4. Richard Thurnwald, *Economics in Primitive Communities*, Oxford University Press, London, 1932; or S. Viljoen, *The Economics of Primitive Peoples*, King, London, 1936. For a brief but broad history of early economic investigations of primitive communities, v. P. W. Koppers, "Die Ethnologische Wirtschaftsforschung" in *Anthropos 10-11* (1915-6): 611-651, 971-1079. The "stages" of technology are discussed by Leroy Olivier, attacking Karl Bücher (*Industrial Evolution*, Trans. S. M. Wickett, New York, Holt, 1912), *Essai D'Introduction Critique a L'Etude de L'Economie Primitive*, Librairie Orientaliste Paul Guenthner, Paris, 1925.

5. This is, however, a major problem of sociological analysis.

6. In *Coral Gardens* (vol. I, pp. 42, 76-6, etc.) Malinowski points out, as he has elsewhere, the importance of the yam in the social life of the Trobrianders. He notes that white traders consider them "irrational" in their insistence on gardening, instead of working for wages and then trading for yams. The economist cannot call this behavior "irrational."

7. Thus, the Tikopia had no money in the ordinary sense, and did not know its value. Presumably this is true of the Murngin, also.

8. Indeed, the "profit motive" is a prime example of means which have been transformed into an *ultimate* end.

9. Firth, *Primitive Polynesian Economy*, p. 7.

10. *Ibid.*

11. *Ibid.*

12. *Ibid.*

13. R. Firth, *Primitive Economics of the New Zealand Maori*, Dutton, N. Y., 1929, p. 17.

14. This does not mean, of course, there was no evolutionary process. It is simply a recognition of the complexity of cultural reconstructions, and a complete denial of any determinate unilinearity in this evolution. With reference to religion proper, see Appendix III, especially the analysis of Andrew Lang and W. Schmidt, who fought this simple evolutionary idea, even though the latter is perhaps impelled by a doctrinaire sentiment. See also the work of Leslie White, *The Science of Culture*, N. Y., Farrar and Straus, 1949, for a strong re-introduction of problems in social evolution.

15. See, for example, K. Bücher, *op. cit.*, pp. 12-14.

16. In a very strict sense, of course, Warner is correct, since he is apparently talking about an independent market system and money economy, and it is true that "other social institutions" regulate economic processes. However, a better

understanding of economic theory would indicate that the first is not equated with an economic system, being only one aspect of it, and the latter proposition is true of any society. The lack of orientation toward these problems, however, makes the analysis of such phenomena difficult in the case of the Murngin.

17. After Weber's work there can no longer be any doubt that such effects are to be found even in our own rationalistic culture. Durkheim, also, in his *De la Division de la Travail* devoted some discussion to the institutional structure in which economic contracts take place, part of which is derived from the Christian tradition.

18. Herskovits, *op. cit.*, vol. I, p. 30.

19. The wives might work, though their production was restricted (as well as their freedom of movement). However, the army had to be supported, as well as (at present) the administrators, etc.

20. Herskovits, *op. cit.*, vol. I, p. 40.

21. Most of these data are noted by Burton, Bosman, Skertchly, Duncan, Forbes, etc., all of whom remarked on the economic life of Dahomey. For an account of a variant, that of South Togoland, see Alfons Wucherer, "Der Markt in Süd-Togo," *Zeitschrift Für Ethnologie* 67 (1935): 32-43. See Herskovits, *op. cit.*, vol. I, pp. 29-50, where these data are most conveniently summarized.

22. It must be pointed out, however, that even though such a functional relationship exists, the Dahomean society would probably furnish enough incentive for the labor, anyway. This may not be true to the same degree of Tikopia.

23. It must be remarked that this is less true of Tikopia, where the ends are not so definitely those of mere production and increase; there are more religious overtones to the goals, and many of the ceremonials are not pointed in that direction to any significant extent, as will be described.

24. Herskovits, *op. cit.*, vol. I, p. 51.

25. The four-day week is the one used for determining "good" and "evil" days, and the time of religious ceremonials. The days are Mioxi, Adókwin, Zogodú, and Adjaxi (*ibid.*, pp. 51 ff.).

26. The extent of anthroposocial formulation is seen in this idea that the deities must also shop, and that "visiting" would be discourteous when it is known that someone is not "at home." The Dahomean practices are thus clearly mirrored.

27. Herskovits, *op. cit.*, vol. I, p. 53. The construction of a physical representation of a *vodun* is described in vol. II, pp. 301-3.

28. This is, as Herskovits notes (*ibid.*, I, p. 53), a case of sympathetic magic. One may even scold the *aizan* if success is not attained during the day's marketing.

29. Herskovits, *op. cit.*, vol. I, p. 54.

30. This is interestingly documented by Herskovits' comment on the "rural-urban" attitudes: the arrogance of the city folk, and the suspicion and lack of responsiveness of the villagers (vol. I, p. 55).

31. For a comment on Herskovits' conception of *vodun*, see the brief note by Bernard Maupoil, "Le culte du Vaudou. M. J. Herskovits et l'ethnographie afro-americaine," in *L'Afrique Francaise* 9 (1937): 358-360. Maupoil has corresponded with Herskovits on many of the points contained in his researches, and has attempted to test many of them by questioning informants of his own.

32. Herskovits, *op. cit.*, vol. I, p. 60.

33. Cf. Wucherer, *op. cit.*, pp. 32-43.

34. Herskovits, *op. cit.*, vol. I, p. 60-1.

35. Herskovits, *op. cit.*, vol. II, pp. 209-10.

36. Le Herissé in 1911 comments on the continuance of the ritual for the royal dead, though the king was not there, thus indicating the strength of these patterns in spite of their expense: "Aujourd'hui, le roi est représenté par son trone et par son hamac recouvert entierement d'un voile; mais, tout se passe comme s'il etait réclement la, en moins la foule délirante et en plus l'indifference des passants que rencontre le cortége, formé seulement de membres de la famille royal et de quelques serviteurs fideles au souvenir" (*op. cit.*, p. 190).

37. Herskovits, *op. cit.*, vol. I, p. 210.

38. Herskovits, *op. cit.*, vol. I, p. 217.

39. For another account of some aspects of the ceremonies, including that of human sacrifice, see Le Herissé's brief account of the cult of the dead, *op. cit.*, pp. 157-194, esp. p. 194.

40. See the chapter in Herskovits, *op. cit.*, vol. I, pp. 63-77, "The Cooperative Element in Dahomean Life." No writer previous to the Herskovits's, not even Le Herissé, has described this institution in such a manner, and only a few devote more than a passing sentence. Maupoil maintains that Herskovits is in error with respect to the cooperative nature of the organization outside of funerary functions. Maupoil is in the French Colonial Service, and certain facts about Dahomey would have been closed to him. On the other hand, it would seem that the dokpwe would be common knowledge, unlike knowledge of religious patterns. Nevertheless, Herskovits seems to be reliable. The facts fit the general organizational character of both Dahomean and other West African group life. Similar organizations may be met with in the same area. Herskovits even collected an appliqué cloth in which such an organization is represented (vol. I, *op. cit.*, p. 68).

41. Herskovits, *op. cit.*, vol. I, p. 68.

42. *Ibid.*, p. 65.

43. *Ibid.*, pp. 357 ff.

44. *Ibid.*, p. 194.

45. *Ibid.*

46. *Ibid.*, pp. 176 ff.

47. From the conclusion of the bush ceremonies, the dokpwegan is considered to be no longer connected with these partly deified dead. The remainder of the ritual process is under the control of the chief priest of the ancestral cult. Cf. *Ibid.*, p. 205.

48. Mead, *Kinship in the Admiralty Islands*, pp. 322, 324, 328.

49. Fortune, *op. cit.*, pp. 5, 13, 20. This problem was difficult to analyze. Although Fortune is usually classified as a "functionalist," he does not always attempt to see the situation "from the point of view of the actor," but attempts often to see what it "actually" is, i.e., as it seems to an outsider. This means concretely that he often expresses cynicism concerning the motives of the actors, since he imputes motivations of a more rationalistic nature than the actor is aware of himself. He is thus introducing a rationalistic bias into the situation, by pointing out what the individual might be attempting to do, *if* the individual were coolly planning the situation. This may sometimes mean that in his writings he implies often that the believer does not think of his values as self-validating, requiring no specific reward.

A further complexity is introduced by the general picture of Manus society given by Mead in *Growing Up in New Guinea*. Several checks on this general picture were utilized, which included Mead's detailed data in that book as well as those in *Kinship in the Admiralty Islands,* various articles, and details of Fortune's material. Nevertheless, the existence of this generalized picture in Mead's book may mean that the casual reader will "see things differently" from the analysis given here. For Mead apparently views Manus society, as crass, rationalistic, unimaginative, and self-seeking, a view which she also holds about contemporary American culture. This view of both cultures as a land of Babbits represents a check on the general Manus picture, also, since far better analyses of our culture exist than those of Sinclair Lewis. Mead's *general* view must therefore be partially discounted by her and Fortune's detailed accounts.

The problem was solved, therefore, partly by attention to the details of action. From this, however, another step was made. A series of propositions was drawn up concerning the relationship of the Manus to his Sir Ghost. These were based on the theory of religion presented here and on the published details, but were not completely to be answered by the published works. These conclusions were then sent to Dr. Fortune with the request that he explain the relationship. His reply approved the propositions, as well as clarifying further the Manus—Sir Ghost relationship.

50. Fortune, personal letter dated November 4, 1943: "The contract idea in Manus religion is not a business contract, but a covenant." For examples of a covenant in the Judaic tradition, see Genesis, 9:8-17; 15:7-18; Jeremiah, 50: 5-46. In Christian exegesis, both the Old Testament and the New Testament are covenants.

51. Fortune, *op. cit.*, p. 46.

52. Fortune, personal letter, November 4, 1943.

53. Fortune, "Manus Religion," *Oceania* 2 (1931): p. 82. Sir Ghost would in this case wander the middle seas for a while, then become a sea slug.

54. Fortune, personal letter, November 4, 1943: "Very rarely a ward may exercise his choice of Sir Ghost." To a limited extent, of course, ward exercises such a right, in that he takes a particular ancestor as Sir Ghost when the relationship begins. However, the determining factors are then the recency of death, prestige, and closeness of relationship of the dead. (Fortune, *op. cit.*, pp. 1, 2, 6, 10, 15-6, 19, 20.)

55. *Ibid.*, pp. 5, 13, 20, 29.

56. This does not mean, of course, that the ordinary contract is immoral. The moral element is simply not the most significant part of it.

57. Mead, *Kinship in the Admiralty Islands,* p. 191.

58. Fortune, *op. cit.*, p. 10.

59. *Ibid.*, p. 40.

60. *Ibid.*

61. See the long and involved case of Alupwai's sin, *Ibid.*, pp. 183 ff., esp. p. 220, when Alupwai finally confesses after terrific pressure is brought to bear against her in the crowded séances.

62. *Ibid.*, pp. 40, 220. Note that great resistance must be broken down by suspicion, recrimination, charge, and threat.

63. She cannot have sinned with her betrothed, since there is rigid avoidance between them. The situation does not charge these plans for marriage, for expiation wipes out the sin.

64. *Ibid.,* pp. 223-4.

65. Actually, Fortune expresses an even more radical point of view concerning this general issue, since he claims that if there is any domination between the Manus religion and some other pattern (daily social patterns, or economic relationships), it is rather the religious pattern in terms of which the others are conceived, and not vice versa (see *ibid.,* pp. 46-7).

66. Note that even Koretan, though blind and old, is not believed to be free of these obligations, and the Manus did not want the situation to be brought before a white court, which would be too soft-hearted (see *ibid.,* pp. 314 ff).

67. *Ibid.,* p. 49. In conformity with the considerable amount of rational calculation entering all aspects of Manus life, this push which Sir Ghost gives his ward toward promptness in paying debts, accumulating riches, etc., is conceived by the ward as being mere selfishness on Sir Ghost's part: Sir Ghost simply wants honor paid to him in the form of funerary feasts, respect and gifts at the marriage of Sir Ghost on the spirit plane, or a great showing of property in important property exchanges (see *ibid.,* pp. 13, 49, 50). Ward does not claim, however, that Sir Ghost does not have this right.

68. *Ibid.,* p. 346.

69. *Ibid.,* p. 50: Mead, *Growing Up in New Guinea,* p. 101.

70. Fortune, *op. cit.,* pp. 50-52.

71. *Ibid.,* pp. 286-8: Mead, *Growing Up in New Guinea,* p. 301.

72. Fortune, *op. cit.,* pp. 292-3.

73. *Ibid.,* p. 344.

74. *Ibid.,* p. 320.

75. Such as the Annual Customs in Dahomey, the Wawilak Cycle in Murngin, the various winter solstice ceremonies in Zuñi most of the work of the Gods in Tikopia, etc. See *ibid.,* p. 343. It is not necessary to extend the discussion at this point in order to explain this lack. Two significant facts are to be noted, however. One is that communal action, always to be found in such great periodic ceremonies, is almost absent in Manus. The other fact is that the Manus are not agriculturists, hunters, or herders, depending on a natural, seasonal cycle only in fishing, and this only partially. Fortune says, "There is no ritual in Manus that is daily, weekly, or annually regulated, except that which is evoked by the recurrence of the high tide which seasonally sweeps the spawning fish over the barrier reef."

76. This religious-familial-economic nexus is interestingly side-lighted by the ban on a widow remarrying until the final mourning feasts (Mead, *Growing Up in New Guinea,* pp. 79-80, *Kinship in the Admiralty Islands,* p. 227, Fortune, *op. cit.,* pp. 322 ff). The recently dead Sir Ghost is more powerful, and expected to be jealous of his widow, and is not "appeased" until the economic exchanges centering about the feast have been made.

# CHAPTER 6

1. Firth, *Economy,* pp. 353-4.

2. *Ibid.,* pp. 354-5.

3. The proposition has wider application than Firth suggests here (p. 357). What is known as "vulgar Marxism" makes an analogous error to this hedonistic bias of classical and later orthodox economics, by claiming that this or that phe-

nomenon is "basically economic." Similarly, various brands of psychoanalytic theory have suggested one or another "basic" factor. These can all be reduced to the same structure: (1) A given phenomenon is basically X; (2) But demonstrably other factors are also playing a part in the phenomenon; (3) These factors are also X; (4) X causes everything, because (5) X is everything. The last propositions are, of course, never made explicit, since the first is usually a widespread sentiment generally accepted. This is true of the maximization of satisfactions, which turns out to mean that we do whatever we do because we want to do so, proved by the fact that we actually do it: an operationally meaningless, logically closed circle of reasoning.

4. Firth, *Economy*, p. 33.

5. See chs. VII and VIII on the function of the chief as lawmaker with reference to economic enterprise.

6. It must be repeated that at no point is the thesis maintained, that "social action is 'basically' religious." This would be notably inaccurate, and at several stages care has been taken to insist that certain actions were secular—political, economic, technological, etc. It is rather that at the various levels of social action some elements of religious belief and emotion do play a significant part, which must be emphasized in our age because of the widespread and insistent stress on rational factors.

7. Firth, *Work*, vol. I, p. 91.

8. *Ibid.*

9. Firth, *Work*, vol. I, p. 68. Note also similar and longer formulae, pp. 62-90, with much the same suggestion.

10. *Ibid.*, p. 90.

11. Firth, *Work*, p. 90. See also the more detailed description of the inspection and repair of a canoe, in *Economy*, pp. 117-131.

12. This is interestingly intensified by the attitude which dictates the fast walk as the *tapu* or sacred stride, not the slow and stately walk of our culture. The movement must be hurried, jerky, fast, and efficient, with the weight on the toes and ball of the foot (*Work*, vol. II, p. 230): "The object was to convey the impression to the gods that the person was moving rapidly about their business, yet with due regard for the sacredness of the ground on which he treads."

13. *Ibid.*, p. 319.

14. *Ibid.*, vol. I, p. 62.

15. Somosomo is no longer a sacred house, only its former site. The mats are used for the site, as they are for any other temple. (See *Work*, vol. II, p. 304.) It was built, according to legend, by the Atua i Kafika.

16. The whole scene is given in *Work*, vol. II, p. 307.

17. Firth, *Work*, vol. I, p. 21.

18. That is, enough time to cut, dry, and plait the leaf.

19. Roi: "Taro or breadfruit are sliced, or ripe bananas (green bananas are not used for roi)." (*We the Tikopia*, p. 105.) After the coconut cream and sago flour have been poured over the ingredients, "the dish is then wrapped up and cooked ten hours or so."

20. Firth rightly insists (*Primitive Polynesian Economy*, pp. 168-186, "Ritual in Productive Activity") on a deterrent effect caused by much of ritual, and this negative function has been noted at several points in this study. Asking the aid of the deities is technologically ill conceived, judged by the canons of science,

and in terms of the allocation of the resource of time and food (libations) is uneconomically irrational. It is, however, irrational only to the extent that such ceremonies are thought to be means, not ends in themselves. When the ritual is negative in its economic function, it is no less important in other aspects.

21. The food is for both ritual exchanges (secular, for the most part), ritual offerings, and homage to the chief. Bark cloth is produced to "top" the gifts of food, as a mark of prestige, while the mats are necessary for "recarpeting" the temples and replacing the mats of the sacred ancestors.

22. No claim need be made that these particular tasks could not be mostly secular in another society. What could be claimed, however, is that in any society there will be important economic activities which are directed by the demands of religious beliefs and rituals. This does not simply at all that either "causes" the other.

23. *Primitive Polynesian Economy*, p. 202.

24. This planting is not accompanied by a complex ritual, and the chief goes alone merely because of the small amount of work involved. Cf. *Work of the Gods*, vol. II, p. 333.

25. The extraction is further based on purely secular economic factors, since the ownership of a spring for the washing, and of costly equipment, particularly the large troughs, are also important in the organization of the process. This is one ritual process which may be under the leadership of a commoner, at least in the technical phases.

26. Firth, *Work of the Gods*, vol. II, p. 335.

27. *Ibid.*, p. 337.

28. This whole discussion is taken from the detailed description given by Firth, pp. 332-373.

29. *Ibid.*, p. 344.

30. "Hot" is not a *descriptive*, but a *ritual*, term, since the food when eaten may actually be cold (*ibid.*, p. 344). It is, however, cooked specially for "those within," and is thus not the usual Tikopia cold food, which is merely a morning remnant from the previous afternoon's oven. Some relation may be considered in terms of sex and age divisions, since children in particular symbolize "cold food."

31. *Ibid.*, p. 346.

32. *Ibid.*, p. 349.

33. *Ibid.*, p. 350.

34. *Ibid.*, p. 354.

35. Firth notes (*ibid.*, p. 355) two cases where a very tiny amount was not allowed to be wasted, and maintains (p. 366) that in no case is turmeric thrown away because it did not turn out well in the oven: it is reworked and again baked, thus increasing production because of the sacred character of the product.

36. Firth, *ibid.*, p. 356. The Kafika chief demonstrated his great conscientiousness throughout the Work of the Gods.

37. Firth, *Primitive Polynesian Economy*, p. 213.

38. *Ibid.*, p. 213.

39. Firth says only (*ibid.*, p. 213), "To some extent" is this true. However, the process of receiving and giving as he describes it, coupled with the chief's relatively small consumption, his own and his family's production for their own use, etc., leave little room for doubt that his function as "agent" is rather marked.

40. As would be expected in this rather light-hearted culture, the tabus of

mourning are lessened by the chief's kin, who press him to eat, anyway, his acceptance being rationalized as merely an effort to avoid offending his own kin. This is not true of the younger members of the family at that time (*ibid.*, p. 216).

41. *Ibid.*, p. 221.

42. One might, though doubtfully, include *monotanga* from initiations and funerals, since in both cases the sacred ancestors figure.

43. A complete list is given by Firth in *ibid.*, pp. 221-2.

44. Firth, *Work of the Gods,* vol. I, p. 158.

45. *Ibid.*, p. 164.

46. *Ibid.*

47. *Primitive Polynesian Economy*, p. 337.

48. *Ibid.*

49. *Ibid.*, pp. 320-332. Note especially the complex character of this type of exchange, in which the relationship to common and sacred ancestors is emphasized, stressing mostly the kinship ties.

50. The explanation may conceivably lie in the realm of the esthetic, in that the hook must be a special kind, "with the turtleshell barb attached to the shell shank. (The shank is frequently worn separately, as an ornament.)" See *Ibid.*, p. 339.

51. *Ibid.*, p. 342.

52. *Ibid.*, p. 338.

53. As a matter of fact, the question of the bonito hook raises another serious question which Firth attempts to answer (*Economy*, p. 342), as to the cause for such a small production of such valuable objects. The amount of labor put into them is much smaller than their equivalent value in terms of canoes, for example, and comparatively little skill is required. He suggests that there is little response of supply to demand because, mainly, of an indifference which amounts to a philosophy of life. That is, there is little stimulus to such acquisition, since their interests have other channels of expression. He suggests this as a hypothesis, though this study has documented it in several other connections, mostly religious. Their interest is much less in the economic effects of the ritual or the exchange, and much more in the devotion to the gods, the attainment of their favor, and the renewal of social and kinship ties. These latter are further emphasized, and the pattern of exchange leaves no one with what might be called a "profit," thus forcing motivation from the economic aspect of the ceremony.

54. *Ibid.*, p. 344.

55. The lack of equivalence between different series is expressed by Firth's statement that one cannot "express the value of a bonito hook in terms of a quantity of food, since no such exchange is ever made and would be regarded by the Tikopia as fantastic" (*ibid.*, p. 340).

56. This is true, even though commoners may actually own any of them, and may in fact be rather wealthy.

57. This does not imply social mobility, however, since rank is fixed by tradition, legend and religious belief. One can, however, live up to the fullest expectations of one's status, or fail to do so. In this, there can be considerable social emulation.

58. There is, of course, as in any culture, some evasion of these limitations, as in the case of fishing, where an individual may hide a big fish (which should go only to a chief) from the community and eat it with his family (*ibid.*, p. 364).

59. Parsons, *Pueblo Indian Religion*, vol. I, p. 112.

60. Parsons, *Zuñi and Hopi Ceremonialism*, p. 41.

61. *Ibid.*, p. 83.

62. Ruth L. Bunzel, "Zuñi Katchinas," in *Bureau of American Ethnology Reports*, vol. XLVII (1929-30), p. 905. The "crook" or staff is a formal symbol of handing over an obligation.

63. M. C. Stevenson, *The Zuñi Indians*, p. 23.

64. E.g., the Navahos often drop in, and Zuñi accept them as guests. See *ibid.*, p. 231.

65. *Ibid.*, pp. 97-98.

66. Bunzel, "Zuñi Katchinas," in *Bureau of American Ethnology Reports*, vol. XLVII (1929-30).

67. *Ibid.*, pp. 602-3.

68. Stevenson, *op. cit.*, p. 223.

69. *Ibid.*, p. 145.

70. *Ibid.*, p. 141; Kothluwalawa is the sacred place from which the gods came.

71. *Ibid.*, pp. 229-230.

72. *Ibid.*, p. 115.

73. A few of these rabbits are used exclusively for ceremonial purposes. See *ibid.*, pp. 89 ff.

74. *Ibid.*, p. 120. A parallel to this is that no ashes or sweepings may be taken from the house, either.

75. Bunzel, "Introduction to Zuñi Ceremonialism," *Bureau of American Ethnology Reports*, vol. XLVIII (1929-30), p. 501.

76. F. H. Cushing, "Outline of Zuñi Creation Myths" in *Bureau of American Ethnology Reports*, vol. XIII (1891-92), pp. 352-55.

77. For the attention given the growing corn, see Parsons, *Pueblo Indian Religion*, vol. II, pp. 791-2. For resistance to innovations in Zuñi and other pueblos, see chs. VIII and IX.

78. Bunzel, "Zuñi Katchinas," in *Bureau of American Ethnology Reports*, vol. XLVII (1929-30).

79. *Ibid.*

80. Ruth L. Bunzel, "Zuñi Ritual Poetry," in *Bureau of American Ethnology Reports*, vol. XLVII (1929-30), p. 791.

81. *Ibid.*, pp. 802-3.

82. Small animals are easier to catch, since the dry grass allows vast areas to be burned over, driving out such animals. The dry land also allows greater mobility. The wet season brings floods which drive the Murngin from the lower coastal plain into higher ground (see Warner, *op. cit.*, pp. 259, 380 ff.), though the plains are thereby rendered fruitful.

83. *Ibid.*, pp. 145, 290, 298, 300, 306, 355, 356, 395.

84. *Ibid.*, p. 19.

85. *Ibid.*

86. *Ibid.*, p. 18. Note that it is near such bodies that the food supply is sufficient for larger groups to maintain themselves. Although the dry season is one of plenty, it can be that only because of the wetting of the land prior to that season. Similarly as these bodies of water dry, they are sources of food.

87. *Ibid.*, p. 147.

88. Warner's statement (*ibid.*, p. 148) that the "ultimate value" in Murngin society is freedom of physical mobility seems exaggerated, and is certainly disproved by his data, which show religious and kinship structures as being far more important. Nevertheless, the desire for mobility is undoubtedly important enough to prevent much accumulation.

89. *Ibid.*, pp. 138-9.

90. This is the *makarata*, which is discussed in the section on religio-political interrelationships.

91. *Ibid.*, p. 139.

92. *Ibid.*, pp. 140, 347.

93. However, the men do not think of the women as being *ritually* important at this ritual period.

94. *Ibid.*, pp. 340-356. The latter section is similar to the end of the Ulmark ceremony.

95. *Ibid.*, pp. 354-5.

96. *Ibid.*, p. 356.

97. *Ibid.*, p. 355.

98. *Ibid.*, pp. 356-370. Preparations for this ceremony are similar to those before Dua Narra ceremony.

99. *Ibid.*, p. 364.

100. *Ibid.*, p. 365. In the "old days," i.e., the ancient, mythological period, the great totem Banitja is supposed to have come out to look for food because he smelled it cooking. All the young men painted as bandicoot have in addition yellow lines and white dots to indicate both barrimundi and the white foam the fish makes when it bites.

101. *Ibid.*, p. 370, as also p. 356, in the Dua Narra ceremony; and pp. 328-9 in the Ulmark.

102. See *ibid.*, Appendix II, on "Murngin Artifacts," pp. 471-505, as also ch. V. Note especially the various uses for string.

103. *Ibid.*, p. 145.

104. *Ibid.* It is to be noted that even in this economic relationship the matter of prestige is more important than "profit."

105. *Ibid.*, p. 145. Note that as in exchange for profit in other economies, the idea of exchanging like values is expressed here, with the qualification that it is an exchange of equal *ritual* or *sacred* value.

106. *Ibid.*, p. 146.

107. *Ibid.*, pp. 290-311. The ceremony lasts for an indefinite period of time, centering about initiation and including a great number of references to sex, with a final period of licensed exchange of wives.

108. *Ibid.*, p. 292.

109. The sisters sang these rituals to prevent the flood, and to prevent the snake from swallowing them. Later, in a spirit dream, they taught the men all the songs and dances of the Wawilak constellation.

110. The gifts are symbolic of the Wawilak sisters, who were also "taken" or swallowed by the great snake, Muit.

111. *Ibid.*, pp. 306-8. The importance of selecting only *distant* relatives for such intercourse is obvious as a factor in avoiding later sexual competition.

112. *Ibid.*, p. 396.

# CHAPTER 7

1. Some interesting points have been raised, which are not immediately relevant, in these polemics. Cf., for example, Malinowski's *Crime and Punishment in Savage Society*, Harcourt, N. Y., 1926, and Wm. Seagle, "Primitive Law and Professor Malinowski," *Am. Anthrop.* 39:280 ff.; as well as A. R. Radcliffe-Brown, "Primitive Law" in the *Enc. Soc. Sci.* Note Malinowski's Introduction to H. Ian Hogbin's *Law and Order in Polynesia*, Christopher's, London, 1934. An interesting treatment is that of K. N. Llewellyn and E. Adamson Hoebel, *The Cheyenne Way*, University of Oklahoma, Norman (Okla.), 1941, pp. 20-65. For more concrete materials, v. Bruno Gutmann, *Das Recht der Dschagga*, Beck, München, 1926; Albert Harrasser, "Die Rechtsverletzung bei den australischen Eingeborenen," Beilageheft zur *Zeitschrift f. Vergleichende Rechtswissenschaft*, Bd. 50 (1936) Stuttgart; "Les derniers rois du Dahomey," by Henri Lefaivre, in *Revue d'Histoire des Colonies* 25 (1937): pp. 25-76; G. Härtter, "Das Gottesgericht bei den Ewe," in *Zeitschrift f. Ethnologie* 69 (1937): 62-72; or, among a much less "developed" group, Herbert König's "Das Recht der Polarvölker" in *Anthropos* 22:689-746.

2. It is not certain that the basis of the distinction lies, analytically, in the presence of a writing system.

3. As is done, for example, by Malinowski (*Crime and Custom*), p. 28: ". . . a body of binding obligations, regarded as right by one party and acknowledged as a duty by the other, and kept in force by a specific mechanism of reciprocity [contractualism] and publicity inherent in the structure of their society"; or *The Family Life of the Australian Aborigines*, Hodder, London, 1913, p. 115: "A given social norm or rule is legal if it is enforced by a direct, organized, and definite social sanction." This leaves no analytical distinction between a spanking and an electrocution, though the answer might be made that ultimately there is little, both being concerned with order and social discipline.

4. As is done by Seagle, *op. cit.* This approach is simpler, but on the other hand excludes most societies, where nevertheless there are phenomena *analytically* similar.

5. Hogbin, *op. cit.*, pp. lxv-lxvi, *infra et supra.*

6. In our society. The Murngin have a different attitude, somewhat like ours in a situation of border skirmishes.

7. Cf. Max Weber, *Wirtschaft u. Gesellschaft*, pp. 642-9.

8. It becomes evident that the lawyers and the sociologists may easily bark up different trees. If there is a varying degree of explicitness, as seems obvious, then the sociologist or anthropologist is likely to see the degrees as being *only* degrees, while the legalist will note the differences between the extremes while failing to see the sameness of pattern.

9. Unpub. seminar discussion by Prof. W. E. Moore, Pennsylvania State College, Winter, 1941. I judge that both Llewellyn and Hoebel (E. Adamson Hoebel, *The Political Organization and Law-Ways of the Comanche Indians*, *Am. Anthrop. Ass. Mem.* No. 54, 1940, p. 47; Llewellyn and Hoebel, *op. cit.*, p. 23) would agree in general to this statement. Both criticize Malinowski in terms somewhat different from Seagle's, and emphasize the fact of authority or force as well as that of (court) conflict. The latter point is also made, as is known,

by Vinogradoff (*Outlines of Historical Jurisprudence*, 2 vols., Oxford U., London, 1920-2).

10. Cf. Wilson D. Wallis, *Messiahs: Christian and Pagan*, Badger, Boston, 1918; Curt Nimuendaju, "Die Sagen von der Erschaffung und Vernichtung der Welt als Grundlagen der Religion der Apapoçuva-Guarani," *Zeitschrift f. Ethnologie* 46 (1914): 284-403; Weston LaBarre, *The Peyote Cult* (Yale U. Pub. Anthrop.), New Haven, 1938; James Mooney, "The Ghost Dance Religion and Sioux Outbreak of 1890" (*Bur. Am. Ethn. Rep.*), 1892. Cf. Chester I. Barnard, *The Functions of the Executive*, Cambridge, Harvard University Press, 1938, esp. pp. 162-168.

11. Furnishing a good example, under the autocratically harsh Shaka, as is known, many Zulu left the country, forming the Matabele, Nguni, and Shangana. Note that (theoretically) great powers are usually hamstrung by the existence of number of officials who carry out the threat of those powers (or who sabotage them). Cf. the Dahomey king in this regard. The group gives the power, but *under conditions*, however implicit.

12. Weber, *op. cit.*, pp. 250-7, 201-3, 753-7.

13. See Ralph Linton's discussion of explicitness as it relates to the Comanche when compared to the highly organized West African cultures, in *The Study of Man*, Appleton-Century, N. Y., Stu. ed., 1936, pp. 227-9. This whole discussion as it deals with Tikopia will not be as complete as would be desired in the light of Firth's *Rank and Religion in Tikopia*. As yet unpublished.

14. For example, the "power behind the throne," the ultimate authority, may be presumed in some cases to be divine, but the bureaucratic structure becomes autonomous. More to home, the Menabe Tanala, the Tallensi, the Nguato, and the Zulu all have as "ultimate authorities" the French and British Governments, and this is true of Dahomey as well. The political structures of these tribes seem to operate more smoothly, however, when the ultimate authority stays out of the picture. *Vide* M. Fortes and E. E. Evans-Pritchard, *African Political Systems*, Oxford U., London, 1941, pp. 25-82, 239-71, as also the interesting discussion of recent trends in colonial rule, in L. P. Mair, *Native Policies in Africa*, Routledge, London, 1936. Cf. Weber, *Wirtschaft u. Gesellschaft*, pp. 150 ff.

15. E.g., the Fono of Rarokoka, to be discussed later, in Firth, *Work of the Gods*, vol. II, pp. 189-205.

16. It is difficult to avoid in such analyses the temptation of referring to the immediate past, and describing those patterns as though they existed today. This is particularly true of Dahomey, whose autonomy was lost only in 1894, and whose inhabitants number many who lived in that former regime. Further, one thinks of changes forced on a group from the outside as being somehow less a part of the "real" society. It is possible to steer a middle ground, of making clear the temporal referent in any given case. For an interesting example of the vividness of Dahomean history to a native, cf. Le Herissé, *op. cit.*, pp. 271-352, "Histoire du Dahomey raconteé par un Dahomean."

17. Though the present tense is used, it must be understood that the ordeal is not used now, ". . . except where fear of discovery is slight because of the remoteness of European officials, or the absence of French-speaking inhabitants . . ." (Herskovits, *op. cit.*, vol. II, p. 18, "Knowledge of this judicial magic, and the formulae for the manipulation of it, has been far from forgotten, however, and it is not without significance that in discussing the ordeals informants invariably used the present tense."

18. Of course, in terms of the purposes and knowledge of a ruler, the choice of the ordeal then becomes a useful judicial tool, though the trial is made *after* his private decision of guilt.

19. Similarly, cf. Malinowski, *Crime* . . . , pp. 85-92, and Hogbin, *op. cit.*, pp. 216-22, though of course the conception of magic is slightly different as it leads to this conclusion.

20. This repeats in vividly concrete form the point mentioned above, that in a highly structured system the top power can be changed without the total pattern being destroyed. The modern fascistic or communist coup d'etat is of the same nature.

21. Here, as in the case of the village ordeals, there was ample opportunity for determining the decision by manipulation. Le Herissé notes (p. 75, as Herskovits quotes) that the one who administered the ordeal could easily choke the bird. The administerer received a fee before the ritual.

22. Herskovits, *op. cit.*, vol. II, p. 20.

23. On the analytical level, such limitations always exist, in that neither can completely usurp all man's activity. On the concrete level, except where the most powerful religious practitioner is also the political leader, conflicts or limitations are always potential between "king" and "high priest."

24. Herskovits, *op. cit.*, vol. II, p. 9.

25. Herskovits, *ibid.*, p. 12.

26. *Ibid.*, p. 14.

27. These were the property of the monarchy.

28. Herskovits, *op. cit.*, vol. I, p. 121.

29. *Ibid.*, p. 122. It should be emphasized, as Herskovits does not here, how signal an occasion this was, when the king allowed others to drink with him.

30. Again, here, Herskovits does not remark on the symbolic significance of the occasion, as indicated by the sprinkling of sacrificial blood on particular objects (akin, of course, to the Ashanti consecration of the stool).

31. There were only twelve which did not make hoes, and these were supervised closely. Cf. Herskovits, *op. cit.*, vol. I, p. 126.

32. Herskovits, *ibid.*, p. 127.

33. This case interestingly documents the worldly importance of religion. Even in this most secular of societies, where the king was ultimately powerful and just possibly somewhat more synical or sceptical than others, religious powers are being used as means for secular ends (which might be superficially thought to be more easily attained by secular means); and, more important, the secular leader considered it necessary to guard against the power of religious action.

34. "Sacred," but possibly occurring in this world, and thus potentially competitive with the secular.

35. "Customs" is a frequently used term in the literature on Dahomey, referring to both the funeral ceremonies for a king, and the annual ceremonies in the kingly ancestral cult. Herskovits witnessed a one-day ceremonial (*op. cit.*, pp. 57-69) which was much like these. They were once very spectacular, and involved some human sacrifice (exaggerated in report), human beings constituting the most worthy gift for a kingly ceremony. Descriptions occur in Burton and Skertchly, as well as Forbes, though their reports differ as to the number killed. Cf. R. F. Burton, *A Mission to Gelele, King of Dahomey* etc. 2 vols. (III and IV of the Memorial Edition), London, 1893, vol. II, pp. 58 ff.; as well as

vol. I, pp. 228 ff.; and J. A. Skertchly, *Dahomey*, London, 1874, pp. 178 ff., and pp. 383 ff.

36. A sacred number.

37. Herskovits, *op. cit.*, vol. I, p. 134.

38. *Ibid.*

39. "The political hierarchy of Dahomey may be thought of in a general way as comprising three ranks. The highest of these, where position was shared with no one, was occupied by the King." (Herskovits, *Dahomey*, vol. II, p. 22.) Compare his statements with more isolated and less systematic comments on regions nearer the coast, in A. Bartet, "Les rois du Bas-Dahomey, *Soc. D. Geogr. D. Rochefort Bull.* (Rochefort), vol. 30 (1908): 179-216; also Henri Lefaivre, "Les dernier . . . ," *op. cit.* The earlier traveler's reports, of course, emphasized these aspects more than any others.

40. This was one of the most striking elements of the political life of Dahomey, to an outsider, since early reports emphasize the ceremony of throwing dirt on the head, etc. Herskovits points out, and photographs show, how Dahomeans "still prostrate themselves before a superior," *op. cit.*, p. 33.

41. One must be cautious, however, in interpreting this since certainly the larger part of this deep respect was not alone religious in character (i.e., consciously), but a reflection of the extreme power of life and death—even though this secular power had certain bases even further removed, i.e., the religious.

42. Herskovits, *ibid.*, p. 36.

43. *Ibid.*

44. There are, of course, suggestions in Robert S. Rattray, *Religion and Art in Ashanti*, Oxford, Clarendon, 1927, and *Ashanti Law and Constitution*, Oxford, Clarendon, 1929, in that some of the same symbolisms are used in the two cultures, particularly the consecration by blood. Cf. also in this regard, Paul Hazoumé, "Le pacte de sang au Dahomey," *Trav. Et. Memoires d'Ethn.* 25 (1937): viii-170.

45. Le Herissé, *op. cit.*, pp. 271-2.

46. Herskovits, *op. cit.*, vol. II, p. 49. The "apartness" of this group is accentuated by the fact that ". . . no prince, and no child of a prince, may become a cult member of any of the gods. He may not even be vowed as a cult member of the royal Tɔhwiyo, for the relationship of cult-member to his *Vodun* is that of servant, and no one of royal blood may affiliate himself with a *Vodun* and serve him publicly, for royal blood, even in the living, partakes of godly qualities" (Herskovits and Herskovits, *op. cit.*, p. 30).

47. *Ibid.*

48. *Ibid.*

49. Herskovits claims (*op. cit.*, vol. II, p. 68) that Behanzin's family had been impoverished by the "Great Customs" at Behanzin's death, in accordance with the Dahomean notion of having an incredibly impressive funeral. This ceremony was a commemoration of Behanzin's funeral.

50. Now a chief of one of the quarters in Abomey.

51. Later attention will be given to sex position, though it may be noted here that in spite of the "masculinity" of the society, women, especially elder women, held important positions in the political hierarchy, usually as quasi-official checkers or inspectors of affairs entrusted to various officials.

52. Herskovits, *op. cit.*, vol. II, p. 62; for his description, see pp. 57-69; sources for earlier descriptions of these and the "Great Customs" have been previ-

ously noted. These seem to have been ritualized expressions of the wealth, secular power, and sacredness of the king.

53. Animals now; though, as noted, human sacrifices played a part under the monarchy. These were often substituted for by animals.

54. The tragedy of this, in Dahomean terms, ought to be kept in mind. They would therefore lack the proper funeral ceremonies, and would not (probably) ever be a central figure in deification ceremonies.

55. Herskovits calls his movements (*op. cit.*, vol. II, p. 67) "ritually awkward," and this may be a proper characterization. However, the awkwardness may be indeed real, since the king (or chief) could not be expected to be capable of priestly grace.

56. *Ibid.*, p. 68.

57. Herskovits mentions (*op. cit.*, vol. II, p. 75) that "even under the present European regime this official exists, though he has no standing with the government." He represents an excellent example of the insight of the monarchy into the pervasiveness of religious activities, and the possibility of utilizing them.

58. Herskovits makes no such qualification, yet the possessors of such an esoteric lore as was under the control of the priests, and the holders of such power in other directions, would certainly reduce in actuality much of this theoretical secular power. This would be further true, since the followers could not be allowed to know much about this control, else the religious control would wane. Actually, there seems to have been no need for any constantly *active* control. Cf. Herskovits, *op. cit.*, vol. II, p. 175.

59. These were the abnormally born.

60. Herskovits, *op. cit.*, vol. II, p. 175.

61. He might also be removed if there were—the other side of the inter-relationship—signs of divine displeasure with the officiant.

62. Though many ceremonies are "secret," i.e., not open to the uninitiate, the Dahomeans do not consider them secret. See Herskovits, *op. cit.*, vol. II, p. 194.

63. This does not mean, however, that the upper class did or does not patronize the diviner: Even the diviner patronizes another diviner, if a crisis arises (Herskovits, *op. cit.*, vol. II, p. 215).

64. *Ibid.*

65. Herskovits, *op. cit.*, vol. I, pp. 118-9. This was only one such technique. Since taxation of livestock took place only once in about three years, variations of this false alarm could be used: floods, general misfortunes, etc., there being some difference in what was done to avert the calamities. In each case, however, the supernatural, administered by official religious practitioners, was utilized for political ends, thus emphasizing the wide uses of the religious beliefs. The particular deity involved also varied.

# CHAPTER 8

1. Mead, *Growing Up in New Guinea*, pp. 302-304.
2. *Ibid.*, p. 302.
3. *Ibid.*, pp. 303-4; Fortune, *Manus Religion*, pp. 128- 217-8, 314.
4. Mead, *Growing Up in New Guinea*, p. 304.
5. Mead, *Kinship in the Admiralty Islands*, p. 195.

6. Fortune, *Manus Religion*, p. 128; Mead, *Growing Up in New Guinea*, p. 304.

7. Fortune, *Manus Religion*, p. 128. Fortune also notes: They ". . . stand alone in their respect for the courts of the Australian Administration and for their almost inordinate love of using them."

8. See *ibid.*, pp. 314-321, for details.

9. *Ibid.*, pp. 128-9.

10. Note how the constable may stand by (in the seduction case, see *ibid.*, pp. 124 ff.) or even take an active part (as in the incest case, pp. 145 ff.), but in either case he is backing the native opinion and idea of justice as expressed by Sir Ghost.

11. There may be more conflict in the future, since the mediums will sometimes blame an illness on the use of the white man's justice instead of native, or vice versa. In the case of the seduction mentioned above, the seducer might have been jailed instead of there being an expiatory payment. See *ibid.*, p. 136.

12. *Ibid.*, p. 52.

13. Mead, *Growing Up in New Guinea*, pp. 10, 47-48.

14. The entire case is given in Fortune, *Manus Religion*, pp. 145-183.

15. *Ibid.*, p. 148.

16. *Ibid.*, p. 152.

17. However, since it was becoming plain that Popwitch was not going to recover, an explanation had to be made in terms of ghostly motives. With confession and expiation (i.e., acceptance of the charge of guilt, and punishment), the original sin was held to be without further effect.

18. *Ibid.*, pp. 2, 3.

19. *Ibid.*, pp. 113-15.

20. *Ibid.*, pp. 64 ff. Mead, *Growing Up in New Guinea*, pp. 32-4, describes how the Manus attempt to prevent stealing at even the earliest ages, so that in this field of activity there are really few transgressors.

21. Fortune, *Manus Religion*, p. 69.

22. *Ibid.*, pp. 57, 80.

23. R. Firth, *Primitive Polynesian Economy*, Routledge, London, 1939, p. 231.

24. *Ibid.*, p. 233.

25. Firth, *Work of the Gods*, vol. II, pp. 189-205. This ceremony has been mentioned before.

26. *Ibid.*, p. 189.

27. Firth, *Work of the Gods*, vol. II, pp. 200-1. The technique is *coitus interruptus*. See *We, the Tikopia*, pp. 490-3, 515, 524. Infanticide is also utilized: pp. 527-30.

28. Firth, *Work of the Gods*, vol. II, p. 201.

29. *Ibid.*, p. 196.

30. Firth, *Ibid.*, p. 198.

31. Firth, *Ibid.*, p. 203.

32. Though this is a customary way of reinstating oneself in the chief's graces, it must be noted that this is not a mere case of personal insult, which would be the usual situation giving rise to this scene. The punishment does not distinguish this situation, but the public breach of important rules, leading to a secular official (the ariki is certainly not the representative of the *Atua i Tafua* when he begins scolding the culprit) taking direct and publicly sanctioned action

against the violator. This fact is further set off by the occasional case of a wealthy man who deliberately commits this offence in order "conspicuously to consume" in payment and gain a reputation. Here, however, the commoner would not dare to follow. (*Ibid.*, p. 204.)

33. Firth, *Primitive Polynesian Economy*, p. 231.

34. Firth, *We, the Tikopia*, pp. 380-1, where the case is given in detail.

35. Firth, *We, the Tikopia*, p. 380. The function of this shouting is clear: the order then becomes a public, official measure, not a merely personal one. The whole group is then party to the judgment, while the culprit has little recourse.

36. *Ibid.*, p. 381.

37. Firth, *We, the Tikopia*, p. 381. This, even though the personality of the chief was criticized at the same time.

38. Firth, *We, the Tikopia*, p. 384.

39. *Ibid.* That is, the chief intervenes when there is actually a "public" disorder, not one which is part of ordinary social interaction and thus resolved in the usual course of things.

40. Firth, *We, the Tikopia*, p. 350.

41. Firth, *Work of the Gods*, vol. 5, p. 16; *Primitive Polynesian Economy*, p. 202. Firth does not suggest, though it may be true, that these symbolize the usual binding of a frond about a tree.

42. Firth, *Work of the Gods*, vol. I, pp. 19-20.

43. But a man should not starve merely that more coconut shall accumulate. Obedience is in direct proportion to the rank of the imposer of the tapu, and he may lift it briefly for certain reasons. Further, some tapu rest only on the respect for a man of rank (See *Primitive Polynesian Economy*, pp. 207-10).

44. It is to be regretted, as stated before, that Firth's *Rank and Religion in Tikopia* is not published. Of great aid in this might also be his *History and Traditions of Tikopia*, also as yet unpublished.

45. Firth, *Primitive Polynesian Economy*, p. 223.

46. Though, as will be pointed out in more detail later, there is only one real "gift," which is given twice a year. All others are reciprocated or redistributed almost immediately.

47. Firth, *Primitive Polynesian Economy*, p. 225.

48. *Ibid.*, pp. 225-6.

49. *Ibid.*, pp. 226-7.

50. Firth, *Primitive Polynesian Economy*, p. 232.

51. That is, true brother and sister; Firth, *We, the Tikopia*, p. 329.

52. *Ibid.*

53. Since Tikopia is so completely isolated in the ocean, there is almost no chance of reaching land.

54. *Ibid.*, p. 333.

55. *Ibid.*

56. *Ibid.*, pp. 333-4.

57. *Ibid.*, p. 335. As he points out, and as has been suggested before, the spirits (or deities) feel about such laws just as do ordinary individuals: "The spirits, just as men, respond to a norm of conduct of an external character. The moral law exists in the absolute, independent of the gods." That is, independent so far as conscious motivation is concerned.

58. Firth, "The Meaning of Dreams in Tikopia" in *Essays Presented to C. G. Seligman*, 1934, pp. 63-74.

59. Nor is mother-son or father-daughter incest known as a public and historical (official) fact, though Firth found one suggestion of mother-son incest (*We, the Tikopia*, p. 327).

60. Stevenson, *op. cit.*, p. 289.

61. Bunzel, "Introduction to Zuñi Ceremonialism," *Bureau of American Ethnology Reports*, vol. XLVII, p. 478.

62. *Ibid.*, p. 479.

63. *Ibid.*

64. Parsons, *Pueblo Indian Religion*, vol. I, p. 157.

65. Stevenson, *op. cit.*, p. 290.

66. Impeachment proceedings may also be brought against a religious leader. In 1890, a ceremony for the third coming of the Corn Maidens was being held so that the new sun priest might learn the ceremony, the previous sun priest having been impeached for having caused a drought (see *ibid.*, p. 180).

67. Parsons, *Pueblo Indian Religion*, vol. I, p. 145; Bunzel, "Introduction to Zuñi Ceremonialism," *Bureau of American Ethnology Reports*, vol. XLVII, p. 478. Actually, only the "chiefs of the rain societies identified with the six cardinal directions," with the heads of the three other priesthoods, are included in the council, not all rain priests.

68. Parsons, *Notes on Zuñi*, pt. II, pp. 264-277.

69. Bunzel, "Introduction to Zuñi Ceremonialism," *Bureau of American Ethnology Reports*, vol. XLVII, p. 479.

70. The last such case of torture in the pueblo resulted when a man boasted while drunk of his powers. After being hung, then later beaten with the clubs of the War chiefs, he still would not talk. However, he had sent to Fort Wingate for help, and the troops who finally came jailed three of the principals. See Parsons, *Pueblo Indian Religion*, pp. 64-5.

71. Stevenson, *op. cit.*, p. 393.

72. Parsons, *Pueblo Indian Religion*, p. 66.

73. Bunzel, "Introduction to Zuñi Ceremonialism," *Bureau of American Ethnology Reports*, vol. XLVII, p. 479.

74. Stevenson, *op. cit.*, pp. 392-406, gives several such cases, showing how ready the officials were to kill witches.

75. Bunzel, "Introduction to Zuñi Ceremonialism," *Bureau of American Ethnology Reports*, vol. XLVII, p. 480. This, of course, is a general impression made on all visitors to Zuñi.

76. *Ibid.*, p. 501. Sexual intercourse during this period is also forbidden.

77. *Ibid.*, p. 515.

78. Stevenson, *op. cit.*, p. 216-7. The "police" are, of course, the Bow priests. See Parsons, *Hopi and Zuñi Ceremonialism*, p. 57.

79. Bunzel, "Introduction to Zuñi Ceremonialism," *Bureau of American Ethnology Reports*, vol. XLVII, p. 479.

80. Stevenson, *op. cit.*, pp. 386-7. Parsons says (*Pueblo Indian Religion*, vol. I, p. 116) that by narcotics the "lost, strayed, or stolen" may be also found.

81. Bunzel, "Introduction to Zuñi Ceremonialism," *Bureau of American Ethnology Reports*, vol. XLVII, p. 479.

82. Stevenson, *op. cit.*, p. 234. With the council were the individuals who were "to impersonate the Council of the Gods and the Shalako."

83. Bunzel, "Zuñi Katcinas," *Bureau of American Ethnology Reports*, vol. XLVII, p. 963. Bunzel calls this a "grave offense," but adds that "hardly a year passes" without its occurrence.

84. Bunzel, "Introduction to Zuñi Ceremonialism," *Bureau of American Ethnology Reports*, vol. XLVII, p. 479.

85. Parsons, *Pueblo Indian Religion*, vol. I, p. 434.

86. One of Bunzel's informants died after having given her considerable information, and it was his opinion as well as that of the pueblo that he had lost his protection thereby. See Bunzel, "Introduction to Zuñi Ceremonialism," *Bureau of American Ethnology Reports*, vol. XLVII, p. 494.

87. It must be kept in mind, however, that validation is necessary for such ritual to be legitimate, i.e., potent. Many rituals are known to those not empowered to use them, and these remain valueless to such individuals.

88. *Ibid.*, p. 479.

89. See the various stories with this theme, in Bunzel, "Zuñi Katcinas," *Bureau of American Ethnology Reports*, vol. XLVII, pp. 999-1005.

90. However, flogging is also purificatory, especially when the spikes of the giant yucca are used. An example is initiation proceedings. Stevenson (*op. cit.*, pp. 240-1) relates that when a non-initiate happens to be present when the sacred paint is applied to masks for the Shalako, he must be whipped. It is possible to maintain, with Durkheim, although the point is too complex to be dealt with here, that punishment very generally figures as a purifier or at least cathartic for the emotions of any society.

91. It may be regretted that Warner has not published his field notes, or made them available. A. R. Radcliffe-Brown mentions them several times in his "The Social Organization of Australian Tribes," *Oceania I* (1930-1): 34-63; 206-256; 426-456. Since he spent such a long and intensive research period among them, his analysis of the Murngin may be considered reliable, as frequent references to it in *Oceania*, the journal containing the most intensive studies of the area, would indicate. However, this allows less of an independent check on his analyses, through the intimate details themselves.

92. Warner, *op. cit.*, p. 35.

93. *Ibid.*, p. 36. See, also, T. Theodor Webb, "Tribal Organization in East Arnhem Land," *Oceania III* (1932-3): 466-79.

94. Warner, *op. cit.*, p. 5.

95. *Ibid.*, p. 79.

96. *Ibid.*, pp. 79-81.

97. As a matter of fact, this same pattern is repeated often in other, secularized, societies, such as our own, where the situation "by custom" is not always a legal one (i.e., we have translated certain moral propositions into law). The situation *can* become legal, but the immediate and supported action is direct and indignant. Generally, in our society the man who makes a legal matter of this situation from the first will be despised by the community.

98. *Ibid.*, p. 81.

99. *Ibid.*, p. 129.

100. *Ibid.*, p. 174-6.

101. *Ibid.*, p. 174.
102. *Ibid.*, p. 175.
103. *Ibid.*, pp. 175-6.
104. This is the ideal version, which deviates, like all patterns in all societies, from the "proper" fashion. For there will be young hotheads, accidents, or treachery, which can start a general battle. This does not negate the usual efficacy of the pattern of expiation and catharsis. A case of treachery is given on pp. 177-81.
105. *Ibid.*, p. 139.
106. *Ibid.*, p. 139.
107. *Ibid.*, p. 156.
108. The qualification is necessary, since out-group antagonism may be and often is expressed in or intensified by sacred rituals. Nazism, e.g., became a nationalist religion, glorifying war—but war toward members of *other* groups.
109. *Ibid.*, p. 157.
110. *Ibid.*, p. 131.
111. *Ibid.*, pp. 131, 157, 232, etc. It must be noted that the Murngin are "bloody minded," and often threaten to kill when they do not carry out the threat. This type of exaggeration may be whimsically compared to the Dahomean pattern of number-exaggeration, or the Tipokia food-exaggeration.
112. *Ibid.*, p. 157.
113. *Ibid.*, p. 78.
114. *Ibid.*, p. 162.
115. *Ibid.*, p. 162; he gives specific cases on p. 160.
116. *Ibid.*, p. 130.
117. Nevertheless, and of course, this does not mean that a given social science, or scientist, may not orient himself with respect to only one such sphere or level, for purposes of investigation. Indeed, his work will have little value unless it is strictly formulated from some one explicit point of observation.

# CHAPTER 9

1. See Sigmund Freud, *Die Zukunft Einer Illusion*, Leipzig, Intern. Psychoan. Verlag, 1927. This theory is discussed more fully in Appendix II.
2. See Kingsley Davis' *Human Society*, ch. XIII ("Marriage and the Family").
3. Arnold van Gennep, *Les Rites de Passage*, Librairie Critique (Emile Nourry), Paris, 1909, p. 3.
4. Although, as has been noted, the Zuñi do not think of marriage as having great social importance.
5. Not, of course, to the same degree. The Zuñi do not have elaborate ceremonies for this situation. The ceremonies may in some societies be given for the mother or father, not the child (See Margaret Mead, *Social Organization of Manua, Bishop Museum Bulletin No. 76*, Honolulu, 1930, p. 89). Gregory Bateson reports that the Iatmul celebrate the *naven* "for a girl . . . when she gives birth to a child," though not for the father when his first son is born (*Naven*, Cambridge: Cambridge Univ. Press, 1936, p. 48).
   It is clear that this is a question of *social* birth far more than of *physical* birth. The parturition of a still-born child, or of twins in the eastern tribes of Western Nigeria or (in earlier times) among the Ba-Thonga (Junod, *op. cit.*, vol. II,

pp. 433-40), or of the *tɔxɔsu* who are fated ill among the Dahomey (Herskovits, *Dahomey*, I, p. 262) may be properly considered a physical birth, but not at all a social one: no new member is being accepted, and no charge of rearing a child is being delegated.

6. See Kingsley Davis' exposition, "A Conceptual Analysis of Stratification," in *American Sociological Review*, vol. VII (June 1942), pp. 309-322.

7. Note, for example, the sub-incision rites. In this connection, see M. F. Ashley-Montagu's exposition of the meaning of the ceremony, in *Coming Into Being Among the Australian Aborigines*, Routledge, London, 1937.

8. See the elaborate analysis of this in George Peter Murdock, *Social Structure*, New York: Macmillan, 1949.

9. A more extended statement of this may be found in various of Malinowski's works. Cf., e.g., "Parenthood—the Basis of Social Structure," in V. F. Calverton and S. D. Schmalhausen, *The New Generation*, Macauley, N. Y., 1930, or *Sex and Repression*, Harcourt, Brace, N. Y., 1927, pp. 212-217.

10. Malinowski, "Parenthood . . . ," p. 135. It is interesting to note that Rivers, making his investigations shortly after the turn of the century and without this principle to guide him, found while investigating polyandry among the Todas that any man born of such a family arrangement always gave the name of *only one* of his potential fathers when asked his father's name (W. H. R. Rivers, *The Todas*, Macmillan, London, 1906, p. 516). Rivers was insistent on the point, and discovered several rules governing *which* man it is who will be considered "father." There is, however, always *someone*, and it seems to be *only one*—even though that one may change during the lifetime of the Toda child.

11. Paul Radin claims ("Ancestor Worship," in the *Encyclopedia of the Social Sciences*) that true cases of ancestor worship are rare.

12. In spite of the meager nature of Zuñi funeral ceremonies, it will be seen that they fit this description.

13. Cf. Durkheim, *op. cit.*, pp. 399 ff.

14. The functions of mourning have been treated more fully by Willard Waller, *The Family*, Cordon, N. Y., 1938, pp. 491-523, as well as by Sigmund Freud, "Mourning and Melancholia," in *Collected Papers*, vol. IV. Int. Psychoan., Press, London, 1924-5, pp. 152-170, and Howard Becker, "The Sorrow of Bereavement," *Journal of Abnormal Psychology*, vol. XXVII, pp. 391-410.

15. Herskovits, *op. cit.*, vol. I, p. 302. There are, according to Herskovits, thirteen marriage types. These differ from previous descriptions (for example, cf. Le Herissé, *op. cit.*, pp. 203 ff.) in details. Neither Burton nor Skertchly attempted such a detailed description. However, Le Herissé does agree that there are two classes of marriage forms, according to whether the father's family or the mother's has control over the children. It is to be expected, of course, that in such a patriarchal, patrilineal, patrilocal culture there would be strong pressures toward paternal control. This is even seen in the fact that the other marriage forms can become like the *akwenusi* through certain ceremonies.

16. Herskovits, *op. cit.*, vol. I, pp. 303-4. These may include taking part in funeral rites, and in making gifts for these ceremonials.

17. It is the sib head and not the father who receives the presents, since the goat is to be sacrificed to the founding sib ancestor (*tɔhwiyo*), and the sib head officiates in this capacity. The caury shells are also given to the ancestors.

18. *Ibid.*, p. 309.

19. Without, however, any elaborate ceremony with drums and dancing.

20. This is usual, since Lεgba is the messenger of the gods, and it is felt that without his assistance many requests or prayers would never be heard.

21. *Loc. cit.*

22. This point is interesting, in that newly dedicated shrines are also given this simple dish as a first offering, in order that the spirit may not always expect expensive gifts.

23. If the woman was not a virgin, and it was not the husband himself who had first access to her (in which case he must have saved the first mat), he may even reject her. In any case, the occasion is less elaborate, and the man's society does not offer many gifts (*ibid.*, pp. 308-9).

24. *Ibid.*, pp. 341-2.

25. *Ibid.*, pp. 343-4.

26. If a serious quarrel occurs between his family and hers, whether caused by him or not, the sib head of her family may declare a divorce between all women from that sib who are married to any members of his sib. This may be used, for example, in the case of the *adomevodida* marriage form, where a long-standing promise of a woman from one sib to another is finally broken or remains unfulfilled. The sib ancestors enforce this decree until conformity is achieved (see *Ibid.*, pp. 313-6).

27. Although this holds in many cases where the women retain control over the children, the case is not so clear with the "free" relationship, or *xadudo*. This conformity is not so easily forced, since the woman broke with her sib when she became the man's wife. Just as she did not make her ancestral spirits a party to her marriage, so she is not protected by them in the same fashion as in most other marriage forms.

28. *Ibid.*, p. 259.

29. Skertchly, *op. cit.*, p. 500; Herskovits, *op. cit.*, vol. I, pp. 260-1.

30. *Ibid.*, vol. II, p. 216.

31. Le Herissé, *op. cit.*, pp. 235-42; Herskovits, *op. cit.*, vol. I, pp. 263 ff.

32. This is the spirit of an ancestor, remolded by Mawu into a new being.

33. The series of ceremonies for twins, or for children who come under the category of twins, are much more elaborate, and more closely related to the religious system. They are thought to be specially favored, and there is even a twin cult. (See *Ibid.*, pp. 270-2.)

34. *Ibid.*, vol. II, p. 218.

35. And even these cases obtain it from a male relative.

36. The importance of Lεgba has been mentioned, as the messenger to other spirits.

37. The fact that these ceremonies seem to be unconnected with the religious pattern is of interest, in that circumcision and cicatrization (especially the former) are often so related. The solution may lie in the fact that the ceremonies do not mark definitely the stage of adulthood, and that moreover the Dahomeans feel the ceremonies are performed for erotic and hygienic reasons. That is, they do not have the deep significance that they have in many other societies, and likewise do not become occasions for sacred rites. (See *Ibid.*, vol. I, pp. 291 ff.)

38. The cicatrizations noted here are not those made on cult or sib and tribal

members. These latter, as well as certain special cuts for particular purposes, relate much more definitely to the supernatural.

39. Determination of a date by a diviner is not, it must be noted, proof that an event in Dahomey has religious significance. Divination is so much a part of tribal life, that any sort of secular or sacred event may be explained or initiated through the diviner.

40. *Ibid.*, p. 296.

41. However, princes do not participate in any ceremony, and no offerings are made, when they are circumcised. The fact that there is disagreement as to the details of the operation may indicate that attitudes toward circumcision are changing, probably toward secularization.

42. The function of this intercourse is not clear. Herskovits claims (*Ibid.*, p. 297) that though this is dangerous for the woman there is no idea of fertility rites or of assuring boys of sexual potency.

43. The others are the djɔtɔ, which is at first the sɛmɛkɔkɑto with the task of finding substance for an individual's body, but which is later the guardian spirit; the sɛmɛdon, which is the personal soul or personality; and the sɛlidɔn, or the individual's intellect or intuition, the "great soul" or *se*. Only men have all four souls.

44. *Ibid.*, vol. II, p. 219.

45. *Ibid.*, p. 395.

46. Such as death in childbirth, or by lightning, leprosy or smallpox.

47. *Ibid.*, pp. 398-401.

48. Reo F. Fortune, "Manus Religion," *Oceania*, vol II (1931), pp. 83 ff.

49. Mead, *Growing Up in New Guinea*, p. 109.

50. Among other diseases, malaria in a virulent form seems to exist, according to personal communications (Nov. 4, 1943, and March 22, 1946) and personal marginal notes for his article on Manus religion (*Oceania*, vol. II, p. 84).

51. Fortune, *Manus Religion*, p. 5.

52. *Ibid.*, p. 18.

53. Mead, *Kinship in the Admiralty Islands*, pp. 315 ff.

54. *Ibid.*, pp. 227-8.

55. Fortune, *Manus Religion*, p. 79.

56. *Ibid.*, p. 79.

57. *Ibid.*, p. 341.

58. Mead, *Growing Up in New Guinea*, p. 154.

59. Fortune, *Manus Religion*, p. 338.

60. *Ibid.*, p. 337.

61. *Ibid.*, p. 338.

62. *Ibid.*, p. 339.

63. Mead, *Growing Up in New Guinea*, p. 163; Mead, *Kinship in the Admiralty Islands*, p. 248.

64. *Ibid.*, p. 253.

65. Fortune, *Manus Religion*, p. 13.

66. Mead, *Growing Up in New Guinea*, p. 318.

67. Fortune, *Manus Religion*, p. 13.

68. Mead, *Growing Up in New Guinea*, p. 318.

69. Mead, *Kinship in the Admiralty Islands*, p. 227

70. Fortune, *Manus Religion*, p. 277.

# CHAPTER 10

1. Firth, *We the Tikopia*, p. 346.
2. *Ibid.*, p. 359.
3. Firth, *Work of the Gods*, p. 304.
4. Firth, *We the Tikopia*, p. 182.
5. *Ibid.*, p. 183.
6. Firth, *Work of the Gods*, I, p. 25.
7. It is perhaps of interest to note that an important female diety is dangerous, having a white body and a predilection for carrying men off or having sexual intercourse with them. She is the guardian of the heavenly dwelling of women dying in childbirth. The death motif is common in stories about her. See *ibid.*, II, p. 327 ff.
8. Although the women may take some part in the ceremonies for the female diety, they may not do so when they are menstruating, possibly because this, like childbirth, is a secular and female activity par excellence. See Firth, *We the Tikopia*, p. 476.
9. *Ibid.*, p. 145.
10. *Ibid.*, p. 135.
11. *Ibid.*, pp. 203-6.
12. *Ibid.*, p. 150.
13. *Ibid.*, p. 180.
14. *Ibid.*, p. 210.
15. This particular dance is performed in the same way for girls though they do not dance in the midst of the main body of men. See *Ibid.*, pp. 211 ff.
16. *Ibid.*, p. 108.
17. *Ibid.*, p. 186.
18. The Christians of the island also take part in the ceremony. See *Ibid.*, p. 434.
19. *Ibid.*, p. 464.
20. *Ibid.*, p. 466.
21. *Ibid.*, p. 466.
22. Firth, *Work of the Gods*, II, pp. 243-4.
23. Past tense, of course, since the Christianizing of the Tafua chief has meant the actual address is no longer given to the assembled people. See *Ibid.*, Chapter VII. The chiefs still assemble.
24. Bunzel, "Introduction to Zuñi Ceremonialism," *Bureau of American Ethnology Reports*, vol. XLVII, p. 476.
25. Kroeber, *Zuñi Kin and Clan*, p. 47.
26. *Ibid.*, p. 91. There is, of course, some participation through the fact that a particular ritual act must be performed by a member of a certain clan.
27. Bunzel, "Introduction to Zuñi Ceremonialism," *Bureau of American Ethnology Reports*, vol. XLVII, pp. 535-6.
28. Stevenson, *op. cit.*, p. 298.
29. *Ibid.*, p. 301.
30. Bunzel, "Zuñi Katchinas," *Bureau of American Ethnology Reports*, vol. XLVII, p. 975. The year is uncertain now, since the ceremony has not been held regularly every four years in recent times.

31. *Loc. cit.*

32. *Ibid.*, p. 980.

33. *Ibid.*, p. 999.

34. Bunzel, "Zuñi Ritual Poetry," *Bureau of American Ethnology Reports,* vol. XLVII, p. 795.

35. *Ibid.*, pp. 802-3.

36. Bunzel, "Introduction to Zuñi Ceremonialism," *Bureau of American Ethnology Reports,* vol. XLVII, p. 504.

37. Stevenson, *op. cit.*, p. 306.

38. Kroeber, *op. cit.*, p. 90.

39. *Loc. cit.*

40. Bunzel, "Introduction to Zuñi Ceremonialism," *Bureau of American Ethnology Reports,* vol. XLVII, p. 543.

41. Bunzel, "Zuñi Ritual Poetry" (p. 705) and "Zuñi Katchinas" (p. 955), in *Bureau of American Ethnology Reports,* vol. XLVII.

42. Stevenson (*op. cit.*, p. 293) says that in all her years with the Zuñi she saw only one parent strike a child or use harsh words against it.

43. *Ibid.*, p. 228.

44. Parsons, *Pueblo Indian Religion,* vol. I, p. 51.

45. Parsons, *Notes on Zuñi,* Pt. I, pp. 153, 172-3: Bunzel, "Zuñi Katchinas," *Bureau of American Ethnology Reports,* vol. XLVII, pp. 936-941; Parsons, "The Zuñi adoshle and suuke," *American Anthropologist,* 18:338-347.

46. Bunzel, "Zuñi Katchinas," *Bureau of American Ethnology Reports,* vol. XLVII, pp. 889, 1018-20.

47. *Ibid.*, p. 1020.

48. Parsons, *Pueblo Indian Religion,* vol. I, p. 343.

49. Or it may be performed by a "child of clan, i.e, one whose paternal clan is Badger (see *Ibid.*, p. 161).

50. Bunzel, "Zuñi Ritual Poetry," *Bureau of American Ethnology Reports,* vol. XLVII, p. 616.

51. The term "ceremonial father" is significant in this regard, since the respect given the father is thus parallel to that given the priest. "My child," and "my father," are terms frequently noted in the prayers when respect is paid or received.

52. A. R. Radcliffe-Brown, "The Sociological Theory of Totemism," *Proceedings of the Fourth Pacific Science Congress,* vol. III, *Biological Papers,* Maks and Van Der Klits, Batavia-Bandoeng, 1930, p. 301.

53. The literature on totemism is extensive, since an earlier generation of anthropologists, seeking evolutionary "solutions," considered this system as the earliest and most "primitive" type of religion. For interesting discussions of totemism, see: A. R. Brown, "The Definition of Totemism," *Anthropos,* vol. IX (1914), pp. 622-30; "Das Problem des Totemismus," by Mödling, Swanton, Wundt, Rivers, Goldenweiser, Bas, and others, in *Anthropos,* same volume; A. P. Elkin, "Studies in Australian Totemism," *Oceania,* vol. IV (1933-4), pp. 113-131; or D. F. Thompson, "The Hero Cult, Initiation and Totemism of Cape York," *Journal of the Royal Anthropological Institute,* vol. LXIII (1933), pp. 453-538. The problem particularly occupied the attention of Continental scholars.

54. Warner, *op. cit.*, p. 260.

55. *Ibid.*, p. 252.

56. *Ibid.*, p. 386.
57. *Ibid.*, p. 394.
58. See also W. Lloyd Warner, "Murngin Warfare," *Oceania*, vol. I (1930), pp. 457-494.
59. Warner, *op. cit.*, pp. 79-81.
60. *Ibid.*, p. 128.
61. *Ibid.*, p. 127.
62. *Ibid.*, p. 70.
63. For a broader discussion of the social organization of the tribes in Australia, see A. Radcliffe-Brown, "The Social Organization of Australian Tribes," *Oceania*, vol. I (1930-31), pp. 34-63; 206-246; 426-456.
64. Warner, *op. cit.*, p. 130.
65. *Ibid.*, p. 284.
66. *Ibid.*, p. 386.
67. *Ibid.*, p. 307.
68. *Loc. cit.*
69. *Ibid.*, p. 71.
70. For further discussion of the relationship between the individual and the totemic elements, see A. R. Radcliffe-Brown, "Notes on Totemism in Eastern Australia," *Journal of the Royal Anthropological Institute*, vol. LIX (1929), pp. 399-415.
71. Warner, *op. cit.*, pp. 417-432.

# APPENDIX I

1. Fortune, *Manus Religion*, pp. 32, 34, 39.
2. Margaret Mead, *Growing Up in New Guinea*, in *From the South Seas*, Morrow, New York, 1939, pp. 23-50.
3. M. J. Herskovits, *Dahomey*, Augustin, New York, 1938, vol. II, pp. 170, 179-180, 186-188.
4. *Ibid.*, pp. 110, 181, 183.
5. *Ibid.*, p. 218; vol. I, pp. 210, 212; however, women with few exceptions do not obtain a Fa (II, 219), and although they predominate in cult membership, only about one-fourth of the female population during Burton's visit were estimated to be ordinary cult-members. (Richard F. Burton, *A Mission to Gelele King of Dahome*, 2d ed., Tinsley, London, 1864, vol. II, p. 155.)
6. Raymond Firth, *We, the Tikopia*, American, 1936, p. 148.
7. Actually, of course, there are no "schools" like the Maori "College." On the other hand, it is explicitly recognized that there is a definite body of lore, sacred and secular, and that certain people must acquire it. Boys are almost always allowed to attend religious ceremonies. Girls are almost never so allowed (*Ibid.*, p. 145). Parents are assumed to be the main source of all information. Details of the family ritual are given by the father, since these are sacred property and almost without exception patrilineal (*Ibid.*, p. 148). The premature death of a father may thus diminish considerably the effective ritual knowledge of a son. As is seen throughout the *Works of the Gods*, it is the elders and chiefs who actually perform the main elements of the ceremonies, while commoners participate only peripherally or as spectators. Thus, in the ritual at Somosomo (*Work of the Gods*, Lund,

Humphries, London, 1940, vol. II, p. 304), of the Kafika representatives, only the Ariki Kafika, and the elders of Tavi, Rarovi and Porima were allowed to take part in the work. There are a few elements of the rituals performed only by women, although they are not fundamental (*We, the Tikopia*, p. 471). It is the chiefs, of course, who acquire the most information, including many words not used by commoners (*Work of the Gods*, vol. I, pp. 26, 54-55, 74, 108, vol. II, 236). A probable heir to the chieftainship (or, of course, to a position as elder) will have to be taught much more than others, by his father as well as other elders, in order to preside at important rituals (*Primitive Polynesian Economy*, Routledge, London, 1939, p. 103). Since many rituals are public or only semi-private, much ritual knowledge is "picked up" by others who, however, do not accept any right to use it (see *We, the Tikopia*, p. 7-8).

8. Warner, W. L., *A Black Civilization*, Harpers, N. Y., 1937, p. 6-7.

9. *Ibid.*, pp. 125 ff., esp. 128 and 131.

10. *Ibid.*, pp. 6, 387.

11. Herskovits, *op. cit.*, vol. II, pp. 110, 181, 183, 218-219; Burton, *op. cit.*, p. 155; only a few women are permitted to dance *kachina* (Ruth L. Bunzel, "Introduction to Zuñi Ceremonialism" in *47th Annual Report of the Bureau of American Ethnology, 1929-30*, Washington, 1932, p. 517). However, there are many women in the medicine societies which Bunzel calls the Cult of the Beast Gods (*Ibid.*, p. 528). These societies have the most esoteric knowledge and the most elaborate ritual. Such knowledge is paid for, though all offices are held by men (*Ibid.*, pp. 529, 542). In general Zuñi women have a minor role (Elsie Clews Parsons, *Pueblo Indian Religion*, University of Chicago, Chicago, 1939, p. 40), as do the Dahomean women, in that the highest positions are usually held by men. However, and bearing out the ranking given here, the Dahomean women have considerably more freedom (Herskovits, *op. cit.*, vol. I, pp. 56-7, 254-5, vol. II, pp. 112-127; Bunzel, *loc. cit.*, pp. 543-4), and thus can spend more time in ritual activity. Bunzel points out several powerful indirect roles of certain Zuñi women (*Ibid.*, p. 544).

12. Herskovits, *op. cit.*, Vol. II, pp. 111-127. Ruth L. Bunzel, "Zuñi Ritual Poetry," *47th Annual Report of the Bureau of American Ethnology, 1929-30*, Washington, 1932, pp. 795-827, gives the linguistic elements of initiation into a medicine society and, in footnotes, much of the overt ceremonial. This, as well as the comments on the first steps in *kachina* initiation ("Introduction to Zuñi Ceremonialism," p. 541), as on the acquisition of esoteric knowledge (*Ibid.*, p. 542), suggests how little even some members of societies must learn. Of course, as in Tikopia, many "pick up" more ritual knowledge than they have been formally taught by their elders (*Ibid.*, p. 494).

13. Herskovits, *op. cit.*, Vol. I, pp. 99-106.

14. Firth, *We, the Tikopia*, pp. 7-8, 145, 148; *Work of the Gods*, Vol. I, pp. 26, 54-55, 74, 108, Vol. II, p. 304; *Primitive Polynesian Economy*, p. 103.

15. Warner, *op. cit.*, pp. 6-7, 125 ff.

16. The "likeliness" of this identification in Zuñi life is peculiar, in that there must be an entirely secular representative to deal with the U. S. government. Although this person, the governor, is presumably still increasing in influence, his prestige was reported by Bunzel to be small in 1928. ("Introduction to Zuñi Ceremonialism," p. 479.) Presumably this situation might continue indefinitely, since the real power (council of priests, or its head, *pekwin* or chief priest) could

not be the "American chief" (Parsons, *op. cit.*, pp. 156-7). Although the council has the ultimate political authority, it actually delegates secular affairs to the civil officers, because it is too sacred to mix in such affairs (Bunzel, "Introduction to Zuñi Ceremonialism," p. 478). Crime and warfare are the field of the bow priests, the executive arm of the council (*Ibid.*, pp. 478-9). But religious knowledge and action touch everyone in Zuñi, so that secular power does not necessarily follow from ritual position. Therefore, the situation is this: The indirect source of political power is the council of priests, which may not exercise it except through secular officers who themselves have some influence by virtue of their position. Religious decisions may be implemented by the bow priests, while secular affairs are administered by the civil officers, who do not themselves hold high ritual office (though of course they do participate in rituals).

17. Thus, e.g., Korotan had been the greatest man of rank (*lapan*), a war leader, a sorcerer and magician (Fortune, *op. cit.*, pp. 217, 314 ff.). Mbosai, the most prominent man of Matchupal, had been a diviner (*Ibid.*, p. 124). Nane, who was enjoying great economic success, though not a man of rank, was also a diviner (*Ibid.*, pp. 123, 244).

18. These are modes of variation used by Talcott Parsons in analyzing institutions, in his Social Institutions course (Harvard, spring of 1939). For institutional analysis, another mode was used by him, that of inferiority-superiority in social relationships. Professor Parsons is not responsible for this adaptation to the larger problem of classifying the social context. Each variable may be applied to the general patterns of action to be observed in a society. Even though put in rough terms, a judgment as to the relative position with respect to each variable gives a useful orienting point to one not familiar with the society.

19. Early in the 18th century William Bosman (*New and Accurate Description of the Coast of Guinea, Divided Into the Gold, the Slave, and the Ivory Coasts,* 2d ed., London, 1721) had written in detail of the active trade with the Dahomean kingdom, especially the slave trade. Burton (*op. cit.,* vol. I, p. 29) mentions a log-book which "supplies a good account of independent Whydah," which was published in London, 1693-4. This I have not seen, but the date is significant.

20. See Herskovits, *op. cit.,* vol. I, pp. 107-136 for the ingenious statistical and fiscal system evolved, as well as vol. II, chs. XXII-III and XXV, where the detailed plan of the civil administration is outlined. Especially significant for determining an approach to our Western type of culture is the census system discussed in Ch. XXV. See also his "Population Statistics in the Kingdom of Dahomey," *Human Biology,* vol. IV (1932), pp. 252-61.

21. Note the purely economic arguments given to Herskovits (*op. cit.,* vol. I, p. 61) against price-cutting in the Abomey market. The sheer number of people attending a market (an estimate suggests ten thousand on some days) would tend to make most relationships contractual, or economic, or self-interested. The legal system is interesting for its attempted approach to abstract justice without regard to position or personal relationships, in a purely disinterested fashion. See *Ibid.,* vol. II, pp. 10 ff., especially the ordeal system, pp. 16 ff.

22. Of particular importance for the high rating of its technology are its iron, brass, and cloth achievements. See *Ibid.,* vol. I, pp. 44-6, as well as the numerous photographs of Dahomean work. Technical and artistic aspects of some of this work are treated by Herskovits with Frances S. Herskovits, "The Art of Dahomey:

I—Brass-casting and Appliqué Cloths, II—Wood Carving," *American Magazine of Art*, Vol. 27 (1934: 67-76, 124-131).

23. Warner, *op. cit.*, pp. 3-4.

24. Thus, the kinship rules regulate even "the social goods produced by the technology," and "demand certain divisions of foods, other creature necessities, and services" (*Ibid.*, p. 395). As Warner emphasizes, the hundred-year contact of the Malay traders has not changed the type of trade in northeastern Arnhem Land. Instead of becoming a social relationship of self-interest, functionally specific, and universalistic to fit the purely economic ends of the Malays, the trade of the Murngin (which is with other Australian groups) remains ritualized, a social bond of reciprocity, and "may be an exchange of the same objects" (*Ibid.*, p. 458).

25. *Ibid.*, pp. 4, 52-124.

26. The marked character of this solidarity is seen in the very fact of the persistence of their culture for nearly four centuries after being "conquered." The secretiveness of a whole society as against the outsider is not merely based on fear that giving knowledge of prayers will destroy the power of the prayer. Actually, many who know prayers belonging to others would not lose in the process. This solidarity goes beyond this, and E. C. Parsons could report, "So inconspicuous are these high chiefs of Zuñi that a storekeeper who had lived in the town thirty years did not know of their offices" (*op. cit.*, vol. I, p. 151). The widespread Pueblo rule against leaving the pueblo without permission is part of this same solidarity, whose other side is the rule against foreigners entering (e.g., for marriage). Parsons notes some of the ways in which each Pueblo group maintains its own individuality against the others (*Ibid.*, pp. 6, 7, 8).

27. Although this characteristic is already well known, one fact brings it into sharp focus. In Zuñi, following the general pattern that anything individual is of no importance, marriages play no part in local gossip, though initiations do, as well as births and deaths. (Bunzel, *Ibid.*, "Introduction to Zuñi Ceremonialism," p. 476). What makes this fact so significant is that courtship and marriage are matters of individual choice, not tied with religious or group activity. Hopi, however, use marriage as an occasion for group relationships, including gift exchange between the two clans—and weddings become "one of the most frequent topics of conversation" (*Ibid.*, pp. 476-7).

28. Many of the changes made have come through trade and the spread of sheep-raising, but many seemingly innocuous changes are opposed, such as wheat threshers, railroads, etc. (Parsons, *op. cit.*, vol. I, pp. 19, 23; vol. II, pp. 1082-3; Bunzel, "Introduction to Zuñi Ceremonialism," p. 475). Such resistance increases for elements which touch ritual. Nevertheless, as would be obvious, many changes have been made in the past four centuries, not all of which can be known. One important aspect of this change is that, once a change is made, Zuñi do not think of it as a change, or foreign, but entwine it carefully with other Zuñi traits (A. L. Kroeber, *Zuñi Kin and Clan*, Anthrop. *Papers of the American Museum of Natural History*, vol. XVIII, Pt. II, New York, 1917, pp. 203-4).

29. As, for example, in the working party, a form of cooperation spread throughout the Pueblo culture, or in interpueblo mutual aid (in legends), e.g., when Zuñi asked for help from Hopi after a—mythical—earthquake, see Bunzel, "Zuñi Katchinas," *47th Annual Report of the Bureau of American Ethnology, 1929-30*, p. 1037. In conformity with this tendency is the fact that a great part of a man's time is spent in participating in joint activities, besides the broad

obligations to his household (Bunzel, "Introduction to Zuñi Ceremonialism," p. 476).

30. Firth, *Primitive Polynesian Economy*, pp. 88, 314.

31. E.g., the "race" to swallow a bit of hot yam (Firth, *Work of the Gods*, vol. I, p. 101); or to the personal prestige in catching the first flying fish (*Ibid.*, p. 55) as part of the ritual for "revivifying" the canoes. See especially page 88, where the possibility is mentioned of a wealthy commoner achieving prestige by *breaking* a rule, and then offering an impressive gift to the chief. It is a form of self-advertisement which would be shocking to Zuñi. A test of such prestige may be made when an individual attempts to set a *tapu* of his own (*Primitive Polynesian Economy*, p. 211).

32. The great power of the chiefs allows them to impose their will at many points where the group does not agree justice is being rendered (see *We, the Tikopia*, pp. 381-2, for one case where there was such agreement, and where comment suggests how far a chief may act arbitrarily). This means, in effect, that the immediately effective decision of a chief far outweighs the general public opinion in most affairs, so that subordination is to him, not the solidary group.

33. The wider group of relatives actually attempts to prevent close personal ties within the immediate family, by gaining the affection of the child, or by adopting the child (*Ibid.*, pp. 203-5). Firth claims (*Ibid.*, pp. 205-6) that the Tikopia themselves recognize the function of this: ". . . To preserve as far as possible uniformity of conduct and attitudes within the larger social group and not allow the bonds of the individual family to become so strong as to threaten the wider harmony."

34. For the most part, this is in tumeric-making, canoe-building, net-making, working of bowls, certain types of sinnet lashings, fishing, and tattooing, although as Firth states explicitly, what the expert does very well is also done with lesser competence by the ordinary Tikopia (*Primitive Polynesian Economy*, pp. 112-5).

35. Firth, *Work of the Gods*, vol. I, p. 29. Even more interestingly, the working-adze (iron or steel) of the Taumako chief is associated with the Eel God, which is often evil. Also the "sacred things," taken down for the canoe rites, are iron spikes probably antedating white contact with the Tikopia, but now given a supernatural origin by the Tikopia (*Ibid.*, p. 53).

36. This is aside from changes in the detail of Pueblo ritual. Parsons' theory of a widespread borrowing from Spanish-Catholic ceremonial ("Spanish Elements in the Kachina Cult of the Pueblos," *Proceedings of the Twenty-third International Congress of Americanists*, 1928, pp. 582-603; see especially *op. cit.*, vol. II, pp. 1064 ff.) appears highly unlikely to the present author although the point is not important enough to pursue here. Bunzel seems ironic (*op. cit.*, "Zuñi Katchinas," p. 903) in her approval of Parsons' theory, when she emphasizes that Parsons found the kachina cult most developed where "Church contacts were brief and superficial." Similarly, she says (*Ibid.*), "One is struck, too, at the enormous impetus which contact with the Catholics gave to the growth of the cult in those villages where it could develop unhampered by the church."

Parsons claims that twenty years ago (*Pueblo Indian Religion*, vol. II, p. 1142-3) the ritualistically designed corn meal bowls were giving way to glass containers. "Zuñi masks may be made of cowhide instead of buffalo hide or buckskin" (*Ibid.*, p. 1148). Likewise, the introduction of the Julian calendar breaks seriously with tradition, since the ritual dates are supposed to be set by the priests. Similarly, the introduction of a government mill, since corn grinding by the women is supposed to be an important ritual element.

37. This is true even to the point where Western society would consider heartless the fulfillment of the obligation. The case of Korotan (Fortune, *Manus Religion*, pp. 314-21) would certainly call for mitigation in a white court, even if he were white. Since he was not white, the Manus knew too well the unwillingness of the white court to make him pay everything. "But the Manus are not any more benevolent than we in economic affairs, and they have as firm an idea of justice though the heavens fall, as we" (*Ibid.*, p. 320). Self-interest is followed to the extent that in the larger enterprises, involving the labor of dependent relatives, these less efficient relatives do not gain from the man's success. The affinal exchanges themselves ". . . do not represent the pooled wealth of the entire kinship group . . . but the aggregate of individual contributions," each made individually and so reciprocated (Margaret Mead, *Kinship in the Admiralty Islands, Anthropological Papers of the American Museum of Natural History*, 1934, pp. 190-1).

38. Manus must be honest with both friend and stranger, referring to economic obligations, theft, or simple lying (*Manus Religion*, pp. 345-6). Obviously, however, there are many other relationships which are particularistic. The universalism of some relationships facilitates greatly the extended trade relations of the Manus, with other societies as among themselves. This has an interesting aspect with regard to the inland Usiai, with whom the Manus trade fish for land products. Although the Usiai are enemies, the Manus tradesman deals with one of them as his special trading partner. (However, sexual affairs with foreign women are not of interest to Manus ghosts. See *Ibid.*, p. 219.)

39. Cf. Max Weber, *The Protestant Ethic and the Spirit of Capitalism*, trans. Talcott Parsons, George Allen and Unwin, London, 1930. The asceticism lies not only in Manus restrictions on sex (*Manus Religion*, pp. 344-6), but also in the emphasis on thirft and hard work (*Ibid.*, pp. v, 49, 50, 52, 144, 145, 344; Margaret Mead, *op. cit.*, pp. 9, 83, 208).

40. *Manus Religion*, pp. v, 128.

41. *Ibid.*, pp. 7, 8.

42. James G. Frazer, *The Golden Bough*, 3d ed., 12 vols., Macmillan, London, 1911-1914.

43. More extended characterizations are given in the text, which includes summaries of these religious systems.

44. Herskovits, *op. cit.*, vol. II, pp. 222, 223, 225-9, 291.

45. *Ibid.*, vol. I, pp. 196 ff., 205-9, 237-9; vol. II, p. 297.

46. Raymond Firth, "Report on Research in Tikopia," *Oceania*, vol. I, pp. 113-117; "Totemism in Polynesia," *Oceania*, vol. I, pp. 291-321, 377-98.

47. As J. J. Williams does for the Dahomey ("Africa's God: II—Dahomey," *Boston College Graduate School, Anthropological Series*, vol. I, No. 2, Boston, 1936; or as Pater W. Schmidt does for all primitive religions (*Der Ursprung der Gottesidee*, 6 vols., Munster I. W., Aschendorff, 1926-35).

48. Without at all making it fit the "monotheism" of Williams or Schmidt. See Melville J. and Frances S. Herskovits: *An Outline of Dahomean Religious Belief, Memoirs of the American Anthropological Association*, No. 41, 1933.

49. Bunzel, "Introduction to Zuñi Ceremonialism," *op. cit.*, pp. 509-510, 515, etc.

50. *Ibid.*, pp. 486-7.
51. Firth, "Report on Research in Tikopia," *op. cit.*, pp. 113-4. The emphasis is even greater than is apparent at first, as will be seen later, since all clans have this deity as their head, under different names.
52. Fortune, *Manus Religion*, p. 1.
53. *Ibid.*, pp. 29-37, 343.
54. Warner, *op. cit.*, pp. 249-370. With reference to the seasonal aggregation, see pp. 378 ff.
55. *Ibid.*, pp. 413-442.
56. Bunzel, "Introduction to Zuñi Ceremonialism," *op. cit.*, p. 508.
57. *Ibid.*
58. Parsons, *op. cit.*, vol. I, p. 268.
59. Herskovits, *op. cit.*, vol. I, pp. 170-1, 174-5, 189-90. Of course, there may be highly elaborate rituals which no outsider has yet seen.
60. E.g., *Ibid.*, pp. 123-5.
61. *Ibid.*, vol. II, pp. 68-9.
62. In simple terms, a story is any tale related about any entity, told usually for amusement, and without any further religious implications. The legend usually deals with heroes and men, sometimes with their contacts with the gods, but usually with a feeling for amusement and history. Its happenings are not usually in the supernatural, and it may become simply a traditionalized tale. The myth, of course, deals more definitely with supernatural events and entities, and endows rituals, or sacred objects and places, with religious significance. It would be distinguished from sacred history only in that the latter implies the existence of a recognized body of lore, intellectualized and related as an integrated body of knowledge, with an authoritative acceptance, as in scriptures.

## APPENDIX II

1. But see Leslie White's able reintroduction of the evolution problem, on a more feasible basis, in *The Science of Culture*, New York, Farrar Straus, 1949; as also Lowie, *History*, pp. 283-291.
2. See, for example, W. Schmidt, "L'origine de l'Idée de Dieu," trans. P. J. Pietsch, in *Anthropos* 3 (1908), pp. 125-163; 336-368; 559-611; 801-836; 1081-1120; 4 (1909): 207-250; 505-524; 1075-1091; 5 (1910): 231-246; (this becomes the historical-theoretical volume in the 6-volume edition of *Der Ursprung der Gottesidee;* see *infra*); also, Paul Radin, *Primitive Religion, op. cit.;* Robert H. Lowie, *History*, as also his *Primitive Religion*, Boni and Liveright, N. Y., 1924, Part II; Durkheim, *Elementary Forms of the Religious Life*, trans. J. W. Swain, Macmillan, N. Y., 1915. Chapters 2 and 3; etc. Further: J. Röhr, "Das Wesen des Mana," *Anthropos*, 14-15 (1919-20), pp. 97-124; K. Beth, *Religion u. Magie Bei den Naturvölkern*, Leipzig, Teubner, 1914. In addition, see the series by K. Th. Preuss, in *Globus*, vols. 86 and 87 (1905, 1906), "Der Ursprung der Religion und der Kunst"; and Talcott Parsons, "The Theoretical Development of the Sociology of Religion," in *Essays in Sociological Theory Pure and Applied*, Glencoe, Illinois, The Free Press, 1949, pp. 52-66.
3. The best such classification is that by Talcott Parsons, *Structure of Social Action*, pp. 77-82. In his terms, the animists and naturists are to be generally

classified as "rationalistic, individualistic, statistical positivists." Both the psycho-analytic and socialist-communist groups are radical anti-intellectual positivists. Both Durkheim and Smith, of the sociological group, at times take positions which are classifiable as radical, rationalistic, sociologistic, positivism, etc. However, such a classification has other goals than those of the present critique.

4. Edward B. Tylor, *Primitive Culture* (first ed. 1871), 2 vols., 3rd Am. ed., N. Y., Holt, 1889, vol. I, p. 428. *Vide* Herbert Spencer, *The Principles of Sociology*, 3 vols. in 5, N. Y., Appleton, 1880-96, vol. II, pt. 4, vol. III, pt. 6, as also Lowie, *Primitive Religion*, *op. cit.*, pp. 106 ff., and Durkheim, *Forms*, *op. cit.*, Chapters 2 and 3.

5. *Ibid.*, p. 429.

6. *Ibid.*, p. 436.

7. *Ibid.*, p. 445.

8. *Ibid.*, p. 450.

9. Auguste Comte, *La Philosophie Positive*, 4 vols., Flammarion edition, 1929, Vol. III, Ch. VII. And, of course, Comte took the notion from Saint-Simon. The idea has a long history before that time, as well.

10. As stated in Footnote 3 of this section, this is Talcott Parson's terminology. However, in American sociology, the terms "positivism" and "neo-positivism" have come to be applied rather to the "Lundberg school," which denies that science can solve moral problems directly.

11. Tylor, *op. cit.*, vol. I, p. 427.

12. *Ibid.*, p. 135.

13. This tradition is most systematically analyzed in Talcott Parsons, *The Structure of Social Action*.

14. Tylor, *op. cit.*, vol. I, p. 427.

15. *Ibid.*, p. 418.

16. Durkheim, *Forms*, p. 73, comments that Müller begins with a contrary principle, that "religion reposes upon an experience, from which it draws all its authority." Actually, they differ only in the *type* of experience.

17. For a modern exponent, see Wilson D. Wallis, *Religion in Primitive Society*, N. Y., Crofts, 1939, pp. 11 ff., and esp. Ch. II. Lowie accepts this as *one* source, as he does dreams and visions; see *Primitive Religion*, pp. 108, 112, etc.

18. Using mythology as his subject, and comparative philology as tool, he first elaborated these ideas in 1856, in an essay, "Comparative Mythology," *Oxford Essays*, vol. II (1856) pp. 1-87, esp. pp. 34, 46, 59-60, 66, 82, etc. These ideas were developed by Adalbert Kuhn, *Herabkunft des Feuers und Goettertranks*, Berlin, Dümmler, 1859, again concentrating on the Indo-Iranian groups; and by W. Schwartz, *Der Ursprung der Mythologie*, Berlin, Hertz, 1860; Michael Breal, *Hercule et Cacus, Etude de Mythologie Comparée*, Paris, Durand, 1863. Müller, of course, continued to expound these ideas in numerous later works, including those on both language and religion, using mainly Indo-Iranian sources: *Lectures on the Origin and Growth of Religion*, London, Longmans, Green, 1878; *Anthropological Religion*, London, Longmans, Green, 1892, etc.

19. Müller, *Contributions to the Science of Mythology*, 2 vols., London, Longmans, Green, 1897, vol. I, pp. 68 ff.

20. The theory may be attacked, of course, on linguistic grounds. *Vide* Schmidt, *Der Ursprung der Gottesidee*, vol. I, pp. 25-6.

21. Durkheim, *Forms*, p. 84.

22. Some of these studies of symbols are ingenious and elaborate. See, for example, Géza Róheim, *Australian Totemism*, London, Allen and Unwin, 1925; Theodor Reik, *The Psychological Problem of Religion*, trans. from 2d German edition, ed. Douglas Bryan, N. Y., Farrar, Straus, 1946. Both of these are psychoanalytic in origin; for a linguistic approach, see: J. Winthuis' many publications, especially *Mythos und Kult der Steinzeit*, Stuttgart, Strecker u. Schröder, 1935. A much older treatment is J. J. Bachofen's involved analysis, *Urreligion und Antike Symbole*, 3 vols., Leipzig, Philipp Reclam, 1926 (edited from various of Bachofen's works up to his death in 1887).

23. Andrew Lang *Custom and Myth*, London, Longmans, Green, 1887, and *Myth, Ritual and Religion*, 2 vols., London, Longmans, Green, 1887. See especially the latter, vol. I (1913 edition), p. 34, where he defines a "savage": one who believes in totemism, regards all natural objects as animated and intelligent beings, believes in ancestral ghosts or spirits of woods and wells (though in certain moods conscious of a higher moral faith), tools of stone and wood, nomadic, etc.

24. Andrew Lang, *Magic and Religion*, London, Longmans, Green, 1901, p. 15.

25. Andrew Lang, *The Making of Religion*, London, Longmans, Green, 1898; *Magic and Religion*, Appendix A and pp. 295-297; against Frazer, pp. 82 *et seq.*

26. Lang, *Magic and Religion*, pp. 59-60, 69, esp. 257-269, "First Fruits and Taboos."

27. *Ibid.*, pp. 3-4, 46 *et. seq.*

28. At one point, he also offers a linguistic explanation similar to one of Müller's: *ibid.*, p. 264.

29. The most convenient American edition is the one-volume Macmillan edition, 1935. See also: "The Beginnings of Religion and Totemism Among the Australian Aborigines," *Fortnightly Review*, 1905, pp. 151-162 and 452-467; and *Totemism and Exogamy*, 4 vols., London, Macmillan, 1910.

30. Bronislaw Malinowski, "Sir James George Frazer," in *A Scientific Theory of Culture*, Chapel Hill, University of North Carolina, 1944, pp. 177-221. See also Robert H. Lowie, *History, op. cit.*, pp. 101-104.

31. Frazer, *op. cit.*, pp. 12, 45-46.

32. By Henri Hubert, Marcel Mauss, and Emile Durkheim in France, and William Robertson Smith and R. R. Marett in England, for example.

33. Frazer, *op. cit.*, p. 50, and "The Ritual of Death and Resurrection," pp. 691-701. Also: Bronislaw Malinowski, *Magic, Science and Religion*, Glencoe, Ill., The Free Press, 1948, pp. 2 ff.; the essay is from 1925.

34. See Theodor Reik, *op. cit.*; Géza Roheim, *op. cit.*; Roheim, "Dying Gods and Puberty Ceremonies," in *Journal of the Royal Anthropological Institute* 59 (1929): pp. 181-197; Otto Rank, *Seelenglaube U. Psychologie*, Leipzig, Deuticke, 1930; Karl Beth "Die Religion im Urteil der Psychoanalyse," *Archiv Fuer Religions-Psychologie* 2 (1929): pp. 76-87. Although Freud's *The Future of an Illusion* (trans. W. D. Robson-Scott, Edinburg, Liveright, 1928) appeared in German in 1927, his explorations began prior to 1910. Two of Reik's essays were developed shortly after that. The reception given by American anthropologists to this body of work has been less than cordial. An amusing case of a change toward "tolerance" may be seen in the A. L. Kroeber's "recantation" of his first review (*Am. Anthrop.*

vol. 22, 1920, pp. 48-55), of *Totem and Taboo* nearly twenty years later (*Am. J. Soc.* vol. 45, 1939, pp. 446-451).

35. Trans. Katherine Jones, N. Y., Knopf, 1939.

36. Freud, *The Future of an Illusion*, p. 26.

37. *Ibid.*, p. 28.

38. This, I gather, is what Parsons considers a major contribution of Max Weber and Malinowski, see his *Essays, op. cit.*, pp. 62 ff.

39. Freud, *Future*, pp. 29-30.

40. What Jane Ellen Harrison and Francis Cornford call *Moira* as it figures in Greek philosophy and religion. Cf. Cornford's *From Religion to Philosophy*, N. Y., Longmans, 1912, and Harrison's *Ancient Art and Ritual*, N. Y., Holt, 1913.

41. Freud, *Future*, p. 30.

42. Compare the similar treatment by J. Kinkel, "The Problem of the Psychological Foundation and of the Origin of Religion," in *Imago*, vol. VIII, Nos. 1 and 2. Similar expositions are to be found in the standard psychoanalytic journals. cf., for example, Theodore Schroeder, "The Psychoanalytic Approach to Religious Experience," in the *Psychoanalytic Review*, vol. 16, pp. 361-76, as also the abstract of a paper by Ernest Jones, read at the International Congress of Psychology in Groningen, "The Psychology of Religion," *Psychoanalytic Review*, vol. 17, p. 356.

43. Freud, *Future*, pp. 51-3.

44. Schmidt, *Ursprung*, vol. I, pp. 69-133, "Die Stellungnahme der theologischen Kreise." His treatment is encyclopedic and therefore sketchy, but the basic facts are evident enough.

45. Perhaps the first of significance was A. Bros, *La Religion des Peuples Non-Civilisés*, Paris, Lethielleux, 1907, who does deal with animism, tho accepting revelation as the beginning of religion. Schmidt himself first began publishing about this time, and in 1908-9 began his long series of articles, "L'Origine de l'Idée de Dieu" in *Anthropos*, culminating in the six-volume work already cited. Cf. also A. LeRoy, *Les Pygmées*, Tours, A. Mame, 1905 and *La Religion des Primitifs*, Paris, 1909, later trans. Newton Thompson, N. Y. Macmillan, 1922. A. Bros continued to publish for a number of years, one of the latest being *L'Ethnologie Religieuse*, Paris, Librairie Bloud et Gay, 1936.

46. Schmidt, *Ursprung*, vol. I, p. 112.

47. Here, as elsewhere, the word "theory" does not mean "speculation," but "a statement of interrelationship between facts."

48. Granted, in part because their ability to raise funds from the bourgeoisie was somewhat limited.

49. In this case, of course, they relied most heavily on Lewis Henry Morgan's *Systems of Consanguinity and Affinity*, 1877.

50. See D. Dietzgen, *Saemtliche Schriften*, 3 vols., Wiesbaden, Dietzgen, 1911, vol. III: "Wie die Gotter entstanden sind." Dietzgen, however, is considered a revisionist. Also: Fr. Lütgenau, *Natuerliche und Soziale Religion*, Stuttgart, Dietz, 1894.

51. Karl Marx, *Capital*, N. Y., Modern Library edition (vol. I), 1936, pp. 91-2.

52. *Loc. cit.*

53. F. Engels, *Der Ursprung der Familie, des Privateigentums und des Staats,* 5th ed., Stuttgart, Dietz, 1892, p. 2. This is called the "Mittelstufe der Wildheit."

54. H. Eilderman, *Urkommunismus und Urreligion,* Internat. Arbeiter-Bibliothek, Berlin, 1921, pp. 18, 21. However, in a somewhat more sophisticated manner, Radin makes a similar guess about this early period: Paul Radin, *Primitive Religion,* N. Y., Viking, 1937, pp. 5-8, 24, 31, 38, 52, pp. 192 ff.

55. Nikolai Lenin, *Imperialism, the State and Revolution,* N. Y., Vanquard, 1929, p. 181.

56. George Plekhanov, "The Materialist Conception of History," in *Essays in Historical Materialism,* N. Y. International, 1940, p. 38. This essay dates from 1897, when, according to Lenin, Plekhanov was still acceptable.

57. Engels, *op. cit.,* p. XIV.

58. *Ibid.,* p. viii.

59. Lenin, *op. cit.,* pp. 119-120.

60. Engels, *op. cit.,* pp. 163-188.

61. Although, as Lowie points out (*History,* chs. 9, 11), Boas independently used similar techniques. See Fritz Graebner, "Kulturkreise und Kulturschichten in Ozeanien," *Zeitschrift Für Ethnologie,* 1905, pp. 28 ff.; *Methode der Ethnologie,* Heidelberg, Winter, 1911.

62. However, as Lowie cogently argues (*Religion,* pp. 124 ff.), the classification is at best somewhat doubtful.

63. Lowie, *Religion,* pp. 125-6. We will not know, however, *which* elements have been preserved.

64. On the whole, this would be true. However, in an absolute sense, no group is more ancient, following the idea that all modern men are of the same species. The problem is not age as such, but the point at which technological (the only observable criterion) development stopped. As to other elements, we can not answer the question.

65. This is not surprising, considering the really human attributes of the Christian God, which is supposed to be the epitome of such a high-god. He has a *son,* and does not merely create him out of nothing. He becomes angry, is vengeful, has tabus, and so forth.

66. Lowie, *Religion,* p. 133.

67. F. Graebner, *Das Weltbild der Primitiven,* München, Reinhardt, 1924.

68. Henri Hubert and Marcel Mauss, "Esquisse d'une Théorie Générale de la Magie," *L'Année Sociologique,* vol. VII (1902-3), pp. 1-146; and "Essai sur la nature et la fonction du sacrifice," vol. II (1897-8), pp. 29-138; Lucien Levy-Bruhl, *Primitive Mentality,* trans. L. A. Clare, N. Y., Macmillan, 1923, and *La Mythologie Primitive,* 2nd ed., Paris, Alcan, 1935. The impact on the work of Maurice Halbwachs need not concern us here. Most of Durkheim's later work on religion can be seen in its conceptual beginnings, in "De la definition des Phénomènes Religieux," *L'Année Sociologique,* vol. II (1897-8), pp. 129-132. The standard elucidation of Durkheim's work on religion is Parsons' *Structure of Social Action,* where this task is not the central focus. An excellent, simpler exposition is that of Harry Alpert, *Emile Durkheim and His Sociology,* N. Y., Columbia University, 1939.

69. See the sweeping rejection of Durkheim's work in A. A. Goldenweiser, "Religion and Society: a Critique of Durkheim's Theory of the Origin and

Nature of Religion," *J. Philos., Psych. and Sci. Meth.*, vol. IV (1917), pp. 113-124; or Lowie's somewhat gentler treatment, in *Religion*, ch. VII. See also Clement C. J. Webb, *Group Theories of Religion and the Individual*, N. Y., Macmillan, 1916, chs. 3, 4, 8. Risking a guess, I suspect that a large part of the difficulty lay in his style. It has the deceptive simplicity which is to be found in John Dewey. One is always certain that one understands any given statement, and many of them have the unqualified, and therefore annoying, quality of an epigram.

70. Harrison's best known works are *Prolegomena to the Study of Greek Religion*, Cambridge, University Press, 1903; and *Themis*, Cambridge, University Press, 1912. Cf. Gilbert Murray, *The Rise of the Greek Epic*, Oxford, Clarendon, 1907; and *Five Stages of Greek Religion*, Oxford, Clarendon, 1925 (lectures of 1912); and Francis M. Cornford, *From Religion to Philosophy*, N. Y., Holt, 1913.

71. Most of these men implicitly followed Tylor's reasoning in his classic article, "On a Method of Investigating the Development of Institutions; applied to Laws of Marriage and Descent," *Journal of the Royal Anthropological Institute*, vol. 18 (1878), pp. 245-272. See Smith, *Lectures on the Religion of the Semites*, 3rd ed., Edinburgh, Black, 1889, pp. 58-9, 312, 345, 357, etc.; Durkheim, *Forms*, pp. 1-8, *et. seq.*, 88-97.

72. Only in part, since some elements of Durkheim's sociology of knowledge, generalized, have become part of modern sociology. Cf. Smith, *Ibid.*, pp. 41ff., 85ff., 264, 275, 287; and Durkheim, *Ibid.*, pp. 10ff., 440ff. Some of this notion of the primitive's inability to think "logically" may have come from reports of missionaries, who found them unreceptive to enlightenment. A good example of masterful handling of logic by a native is actually given in Levy-Bruhl, *op. cit.*, p. 321, though Levy-Bruhl obviously does not see its significance.

73. Smith, *Ibid.*, esp. p. 274, as well as pp. 28, 151, 275, etc., and Durkheim, *Ibid.*, pp. 188ff., 199-201. Although Smith emphasizes the communal feast and sacrifice, and Durkheim the totem, their conceptions are very similar. Smith recognized that individuals differed in religiosity.

74. See "Personal Reminiscences of a Winnebago Indian" (*University of California Bureau of American Archeology and Ethnology*), vol. 26 (1913), pp. 243-318; and *Primitive Man as Philosopher*, N. Y., Appleton-Century, 1927. Schmidt and Koppers also pointed out the fact.

75. Smith, *Ibid.*, pp. 55, 90, 154-5, 265-6.

76. *Ibid.*, pp. 154, 265; Durkheim, *Ibid.*, pp. 43ff.

77. Smith, *Ibid.*, pp. 184ff., 195, 199, 206-8, 260ff.; and Durkheim, *Ibid.*, pp. 103ff., 168-188.

78. *Ibid.*, pp. 2-3.

79. Parsons, *Structure of Social Action*, p. 420.

80. *Ibid.*, p. 427.

81. Whereby, for example, the word *lamb* in many Christian services refers not only to the animal, but also (a secondary symbolism) is related to the development of symbolisms regarding flocks of sheep, Jesus as shepherd, the blood of the lamb at Passover, etc.

82. Parsons, *op. cit.*, p. 427. (Italics mine.)

# INDEX

317

# FREE PRESS PAPERBACKS

## A NEW SERIES OF PAPERBOUND BOOKS
### IN THE SOCIAL AND NATURAL SCIENCES, PHILOSOPHY, AND THE HUMANITIES

These books, chosen for their intellectual importance and editorial excellence, are printed on good quality book paper, from the large and readable type of the cloth-bound edition, and are Smyth-sewn for enduring use. *Free Press Paperbacks* conform in every significant way to the high editorial and production standards maintained in the higher-priced, case-bound books published by *The Free Press of Glencoe*.

*For information address:*

## THE FREE PRESS OF GLENCOE
*A Division of The Macmillan Company, 60 Fifth Avenue, New York, N. Y. 10011*